PARABLES FROM NATURE

Mrs. Gatty T. Nelson & Sons

For information regarding special discounts for bulk purchases, please contact BN Publishing at info@bnpublishing.com

www.bnpublishing.com

Printed in the U.S.A.

Table of Contents

A LESSON OF FAITH

"If a man die, shall he live again? All the days of my appointed time will I wait, till my change come."–JOB xiv. 14.

"LET me hire you as a nurse for my poor children," said a Butterfly to a quiet Caterpillar, who was strolling along a cabbage-leaf in her odd lumbering way. "See these little eggs,?" continued the Butterfly; "I don't know how long it will be before they come to life, and I feel very sick and poorly, and if I should die, who will take care of my baby butterflies when I am gone? Will you, kind, mild, green Caterpillar? But you must mind what you give them to eat, Caterpillar! They cannot, of course, live on your rough food. You must give them early dew, and honey from the flowers; and you must let them fly about only a little way at first; for, of course, one can't expect them to use their wings properly all at once. Dear me! It is a sad pity you cannot fly yourself. But I have no time to look for another nurse now, so you will do your best, I hope. Dear! Dear! I cannot think what made me come and lay my eggs on a cabbage-leaf! What a place for young butterflies to be born upon! Still you will be kind, will you not, to the poor little ones? Here, take this gold-dust from my wings as a reward. Oh, how dizzy I am! Caterpillar! You will remember about the food–"

And with these words the Butterfly closed her eyes and died; and the green Caterpillar who had not had the opportunity of even saying Yes or No to the request, was left standing alone by the side of the Butterfly's eggs.

"A pretty nurse she has chosen, indeed, poor lady!" exclaimed she, "and a pretty business I have in hand! Why, her senses must have left her, or she never would have asked a poor crawling creature like me to bring up her dainty little ones! Much they'll mind me, truly, when they feel the gay wings on their backs, and can fly away out of my sight whenever they choose! Ah! How silly some people are, in spite of their painted clothes and the gold-dust on their wings!"

However, the poor Butterfly was dead, and there lay the eggs on the cabbage-leaf; and the green Caterpillar had a kind heart, so she resolved to do her best. But she got no sleep that night, she was so very anxious. She made her back quite ache with walking all night long round her little charges, for fear any harm should happen to them; and in the morning says she to herself–"Two heads are better than one. I will consult some wise animal upon the matter, and get advice. How should a poor crawling creature like me know what to do without asking my betters?"

But still there was a difficulty–whom should the Caterpillar consult? There was the shaggy Dog who sometimes came into the garden. But he was so rough! He would most likely whisk all the eggs off the cabbage-leaf with one brush of his tail, if she called him near to talk to her, and then she should never forgive herself. There was the Tom Cat, to be sure, who would sometimes sit at the foot of the apple-tree, basking himself and warming his fur in the sunshine; but he was so selfish and indifferent! There was no hope of his giving himself the trouble to think about butterflies' eggs. "I wonder which is the wisest of all the animals I know," sighed the Caterpillar, in great distress; and then she thought, and thought, till at last she thought of the Lark; and she fancied that because he went up so high, and nobody knew where he went to, he must be very clever, and know a great deal; for to go up very high (which *she* could never do) was the Caterpillar's idea of perfect glory.

Now, in the neighbouring cornfield there lived a Lark, and the Caterpillar sent a message to him, to beg him to come and talk to her; and when he came she told him all her difficulties, and asked him what she was to do, to feed and rear the little creatures so different from herself.

"Perhaps you will be able to inquire and hear something about it next time you go up high," observed the Caterpillar timidly.

The Lark said, "Perhaps he should", but he did not satisfy her curiosity any further. Soon afterwards, however, he went singing upwards into the bright, blue sky. By degrees his voice died away in the distance, till the green Caterpillar could not hear a sound. It is nothing to say she could not see him; for, poor thing! She never could see far at any time and had a difficulty in looking upwards at all, even when she reared herself up most carefully, which she did now; but it was of no use, so she dropped upon her legs again, and resumed her walk round the Butterfly's eggs, nibbling a bit of the cabbage-leaf now and then as she moved along.

"What a time the Lark has been gone!" she cried, at last. "I wonder where he is just now! I would give all my legs to know! He must have flown up higher than usual this time, I do think! How I should like to know where it is that he goes to, and what he hears in that curious blue sky! He always sings in going up and coming down, but he never lets any secret out. He is very, very close!"

And the green Caterpillar took another turn round the Butterfly's eggs.

At last the Lark's voice began to be heard again. The Caterpillar almost jumped for joy and it was not long before she saw her friend descend with hushed note to the cabbage bed.

"New, news, glorious news, friend Caterpillar!" sang the Lark; "but the worst of it is, you won't believe me!"

"I believe everything I am told," observed the Caterpillar hastily.

"Well, then, first of all, I will tell you what these little creatures are to eat"–and the Lark nodded his beak towards the eggs. "What do you think it is to be? Guess!"

"Dew, and the honey out of flowers, I am afraid," sighed the Caterpillar.

"No such thing, old lady! Something simpler than that. Something that you can get at quite easily."

"I can get at nothing quite easily but cabbage-leaves," murmured the Caterpillar, in distress.

"Excellent! My good friend," cried the Lark exultingly; "you have found it out. You are to feed them with cabbage-leaves."

"*Never!* " said the Caterpillar indignantly. "It was their dying mother's last request that I should do no such thing."

"Their dying mother knew nothing about the matter," persisted the Lark; "but why do you ask me, and then disbelieve what I say? You have neither faith nor trust."

"Oh, I believe everything I am told," said the Caterpillar.

"Nay, but you do not," replied the Lark; "you won't believe me even about the food, and yet that is but a beginning of what I have to tell you. Why, Caterpillar, what do you think those little eggs will turn out to be?"

"Butterflies, to be sure," said the Caterpillar.

"*Caterpillars!* " sang the Lark; "and you'll find it out in time;" and the Lark flew away, for he did not want to stay and contest the point with his friend.

"I thought the Lark had been wise and kind," observed the mild green Caterpillar, once more beginning to walk round the eggs, "but I find that he is foolish and saucy instead. Perhaps he went up too high this time. Ah, it's a pity when people who soar so high are silly and rude nevertheless! Dear! I still wonder whom he sees, and what he does up yonder."

"I would tell you, if you would believe me," sang the Lark, descending once more.

"I believe everything I am told," reiterated the Caterpillar, with as grave a face as if it were a fact.

"Then I'll tell you something else," cried the Lark; "for the best of my news remains behind. *You will one day be a Butterfly yourself.* "

"Wretched bird!" exclaimed the Caterpillar, "you jest with my inferiority–now you are cruel as well as foolish. Go away! I will ask your advice no more."

"I told you, you would not believe me," cried the Lark, nettled in his turn.

"I believe everything that I am told," persisted the Caterpillar; "that is"–and she hesitated–"everything that it is reasonable to believe. But to tell me that butterflies' eggs are caterpillars, and that caterpillars leave off crawling and get wings, and become butterflies! Lark! You are too wise to believe such nonsense yourself, for you know it is impossible."

"I know no such thing," said the Lark, warmly. "Whether I hover over the cornfields of earth, or go up into the depths of the sky, I see so many wonderful things, I know no reason why there should not be more. Oh, Caterpillar! It is because you crawl, because you never get beyond your cabbage-leaf, that you call any thing impossible."

"Nonsense!" shouted the Caterpillar. "I know what's possible, and what's not possible, according to my experience and capacity, as well as you do. Look at my long green body and these endless legs, and then talk to me about having wings and a painted feathery coat! Fool!"

"And fool you! You would-be-wise Caterpillar!" cried the indignant lark. "Fool, to attempt to reason about what you cannot understand! Do you not hear how my song swells with rejoicing as I soar upwards to the mysterious wonder-world above? Oh, Caterpillar! What comes to you from thence, receive, as I do, upon trust."

"That is what you call–"

"*Faith*," interrupted the Lark.

At that moment she felt something at her side. She looked round–eight or ten little green caterpillars were moving about, and had already made a show of a hole in the cabbage-leaf. They had broken from the Butterfly's eggs!

Shame and amazement filled our green friend's heart, but joy soon followed; for, as the first wonder was possible, the second might be so too. "Teach me your lesson, Lark!" she would say; and the Lark sang to her of the wonders of the earth below, and of the heaven above. And the Caterpillar talked all the rest of her life to her relations of the time when she should be a Butterfly.

But none of them believed her. She nevertheless had learnt the Lark's lesson of faith, and when she was going into her chrysalis grave, she said–"I shall be a Butterfly some day!"

But her relations thought her head was wandering, and they said, "Poor thing!"

And when she was a Butterfly, and was going to die again, she said–

"I have known many wonders–I have faith–I can trust even now for what shall come next!"

THE LAW OF AUTHORITY AND OBEDIENCE

A FINE young Working-bee left his hive, one lovely summer's morning, to gather honey from the flowers. The sun shone so brightly, and the air felt so warm, that he flew a long, long distance, till he came to some gardens that were very beautiful and gay; and there having roamed about, in and out of the flowers, buzzing in great delight, till he had so loaded himself with treasures that he could carry no more, he bethought himself of returning home. But, just as he was beginning his journey, he accidentally flew through the open window of a country-house, and found himself in a large dining room. There was a great deal of noise and confusion, for it was dinner-time, and the guests were talking rather loudly, so that the Bee got quite frightened. Still he tried to taste some rich sweetmeats that lay temptingly in a dish on the table, when all at once he heard a child exclaim with a shout, "Oh, there's a bee, let me catch him!" on which he rushed hastily back to (as he thought) the open air. But, alas! Poor fellow, in another second he found that he had flung himself against a hard transparent wall! In other words, he had flown against the glass panes of the window, being quite unable, in his alarm and confusion, to distinguish the glass from the opening by which he had entered. This unexpected blow annoyed him much; and having wearied himself in vain attempts to find the entrance, he began to walk slowly and quietly up and down the wooden frame at the bottom of the panes, hoping to recover both his strength and composure.

Presently, as he was walking along, his attention was attracted by hearing the soft half-whispering voices of two children, who were kneeling down and looking at him.

Says the one to the other, "This is a working-bee, Sister; I see the wax-bags under his thighs. Nice fellow! How busy he has been!"

"Does he make the wax and honey himself?" whispered the Girl.

"Yes, he gets them from the insides of the flowers. Don't you remember how we watched the bees once dodging in and out of the crocuses, how we laughed at them, they were so busy and fussy, and their dark coats looked so handsome against the yellow leaves? I wish I had seen this fellow loading himself today. But he does more than that. He builds the honeycomb, and does pretty nearly everything. He's a working-bee, poor wretch!"

"What is a working-bee? And why do you call him 'Poor wretch,' Brother?"

"Why, don't you know, Uncle Collins says, all people are poor wretches who work for other people who don't work for themselves? And that is just what this bee does. There is the queen-bee in the hive who does nothing at all but sit at home, give orders, and coddle the little ones; and all the bees wait upon her, and obey her. Then there are the drones–lazy fellows, who lounge all their time away. And then there are the working-bees, like this one here, and they do all the work for everybody. How Uncle Collins would laugh at them, if he knew!"

"Doesn't Uncle Collins know about bees?"

"No, I think not. It was the gardener who told me. And, besides, I think Uncle Collins would never have done talking about them and quizzing them, if he once

knew they couldn't do without a queen. I heard him say yesterday, that kings and queens were against nature, for that nature never makes one man a king and another a cobbler, but makes them all alike; and so he says, kings and queens are very unjust things."
"Bees have not the sense to know anything about that," observed the little Girl, softly.
"Of course not! Only fancy how angry these working fellows would be, if they knew what the gardener told me!"
"What was that?"
"Why, that the working-bees are just the same as the queen when they are first born, just exactly the same, and that it is only the food that is given them, and the shape of the house they live in, that makes the difference. The bee-nurses manage that; they give some one sort of food, and some another, and they make the cells different shapes, and so some turn out queens, and the rest working-bees. It's just what Uncle Collins says about kings and cobblers–nature makes them all alike. But, look! The dinner's over–we must go."
"Wait till I let the Bee out, Brother," said the little Girl, taking him gently up in a soft handkerchief; and then she looked at him kindly and said, "Poor fellow! So you might have been a queen if they had only given you the right food, and put you into a right-shaped house! What a shame they didn't! As it is, my good friend," (and here her voice took a childish mocking tone)–"As it is, my good friend, you must go and drudge away all your life long, making honey and wax. Well, get along with you! Good luck to your labours!" And with these words she fluttered her handkerchief through the open window, and the Bee found himself once more floating in the air.
Oh, what a fine evening it was! But the liberated Bee did not think so. The sun still shone beautifully though lower in the sky, and though the light was softer, and the shadows were longer; and as to the flowers, they were more fragrant than ever; yet the poor Bee felt as if there were a dark heavy cloud over his own heart, for he had become discontented and ambitious, and he rebelled against the authority under which he had been born.
At last he reached his home–the hive which he had left with such a happy heart in the morning–and, after dashing in, in a hurried and angry manner, he began to unload the bags under his thighs of their precious contents, and as he did so he exclaimed, "I am the most wretched of creatures!"
"What is the matter? What have you done?" cried an old Relation who was at work near him; "Have you been eating the poisonous kalmia flowers, or have you discovered that the mischievous honey-moth has laid her eggs in our combs?"
"Oh, neither, neither!" answered the Bee, impatiently; "only I have traveled a long way, and have heard a great deal about myself that I never knew before, and I know now that we are a set of wretched creatures!"
"And, pray, what wise animal has been persuading you of that, against your own experience?" asked the old Relation.
"I have learnt a truth," answered the Bee, in an indignant tone, "and it matters

not who taught it me."
"Certainly not; but it matters very much that you should not fancy yourself wretched merely because some foolish creature has told you you are so; you know very well that you never were wretched till you were told you were so. I call that very silly; but I shall say no more to you." And the old Relation turned himself round to his work, singing very pleasantly all the time.
But the Traveler-bee would not be laughed out of his wretchedness; so he collected some of his young companions around him, and told them what he had heard in the large dining room of the country-house; and all were astonished, and most of them vexed. Then he grew so much pleased at finding himself able to create such excitement and interest, that he became sillier every minute, and made a long speech on the injustice of there being such things as queens, and talked of nature making them all equal and alike, with an energy that would have delighted Uncle Collins himself.
When the Bee had finished his speech, there was first a silence and then a few buzzes of anger, and then a murmured expression of plans and wishes. It must be admitted; their ideas of how to remedy the evil now for the first time suggested to them, were very confused. Some wished Uncle Collins would come and manage all the beehives in the country, for they were sure he would let *all* the bees be queens, and then what a jolly time they should have! And when the old Relation popped his head round the corner of the cell he was building, just to inquire, "What would be the fun of being queens, if there were no working-bees to wait on one?" the little coterie of rebels buzzed very loud, and told him he was a fool, for, of course, Uncle Collins would take care that the tyrant who had so long been queen, and the royal children, now ripening in their nurse-cells, should be made to wait on them while they lasted.
"And when they are finished?" persisted the old Relation, with a laugh.
"Buzz, buzz," was the answer; and the old Relation held his tongue.
Then another Bee suggested that it would, after all, be very awkward for them all to be queens; for who would make the honey and wax, and build the honeycombs, and nurse the children? Would it not be best, therefore, that there should be no queens whatever, but that they should all be working-bees?
But then the tiresome old Relation popped his head round the corner again, and said, he did not quite see how that change would benefit them, for were they not all working-bees already? On which an indignant buzz was poured into his ear, and he retreated again to his work.
It was well that night at last came on, and the time arrived when the labours of the day were over, and sleep and silence must reign in the hive. With the dawn of the morning, however, the troubled thoughts unluckily returned, and the Traveler-bee and his companions kept occasionally clustering together in little groups, to talk over their wrongs and a remedy. Meantime, the rest of the hive were too busy to pay much attention to them, and so their idleness was not detected. But, at last, a few hot-headed youngsters grew so violent in their different opinions, that they lost all self-control, and a noisy quarrel would have broken out, but that the Traveler-bee flew to them, and suggested that, as they

were grown up now, and could not all be turned into queens, they had best sally forth and try the republican experiment of all being working-bees without any queen whatever. With so charming an idea in view, he easily persuaded them to leave the hive; and a very nice swarm they looked as they emerged into the open air, and dispersed about the garden to enjoy the early breeze. But a swarm of bees, without a queen to lead them, proved only a helpless crowd, after all. The first thing they attempted, when they had re-collected to consult, was, to fix on the sort of place in which they should settle for a home.

"A garden, of course," says one. "A field," says another. "There is nothing like a hollow tree," remarked a third. "The roof of a good outhouse is best protected from wet," thought a fourth. "The branch of a tree leaves us most at liberty," cried a fifth. "I won't give up to anybody," shouted all.

They were in a prosperous way to settle, were they not?

"I am very angry with you," cried the Traveler-bee, at last; "half the morning is gone already, and here we are as unsettled as when we left the hive!"

"One would think you were going to be queen over us, to hear you talk," exclaimed the disputants. "If we choose to spend our time in quarrelling, what is that to you? Go and do as you please yourself!"

And he did; for he was ashamed and unhappy; and he flew to the further extremity of the garden to hide his vexation; where, seeing a clump of beautiful jonquils, he dived at once into a flower to soothe himself by honey-gathering. Oh, how he enjoyed it! He loved the flowers and the honey-gathering more than ever, and began his accustomed murmur of delight, and had serious thoughts of going back at once to the hive as usual, when as he was coming out of one of the golden cups, he met his old Relation coming out of another.

"Who would have thought to find you here alone?" said the old Relation. "Where are your companions?"

"I scarcely know; I left them outside the garden."

"What are they doing?"

". . . Quarrelling . . . " murmured the Traveler-bee.

"What about?"

"What they are to do."

"What a pleasant occupation for bees on a sunshiny morning!" said the old Relation, with a sly expression.

"Don't laugh at me, but tell me what to do," said the puzzled Traveler. "What Uncle Collins says about nature and our all being alike, sounds very true, and yet somehow we do nothing but quarrel when we try to be all alike and equal."

"How old are you?" asked the old Relation.

"Seven days," answered the Traveler, in all the sauciness of youth and strength.

"And how old am I?"

"Many months, I am afraid."

"You are right, I am an oldish bee. Now, my dear friend, let us fight!"

"Not for the world. I am the stronger, and should hurt you."

"I wonder what makes you ask advice of a creature so much weaker than yourself?"

"Oh, what can your weakness have to do with your wisdom, my good old Relation? I consult you because I know you are wise; and I am humbled myself, and feel that I am foolish."
"Old and young–strong and weak–wise and foolish–what has become of our being alike and equal? But never mind; we can manage. Now let us agree to live together."
"With all my heart. But where shall we live?"
"Tell me first which of us is to decide, if we differ in opinion?"
"You shall; for you are wise."
"Good! And who shall collect honey for food?"
"I will; for I am strong."
"Very well; and now you have made me a queen, and yourself a working-bee! Ah! You foolish fellow, won't the old home and the old queen do? Don't you see that if even two people live together, there must be a head to lead and hands to follow? How much more in the case of a multitude!"
Gay was the song of the Traveler-bee as he wheeled over the flowers, joyously assenting to the truth of what he heard.
"Now to my companions," he cried at last. And the two flew away together and sought the knot of discontented youngsters outside the garden wall.
They were still quarrelling, but no energy was left them. They were hungry and confused, and many had flown away to work and go home as usual.
And very soon afterwards a cluster of happy buzzing bees, headed by the old Relation and the Traveler, were seen returning with wax-laden thighs to their hive.
As they were going to enter, they were stopped by one of the little sentinels who watch the doorway.
"Wait," cried he; "a royal corpse is passing out!"
And so it was; a dead queen soon appeared in sight, dragged along by working-bees on each side; who, having borne her to the edge of the hive-stand, threw her over for interment.
"How is this? What has happened?" asked the Traveler-bee, in a tone of deep anxiety and emotion: "Surely our queen is not dead?"
"Oh, no!" answered the sentinel; "but there has been some accidental confusion in the hive this morning. Some of the cell-keepers were unluckily absent, and a young queen-bee burst through her cell, which ought to have been blocked up for a few days longer. Of course the two queens fought till one was dead; and, of course, the weaker one was killed. We shall not be able to send off a swarm quite so soon as usual this year; but these accidents can't be helped."
"But this one might have been helped," thought the Traveler-bee to himself, as with a pang of remorse he remembered that he had been the cause of the mischievous confusion.
"You see," buzzed the old Relation, nudging up against him, "You see even *queens are not equal!* And that there can be but one ruler at once!"
And the Traveler-bee murmured a heart-wrung "Yes."
And thus the instincts of nature confirm the reasoning conclusions of man.

THE UNKNOWN LAND

IT mattered not to the Sedge Warbler whether it was night or day!
She built her nest down among the willows, and reeds, and long thick herbage that bordered the great river's side, and in her sheltered covert she sang songs of mirth and rejoicing both by night and day.
"Where does the great river go to?" asked the little ones, as they peered out of their nest one lovely summer night, and saw the moonbeams dancing on the waters as they hurried along. Now, the Sedge Warbler could not tell her children where the great river went to; so she laughed, and said they must ask the Sparrow who chattered so fast, or the Swallow who traveled so far, next time one or other came to perch on the willow-tree to rest. "And then," said she, "you will hear all such stories as these!" And thereupon the Sedge Warbler tuned her voice to the Sparrow's note, and the little ones almost thought the Sparrow was there, the song was so like his–all about towns, and houses, and gardens and fruit-trees, and cats, and guns; only the Sedge Warbler made the account quite confused, for she had never had the patience to sit and listen to the Sparrow, so as really to understand what he said about these matters.
But imperfect as the tale was, it amused the little ones very much, and they tried then to sing like it, and sang till they fell asleep and when they awoke, they burst into singing again; for, behold! The eastern sky was red with the dawn, and they knew the warm sunbeams would soon send beautiful streaks of light in among the reeds and flags that sheltered their happy home.
Now, the Mother-bird would sometimes leave the little ones below, and go up into the willow-branches to sing alone; and as the season advanced she did this oftener and oftener; and her song was plaintive and tender then, for she used to sing to the tide of the river, as it swept along she knew not whither, and think that some day she and her husband and children should all be hurrying so onward as the river hurried–she knew not whither also–to the Unknown Land whence she had come. Yes! I may call it the Unknown Land; for only faint images remained upon her mind of the country whence she had flown.
At first she used to sing these ditties only when alone, but by degrees she began to let her little ones hear them now and then, for were they not going to accompany her? And was it not as well, therefore, to accustom them gradually to think about it?
Then the little ones asked her where the Unknown Land was. But she smiled, and said she could not tell them, for she did not know.
"Perhaps the great river is traveling there all along," thought the eldest child. But he was wrong. The great river was rolling on hurriedly to a mighty city, where it was to stream through the arches of many bridges, and bear on its bosom the traffic of many nations; restless and crowded by day; gloomy, dark, and dangerous by night! Ah! What a contrast were the day and night of the mighty city, to the day and night of the Sedge Warbler's home, where the twenty-four hours of changes God has appointed to nature were but so many changes of beauty!

"Mother, why do you sing songs about another land?" asked a young tenderhearted fledgling one day. "Why should we leave the reed-beds and the willow-trees? Cannot we all build nests here, and live here always? Mother, do not let us go away anywhere else. I want no other land, and no other home but this. There are all the baits in the great river to choose from, where we shall each settle; there can be nothing in the Unknown Land more pleasant than the reed-beds and the willow-trees here. I am so happy! Leave off those dreadful songs!"
Then the Mother's breast heaved with many a varied thought, and she made no reply. So the little one went on–
"Think of the red glow in the morning sky, Mother, and the soft haze–and then the beautiful rays of warm light across the waters! Think of the grand noonday glare, when the broad flags and reeds are all burnished over with heat. Think of these evenings, Mother, when we can sit about in the branches–here, there, anywhere–and watch the great sun go down behind the sky or fly to the great river, and sing in the long green herbage there, and then come home by moonlight and sing till we fall asleep; and wake singing again, if any noise disturb us, if a boat chance to paddle by, or some of those strange bright lights shoot up with a noise into the sky from distant gardens. Think, even when the rain comes down, how we enjoy ourselves, for then how sweet it is to huddle into the soft warm nest together, and listen to the drops pattering upon the flags and leaves overhead! Oh, I love this dear, dear home so much! Sing those dreadful songs about another land no more!"
Then the Mother said–
"Listen to me, my child, and I will sing you another song."
And the Sedge Warbler changed her note, and sang to her tender little one of her own young days, when she was as happy and as gay as now, though not here among the reed-beds; and how, after she had lived and rejoiced in her happiness many pleasant months, a voice seemed to rise within her that said–"*This is not your Rest!* " And how she wondered, and tried not to listen, and tried to stop where she was, and be happy there still. But the voice came oftener and oftener, and louder and louder; and how the dear partner she had chosen heard and felt the same; and how at last they left their home together, and came and settled down among the reed-beds of the great river. And, oh, how happy she had been!
"And where is the place you came from, Mother?" asked the little one. "Is it anywhere near, that we may go and see it?"
"My child," answered the Sedge Warbler, " it is the Unknown Land! Far, far away, I know: but where, I do not know. Only the voice that called me thence is beginning to call again. And, as I was obedient and hopeful once, shall I be less obedient and hopeful now–now that I have been so happy? No, my little one, let us go forth to the Unknown Land, wherever it may be, in joyful trust."
"You will be with me, so I will," murmured little Sedge Warbler in reply; and before she went to sleep she joined her young voice with her mother's in the song of the Unknown Land.
One day afterwards, when the parent birds had gone off to the sedgy banks of a neighbouring stream, another of the young ones flew to the topmost branches of

some willow-trees, and, delighted with his position, began to sing merrily, as he swung backwards and forwards on a bough. Many were the songs he tried, and well enough he succeeded for his age, and at last he tried the song of the Unknown Land.

"A pretty tune, and a pretty voice, and a pretty singer!" remarked a Magpie, who unluckily was crossing the country at the time, and whose mischievous spirit made him stop to amuse himself, by showing off to the young one his superior wisdom, as he thought it.

"I have been in many places, and even once was domesticated about the house of a human creature, so that I am a pretty good judge of singing," continued Mr. Mag, with a cock of his tail, as he balanced himself on a branch near the Sedge Warbler; "but, upon my word, I have seldom heard a prettier song than yours–only I wish you would tell me what it is all about."

"It is about the Unknown Land," answered the young Warbler, with modest pleasure, and very innocently.

"Do I hear you right, my little friend?" inquired the Magpie with mock solemnity–"The *Unknown* Land, did you say? Dear, dear! To think of finding such abstruse philosophy among the marshes and ditches! It is quite a treat! And pray, now, what is there that you can tell an odd old fellow like me, who am always anxious to improve myself, about this Unknown Land?"

"I don't know, except that we are going there some day," answered the Sedge Warbler, rather confused by the Magpie's manner.

"Now, that is excellent!" returned the Magpie, chuckling with laughter. "How I love simplicity, and, really, you are a choice specimen of it, Mr. Sedge Warbler. So you are thinking of a journey to this Unknown Land, always supposing, of course, my sweet little friend, that you can find the way to it, which, between you and me, I think there must naturally be some doubt about, under the circumstances of the place itself being unknown! Good evening to you, pretty Mr. Sedge Warbler. I wish you a pleasant journey!"

"Oh, stop, stop!" cried the young bird, now quite distressed by the Magpie's ridicule; "don't go just yet, pray. Tell me what you think yourself about the Unknown Land."

"Oh, you little wiseacre, are you laughing at me? Why, what can any body, even so clever a creature as yourself think about an unknown thing? You can guess, I admit, anything you please about it, and so could I, if I thought it worthwhile to waste my time so foolishly. But you will never get beyond guessing in such a case–at all events, I confess my poor abilities can't pretend to do anything more."

"Then you are not going there yourself? " murmured the overpowered youngster.

"Certainly not. In the first place, I am quite contented where I am; and, in the second place, I am not quite so easy of belief as you seem to be. How do I know there is such a place as this Unknown Land at all?"

"My father and mother told me that," answered the Sedge Warbler, with more confidence.

"Oh, your father and mother told you, did they?" sneered the Magpie, scornfully. "And you're a good little bird, and believe everything your father and mother tell

you. And if they were to tell you, you were going to live up in the moon, you would believe them, I suppose?"
"They never deceived me yet!" cried the young Sedge Warbler firmly, his feathers ruffling with indignation as he spoke.
"Hoity, toity! What's the matter now, my dainty little cock? Who said your father and mother had ever deceived you? But, without being a bit deceitful, I take the liberty to inform you that they may be extremely ignorant. And I shall leave you to decide which of the two, yourself; for, I declare, one gets nothing but annoyance by trying to be good-natured to you countrified young fellows. You are not fit to converse with a bird of any experience and wisdom. So, once for all, good-bye to you!"
And the Magpie flapped his wings, and was gone before the Sedge Warbler had half recovered from his fit of vexation.
There was a decided change in the weather that evening, for the summer was now far advanced, and a sudden storm had brought cooler breezes and more rain than usual, and the young birds wondered, and were sad, when they saw the dark sky, and the swollen river, and felt that there was no warm sunshine to dry the wet, as was usual after a mid-day shower.
"Why is the sky so cloudy and lowering, and why is the river so thick and gloomy, and why is there no sunshine, I wonder?" said one.
"The sun will shine again tomorrow, I dare say," was the Mother's answer; "but the days are shortening fast; and the storm has made this one very short; and the sun will not get through the clouds this evening. Never mind! the wet has not hurt the inside of our nest. Get into it, my dear ones, and keep warm, while I sing to you about our journey. Silly children, did you expect the sunshine to last here for ever?"
"I hoped it might, and thought it would, once, but lately I have seen a change," answered the young one who had talked to her mother so much before. "And I do not mind now, Mother. When the sunshine goes, and the wet comes, and the river looks dark and the sky black, I think about the Unknown Land."
Then the Mother was pleased, and, perched upon a tall flag outside the nest, she sang a hopeful song of the Unknown Land; and the father and children joined–all but one! He, poor fellow, would not, could not sing; but when the voices ceased, he murmured to his brothers and sisters in the nest–
"This would be all very pleasant and nice, if we could know anything about the Land we talk about."
"If we were to know too much, perhaps we should never be satisfied here," laughed the tender little one, who had formerly been so much distressed about going.
"But we know nothing," rejoined the other bird; "indeed, how do we know there is such a place as the Unknown Land at all?"
"We feel that there is, at any rate," answered the Sister-bird. "I have heard the call our mother tells about, and so must you have done."
"You fancy you have heard it, that is to say," cried the Brother; "because she told you. It is all fancy, all guesswork; no knowledge! I could fancy I heard it too,

only I will not be so weak and silly; I will neither think about going, nor will I go."
"*This is not your Rest*," sang the Mother, in a loud clear voice, outside; and "*This is not your Rest*," echoed the others in sweet unison; and "*This is not your Rest*," sounded in the depths of the poor little Sedge Warbler's own heart.
"This is not our Rest!" repeated the Mother. "The river is rushing forward; the clouds are hurrying onward; the winds are sweeping past, because here is not their Rest. Ask the river, ask the clouds, ask the winds, where they go to: Another Land! Ask the great sun, as he descends away out of sight, where he goes to: Another Land! And when the appointed time shall come, let us also arise and go hence."
"Oh! Mother, Mother, would that I could believe you! Where is that other Land?" Thus cried the distressed doubter in the nest. And then he opened his troubled heart, and told what the Magpie had said, and the parent birds listened in silence, and when he ceased–
"Listen to me, my son," exclaimed the Mother, "and I will sing you another song."
Whereupon she spoke once more of the land she had left before; but now the burden of her story was that she had left it without knowing why. She "went out not knowing whither,"–in blind obedience, faith, and hope. As she traversed the wide waste of waters, there was no one to give her reasons for her flight, or tell her, "This and this will be your lot." Could the Magpie have told her, had he met her there? But had she been deceived? No! The secret voice which had called and led her forth, had been one of Kindness. When she came to the reed-beds she knew all about it. For then arose the strong desire to settle. Then she and her dear partner lived together. And then came the thought that she must build a nest. Ah! Had the Magpie seen her then, building a home for children yet unborn, how he would have mocked at her! What could she know, he would have asked, about the future? Was it not all guesswork, fancy, folly? But had she been deceived! No! It was that voice of Kindness that had told her what to do. For did she not become the happy mother of children? And was she not now able to comfort and advise her little ones in their troubles? For, let the Magpie say what he would, was it likely that the voice of Kindness would deceive them at last? "No!" cried she; "in joyful trust let us obey the call, though now we know not why. When obedience and faith are made perfect, it may be that knowledge and explanation shall be given." So ended the Mother's strain, and no sad misgivings ever clouded the Sedge Warbler's home again.
Several weeks of changing autumn weather followed after this, and the chilly mornings and evenings caused the songs of departure to sound louder and more cheerily than ever in the reed-beds. They knew, they felt, they had confidence, that there was joy for them in the Unknown Land. But one dark morning, when all were busy in various directions, a sudden loud sound startled the young ones from their sports, and in terror and confusion they hurried home. The old nest looked looser and more untidy than ever that day, for some water had oozed in through the half-worn bottom. But they huddled together into it, as of old, for

safety. Soon, however, it was discovered that neither Father nor Mother were there; and after waiting in vain some time for their return, the frightened young ones flew off again to seek them.

Oh! Weary, weary search for the missing ones we love! It may be doubted whether the sad reality, when they came upon it, exceeded the agony of that hour's suspense.

It ended, however, at last! On a patch of long rank herbage which covered a mud bank, so wet that the cruel sportsman could not follow to secure his prey, lay the stricken parent birds. One was already dead, but the mother still lived, and as her children's wail of sorrow sounded in her ear, she murmured out a last gentle strain of hope and comfort.

"Away, away, my darlings, to the Unknown Land. The voice that has called to all our race before, and never but for kindness, is calling to you now! Obey! Go forth in joyful trust! Quick! Quick! There's no time to be lost!"

"But my Father–you–oh, my Mother!" cried the young ones.

"Hush, sweet ones, hush! We cannot be with you there. But there may be some other Unknown Land which this may lead to;" and the Mother laid her head against her wounded side and died.

Long before the sunbeams could pierce the heavy haze of the next autumn morning, the young Sedge Warblers rose for the last time o'er their much loved reed-beds, and took flight–"they knew not whither."

Dim and undefined hope, perhaps, they had that they might find their parents again in the Unknown Land. And if one pang of grief struck them when these hopes ended, it was but for a moment, for, said the Brother-Bird–

"There may be some other Unknown Land, better even than this, to which they may be gone."

KNOWLEDGE NOT THE LIMIT OF BELIEF

"Canst thou by searching find out God?"–JOB xi. 7.

IT was but the banging of the door, blown to by a current of wind from the open window that made that great noise, and shook the room so much!

The room was a naturalist's library, and it was a pity that some folio books of specimens had been left so near the edge of the great table, for, when the door clapt to, they fell down, and many plants, sea-weeds, etc., were scattered on the floor.

And, "Do we meet once again?" said a zoophyte to a seaweed (a *Corallina*) in whose company he had been thrown ashore, "Do we meet once again? This is a real pleasure. What strange adventures we have gone through since the waves flung us on the sands together!"

"Ay, indeed," replied the Seaweed, "and what a queer place we have come to at last! Well, well–but let me first ask you how you are this morning, after all the washing, and drying, and squeezing, and gumming, we have undergone?"

Zoophyte. "Oh, pretty well in health, Seaweed, but very, very sad. You know there is a great difference between you and me. You have little or no cause to be sad. You are just the same now that you ever were, excepting that you can never grow any more. But I! Ah, I am only the skeleton of what I once was! All the merry little creatures that inhabited me are dead and dried up. They died by hundreds at a time soon after I left the sea; and even if they had survived longer, the nasty fresh water we were soaked in by the horrid being who picked us up, would have killed them at once. What are you smiling at?"

Seaweed. "I am smiling at your calling our new master a horrid being, and also at your speaking so positively about the little creatures that inhabited you."

"And why may I not speak positively of what I know so well? " asked the other.

Seaweed. "Oh, of what you know, by all means! But I wonder what we do know! People get very obstinate over what they think they know, and then, lo and behold! It turns out to be a mistake."

Zoophyte. "What makes you say this?"

Seaweed. "I have learnt it from a very curious creature I have made acquaintance with here–a bookworm. He walks through all the books in this library just as he pleases, and picks up a quantity of information, and knows a great deal. And he's a mere nothing, he says, compared to the creature who picked us up–the 'horrid being' as you call him. Why, my dear friend, the Bookworm tells me that he who found us is a man, and that a man is the most wonderful creature in all the world; that there is nothing in the least like him. And this particular one here is a naturalist; that is, he knows all about living creatures, and plants, and stones, and I don't know what besides. Now, wouldn't you say that it was a great honour to belong to him, and to have made acquaintance with his friend the Bookworm?"

Zoophyte. "Of course I should, and do."

Seaweed. "Very well, I know you would; and yet I can tell you that this naturalist and his bookworm are just instances of what I have been saying. They fancy that betwixt them they know nearly everything, and get as obstinate as possible over the most ridiculous mistakes."

Zoophyte. "My good friend, are you a competent judge in such matters as these?"

"Oh, am I not!" the Seaweed rejoined. "Why now, for instance, what do you think the Bookworm and I have been quarrelling about half the morning? Actually as to whether *I* am an animal or a vegetable. He declares that I am an animal full of little living creatures like yours, and that there is a long account of all this written on the page opposite the one on which I am gummed!"

"Of all the nonsense I ever listened to!" began the Zoophyte, angrily, yet amused–but he was interrupted by the Seaweed–

"And as for *you*–I am almost ashamed to tell you–that you and all your family and connections were, for generations and generations, considered as vegetables. It is only lately that these naturalists found out that you were an animal. May I not well say that people get very obstinate about what they think they know, and after all it turns out to be a mistake? As for me, I am quite confused with these blunders."

"O dear, how disappointed I am!" murmured the Zoophyte. "I thought we had really fallen into the hands of some very interesting creatures. I am very, very sorry! It seemed so nice that there should be wonderful, wise beings, who spend their time in finding out all about animals, and plants, and such things, and keep us all in these beautiful books so carefully. I liked it so much and now I find the wonderfully wise creatures are wonderfully stupid ones instead."

"Very much so," laughed the Seaweed, "though our learned friend, the Bookworm, would tell you quite otherwise; but he gets quite muddled when he talks about them, poor fellow!"

"It is very easy to ridicule your betters," said a strange voice; and the Bookworm, who had just then eaten his way through the back of Lord Bacon's *Advancement of Learning*, appeared sitting outside, listening to the conversation. "I shall be very sorry that I have told you anything, if you make such a bad use of the little bit of knowledge you have acquired."

"Oh, I beg your pardon, dear friend!" cried the Seaweed. "I meant no harm. You see it is quite new to us to learn anything; and, really, if I laughed, you must excuse me. I meant no harm–only I *do* happen to know–really for a fact–that I never was alive with little creatures like my friend the Zoophyte; and he happens to know–really for a fact–that he never was a vegetable; and so you see it made us smile to think of your wonderful creature, man, making such wonderfully odd mistakes."

At this the Bookworm smiled; but he soon shook his head gravely, and said–"All the mistakes man makes, man can discover and correct–I mean, of course, all the mistakes he makes about creatures inferior to himself, whom he learns to know from his own observation. He may not observe quite carefully enough one day, but he may put all right when he looks next time. I never give up a statement when I know it is true: and so I tell you again–laugh as much as you please–that, in spite of all his mistakes, man is, without exception, the most wonderful and

the most clever of all the creatures upon earth!"
"You will be a clever creature yourself if you can prove it!" cried both the Zoophyte and Seaweed at once.
"The idea of taking me with my hundreds of living inhabitants for a vegetable!" sneered the Zoophyte.
"And me with my vegetable inside, covered over with lime, for an animal!" smiled the Seaweed.
Bookworm. "Ah! Have your laugh out, and then listen. But, my good friends, if you had worked your way through as many wise books as I have done, you would laugh less and know more."
Zoophyte. "Nay, don't be angry, Bookworm."
Bookworm. "Oh, I am not angry a bit. I know too well the cause of all the folly you are talking, so I excuse you. And I am now puzzling my head to find out how I am to prove what I have said about the superiority of man, so as to make you understand it."
Seaweed. "Then you admit there is a little difficulty in proving it? Even you confess it to be rather puzzling."
Bookworm. "I do; but the difficulty does not lie where you think it does. I am sorry to say it–but the only thing that prevents your understanding the superiority of man, is your own immeasurable inferiority to him! However many mistakes he may make about you, he can correct them all by a little closer or more patient observation. But no observation can make you understand what man is. You are quite within the grasp of his powers, but he is quite beyond the reach of yours."
Seaweed. "You are not over-civil, with all your learning, Mr. Bookworm."
Bookworm. "I do not mean to be rude, I assure you. You are both of you very beautiful creatures, and, I dare say, very useful too. But you should not fancy either that you do know everything, or that you are able to know everything. And, above all, you should not dispute the superiority and powers of another creature merely because you cannot understand them."
Seaweed. "And am I then to believe all the long stories anybody may choose to come and tell me about the wonderful powers of other creatures? And, when I inquire what those wonderful powers are, am I to be told that I can't understand them, but am to believe them all the same as if I did?"
Bookworm. "Certainly not, unless the wonderful powers are proved by wonderful results; but if they are, I advise you to believe in them, whether you understand them or not."
Seaweed. " I should like to know how I am to believe what I don't understand."
Bookworm. "Very well, then, don't! And remain an ignorant fool all your life. Of course, you can't really understand anything but what is within the narrow limits of your own powers; so, if you choose to make those powers the limits of your belief, I wish you joy, for you certainly won't be overburdened with knowledge."
Seaweed. "I will retort upon you that it is very easy to be contemptuous to your inferiors, Mr. Bookworm. You would do much better to try and explain to me those wonderful powers themselves, and so remove all the difficulties that stand

in the way of my belief."

Bookworm. "If I were to try ever so much, I should not succeed. You can't understand even *my* superiority."

Seaweed. "Oh, Bookworm! Now you are growing conceited."

Bookworm. "Indeed I am not; but you shall judge for yourself. I can do many things you can't do; among others, I can see."

Seaweed. "What is that?"

Bookworm. "There, now! I knew I should puzzle you directly! Why, seeing is something that I do with a very curious machine in my head, called an eye. But as you have not got an eye, and therefore cannot see, how am I to make you understand what seeing is?"

Seaweed. "Why, you can tell us, to be sure."

Bookworm. "Tell you what? I can tell you I see. I can say, now I see; now I see, as I walk over you and see the little bits of you that fall under my small eye. Indeed, I can also tell you what I see; but how will that teach you what seeing is? You have got no eye, and therefore you can't see, and therefore also you can never know what seeing is."

Zoophyte. "Then why need we believe there is such a thing as seeing?"

Bookworm. "Oh, pray, don't believe it! I don't know why you should, I am sure! There's no harm at all in being ignorant and narrow-minded. I am sure I had much rather you took no further trouble in the matter; for you are, both of you, very testy and tiresome. It is from nothing but pride and vanity, too, after all. You want to be in a higher place in creation than you are put in, and no good ever comes of that. If you'd be content to learn wonderful things in the only way that is open to you, I should have a great deal of pleasure in telling you more."

Zoophyte. "And pray what way is that?"

Bookworm. "Why, from the effects produced by them. As I said before, even where you cannot *understand* the wonderful powers themselves, you may have the grace to believe in their existence, from their wonderful results."

Seaweed. "And the results of what you call 'seeing' are–"

"In man," interrupted the Bookworm, "that he gets to know everything about you, and all the creatures, and plants, and stones he looks at; so that he knows your shape, and growth, and colour, and all about the cells of the little creatures that live in you–how many feelers they have, what they live upon, how they catch their food, how the eggs come out of the egg-cells, where you live, where you are to be found, what other zoophytes are related to you, which are most like you–in short, the most minute particulars; so that he puts you into his collections, not among strange creatures, but near to those you are nearest related to; and he describes you, and makes pictures of you, and gives you a name so that you are known for the same creature, wherever you are found, all over the world. And now, I'm quite out of breath with telling you all these wonderful results of seeing."

"But he once took me for a vegetable," mused the Zoophyte.

"Yes; as I said before, he had not observed quite close enough, nor had he then invented a curious instrument which enables his great big eye to see such little

fellows as your inhabitants are. But when he made that instrument, and looked very carefully, he saw all about you."
"Ay, but he still calls me an animal," observed the Seaweed.
"I know he does, but I am certain he will not do so long! If you are a vegetable, I will warrant him to find it out when he examines you a little more."
"You expect us to believe strange things, Bookworm," observed the Zoophyte.
"To be sure, because there is no end of strange things for you to believe! And what you can't find out for yourself, you must take upon trust from your betters," laughed the Bookworm. "It's the only plan. *Observation and Revelation are the sole means of acquiring knowledge.*"
Just at that moment the door opened, and two gentlemen entered the room.
"Ah, my new specimens on the floor!" observed the Naturalist; "but never mind," added he, as he picked them up; "Here is the very one we wanted; it will serve admirably for our purpose. I shall only sacrifice a small branch of it, though."
And the Naturalist cut off a little piece of the Seaweed and laid it in a saucer, and poured upon it some liquid from a bottle, and an effervescence began to take place forthwith, and the Seaweed's limy coat began to give way; and the two gentlemen sat watching the result.
"Now," whispered the Bookworm to the Zoophyte, "those two men are looking closely at your Seaweed friend, and trying what they call experiments, that they may find out what he is; and if they do not succeed, I will give up all my arguments in despair."
But they did succeed.
The gentlemen watched on till all the lime was dissolved, and there was nothing left in the saucer but a delicate red branch with little round things upon it, that looked like tiny apples.
"This is the fruit decidedly," remarked the Naturalist; "and now we will proceed to examine it through the microscope."
And they did so.
And an hour or more passed, and a sort of sleepy forgetfulness came over the Bookworm and his two friends; for they had waited till they were tired for further remarks from the Naturalist. And, therefore, it was with a start they were aroused at last by hearing him exclaim, "It is impossible to entertain the slightest doubt. If I ever had any, I have none now; and the *Corallinas* must be removed back once more to their position among vegetables!"
The Naturalist laughed as he loosened the gum from the specimen, which he placed on a fresh paper, and classed among Red Seaweeds. And soon after, the two gentlemen left the room once more.
"So he has really found our friend out!" cried the Zoophyte; "and he was right about the fruit, too! Oh, Bookworm, Bookworm! Would that I could know what seeing is!"
"Oh, Zoophyte, Zoophyte! I wish you would not waste your time in struggling after the unattainable! You know what feeling is. Well, I would tell you that seeing is something of the same sort as feeling, only that it is quite different.

Will that do?"
"It sounds like nonsense."
"It is nonsense. There can be no answer but nonsense, if you want to understand 'really for a fact,' as you call it, powers that are above you. Explain to the rock on which you grow, what feeling is!"
"How could I?" said the Zoophyte; "it has no sensation."
"No more than you have sight," rejoined the Bookworm.
"That is true indeed," cried the Zoophyte. "Bookworm! I am satisfied–humbled, I must confess, but satisfied. And now I will rejoice in our position here, glory in our new master, and admire his wonderful powers, even while I cannot understand them."
"I am proud of my disciple," returned the Bookworm kindly.
"I also am one of them," murmured the Seaweed; "but tell me now, are there any other strange powers in man?"
"Several," was the Bookworm's answer; "but to be really known they must be possessed. A lower power cannot compass the full understanding of a higher. But to limit one's belief to the bounds of one's own small powers, would be to tie oneself down to the foot of a tree, and deny the existence of its upper branches."
"There are no powers beyond those that man possesses, I suppose," mused the Zoophyte.
"I am far from saying that," replied the Bookworm; "on the contrary–"
But what he would have said further no one knows, for once more the door opened, and the Naturalist, who now returned alone, spent his evening in putting by the specimens in their separate volumes on the shelves. And it was a long, long time before the Bookworm saw them again; for the volumes in which they were kept were bound in Russia leather, to the smell of which he had a particular dislike, so that he never could make his way to them for a friendly chat again.

TRAINING AND RESTRAINING

"Train up a child in the way he should go."–PROV. xxii. 6.

"WHAT a fuss is made about you, my dear little friends!" murmured the Wind, one day, to the flowers in a pretty villa garden. "I am really quite surprised at your submitting so patiently and meekly to all the troublesome things that are done to you! I have been watching your friend the Gardener for some time today; and now that he is gone at last, I am quite curious to hear what you think and feel about your unnatural bringing up."

"Is it unnatural?" inquired a beautiful Convolulus Major, from the top of a tapering fir-pole, up which she had crept, and from which her velvet flowers hung suspended like purple gems.

"I smile at your question," was the answer of the Wind. "You surely cannot suppose that in a natural state you would be forced to climb regularly up one tall bare stick such as I see you upon now. Oh dear, no! Your cousin, the wild Convolvulus, whom I left in the fields this morning, does no such thing, I assure you. She runs along and climbs about, just as the whim takes her. Sometimes she takes a turn upon the ground; sometimes she enters a hedge, and plays at bo-peep with the birds in the thorn and nut-trees–twisting here, curling there, and at last, perhaps coming out at the top, and overhanging the hedge with a canopy of green leaves and pretty white flowers. A very different sort of life from yours, with a Gardener always after you, trimming you in one place, fastening up a stray tendril in another, and fidgeting you all along–a sort of perpetual 'mustn't go here'–'mustn't go there.' Poor thing! I quite feel for you! Still I must say you make me smile; for you look so proud and self-conscious of beauty all the time, that one would think you did not know in what a ridiculous and dependent position you are placed."

Now the Convolvulus was quite abashed by the words of the Wind, for she was conscious of feeling very conceited that morning, in consequence of having heard the Gardener say something very flattering about her beauty; so she hung down her rich bell-flowers rather lower than usual, and made no reply.

But the Carnation put in her word: "What you say about the Convolvulus may be true enough, but it cannot apply to me. I am not aware that I have any poor relations in this country, and I myself certainly require all the care that is bestowed upon me. This climate is both too cold and too damp for me. My young plants require heat, or they would not live; and the pots we are kept in protect us from those cruel wire-worms who delight to destroy our roots."

"Oh!" cried the Wind, "our friend the Carnation is quite profound and learned in her remarks, and I admit the justice of all she says about damp and cold, and wire-worms; but,"–and here the Wind gave a low-toned whistle as he took a turn round the flower-bed–"but what I maintain, my dear, is that when you are once strong enough and old enough to be placed in the soil, those gardeners ought to let you grow and flourish as Nature prompts, and as you would do were you left alone. But no! Forsooth, they must always be clipping, and trimming, and twisting up every leaf that strays aside out of the trim pattern they have chosen for you to grow in. Why not allow your silver tufts to luxuriate in a natural manner? Why must every single flower be tied up by its delicate neck to a stick the moment it begins to open? Really, with your natural grace and beauty, I think you might be trusted to yourself a little more!"

And the Carnation began to think so too; and her colour turned deeper as a feeling of indignation arose within her at the childish treatment to which she had been subjected. "With my natural grace and beauty," repeated she to herself, "they might certainly trust me to myself a little more!"

Still the Rose-tree stood out that there must be some great advantages in a Gardener's care; for she could not pretend to be ignorant of her own superiority to all her wild relations in the woods. What a difference in size, in colour, and in fragrance!

Then the Wind assured the Rose he never meant to dispute the advantage of her living in a rich-soiled garden; only there was a natural way of growing, even in a garden; and he thought it a great shame for the gardeners to force the Rose-tree into an unnatural way, curtailing all the energies of her nature. What could be more outrageous, for example, than to see one rose growing in the shape of a bush on the top of the stem of another? "Think of all the pruning necessary," cried he, "to keep the poor thing in the round shape so much admired. And what is the matter with the beautiful straggling branches that they are to be cut off as fast as they appear? Why not allow the healthy Rose-tree its free and glorious growth? Why thwart its graceful droopings or its high aspirings? Can it be too large or too luxuriant? Can its flowers be too numerous? Oh, Rose-tree, you know your own surpassing merits too well to make you think this possible!"

And so she did, and a new light seemed to dawn upon her as she recollected the spring and autumnal prunings she regularly underwent, and the quantities of little branches that were yearly cut from her sides, and carried away in a wheel-barrow. "It is a cruel and a monstrous system, I fear," said she.

Then the Wind took another frolic round the garden, and made up to the large white Lily, into whose refined ear he whispered a doubt as to the necessity or advantage of her thick powerful stem being propped up against a stupid, ugly stick! He really grieved to see it! Did that lovely creature suppose that Nature, who had done so much for her that the fame of her beauty extended throughout the world, had yet left her so weak and feeble that she could not support herself in the position most calculated to give her ease and pleasure? "Always this tying up and restraint!" pursued the Wind, with an angry puff. "Perhaps I am prejudiced; but as to be deprived of freedom would be to me absolute death, so my soul revolts from every shape and phase of slavery!"

"Not more than mine does!" cried the proud white Lily, leaning as heavily as she could against the strip of matting that tied her to her stick. But it was of no use–she could not get free; and the Wind only shook his sides and laughed spitefully as he left her and then rambled away to talk the same shallow philosophy to the Honeysuckle that was trained up against a wall. Indeed, not a flower escaped his mischievous suggestions. He murmured among them all–laughed the trim-cut

Box-edges to scorn–maliciously hoped the Sweet-peas enjoyed growing in a circle, and running up a quantity of crooked sticks–and told the flowers, generally, that he should report their unheard-of submission and meek obedience wherever he went.

Then the white Lily called out to him in great wrath, and told him he mistook their characters altogether. They only submitted to these degrading restraints because they could not help themselves; but if he would lend them his powerful aid, they might free themselves from at least a part of the unnatural bonds which enthralled them.

To which the wicked Wind, seeing that his temptations had succeeded, replied, in great glee, that he would do his best; and so he went away, chuckling at the discontent he had caused.

All that night the pretty silly flowers bewailed their lavish condition, and longed for release and freedom; and at last they began to be afraid that the Wind had only been jesting with them, and that he would never come to help them, as he had promised. However, they were mistaken; for, at the edge of the dawn, there began to be a sighing and a moaning in the distant woods, and by the time the sun was up, the clouds were driving fast along the sky, and the trees were bending about in all directions; for the Wind had returned–only now he had come in his roughest and wildest mood–knocking over everything before him. "Now is your time, pretty flowers!" shouted he, as he approached the garden; and "Now is our time!" echoed the flowers tremulously, as, with a sort of fearful pleasure, they awaited his approach.

He managed the affair very cleverly, it must be confessed. Making a sort of eddying circuit round the garden, he knocked over the Convolvulus-pole, tore the strips of bast from the stick that held up the white Lily, loosed all the Carnation flowers from their fastenings, broke the Rose-tree down, and leveled the Sweet-peas to the ground. In short, in one half-hour he desolated the pretty garden; and when his work was accomplished, he flew off to rave about his deed of destruction in other countries.

Meanwhile, how fared it with the flowers? The Wind was scarcely gone before a sudden and heavy rain followed, so that all was confusion for some time. But towards the evening the weather cleared up, and our friends began to look around them. The white Lily still stood somewhat upright, though no friendly pole supported her juicy stem; but, alas! It was only by a painful effort she could hold herself in that position. The Wind and the weight of rain had bent her forward once, beyond her strength, and there was a slight crack in one part of the stalk, which told that she must soon double over and trail upon the ground. The Convolvulus fared still worse. The garden-beds sloped towards the south; and when our friend was laid on the earth–her pole having fallen–her lovely flowers were choked up by the wet soil which drained towards her. She felt the muddy weight as it soaked into her beautiful velvet bells, and could have cried for grief: she could never free herself from this nuisance. O that she were once more climbing up the friendly fir-pole! The Honeysuckle escaped no better; and the Carnation was ready to die of vexation, at finding that her coveted freedom had leveled her to the dirt.

Before the day closed, the Gardener came whistling from his farm work, to look over his pretty charges. He expected to see a few drooping flowers, and to find that one or two fastenings had given way. But for the sight that awaited him he was not prepared at all. Struck dumb with astonishment, he never spoke at first, but kept lifting up the heads of the trailing, dirtied flowers in succession. Then at last he broke out into words of absolute sorrow: "And to think of my mistress and the young lady coming home so soon, and that nothing can be done to these poor things for a fortnight, because of the corn harvest! It's all over with them, I fear;" and the Gardener went his way.

Alas! What he said was true; and before many days had passed, the shattered Carnations were rotted with lying in the wet and dirt on the ground. The white Lily was languishing discoloured on its broken stalk; the Convolvulus' flowers could no longer be recognised, they were so coated over with mud stains; the Honeysuckle was trailing along among battered Sweet-peas, who never could succeed in shaking the soil from their fragrant heads; and though the Rose-tree had sent out a few straggling branches, she soon discovered that they were far too weak to bear flowers–nay, almost to support themselves–so that they added neither to her beauty nor her comfort. Weeds meanwhile sprang up, and a dreary confusion reigned in the once orderly and brilliant little garden.

At length, one day before the fortnight was over, the housedog was heard to bark his noisy welcome, and servants bustled to and fro. The mistress had returned, and the young lady was with her, and hurried at once to her favourite garden. She came bounding towards the well-known spot with a song of joyous delight; but, on reaching it, suddenly stopped short, and in a minute after burst into a flood of tears! Presently, with sorrowing steps, she bent her way round the flower-beds, weeping afresh at every one she looked at; and then she sat down upon the lawn, and hid her face in her hands. In this position she remained, until a gentle hand was laid upon her shoulder.

"This is a sad spectacle, indeed, my darling," said her mother's voice.

"Never mind about the garden, mamma," replied the young girl, lifting up her tearful face; "we can plant new flowers, and tie up even some of these afresh. But what I have been thinking is, that now, at last, I quite understand what you have so often said about the necessity of training, and restraint, and culture, for us as well as for flowers, in a fallen world. The wind has torn away these poor things from their fastenings, and they are growing wild whichever way they please. I know I should once have argued that if it were their natural mode of growing it must therefore be the best. But I cannot say so, now that I see the result. They are doing whatever they like, unrestrained and the end is, that my beautiful GARDEN is turned into a WILDERNESS."

THE LIGHT OF TRUTH

"DETESTABLE phantom!" cried the traveler, as his horse sank with him into the morass; "to what a miserable end have you lured me by your treacherous light!"

"The same old story for ever!" muttered the Will-o'-the-Wisp in reply. "Always throwing blame on others for troubles you have brought upon yourself. What more could have been done for you, unhappy creature, than I have done? All the weary night through have I danced on the edge of this morass to save you and others from ruin. If you have rushed in further and further, like a headstrong fool, in spite of my warning light, who is to blame but yourself?"

"I am an unhappy creature, indeed," rejoined the traveler: "I took your light for a friendly lamp, but have been deceived to my destruction."

"Yet not by me," cried the Will-o'-the-Wisp, anxiously. "I work out my appointed business carefully and ceaselessly. My light is ever a friendly lamp to the wise. It misleads none but the headstrong and ignorant."

"Headstrong! Ignorant!" exclaimed the Statesman, for such the traveler was. "How little do you know to whom you are speaking! Trusted by my King–honoured by my country–the leader of her councils–ah, my country, my poor country, who will take my place and guide you when I am gone?"

"A guide who cannot guide himself! Misjudging, misled, and–though wise, perhaps, in the imperfect laws of society–ignorant in the glorious laws of Nature and of Truth–who will miss you, presumptuous being? You have mistaken the light that warned you of danger for the star that was to guide you to safety. Alas for your country, if no better leader than you can be found!"

The Statesman never spoke again, and the Will-o'the-Wisp danced back to the edge of the black morass; and as he flickered up and down, he mourned his luckless fate–always trying to do good–so often vilified and misjudged. "Yet," said he to himself, as he sent out his beams through the cheerless night, "I will not cease to try; who knows but that I may save somebody yet! But what an ignorant world I live in!"

* * * * *

"Cruel monster!" shrieked the beautiful Girl in wild despair, as her feet plunged into the swamp, and she struggled in vain to find firmer ground, "you have betrayed me to my death!"

"Ay, ay, I said so! It is always some one else who is to blame, and never yourself, when pretty fools like you deceive themselves. You call me 'monster'–why did you follow a 'monster' into a swamp?" cried the poor Will-o'-the-Wisp angrily.

"I thought my betrothed had come out to meet me. I mistook your hateful light for his. Oh, cruel fiend, I know you now! Must I die so young, so fair? Must I be torn from life, and happiness, and love? Ay, dance! Dance on in your savage joy."

"Fool as you are, it is no joy to me to see you perish," answered the Will-o'-the-Wisp. "It is my appointed law to warn and save those who will be warned. It is my appointed sorrow, I suppose, that the recklessness and ignorance of such as you, persist in disregarding that law, and turning good into evil. I shone bright and brighter before you as you advanced, entreating you, as it were, to be warned. But, in willfulness, you pursued me to your ruin. What cruel mother brought you up, and did not teach you to distinguish the steady beam that guides to happiness, from the wandering brilliancy that bodes destruction?"

"My poor mother!" wept the Maiden; "what words are these you speak of her? But you, in your savage life, know nothing of what she has done for me, her only child. Mistress of every accomplishment that can adorn and delight society, my lightest word, my very smile, is a law to the world we move in."

"Even so! Accomplished in fleeting and fantastic arts that leave no memorial behind them–unacquainted with the beauty and purposes of the realities around you, which work from age to age in silent mercy for gracious ends, and put to shame the toil that has no aim or end. Oh that you had but known the law by which I live!"

The Maiden spoke no more, and then she ceased to struggle. The Will-o'-the-Wisp danced back yet another time to the edge of the black morass; "For," said he, "I may save somebody yet. But what a foolish world I live in!"

* * * * *

"The old Squire should mend these here roads," observed Hobbinoll the Farmer to his son Colin, as they drove slowly home from market in a crazy old cart which shook about with such jerks, that little Colin tried in vain to keep curled up in a corner. It was hard to say whether the fault was most in the roads–though they were rather rutty, it must be owned–or in the stumbling old pony who went from side to side, or in the not very sober driver, who seemed unable at times to distinguish the reins apart, so that he gave sudden pulls, first one way and then the other. But through all these troubles it comforted the Farmer's heart to lay all the blame on the Squire for the bad roads that led across the boggy moor. Colin, however, took but little interest in the matter; but at length, when a more violent jerk than usual threw him almost sprawling on the bottom of the cart, he jumped up, laid hold of the side planks, and began to look around him with his half-sleepy eyes, trying to find out where they were. At last he said, "She's coming, father."

"Who's coming?" shouted Hobbinoll.

"T' mother," answered Colin.

"What's she coming for, I wonder," said Hobbinoll; "we've enough in the cart without her."

"But you're going away from her, father," expostulated Colin, half crying. "I see her with the lanthorn, and she'll light us home. You can't see, father; let me have the reins." But Hobbinoll refused to give up the reins, though he was not very fit to drive. In the struggle, however, he caught sight of the light which Colin took

for his mother's lanthorn.
"And is that the fool's errand you'd be going after?" cried he, pointing with his whip to the light. "It's lucky for you, young one, you have not had the driving of us home tonight, though you think you can do anything, I know. A precious home it would have been at the bottom of the sludgy pool yonder, for that's where you'd have got us to at last. Yon light is the Will-o'-the-Wisp, that's always trying to mislead folks. Bad luck befall him! I got halfway to him once when I was a young 'un, but an old neighbour who'd once been in himself was going by just then, and called me back. He's a villain is that sham-faced Will-o'-the-Wisp."
With these words the Farmer struck the pony so harshly with his heavy whip, twitching the reins convulsively at the same time, at the mere memory of his adventure in the bog, that little Colin was thrown up and down like a ball, and the cart rolled forward in and out of the ruts at such a pace, that Hobbinoll got home to his wife sooner than she ever dared to hope for on market evenings.
"They are safe," observed the Will-o'-the-Wisp,' as the cart moved on, "and that is the great point gained! Nevertheless, such wisdom is mere brute experience. In their ignorance they would have struck the hand that helped them. Nevertheless, I will try again, for I may yet save some one else. But what a rude and ungrateful world I live in!"

* * * * *

"I see a light at last, papa!" shouted a little Boy on a Shetland pony, as he rode by his Father's side along the moor. "I am so glad! There is either a cottage or a friendly man with a lanthorn who will help us to find our way. Let me go after him; I can soon overtake him." And the little boy touched his pony with a whip, and in another minute would have been cantering along after the light, but that his Father laid a sudden and a heavy hand upon the bridle.
"Not a step further in that direction, at any rate, if you please, my darling."
"Oh, papa!" expostulated the child, pointing with his hand to the light.
And, "Oh, my son, I see!" cried the Father, smiling; "and well is it for you that I not only see, but know the meaning of what I see at the same time. That light is neither the gleam from a cottage, nor yet a friendly man with a lanthorn as you think, though, for the matter of that the light is friendly enough to those who understand it. It shines there to warn us from the dangerous part of the bog. Kind old Will-o'-the-Wisp!" pursued the Father, raising his voice, as if calling through the darkness into the distance–"Kind old Will-o'-the-Wisp, we know what you mean; we will not come near your deathly swamps. The Old Naturalist knows you well–good-night, and thank you for the warning." So saying, the Naturalist turned the reins of his son's pony the other way, and they both trotted along, keeping the beaten road as well as they could by the imperfect light.
"After all, it was more like a lanthorn than those pictures of the nasty Will-o'-the-Wisp, papa," murmured the little Boy, reluctantly urging his pony on.
"Our friend is not much indebted to you for the pretty name you have called

him," laughed the Father. "You are of the same mind as the poet, who, with the licence of his craft, said–

> *'Yonder phantom only flies*
> *To lure thee to thy doom.'"*

"Yes, papa, and so he does," interposed the Boy.

"But, indeed, he does no such thing, my dear. On the contrary, he spends all his life in shining brightly to warn travelers of the most dangerous parts of the swamp."

"But the shining seems as if he was inviting them to go after him, papa."

"Only because you choose to think so, my dear, and do not inquire. Does the sailor think the shining of the lighthouse invites him to approach the dangerous rocks on which it is built?"

"Oh, no, papa, because he knows it is put there on purpose to warn him away."

"He only knows by teaching and inquiry, Arthur; and so you also by teaching and inquiry will learn to know that this Will-o'-the-Wisp is made to shine for us in swamps and marshes as a land-beacon of danger. The laws of Nature, which are the acted will of God, work together in this case, as in all others, for a good end. And it is given to of us as both a privilege and a pleasure to search them out, and to avail ourselves of the mercies, whilst we admire the wonders of the great Creator. Can you think of a better employment?"

The fire was very bright, and the tea was warm and good, that greeted the travelers, Father and Son, on their arrival at home that night. Many a joke, too, passed with Mamma as to the sort of tea they should have tasted, and the kind of bed they should have laid down in, had they only gone after the Will-o'-the-Wisp, as young Arthur had so much wished to do.

And for just a few days after these events–not more, for children's wisdom seldom does, or ought to, last much longer–Arthur had every now and then a wise and philosophical fit, and on the principle, that, however much appearances might be to the contrary, the laws of Nature were always working to some good and beneficent end, he sagely and gravely reproved his little sister for crying when a shower of hailstones fell; "For surely," said he, "though we cannot go out today, the storm is doing good to something or somebody somewhere."

It was a blessed creed! Though it cost him a struggle to adhere to it, when the lightning flashed round him, and the thunder roared in the distance, and he saw from the windows dark clouds hanging over the landscape. When some one said the storm had been very grand, he thought–yes, but it was grander still to think that all these laws of Nature, as they are called–this acted will of God–was for ever working night and day, in darkness and in light, recognised or unheeded, for some wise and beneficent end.

Yes! When he was older he would try and trace out these ends, a better employment could not be found. And it may be, that in long after years, when the storms and the clouds that gathered round him were harder yet to look through, because they were mental troubles–it may be, that then, from amidst the tender recollections of his infancy, the gleaming of the Will-o'-the-Wisp would suddenly rise and shine before him with comfort. For the Student of Nature who had traced so many blessed ends out of dark and mysterious beginnings, held fast to the humility and faith of childhood; and where his mind was unable to penetrate, his heart was contented to believe.

* * * * *

Meanwhile the Will-o'-the-Wisp had heard the kind goodnight that greeted him as the travelers passed by on that dark evening. And his light shone brighter than ever, as he said, "I am happy now. I have saved the life of one who not only is thankful for it, but knows the hand that saved him." With these words he cheerily danced back again to his appointed post.

WAITING

"It is good that a man should both hope and quietly wait."–LAM. iii. 26

IT was, doubtless, a very sorry life the House Cricket led, before houses were built and fires were kindled. There was no comfortable kitchen-hearth then, in the warm nooks and corners of which he might sit and sing his cheerful song, coming out every now and then to bask himself in the glow of the blazing light. On the contrary, he, so fond of heat, had no place to shelter in but holes in hollow trees, or crevices in rocks and stones, or some equally dull and damp abode. Besides which, he had to bear the incessant taunts and ridicule of creatures who were perfectly comfortable themselves, and so had no fellow feeling for his want of cheerfulness.

"Why don't you go and spring about, and sing in the fields with your cousin, the Grasshopper?" was the ill-natured question of the Spider, as she twisted her web in one of the refuge-holes the Cricket had crept into; "I am sure your legs are long enough, if you would only take the trouble to undouble them. It's nothing but a sulky, discontented feeling that keeps you and all your family moping in these out-of-the-way corners, when you ought to be using your limbs in jumping about and enjoying yourself. And I dare say, too, that you could sing a great deal louder if you chose."

The Cricket thought, perhaps he could, but he must feel very differently to what he did then, before it would be possible to try. Something was so very, very wrong with him, but what that something was he did not know. All the other beasts and birds and insects seemed easy and happy enough. The Spider, for instance, was quite at home and gay in the hole he found so dismal. And it was not the Spider only who was contented: the Flies–the Bees–the Ants–the very Mole, who sometimes came up from burrowing, and told wonderful stories of his underground delights–the birds with their merry songs–the huge beasts, who walked about like giants in the fields–all–all were satisfied with their condition, and happy in themselves. Every one had the home he liked, and no one envied the other.

But with him it was quite otherwise: he never felt at home! On the contrary, it always seemed to him that he was looking out for something that was not there–some place that could never be found–some state where he could rise out of the depression and uneasiness which here seemed to clog him down, though he could not understand why. Poor fellow! As things were now, he felt for ever driven to hide in holes, although he knew that his limbs were built for energy; and few ever heard his voice, though he possessed one fitted for something much better than doleful complaints.

Sometimes a set of House Crickets would meet and talk the matter over. They looked at their long folded-up legs, and could not but see how exactly they were like those of the Grasshopper. And yet the idea of following the Grasshopper into the cool grass, and jumping about all day was odious to them. Once, indeed, a Cricket of great self-denial offered to go into the fields and find one of his green cousins, and ask his opinion on the subject, and whether he could give any reason why the grasshopper life should be so distasteful to such near relations. And he actually went; and when the Grasshopper could be persuaded to stand quiet for a few seconds, and listen, he was so much concerned for the Crickets (for he had a tender heart, from living so much in the grass, and being so musical), that he said he would himself visit his cousins, and see what could be done for them. Perhaps it was some little accidental ailment, or it might be a chronic affection in the family, owing to mismanagement when they were young, but which a little judicious treatment would correct.

With these views he started for the hollow tree in which the Crickets had taken shelter, and soon reached it, for he traveled the whole way in bounds. And the last bound took him fairly into the midst of the family circle, in which indeed he alighted with more vivacity than politeness, for his cousins did not like such startling gaiety. However, he steadied himself carefully, and then began to examine the legs and knees of all the Crickets assembled. He drew them out, and looked them well over; for, thought he, "there is perhaps some blunder or flaw in the way the joints are put together." But he could find nothing amiss. There sat the Crickets with legs and bodies as nicely made as his own, only with no energy for exertion.

What he might have thought, or what he might have said, after this puzzling discovery, no one can tell; for at the end of his examination he was seized with the fidgets, and, "Excuse me, my dear friends," cried he, "I have the cramp in my left leg–I must jump!" And jump he did–once, twice, thrice–and the last jump carried him out of the tree; and either on purpose, or from forgetfulness, he sprang singing away, and returned to his cousins the Crickets no more.

Oh, this yearning after some other better state that lies unrevealed in the indefinite future–how restless and disheartening a sensation! Oh, this painful contrast of perfection in all created things around, to the lonely meditator on so much happiness, who is the solitary exception to the rule–how trying the position! How cruel, how almost overwhelming the struggle between the iron chain of reality and the soaring wing of aspiration!

But, "What is the use, my poor good friends," expostulated a plodding old Mole one day, after coming out to see how the upper world went on, and hearing the Cricket's complaints–"what is the use of all this groaning and conjecturing? You admit that every other creature but yourself is perfect in its way, and quite happy. Well, then, I will tell you that you ought to be quite sure you are perfect in your way too, though you have not found it out yet; and that you will be happy one day or other, although it may not be the case just now. Do you suppose this fine scheme of things we live in is to be soiled with one speck of dirt, as it were for the sake of teasing such a little insignificant creature as yourself! Don't think it for a moment, for it is not at all likely! But you must not suppose that everything goes right at first even with the best of us. I have had some small experience, and I know. But everything fits in at last. Of that I am quite sure. For instance, now, I do not suppose it ever occurred to you to think what a trial it must be to a young Mole when he first begins to burrow in the earth. Do you imagine that he knows what he is doing it for, or what will be the result? No such thing. It is a complete working in the dark, not knowing in the least where he is going. Dear me! If one had once stopped to conjecture and puzzle, what a hardship it would have seemed to drive one's nose by the hour together into unknown ground, for some unexplained reason that did not come out for some time afterwards, and that one had no certainty would ever come out at all! But everything fits in at last. And so it did with us. I remember it quite well in my own case. We drove the earth away and outwards, till the space so cleared proved an absolute palace! By the bye, I must try and get you down into our splendid abode–it will cheer you up, and teach you a useful lesson. Well, so you see we found out at last what all the grubbing had been for–"

Ah! But," interrupted the Cricket, "you were labouring for some purpose all the time, and if I had to labour I could hope. The difficulty is, to sit moping with nothing to do but wait."

"It is nonsense to talk of nothing to do," answered the Mole; "every creature has something to do. You, for instance, have always to watch for the sun. You know you like the beams and warmth he sends out better than anything else in the world, so you should get into the way of them as much as you can. And after the sun has set, you must hunt up the snuggest holes you can find, and so make the best of things as they are; and for the rest, you must wait. And waiting answers sometimes as well as working, I can assure you. There was the young Ox in the plains near here. As soon as he could run about at all, he began driving his clumsy head against everything he met. No one could tell why; but he fidgeted and butted about all day long, and many of his friends and acquaintances were very much offended by his manners. Others laughed. The dogs, indeed, were particularly amused, and used to bark at him constantly–even close to his nose sometimes, as he lowered his head after them. Well, at last, out came the secret. Two fine horns grew out from our friend's head, and people soon understood the meaning of all the butting; and one of the saucy curs who was playing the old barking game with him one day got finely tossed for his pains. Everything fits in at last, my friends! No cravings are given in vain. There is always something in store to account for them, you may be quite sure. You may have to wait a bit–some of you a shorter, some a longer time; but do wait–and everything will fit in and be perfect at last."

It was a most fortunate circumstance for the Crickets that the Mole happened to give them this good advice; for a malicious Ape had lately been suggesting to them, whether, as they were totally useless and very unhappy, it would not be a good thing for them all, to starve themselves to death, or in some other way, to rid the world of their whole race. But the Mole's good sense gave a different turn to their ideas; and hope is so natural and pleasant a feeling, that when once they ventured to encourage it, it flourished and grew in their hearts till it created a sort of happiness of itself. In short, they determined to wait, and meantime to watch for the sun, as their friend had advised.

There are not many records of the early history of the House Crickets; but it is supposed that they traveled about a good deal–preferring always the hottest countries; and rumors of a few straggling families, who had discovered a sort of Cricket Elysium at the mouth of volcanoes, were afloat at one time. But the truth of the report was never ascertained: and as, doubtless, if ever they got there, they were sure to be swept away to destruction by the first eruption that took place, it is no wonder that the fact has never been thoroughly established.

Meanwhile several generations died off; and things remained much as they were. But the words of the Mole were carried down from father to son, and became a by-word of comfort among them: "Everything would fit in at last! No cravings are given in vain. There is always something in store to account for them. Wait–and everything will fit in, and be perfect at last."

Gleams of hope, indeed, were not wanting to our poor little friends, during this time of probation. Wherever fires were kindled by human hands, whether by wanderers in the depths of forests, or sojourners in tents, a stir of excitement and rapturous expectation was caused among such Crickets as were near enough to know and enjoy the circumstance. But, alas! When the travelers journeyed onwards, or the tents were removed elsewhere, the disappointment that ensued was bitter in proportion.

Many an evil hint, too, had they on such occasions from the mischief-making creatures which are to be found in all grades of life, that such, and no better, would be their fate for ever. Rays of joy, beaming only to be extinguished in cruel mockery of their feelings–such was to be their perpetual portion!

"But we will not believe it," cried the Crickets, heart-broken as they were. "Everything will be perfect at last," sang they as loudly as they could. "No cravings are given in vain." And as they always sang this same song, the mischief-makers got tired of listening at last, and left them to sing and weep alone. Ah! It required no small strength of mind to resist, as they did, such plausible insinuations, supported as they were by present appearances.

But, truly, though it tarried, the day of deliverance and joy did come! The first fire that ever warmed the hearthstone that flagged the grand old chimney-arch of ancient times, ended for ever the mystery of the House Crickets' wants and cravings; and when it commonly blazed every winter night in men's dwellings, all the doubts and woes of Cricket life were over. These seemed to have passed away like the dreams of a disturbed night, which had been succeeded by daylight and reality. And oh, what ecstasy of joy the Crickets felt! How loud they shouted, and how high they sprang! "We knew it would be so! The good old Mole was right! The grumbling beasts were wrong! Everything is perfect now, and no one is so happy as we are."

"Grandmother, what creature is it that I hear singing so loudly in the corner by the fire?" inquires the little one of the good old dame who sits musing on the oaken settle.

"I do not hear it, my child, and I do not know," answers the deaf and blind old crone. "But if it be singing, love, it is happy, and enjoys these blessed fires as much as I do. 'Let everything that hath breath praise the Lord.'"

Ah! It was no wonder that amidst the many merry voices that then shouted, and still shout, round those warm and friendly fires, no voice is louder, no joy more grateful, than that of the patient Cricket. He has "waited" through fear and shadows–has hoped through darkness and ignorance–and his abode now glows with warmth and light. And, if he received a lesson of wisdom from a creature more humble and seemingly more blind than himself, it is at least not the only instance in which instruction has been so obtained.

And now we know the reason why the Crickets come by troops into our houses, and live and thrive about our cheering fires, and sing so loud and long that the housewives sometimes (I grieve to say) get weary of the noise, and try to lessen the number of their lively visitors. But yet there is a strange old notion of good fortune attending the presence of these little chirping creatures. They are welcomed as bringing "good luck" to the family about whose hearth they settle. And so they do! They bring with them a tale of promises made good. They sing a song of hope fulfilled; and though in that glad music there be neither speech nor language which we can recognise as such, there is yet a voice to be heard among them by all who love to listen, with reverent delight, to the sweet harmonies and deep analogies of nature.

> *"The bull-calf butts, with smooth and unarmed brow...and no pre-assurance common to a whole species does in any instance prove delusive."–Coleridge's Aids to Reflection.*

A LESSON OF HOPE

"Oh, yet we trust that, somehow, good
Will be the final goal of ill!"

From TENNYSON'S "In Memoriam."

"HOW the rising blast is driving through the ancient forest! What a dismal roaring there is among the pine-trees! What a sharp clattering among the half-dried poplar-leaves! What a sighing among the beeches! A wild mysterious hour, and full of strange fantastic types of mortal life!"

It was thus I spoke, when, having wandered out one gloomy autumn night to muse on Nature and her laws, I found myself contemplating, in the deep recesses of a wood, the progress of a violent storm. And as I paused, I leant back, in sad reflections lost, against an oak, and, looking upwards to the sky, tried to gaze into the depths of those black vapoury masses that had arisen, one knew not how or whence, to darken over the expanse of heaven; when, all at once there shone down upon me, from an opening in the clouds, the full rays of a bright October moon.

The light was sudden, and a sudden revulsion took place within my heart. I had been thinking that, like the cruel storm, and like the heavy clouds, were the troubles and the trials of human existence: and now, when that sweet radiance broke upon my eyes, I heard a voice exclaim, as if in echo to my thoughts–"It is the moon that shone in Paradise!" It was the Bird of Night, quite near me, in the hollow of a tree. Looking to see from whence the sound had come, I met his large, grave, meditative eyes fixed on my moonlit face, and then I heard the voice exclaim again–"The moon that shone in Paradise!"

Oh, what a thought to come across the tumult of that hour! *The moon that shone in Paradise!* Up to whose radiant orb the eyes of countless generations have been turned–from the first glance of spotless innocence, to the last yearning gaze of sorrow-stricken manhood! And why? But that in that calm unchanging glory there shines forth a promise of eternal, everlasting peace. But now another voice was heard, despite the howling of the storm. It was a croaking Raven, swinging on a branch beside me. He came between me and the light and ever and anon his coal-black wings seemed spreading for a flight.

"Deluded fool," he muttered, "with your endless myths! This comes of living in the dark all day, and spending all your time in guesswork! See! Your precious moon is gone!"

"Not gone, though hidden," was the answer.

But I heard no more than this, for here the frightful wind grew louder still. He roared in fury all around, scattering the last leaves from the bending trees, as if he hated the very relics of the gentle summer. And many bowed their heads, and others moaned in grief.

"Hast thou come with mighty news from distant lands," shouted the Pine-tree scornfully, as he tossed his branches to the storm, "that thou bringest such

confusion in thy path? Ambassador of evil, who hast sent thee here?"
"Cannot yonder moon teach thee milder thoughts?" cried the Elm-tree, as he stood majestic in his sorrow and despair.
"Our hour is come," exclaimed the softer Beech. "My leaves lie scattered all around. Our life is closing fast. Naked and forlorn we stand amid the ruins of the past."
"What mockery of existence," stormed the black-leaved Poplar in his wrath, "to be placed here, and clothed in such sweet beauty, nurtured by gentle dews and tender sunshine, and then be left at last the victims of reckless fury, with all our glories torn by force away! Would I had never risen from the ground!"
"Oh, my aspiring friend," the ill-mouthed Raven cried, "the few months' splendour does not satisfy your heart! You aim too high, methinks. Well, well! Aspiring thoughts are very fine; but were I you, I would accommodate myself to facts. A short spring, a shorter summer, and then to perish. Ha! Here you are again, my ancient worthy friend!"
And then another gust broke in with savage fury on the forest, and many a stalwart branch crashed down upon the ground. The wailings of afflicted nature rose amidst the storm.
"Is there no refuge from this end?" inquired the Oak. "Why have I lived at all?"
"Because destruction is the law of life," the Raven uttered, with his fiercest croak. "Where would destruction be, were there no life to be destroyed? It is a glorious law."
"No law, but only an exception," cried the Bird of Night.
And as he spoke there streamed once more from out the clouds that type of peace that passeth not away–the moon that shone in Paradise. Oh, what a silver mantle she let fall upon the disrobed branches of those trees! Wet as they were with raindrops, and waving in the gale, it seemed as if they shone in robes of starlight glory. What gracious promises seemed streaming down with that sweet light!
"Lift up your heads, ye forest trees, once more;" so sang the mild-eyed Bird of Night. "Fury is short-lived–love alone enduring. All that destroys is transitory, but order is everlasting. The unbridled powers of cruelty may rage–it is but for a time! And ye may darken over the blue heavens, ye vapoury masses in the sky. It matters not! Beyond the howling of that wrath, beyond the blackness of those clouds, there shines, unaltered and serene, the moon that shone in Paradise."
"Your myth again, detested Bird of Night! Here to the rescue, ancient friend!"
And louder then than ever came that cruel, cruel wind.
"It matters not," once more the Owl exclaimed. "The stormy winds must cease, the clouds must pass away, and yonder sails the light that tells of harmony restored."
"Infatuated fool, to live on hope, with death around you and before you!" groaned the Raven–and then a crash like thunder rent the air. The Oak had fallen to the ground. I started at the shock.
"Will the day ever come," I cried aloud, as if addressing some mysterious friend, "will the day ever come when storms and woe shall cease? Order and peace

seem meant, but death and ruin come to pass."
"Oh, miserable doubter, do you ask? Must the brute beasts and mute creation rise to give an answer to your fears? Look in the heaven above, and in the earth below, and in the water deep beneath the earth. One only law is given–the law of order, harmony, and joy."
"Alas, how often broken!" I exclaimed.
"Ay, but disturbance is no law, and therefore cannot last. Disorder, death, and destruction–by their own nature they are transitory–rebellious powers that struggle for a time, and frustrate here and there the gracious purposes ordained. But they exist not of themselves; have neither law nor being in themselves; exist but as disturbers of a scheme whose deep foundations cannot be overthrown. Life, order, harmony, and peace; means duly fitting ends; the object, universal joy. This is the law. Believe in it, and live!"
And as the voice grew silent, from the sky beamed over all the scene the placid moon once more. The wind had lulled or passed away to other regions of the earth, and over all the forest streamed the brilliant light. Once more the lit-up trees shone spangled o'er with rays; and happy murmurs broke upon my ear, instead of loud complaints.
"We have been wild and foolish, gracious moon!" exclaimed the tender Beech. "We doubted all the promises and hopes that you shed so freely down. In pity to the terrors of the night, forgive us once again!"
"You have said right, my sister," said the Oak. "That heavenly power, whom neither winds nor storms can reach, will view with tenderness our troubled lot, who live amid the tempests of the earth. She will forgive; she hath forgiven us all. Hath she not clothed us now with robes more brilliant than the summer ones we love?"
"The robes of hope and promise," wept the Poplar, as he spoke, for all his branches trembled with delight, and stars seemed dropping all around.
"I mourn my dark despair," bewailed the Elm. "I should have called the past to memory! We never are deserted in our need. The winter tempests rage, and terrible they are; but always the bright moon from time to time returns, to shed down rays of hope and promises of glory on our heads; and still we doubt and fear, and still the patient moon repeats her tale. And then the spring and summer time return, and life, and joy, and all our beauteous robes. Oh, what weak tremblers we must be!"
And so, through all the rest of that strange night, murmurs of comfort sounded through the wood, and I returned at last to the poor lonely cottage that I called my home, and wept mixed tears of sorrow and of joy. Father and mother lost, swept suddenly away, and I, with straitened means, left alone to struggle through the world! Did I not stand before my desolate hearth, like one awakened from a dream, a vision (surely such it was!) exclaiming in despair, as did the weeping Beech, "Naked and forlorn I stand amid the ruins of the past." But through the casement glided in on me, me also, as I stood, the blessed rays of that eternal moon–the moon that shone in Paradise–the moon that promises a Paradise restored.

And ever and anon, throughout the struggle of my life, I would return for wisdom and for hope to the old forest where I dreamt the dream. As time passed on, and winter snows came down, a cold, unmeaning sleep seemed to bind up the trees–but still, at her appointed time, the moon came out, and lit up even snow with robes of light and hope. And then the springtime burst the cruel bonds that held all nature in a stagnant state. Verdure and beauty came again; and, as I listened to the gales that breathed soft music through the trees, I thought, "If I could dream again, I should hear songs of exquisite delight." But that was not to be. Still, I could revel in the comfort of the sight, and watch the moonbeams glittering in triumphant joy through the now verdant bowers of those woods, playing in happy sport amid the shadows of the leaves.
And to me also came a spring! From me, too, passed away the winter and its chill! And now I take the children of my love, and the sweet mother who has borne them, to those woods; and ever and anon we tell long tales of Nature and her ways, and how the poor trees moan, when storms and tempests come; and how the wise Owl talks to heedless ears his deep philosophy of laws of order that must one day certainly prevail, and how the patient moon is never weary of her task of shedding rays of hope and promise on the world; and even while we speak, the children clap their hands for joy, and say they never will despair for anything that comes, for, lo! Above their heads there suddenly shines out–THE MOON THAT SHONE IN PARADISE!

THE CIRCLE OF BLESSING

"COME back to me, my children let us not part," murmured the Sea to the Vapours, which rose from its surface, drawn upwards by the heat of the tropical sun. "Return to my bosom, and contribute your share to the preservation of my greatness and strength."

"There is no lasting greatness, but in distributed good," replied the Vapours; "behold we carry your cooling influence to the heated air around. Let us alone, oh Sea! The work is good."

"But carried on at my expense," murmured the Sea. "Is the air your parent, and not I, that you are so careful of its interests and so neglectful of mine? Why are you thus ungrateful to me, from whom your very existence springs? O foolish children! By diminishing my power you are sapping the foundations of your own life. Your very being depends on mine."

"Small and great, great and small, we all depend on each other," sang the Vapours as they hovered in the air. "Mighty Ocean, give us of your abundance for those that need. It is but little that we ask."

"Divided interests are the ruin of fools," muttered the angry Sea.

"But extended ones the glory of the wise," replied the Vapours, as they still continued to rise. "See, now, have we not done ourselves, what we would have you also do? Behold, we have left our salts in your bosom for those that need them."

"And I have cast them as a useless burden to my lowest depths," exclaimed the Sea, indignantly. "Have I not enough, already? Superfluous bounties deserve but little thanks, methinks."

"Yet in those depths, perchance they may be as welcome as we to the air above," persisted the Vapours. "It is ever thus: and all will be made good at last. Small and great, great and small, we are dependent on each other evermore."

"Begone, then," moaned the Sea. "You, who are willing to sacrifice a certain good for an uncertain fancy, begone, and be yourselves the first victims of your folly. The breezes that are now driving you forward across my surface, will rise to fury, and blow you into nothingness as you proceed. Lost among the stormy gusts, where will be your use to others or my recompense for your loss? You will not even exist to repent of this mad desertion of your home. Adieu! For ever and for ever, adieu!"

"Adieu, but not for ever," answered the Vapours, as they dispersed before the wind.

It was not a satisfactory parting, perhaps; for, often as their race had made the journey round the earth, it had never fallen within the power of any portion of them to explain the course of their career, to the surface sea, which had originally grudged their departure. However, the Vapours had now commenced their circuit, and were carried onward by the steady south-east trade-winds to the regions of equatorial calms, that wonderful belt of heat and accumulation, where they were met by breezes which in like manner were travelling from the north, and here this meeting caused for a while a lingering in the career of both. But

these opposing winds, laden with vapours from the two hemispheres, had each their mission, and worked under an appointed law.
It was their province to carry the exhalations from north and south into the cooler upper sky where once more their course was free to travel round the world. Lifted up thus, however, no sooner had the Vapours entered a more temperate atmosphere, than their particles expanded, and a portion of them clung together in drops, which, whilst under the influence of excessive heat, was never the case. They thus became much heavier than before; so heavy, indeed, that the winds were not able to bear them aloft.
"You cannot carry us all," said the Vapours to their struggling supporters. "Some of us will, therefore, return with a message of comfort to the mighty Sea, to tell him all is well."
But even when they came down in torrents of rain to his bosom, the Sea grumbled still. "It is well that a part, at least, of what was lost, returns," said he. But he neither knew nor cared what became of the rest.
The rest, however, fared happily and well; for high above earth and sea–so high, indeed, that they in no way interfered with the winds that swept below–they were borne along by the upper currents of air which were traveling to the north, and carried them forward on their journey of beneficence, and never-ceasing good.
Surely, it must have been a sweet sensation to be drifted along by a never-varying breeze through the higher regions of the sky, undisturbed by care, in a dream of delicious idleness and ease. But this was but a portion of the career of the Vapours from the Sea. At the next meeting, at the outskirts of the tropics, with travelers like themselves coming in the opposite direction, there was a fresh pressure of opposing breezes, a temporary lingering, and then a descent, by which they left those higher regions for ever. Henceforth, they were to be dispersed by surface winds on their course of usefulness to man.
And if, when cradled in that blissful, passage high over the tropics, those Vapours had for a time forgotten their mission, there was no possibility of forgetting it henceforth. Taken up with triumphant delight by all the varying breezes that sport over the northern hemisphere, there was no direction in which they were not to be found. A portion was wanted here, another portion there; the snows of Iceland, and the vineyards of Italy, the orange groves of Spain, and the river which pours over the mighty rocks at Niagara, must all be fed at their appointed seasons, and the food was traveling to them now.
But the eye would weary which strove to look sympathisingly round the vast expanse of the globe. It is enough if we can follow the Vapours through some stages of their journey of love.
On the summit of a mountain, over whose sides the gorse and heather were wont to flower together in bright profusion, and with their lovely intermixture of hues, all the ground was parched and dry. A burning sun by day, rarely followed by dewy nights; a summer drought, in fact, had ruled for weeks over the spot, and the shrunken flower-buds and parched leaves bore painful witness to the fact. The little mountain tarn below was almost dry, and the Sundew plants by its

sides, which were wont to revel in the damp surrounding moss, had lost their nature altogether, and never now offered their coronet of sparkling drops to the admiration of those that passed.
The pretty tumbling waterfall lower down, too, which travelers used to delight to visit, and which was fed by streams from the hills, was reduced to a miserable trickle. Cottage children were sent to fetch water from distances so great, that they sat down and wept by the roadside on their errand; and farmers wore a gloomy, anxious look, which told of a thousand fears about their crops and cattle.
But, while they were thus troubled and careful, lo, the rescue was coming from afar! Yea, traveling towards them upon the wings of the wind. Vapours from tropical seas, Vapours which had left behind them their no-longer-needed salt, were coming accumulated as clouds, to fall as gracious rain and dews upon the thirsty regions of the North.
They are variable and fantastic winds, perhaps, that course over the northern hemisphere. Not steady and uniform in their direction, like the trade-winds in the Tropics; nor like those upper currents far above the trade-winds, which carry the Vapours to the second belts of calms. No! Variable and fantastic they certainly are, and, therefore, we cannot reckon on their arrival to a day–nay, not to a month; but on their arrival at last, we may always surely depend, and perhaps, in this trial of patient expectation, a lesson of quiet faith is intended to be learnt.
And so, just as farmers, and cottage children, and the earth, and its flowers, and leaves, and springs of water, had all sunk into a state of dismal distrust and discomfort, the deliverance came to them as they slept!
Slight variations in the wind had been observed for more than a day; but still no change of weather took place, until one night a steady breeze from the southwest set in, and prevailed for hours. And presently there was a gathering up of clouds all over the sky, though in the darkness of the night their arrival passed unobserved.
Gracious clouds! They were the Vapours of the Sea, which, after many wanderings, had found their way here, at last, on their mission of love. And, lo! The sound of waters was heard once more on the dried-up hills, and sweet, heavy showers dropped down on the delighted earth. All night long it continued, and all night long the earth was streaming tears of joy; and another day and another night succeeded, during which more or less of rain or dew continued to descend.
"Welcome, welcome, oh ye showers and dew!" were the Earth's first words; and, "Leave me now no more," her constant after-cry.
"Poor Earth, poor Earth!" murmured the Vapours which, condensed into raindrops, were trembling, like diamonds, on the leaves and flowers in the sunshine of the second dawn. "Poor Earth, poor Earth! You too refuse to learn the law which brought us here. What you have received so freely, will you not freely give?"
"Nay; but linger with me yet," expostulated the Earth; "and let me rather store you up for my own use hereafter. What do I know of the future, and what it may

bring forth? How can I be sure that the fitful winds will supply me again in time of need? I cannot afford to think of others. Leave me, leave me not."
"None must store against an uncertain future evil, when so many are suffering under a present one," replied the Vapours; "nevertheless, a message of comfort will come to you, after we are gone."
And so, when the sun shone out in his heat and glory, the diamond raindrops were drawn upwards from the flowers and leaves into the air once more. Only the little Sundews kept their coronets of crystal beads throughout the day, as was their custom; though how they managed it, it would be hard to say.
Perhaps as their own natural juices are so thick and clammy, these, mingling with the Vapours as they exuded, held them longer fast.
"You are our prisoners," was the triumphant cry of the Sundew leaves, as they glistened in their liquid gems.
"Nay, but why would you detain us, selfish flowers?" exclaimed the Vapours.
"Oh, you shall go, you shall go; but only gradually, as the moisture courses through our veins to re-supply your place. This is our way of life. But we must hear all from you first. All! All! All! And most of all, why you have tarried so long, till we had almost perished in the dreadful drought?"
It was a long story the Vapours had then to tell, of their irregular passage to the Polar Seas; and how, after their chilly sojourn there as snow, they had passed southwards once more on the summits of drifting icebergs, and again been exhaled, and given back to the ministry of the wandering winds.
"Surely," said they, "we have touched no place in all our wild journeyings where we have not left some blessing behind. Here and there, indeed, folks think they have had too much of us, and here and there too little; but, oh, my delicate friends, believe us, we are faithful and true to our mission all over the world. Behold, we pour into the earth as rain, or slide into it as moisture; and lo, the soil gives its gases into our care, and the roots of the plants draw us and them up together, and feeding on them, expand and flourish, and grow; and when the useful deed is done, and the sun shines down on our labour, up we ascend again to its absorbing rays, to be carried forward again and again, to other gracious deeds. Blame us not therefore, if, in turning aside to some other case of need, we have come a little late to your hills. Own that you have not been forgotten!"
"It is true," murmured the Sundews in return; "but remember, we pine and die without your presence."
"Dear little Sundews, there is not a plant in all the boggy heaths that is so dear to us as you are. See now, we linger with you yet; there is moisture in your mossy bed around this tarn to last for many weeks; and ever as a portion of us steals away, its place shall be supplied from below, so that your leaves shall never miss their sparkling diadem of gems."
The Sundews had no need to tremble after that; but as the exhalations went up from the surface-ground, and the moisture sank lower and lower down into it, a fear stole over the Earth, that another thought might arise, for she knew not that all would return to her again in due season. But, when in the cool of the evening the Vapours descended upon her bosom, as refreshing mist and dew, she

received a portion of comfort. Nevertheless, like the Sea, she grumbled on. "It is well that a part, at least, of what was lost, returns!" she remarked in her greedy anxiety, as the Sea had done before; and, like him, she neither knew nor cared what became of the rest.

There was a mission for every portion, however, and through the now saturated ground the rain-drops sank together, amidst roots, and stones, and soil, moistening all before them as they went, and replenishing the springs that ran among the hills.

The tumbling Waterfall had, by this time, well nigh given up hope. The mournful trickle with which it fell, was an absolute mockery of its former precipitous haste, when lo! Some sudden influence is at work, a rush of vigour flows into the exhausted veins; there is a swelling in the distant springs, nearer and nearer it comes, and now over the rocky ledge there is a heavier flow: a little more, and yet a little more; and then, at last, a rush of water full and fresh is heard!

"Welcome, welcome! Oh, ye Springs and Floods," cried the Waterfall, as once more it rolled in its beauty along its precipitous course, scattering foam and spray upon the moss and flowers that graced its edge. "Stay in the mountains always, that I may thirst no more; leave me, leave me not again!"

"You too, who live by giving and receiving," cried the Vapours as they flushed the stream–"you too, wishing to stop the gracious course of good? Oh shame, shame, shame!"

And then, as if in mockery of the request, a playful gust blew off from the waterfall as it descended, some of its glittering spray, and tossed it to the sunshiny air, where it dispersed once more in smoky mist, but only to return again in time of need.

Down in the lower country, where stately houses, enclosed in noble parks, adorned the land, a beautiful lake lay stretched under the noonday sun. It was fed by the stream which, at some miles' distance, received the tumbling waterfall into its course, and then ran through the lake's broad sheet, escaping at the further end in a quick flowing rill. On the placid mirror-like surface majestic swans swept proudly by, not unsusceptible of the freshening in the water from the filling of the springs above.

A little pleasure-boat was floating lazily about, impelled occasionally forward by the stroke of an oar from a youth, who with one companion of his own age, and an elderly man who sat abstractedly reading a book, formed the passengers of this tiny bark.

The rower's young companion was lounging in a half-sitting, half-reclining posture in the bows of the boat, and both were gazing at the old Baronial Hall, which, with its quaint turrets, long terraces, and picturesque gardens, faced the lake at a slightly distant elevation, where it stood embosomed in trees.

"Well! If the place were to be mine," observed the lounger, with his eyes fixed upon it, "I know exactly what I should do. I would throw all your agricultural and educational, and endless improvement schemes overboard at once; leave them for those whose business it is to look after them; and enjoy myself, and live

like a prince while I had the chance."
"And die worse than a beggar at last," cried the other youth, as he rested on his oars and looked at his cousin who had spoken–"I mean without a friend! You cannot secure even enjoyment, in stagnation," added he. "The very pond here is kept pure by giving out through a stream at one end, what it receives through a stream at the other."
"And the stream from which it receives," said the old man, looking up from his book, "is a type of God Himself; and the stream to which it gives, is a type of the human race. Those who receive from the fountain, without giving to the stream, work equally against the laws of Nature and of God."
A few strokes of the oar here carried the boat away, but surely that was the voice of him who, in the bygone year, had startled the ignorant murmurer in the voyage across the Line? Well it is with those who in the secrets of Nature read the wisdom of God!
Softly did that summer evening sink upon the park and the old Baronial Hall, and heavy were the mists and dews that hung over the woods, and gardens, and flowers, and great was the rejoicing in the country round, when after a time, they were followed by fertilizing rains. Fertilizing rains! The words are easily spoken, but who knows their full meaning, save he who has watched over cornfields or vineyards, threatened with ill-timed drought? We take a great deal for granted in this world, and expect that every thing as a matter of course ought to fit into our humours, and wishes, and wants; and it is often only when danger threatens, that we awake to the discovery that the guiding reins are held by One whom we had well-nigh forgotten in our careless ease.
"If it had not thundered, the peasant had not made the sign of the cross," is the rude proverb of a distant land; and peasant and king are alike implicated in its meaning.
"It is all right now," observed the farmer, as he returned home in the evening, after contemplating the goodly acres drenched and dripping with rain.
And it was all right indeed, for, long after the farmer had forgotten his previous anxieties in sleep, the circle of blessing was at work in the length and breadth of his fields. There, the condensed vapours sank into the willing soil, which gave to them her gases and her salts. There, the fibres of the roots of corn and grass sucked up the welcome food which brought strength and power into the juices of the plant; and then, by slow but sure degrees, the stunted ears began to fill, and men said the harvest would be good.
"Stay with us for ever," asked the Corn-ears of the Vapours, as they felt themselves swell under the delicious influence. The Vapours made no answer, for they did not like to speak of death; but they dealt gently with the corn, and did not leave it till it had ripened gradually for the harvest, and no longer needed their aid; and then they exhaled once more into the air, to follow out their mission elsewhere.
A curly-headed urchin stood by a pump, looking disconsolately at the huge heavy handle, which he could not lift. A little watering-pot was grasped in his hands, and it was easy to see what he wanted. Some one passing by observed

him, and with a smile gave him help. A very few strokes of the handle brought up the water from below, the little watering-pot was filled, and the child ran away. He had a garden of his own: a garden in which a few kidney-beans in one place, and sweet-peas in another, with scatterings of mustard and cress, formed a not very usual mixture; but it served its purpose of giving employment and pleasure to the child.

The kidney-beans which he hoped to eat one day at dinner, were evidently the objects of his most attentive care, for he soaked them again and again with the water from his pot, tossing only a few drops of it over the flowers. Little guessed he of the long, long journey the Vapours of the Sea had made before they helped to fill the springs which fed the well over which the pump was built. Little guessed he either of what would become of them when, after helping to fill his kidney-beans with delicate juices, they returned back to the ministry of the winds.

When be touched his pinafore, after he had finished his work, he found it soaked with wet; and when, soon after, he saw it hung in front of the fire to dry, he sat down and amused himself by watching the steam as it rose from the linen, under the influence of heat.

Trifling it seems to tell–an everyday occurrence of life, not worth a record: yet there was a law even for the vapour that rose from the infant's pinafore in front of the nursery fire. Nothing shall be lost of that which God has ordained to good; and the Vapours were soon on their mission again. Through chimney or window they escaped to the cooler air, and returned to their ceaseless work.

"Give us of your salts," was at last their request, as they percolated through the lower ground to join the mighty rivers which ran into the Sea. "Give us of your salts, and lime, and mineral virtues, oh thou Earth! That we may bear them with us to the Sea from whence we came."

"Is not the Sea sufficient to itself?" inquired the jealous Earth.

"None are sufficient to themselves, oh, careful Mother!" answered the Vapours as they streamed in water along their way. "Small and great, great and small, we all depend on each other. How shall the Shells, and Coral Reefs, and Zoophytes of the deep continue to grow and live, if you refuse them the virtues of your soil? Give us of your salts, and lime, and the mineral deposits of your bosom, oh, Mother Earth! That they may live and rejoice."

"Have you nothing to offer in return?" asked the still-hesitating Earth.

"Do you not know that we have left a blessing behind us wherever we have been?" exclaimed the Vapours. "But no matter for the past. See, we will do ourselves as we would have you do. We will bind ourselves in beauty in the caves of your kingdom, and live with you for ever."

So, as they passed on their way, loading themselves with the virtues of the Earth, some turned aside, and sinking to the subterranean depths, oozed with their limy burden through the roofs of caverns and sides of rocks, and hung suspended in graceful stalactites, or shone out in many-sided crystal forms.

"Now I am satisfied," observed the Earth. "What I see I know. They have left me something behind for what they have taken away."

"And now we are satisfied," cried the rest of the Vapours, as they poured into the rivers and were carried out into the Sea. "Have we not returned with a blessing and treasures in our hand?"

And thus, from age to age, ever since the primary mists went up from the earth and watered the whole face of the ground, the mighty work has gone on, and still continues its course. For not to inactivity and idleness did the Vapours now return, but only to recommence afresh their labours of love. Yes! Evermore rejoicing on their way, through all varieties of accident, of climate, and of place, whether as Snow or Hail, as Showers or Dews, as Floods or Springs, as Rivers or as Seas, the waters are still obediently fulfilling His word who called them into being, and are carrying the everlasting Circle of Blessing round the world.

Oh, ye showers and dew; oh, ye winds of God; oh, ye ice and snow; oh, ye seas and floods; verily, even when man is mute and forgetful, ye bless the Lord, ye praise Him and magnify Him forever!

THE LAW OF THE WOOD

"NEVER!"

What a word to be heard in a wood on an early summer morning, before the sun had quite struggled through the mists, and before the dew had left the flowers and while all Nature was passing through the changes that separate night from day, adapting herself gently to the necessities of the hour.

"Never!"

What a word to come from a young creature, which knew very little more of what had gone before, than of what was coming after, and who could not, therefore, be qualified to pronounce a very positive judgment upon any thing. But, somehow or other, it is always the young and inexperienced, who are most apt to be positive and self-willed in their opinions; and so, the young Spruce-fir, thinking neither of the lessons which Nature was teaching, nor of his own limited means of judging stuck out his branches all around him in everybody's face, right and left, and said–

"Never!"

It so startled a squirrels who was sitting in a neighbouring tree, pleasantly picking out the seeds of a fir cone, that he dropped his treasured dainty to the ground and springing from branch to branch, got up as high as he could, and then, looking down, remarked timidly to himself, "What can be the matter with the Spruce-firs?"

Nothing was the matter with the Spruce-firs, exactly; but the history of their excitement was as follows: They, and a number of other trees, were growing together in a pretty wood. There were oaks, and elms, and beeches, and larches, and firs of many sorts; and here and there, there was a silver-barked Birch. And there was one silver-barked Birch in particular, who had been observing the spruce-firs all that spring; noticing how fast they were growing, and what a stupid habit (as he thought) they had, of always getting into everybody's way, and never bending to accommodate the convenience of others.

He might have seen the same thing for some years before, if he had looked; but he was not naturally of an inquisitive disposition, and did not trouble himself with other people's affairs: so that it was only when the Spruce-fir next him had come so close that its branches fridged off little pieces of his delicate paper-like bark, when the wind was high, that his attention was attracted to the subject.

People usually become observant when their own comfort is interfered with, and this was the case here. However little the Birch might have cared for the Spruce-fir's behaviour generally, there was no doubt that it was very disagreeable to be scratched in the face; and this he sensibly felt, and came to his own conclusions accordingly.

At first, indeed, he tried to sidle and get out of the Fir's way, being himself of a yielding, good-natured character, but the attempt was a quite hopeless one. He could not move on one side a hundredth part as fast as the fir branches grew; so that, do what he would, they came pushing up against him, and teased him all day.

It was quite natural, therefore, that the poor Birch should begin to look round him, and examine into the justice and propriety of such a proceeding on the part of the Spruce-firs; and the result was, that he considered their conduct objectionable in every way.

"For," said he, (noticing that there was a little grove of them growing close together just there,) "if they all go on, shooting out their branches in that manner, how hot and stuffy they will get! Not a breath of air will be able to blow through them soon, and that will be very bad for their health; besides which, they are absolute pests to society, with their unaccommodating ways. I must really, for their own sakes, as well as my own, give them some good advice."

And accordingly, one morning–that very early summer morning before described–the Birch, having had his silvery bark a little more scratched than usual, opened his mind to his friends.

"If you would but give way a little, and not stick out your branches in such a very stiff manner on all sides, I think you would find it a great deal more comfortable for yourselves, and it would certainly be more agreeable to your neighbours. Do try!"

"You are wonderfully ready in giving unasked advice!" remarked the young Spruce-fir next the Birch, in a very saucy manner. "We are quite comfortable as we are, I fancy; and as to *giving way,* as you call it, what, or whom are we called upon to give way to, I should like to know?"

"To me, and to all your neighbours," cried the Birch, a little heated by the dispute.

On which the Spruce-fir next the Birch cried "Never!" in the most decided manner possible; and those beyond him cried "Never!" too; till at last, all the Spruce-firs, with one accord, cried, "Never!" "Never!" "Never!" and half frightened the poor squirrel to death. Every hair on his beautiful tail trembled with fright, as he peeped down from the top of the tree, wondering what could be the matter with the Spruce-firs.

And certainly, there was one thing the matter with them, for they were very obstinate; and as nobody can be very obstinate without being very selfish, there was more the matter with them than they themselves suspected, for obstinacy and selfishness are very bad qualities to possess. But, so ignorant were they of their real character, that they thought it quite a fine thing to answer the Birch-tree's mild suggestion in such a saucy manner. Indeed, they actually gave themselves credit for the display of a firm, independent spirit and so, while they shouted "Never!" they held out their branches as stiffly as possible towards each other, till they crossed, and recrossed, and plaited together, On which they remarked–"What a beautiful pattern this makes! How neatly we fit in one with the other! How pretty we shall look when we come out green all over! Surely the Wood-pigeons would have been quite glad to have built their nests here if they had known. What a pity they did not, poor things! I hear them cooing in the elm-tree yonder, at a very inconvenient height, and very much exposed."

"Don't trouble yourselves about us," cooed the Wood-pigeons from their nest in the elm. "We are much happier where we are. We want more breeze, and more

leafy shade, than you can give us in your close thick-growing branches."
"Every one to his taste," exclaimed the young Spruce-fir, a little nettled by the Wood-pigeons' cool remarks; "if you prefer wind and rain to shelter, you are certainly best where you are. But you must not talk about leafy shade, because every one knows that you can have nothing of it where you are, to what you will find here, when we come out green all over."
"But when will that be?" asked the Wood-pigeons in a gentle voice. "Dear friends, do you not know that the spring is over, and the early summer has begun, and all the buds in the forest are turned to leaves? And you yourselves are green everywhere outside, not only with your evergreen hue, but with the young summer's shoots. I sadly fear, however, that it is not so in your inner bowers."
"Perhaps, because we are evergreens, our sprouting may not go on so regularly as with the other trees," suggested one. But he felt very nervous at his foolish remark. It was welcomed, however, as conclusive by his friends, who were delighted to catch at any explanation of a fact which had begun to puzzle them.
So they cried out, "Of course!" with the utmost assurance, and one of them added, "Our outer branches have been green and growing for some time, and doubtless we shall be green all over soon!"
"Doubtless!" echoed every Spruce-fir in the neighbourhood, for they held fast by each other's opinions, and prided themselves on their family attachment.
"We cannot argue," cooed the Wood-pigeons in return. "The days are too short, even for love; how can there ever be time for quarrelling?"
So things went on in the old way, and many weeks passed over; but still the interlaced branches of the Spruce-firs were no greener than before. But beautiful little cones hung along the outermost ones; and, judging by its outside appearance, the grove of firs looked to be in a most flourishing state.
Alas! However, all within was brown and dry; and the brownness and dryness spread further and further, instead of diminishing, and, no wonder, for the summer was a very sultry one, and the confined air in the Fir-grove became close and unhealthy; and after heavy rains, an ill conditioned vapour rose up from the earth, and was never dispersed by the fresh breezes of heaven.
Nevertheless, the Spruce-firs remained obstinate as ever. They grew on in their old way, and tried hard to believe that all was right.
"What can it matter," argued they, "whether we are green or not, inside? We are blooming and well everywhere else, and these dry branches don't signify much that I can see. Still, I do wonder what can be the reason of one part being more green than another."
"It is absurd for you to wonder about it," exclaimed the Birch, who became more irritated every day. "There is not a tree in the world that could thrive and prosper, if it persisted in growing as you do. But it is of no use talking! You must feel and know that you are in each other's way every time you move; and in everybody else's way too. In mine, most particularly."
"My dear friend," retorted the Spruce-fir, "your temper makes you most absurdly unjust. Why, we make a point of never interfering with each other, or with

anybody else! Our rule is to go our own way, and let everybody else do the same. Thus much we claim as a right."

"Thus much we claim as a right!" echoed the Spruce-fir grove.

"Oh, nonsense about a right," persisted the Birch. "Where is the good of having a right to make both yourself and your neighbours miserable? If we each of us lived in a field by ourselves, it would be all very well. Every one might go his own way then undisturbed. But mutual accommodation is the law of the wood, or we should all be wretched together."

"My friend," rejoined the Spruce-fir, "you are one of the many who mistake weakness for amiability, and make a merit of a failing. We are of a different temper, I confess! We are, in the first place, capable of having ideas, and forming opinions of our own, which everybody is not; and, in the second place, the plans and habits we have laid down to ourselves, and which are not wrong in themselves, we are courageous enough to persist in, even to the death."

The Spruce-fir bristled all over with stiffness, as he refreshed himself by this remark.

"Even," inquired the Birch, in an ironical tone; "even at the sacrifice of your own comfort, and that of all around you?"

"You are suggesting an impossible absurdity," answered the vexed Spruce-fir, evasively. "What is neither wrong nor unreasonable in itself can do no harm to anybody, and I shall never condescend to truckle to other people's whims as to my line of conduct. But there are plenty, who, to get credit for complaisance to their neighbours, would sacrifice their dearest principle without a scruple!"

"Come, come!" persisted the Birch; "let us descend from these heights. There are plenty of *other* people my friend, who would fain shelter the most stupid obstinacy, and the meanest selfishness, behind the mask of firmness of character or principle, or what not. Now what principle, I should like to know, is involved in your persisting in your stiff unaccommodating way of growing, except the principle of doing what you please at the expense of the feelings of other people?"

"Insolent!" cried the Spruce-fir; "we grow in the way which Nature dictates; and our right to do so must therefore be unquestionable. We possess, too, a character of our own, and are not like those who can trim their behaviour into an unmeaning tameness, to curry favour with their neighbours."

"I ought to be silent," cried the Birch; "for I perceive my words are useless. And yet, I would like you to listen to me a little longer. Does the Beech-tree sacrifice her character, do you think, when she bends away her graceful branches to allow room for the friend at her side to flourish too? Look, how magnificently she grows, stretching protectingly as it were, among other trees; and yet, who so accommodating and yielding in their habits as she is?"

"It is her nature to be subservient, it is ours to be firm!" cried the Spruce-fir.

"It is her nature to throw out branches all round her, as it is that of every other tree," insisted the friendly Birch; "but she regulates the indulgence of her nature by the comfort and convenience of others."

"I scorn the example you would set me," cried the Spruce-fir; "it is that of the

weakest and most supple of forest trees. Nay, I absolutely disapprove of the tameness you prize so highly. Never, I hope, will you see us bending feebly about, and belying our character, even for the sake of flourishing in a wood!"
It was all in vain, evidently; so the Birch resolved to pursue the matter no further, but he muttered to himself, "Well, you will see the result."
On which the Spruce-fir became curious, and listened for more. The Birch, however, was silent, and at last, the Spruce-fir made a sort of answer in a haughty, indifferent tone–"I do not know what you mean by the result."
"You will know some day," muttered the Birch, very testily, (for the fir branches were fridging his bark cruelly, the wind having risen) "and even I shall be released from your annoyance, before long!"
"I will thank you to explain yourself in intelligible language," cried the Spruce-fir, getting uneasy.
"Oh! In plain words, then, if you prefer it," replied the Birch. "You are all of you dying."
"Never!" exclaimed the Spruce-fir; but he shook all over with fright as he uttered it. And when the other Spruce-firs--according to custom--echoed the word, they were as tremulous as himself.
"Very well, we shall see," continued the Birch. "Every one is blind to his own defects, of course; and it is not pleasant to tell home truths to obstinate people. But there is not a bird that hops about the wood, who has not noticed that your branches are all turning into dry sticks; and before many years are over, there will be no more green outside than in. The flies and midges that swarm about in the close air round you, know it as well as we do. Ask the Squirrel what he thinks of your brown crackly branches, which would break under his leaps. And as to the Wood-pigeons, they gave you a hint of your condition long ago. But you are beyond a hint. Indeed, you are, I believe, beyond a cure."
They were, indeed; but a shudder passed through the Fir-grove at these words, and they tried very hard to disbelieve them. Nay, when the winter came, they did disbelieve them altogether; for, when all the trees were covered with snow, no one could tell a dead branch from a live one; and, when the snow fell off, they who had their evergreen outside, had an advantage over many of the trees by which they were surrounded. It was a time of silence too, and quiet, for the leafless trees were in a half-asleep state, and had no humour to talk. The evergreens were the only ones who, now and then, had spirit enough to keep up a little conversation.
At last, one day, the Spruce-firs decided to consult with a distant relation of their own, the Scotch-fir, on the subject. He formed one of a large grove of his own kind that grew on an eminence in the wood. But they could only get at him through a messenger; and, when the Squirrel who was sent to inquire whether he ever gave way in his growth to accommodate others, came back with the answer that, "Needs must when there was no help!" the Spruce-firs voted their cousin a degraded being even in his own eyes, and scorned to follow an example so base.
Then they talked to each other of the ill-nature of the world, and tried to persuade themselves that the Birch had put the worst interpretation on their

condition, merely to vex them; and told themselves, in conclusion, that they had nothing to fear. But their anxiety was great, and when another spring and summer succeeded to the winter, and all the other trees regained their leaves, and a general waking up of life took place, a serious alarm crept over the Spruce-fir grove; for, alas! the brownness and dryness had spread still further, and less and less of green was to be seen on the thickest branches.

Had they but listened to advice, even then, all might have been well. Even the little birds told them how troublesome it was to hop about among them. Even the squirrel said he felt stifled if he ran under them for a cone. But they had got into their heads that it was a fine thing to have an independent spirit, and not mind what anybody said; and they had got a notion that it was a right and justifiable thing to go your own way resolutely, provided you allowed other people to do the same. But, with all their philosophy, they forgot that abstract theories are only fit for solitary life, and can seldom be carried out strictly in a wood.

So they grew on, as before, and the Birch-tree ceased to talk, for either his silver peel had all come off, and he was hardened; or else, he had taught himself to submit unmurmuringly to an evil he could not prevent. Certain it is, that no further argument took place, and the condition of the Spruce-firs attracted no further notice; till, one spring morning, several seasons later, the whole wood was startled by the arrival of its owner, a new master, who was come to pay his first visit among its glades.

The occasional sound of an axe-stroke, and a good deal of talking, were heard from time to time, for the owner was attended by his woodman: and at last he reached the Spruce-fir grove.

Alas! And what an exclamation he gave at the sight, as well he might; for nearly every one of the trees had fallen a victim to his selfish mistake, and had gradually died away. Erect they stood, it is true, as before, but dried, withered, perished monuments of an obstinate delusion. The owner and the woodman talked together for a time, and remarked to each other that half those trees ought to have been taken away years ago: that they were never fit to live in a cluster together; for, from their awkward way of growing, they were half of them sure to die.

But of all the Grove there was but one who had life enough to hear these words; and to him the experience came too late. All his old friends were in due time cut down before his eyes; and he, who by an accident stood slightly apart, and had not perished with the rest, was only reserved in the hope that he might partially recover for the convenience of a Christmas-tree.

It was a sad, solitary summer he passed, though the fresh air blew freely round him now, and he rallied and grew, as well as felt invigorated by its sweet refreshing breath; and though the little birds sung on his branches and chattered of happiness and love: for those who had thought with him and lived with him, were gone, and their places knew them no more.

Ah, certainly there had been a mistake somewhere, but it did not perhaps signify much now, to ascertain where; and no reproaches or ridicule were cast upon him by his neighbours; no, not even by the freed and happy silver-barked Birch; for a gentler spirit than that of rejoicing in other people's misfortunes, prevailed in the pretty wood.

So that it was not till Christmas came, and his doom was forever sealed, that the Spruce-fir thoroughly understood the moral of his fate.

But then, when the crowds of children were collected in the brightly-lighted hail, where he stood covered with treasures and beauty, and when they all rushed forward, tumbling one over another, in their struggles to reach his branches; each one going his own way, regardless of his neighbour's wishes or comfort; and when the parents held back the quarrelsome rogues, bidding them one give place to another–"in honour preferring one another"–considering public comfort, rather than individual gratification: then, indeed, a light seemed to be thrown on the puzzling subject of the object and rules of social life; and he repeated to himself the words of the silver-barked Birch, exclaiming–

"Mutual accommodation is certainly the law of the wood, or its inhabitants would all be wretched together."

It was his last idea.

ACTIVE AND PASSIVE

"They also serve who only stand and wait."–MILTON.

"RESTLESS life! Restless life!" moaned the Weathercock on the church-tower by the sea, as he felt himself swayed suddenly round by the wind, and creaked with dismay; "restless, toiling life, and everybody complaining of one all the time. There's that tiresome weathercock pointing east, cried the old woman, as she hobbled up the churchyard path to the porch last Sunday; now I know why I have got all my rheumatic pains back again. Then, in a day or two, came the farmer by on his pony, and drew up outside the wall to have a word with the gravedigger. A bad look out, Tomkins, said he, if that rascally old weathercock is to be trusted, the wind's got into the wrong quarter again, and we shall have more rain. Was it my fault if he did find out through me that the wind was in, what he called, the wrong quarter? Besides, the wind always is in somebody's wrong quarter, I verily believe! But am I to blame? Did I choose my lot? No, no! Nobody need suppose I should go swinging backwards and forwards, and round and round, all my life, if I had my choice about the matter. Ah! How much rather would I lead the quiet, peaceful existence of my old friend, the Dial, down below yonder on his pedestal. That is a life, indeed!"

"How he is chattering away up above there," remarked the Dial from below; "he almost makes me smile, though not a ray of sunshine has fallen on me through the livelong day, alas! I often wonder what he finds to talk about. But his active life gives him subjects enough, no doubt. Ah! What would I not give to be like him! But all is so different with me, alas! I thought I heard my own name too, just now. I will ask. Halloo! Up above there. Did you call, my sprightly friend? Is there anything fresh astir? Tell me, if there is. I get so weary of the dark and useless hours; so common now, alas! What have you been talking about?"

"Nothing profitable this time, good neighbour," replied the Weathercock; "for, in truth, you have caught me grumbling."

"Grumbling . . .? Grumbling, you?"

"Yes, grumbling, I! Why not?"

"But grumbling in the midst of an existence so gay, so active, so bright," pursued the Dial; "it seems impossible."

"Gay, active, bright! a pretty description enough; but what a mockery of the truth it covers! Look at me, swinging loosely to every peevish blast that flits across the sky. Turned here, turned there, turned everywhere. The sport of every passing gust. Never a moment's rest, but when the uncertain breezes choose to seek it for themselves. Gay, active, bright existence, indeed! Restless, toiling life I call it, and all to serve a thankless world, by whom my very usefulness is abused. But you, my ancient friend, you, in the calm enjoyment of undisturbed repose, steady and unmoved amidst the utmost violence of storms, how little can you appreciate the sense of weariness I feel! A poor judge of my troubled lot are you in your paradise of rest!"

"My paradise of rest, do you call it?" exclaimed the Dial; "An ingenious title, truly, to express what those who know it practically, feel to be little short of a stagnation of existence. Dull, purposeless, unprofitable, at the mercy of the clouds and shades of night; I can never fulfill my end but by their sufferance, and in the seasons, rare enough at best, when their meddling interference is withdrawn. And even when the sun and hour do smile upon me, and I carry out my vocation, how seldom does any one come near me to learn the lessons I could teach. I weary of the night; I weary of the clouds; I weary of the footsteps that pass me by. Would that I could rise, even for a few brief hours, to the energy and meaning of a life like yours!"

"This is a strange fatality, indeed!" creaked the Weathercock in reply, "that you, in your untroubled calm, should yearn after the restlessness I sicken of. That I, in what you call my gay and active existence, should long for the quiet you detest!"

"You long for it because you are ignorant of its nature and practical reality," groaned the Dial.

"Nay, but those are the very words I would apply to you, my ancient friend. The blindest ignorance of its workings can alone account for your coveting a position such as mine."

"If that be so, then every position is wrong," was the murmured remark in answer; but it never reached the sky, for at that moment the mournful tolling of a bell in the old church-tower announced that a funeral was approaching, and in its vibrations the lesser sound was lost.

And as those vibrations gathered in the air, they grouped themselves into a solemn dirge, which seemed as if it rose in contradiction to what had just been said.

For it gave out to the mourners who were following the corpse to its last earthly resting-place, that every lot was good, and blessed to some particular end.

For the lots of all (it said) were appointed, and all that was appointed was good.

Little, little did it matter, therefore (it said), whether the lot of him who came to his last resting-place had been a busy or a quiet one; a high or a low one; one of labour or of endurance. If that which was appointed to be done had been well done, all was well.

It gave out, too, that every time and season was good, and blessed to some particular purpose; that the time to die was as good as the time to be born, whether it came to the child who had done but little, or to the man who had done much.

For the times and seasons, (it said,) were appointed, and all that was appointed was good.

Little, little did it matter, therefore, (it said,) whether the time of life had been a long one or a short one, if that which was appointed to be used had been rightly used, all was right.

Echoing and re-echoing in the air came these sounds out of the bell-tower, bidding the mourners not to mourn, for both the lots and the times of all things were appointed, and all that was appointed was good.

The mourners wept on, however, in spite of the dirge of the bell; and perhaps it was best that they did so, for where are the outpourings of penitence so likely to be sincere, or the resolutions of amendment so likely to be earnest, as over the graves of those we love?

So the mourners wept; the corpse was interred; the clergyman departed, and the crowd dispersed; and then there was quiet in the churchyard again for a time.

Uninterrupted quiet, except when the wandering gusts drove the Weathercock hither and thither, causing him to give out a dismal squeak as he turned.

But at last there was a footstep in the old churchyard again, a step that paced up and down along the paved path; now westward towards the sea, now eastward towards the Lych-gate at the entrance.

It was a weather-beaten old fisherman, once a sailor, who occasionally made of that place a forecastle walk for exercise and pondering thoughts, since the time when age and growing infirmities had disabled him from following regularly the more toilsome parts of a fisherman's business, which were now carried on by his two grown-up sons.

He could do a stroke of work now and then, it is true, but, the nows and thens came but seldom, and he had many leisure hours on his hands in which to think of the past, and look forward to the future.

And what a place was that churchyard for awakening such thoughts! There, as he walked up and down, his own wife's grave was not many yards distant from his feet; and yet, from amidst these relics and bitter evidences of finite mortality, he could look out upon that everlasting sea, which seems always to stretch away into the infinity we all believe in.

Perhaps, in his own way, the sailor had often felt this, although he might not have been able to give any account of his sensations.

Up and down the path he paced, lingering always a little at the western point ere he turned; and with his telescope tucked under his arm ready for use, he stood for a second or two looking seaward, in case a strange sail should have come in sight.

The sexton, who had come up to the churchyard again to finish the shaping of the new grave, nodded to him as he passed, and the sailor nodded in return; but neither of them spoke, for the sailor's habits were too well known to excite attention, and the sexton had his work to complete.

But presently, when half-way to the Lych-gate, the sailor stopped suddenly short, turned around hastily, and faced the sea, steadying the cap on his head against the gale which was now blowing directly on his face–looked up into the sky–looked all around–looked at the Weathercock, and then stood, as if irresolute, for several seconds.

At last, stepping over the gravestones, he went up to the stone pedestal, on the top of which the Dial lay, waiting for the gleams of sunshine which had on that day fallen rarely and irregularly upon it.

"If the clouds would but break away for a minute," mused the old man to himself.

And soon after they did so, for they had begun to drive very swiftly over the heavens, and the sunlight, streaming for a few seconds on the dial-plate, revealed the shadow of the gnomon cast upon the place of three o'clock.

The sailor lingered by the Dial for several minutes after he had ascertained the hour, examining the figures, inscriptions, and dates. A motto on a little brass plate was let into the pedestal below: *"Watch, for ye know not the hour."* There was some difficulty in reading it, it was so blotched and tarnished with age and long neglect. Indeed, few people knew there was an inscription there at all; but the old sailor had been looking very closely, and so found it out, and then he spelt it all through, word for word.

It was to be hoped that the engraver (one Thomas Trueman), who claimed to have had this warning put up for the benefit of others, had attended to it himself, for he had long ago, nearly a hundred years ago, gone to his last account. The appointed hour had come for him, whether he had watched for it or not.

Perhaps some such thoughts crossed the sailor's mind, for certainly after reading the sentence, he fell into a reverie. Not a long one, however, for it was interrupted by the voice of the sexton, who, with his mattock over his shoulder, was passing back on his way home, and called out to the sailor to bid him good evening.

"Good-night, Mr. Bowman," said he; "we've rather a sudden change in the wind, haven't we?"

"Aye, aye," answered Bowman, by no means displeased at this deference to his opinion, and he stepped back again to the path, and joined his village friend.

"It is a sudden change, as you say, and an awkward one too, for the wind came round at three o'clock, just at the turn of the tide; and it's a chance but what it will keep this way for hours to come; and a gale all night's an ugly thing, Tomkins, when it blows ashore."

"I hope you may be mistaken, Mr. Bowman," rejoined the sexton; "but I suppose that's not likely. However, they say it's an ill wind that blows nobody good, so I suppose I shall come in for something at last," and here the sexton laughed.

"At your age, strong and hearty," observed the sailor, eyeing the sexton somewhat contemptuously, "you can't have much to wish for, I should think."

"Strong and hearty's a very good thing in its way, Mr. Bowman, I'll not deny; but rest's a very good thing, too, and I wouldn't object to one of your idle afternoons now and then, walking up and down the pavement, looking which way the wind blows. That's a bit of real comfort, to my thinking."

"We don't know much of each other's real comforts, I suspect," observed the sailor abstractedly, and then he added–

"You'll soon be cured of wishing for idle afternoons when they're forced upon you, Tomkins. But you don't know what you're talking about. Wait till you're old, and then you'll find it's I that might be excused for envying you, and not you me."

"That's amazing, Mr. Bowman, and I can't see it," persisted Tomkins, turning round to depart. "In my opinion you've the best of it; but anyhow, we're both of us oddly fixed, for we're neither of us pleased."

With a friendly goodnight, but no further remark, the two men parted, and the churchyard was emptied of its living guests.

When the sailor sat down with his sons an hour or two afterwards to their evening meal, said he, "We must keep a sharp look-out, lads, tonight; the wind came round at three with the turn of the tide, and it blows dead ashore. I've been up to the Captain's at the Hall, and borrowed the use of his big boat in case it's wanted, for unless the gale goes down with the next tide–which it won't, I think–we might have some awkward work. Anyhow, boys, we'll watch."

* * * * * *

"Just what I said," muttered the Dial, as the sound of the last footsteps died on the churchyard path. "Just what I said! Everything's wrong, because everybody's dissatisfied. I knew it was so. We're right in grumbling; that's the only thing we're right in. At least, I'm sure I'm right in grumbling. I'm not so certain about my neighbour on the tower above. Halloo! My sprightly friend, do you hear? Did you notice? Isn't it just as I said? Everything's wrong to everybody."

The strong west wind continued to sweep through the churchyard, and bore these observations away; but the Weathercock meanwhile was making his own remarks to himself.

"There, now! There's the old story over again, only now it's the west wind that's wrong instead of the east! I wish anybody would tell me which is the right wind! But this, of course, is an ill wind, and an ugly gale, and they're afraid it will blow all night, (I wonder why it shouldn't, it blows very steadily and well, as I think,) and then they shake their heads at each other, and look up at me and frown. What's the use of frowning? They never saw me go better in their lives. It's a fine firm wind as ever blew, though it does take one's breath rather fast, I own. If it did not make quite so much howling noise, I should have had a word or two about it with my old comrade below, who sits as steady as a rock through it all, I've no doubt. There is one thing I am not quite easy about myself . . . In case this west wind should blow a little, nay, in short, a great deal harder, even than now, I wonder whether there would be any danger of my being blown down? I'm not very fond of my present quarters, it's true, but a change is sometimes a doubtful kind of thing, unless you can choose what it shall be. I wonder, too, whether people would be glad if I was gone; or whether, after all, I mightn't be rather missed? And I wonder, too–"

But it began to blow too hard for wondering, or talking, or doing anything, but silently holding fast, for the gale was rising rapidly; so rapidly, that before midnight a hurricane was driving over land and ocean, and in its continued roaring, mingled as it was with the raging of a tempest-tossed sea, every other voice and sound was lost.

Tracts of white foam, lying like snow-fields on the water, followed the breakers as they fell down upon the shore with a crash of thunder, and were visible even through the gloom of night.

Hour after hour the uproar continued, and hour after hour the church clock struck, and no one heard. Due west pointed the Weathercock, varying scarcely a point. Firm and composed lay the Dial on his pedestal, and the old church on her foundations, mocking the tumult of the elements by their dead, immovable calm.

In the village on the top of the cliff many were awakened by the noise; and one or two, as they lay listening in their beds, forgot for a time their own petty troubles and trifling cares, and uttered wishes and prayers that no vessels might be driven near that rock-bound shore, on that night of storm!
Vain wishes! Vain prayers! As they turned again to their pillows to sleep, with their children around them, housed in security and peace, the blue lights of distress were sent up by trembling hands into the vault of heaven, and agonised hearts wondered whether human eye would see them, or human hand could aid.
And it might easily have happened, that, in that terrible night, no eye had caught sight of the signals, or caught sight of them too late to be of use, or that those who had seen had been indifferent, or unable to help.
But it was not so, or the Weathercock would have pointed, and the Dial have shown the hour, and the sailor looked at both in vain.
And this was not the case!
People were roused from their pillowed slumbers the next morning to hear that a vessel, with a passenger crew on board of her, was driving on the rocks. From cottage casements, and from the drawing-room windows of houses on the top of the cliff, the fatal sight was seen, for the dismasted ship, rolling helplessly on the waters, drifted gradually in front of the village, looking black as with the shadow of death.
Delicate women saw it, who all unaccustomed to such sights, and shuddering at their own helplessness, could only sink on their knees, and ask if there was no mercy with the Most High. Men saw it whom age or sickness had made weak as children, but who had once been brave and strong, and their heart burned within them as they turned away and sickened at the spectacle of misery they could not even try to avert. Children saw it, who, mixing in the village crowd that by degrees gathered on the cliff, never ceased the vain prattling inquiry of why some good people did not go help the poor people who were drowning in the ship?
"Young 'un, you talk," growled one old fellow who was eyeing the spectacle somewhat coolly through a telescope; "and it's for such as you to talk; but who's to get off a boat over such a surf as yon? Little use there'd be in flinging away more lives to save those that's as good as gone already."
"How you go on, Jonas!" cried a woman from the crowd. "Here's a lady has fainted through your saying that and what do you know about it? While there's life there's hope. My husband went down to the shore hours and hours ago, before it was light."
"With coffins, I suppose," shouted someone, and the jest went round, for the woman who had spoken was the sexton's wife. But many a voice cried "shame," as Mrs. Tomkins turned away to lend her aid in carrying the fainting lady to her home.
It was strange how time wore on, and no change for better or worse seemed to take place in the condition of the unhappy vessel, as far as those on land could judge of her. But she was at least a mile from shore; and even with a glass it was impossible to detect clearly the movements and state of her crew.

It was evident at one time that she had ceased to drift, and had become stationary, and all sorts of conjectures were afloat as to the cause; the most popular and dreadful of which being, that she was gradually filling with water, and must go down.
This was the reason (old Jonas said) why part of the crew had got into the boat that was being towed along behind by means of a rope, so that, when every other hope was over, the rest of the men might join them, and make a last desperate effort to escape the fate of the sinking vessel.
But still time wore on, and no change took place, nor did the vessel appear to get lower in the water, although at times the breakers rolled over her broken decks, and cries of "It's all over! There she goes!" broke from the crowd. The man at the wheel seemed still to maintain his post; those in the boat behind still kept their places, and the few visible about the ship were busied, but no one could say how.
At last somebody shouted that they were raising a jury-mast, though whether as a signal to some vessel within sight of them, or for their own use, remained doubtful for a time; but by and by a small sail became visible, and soon after, it was observed that the vessel had resumed her course, and that she was no longer drifting, but steering! It was clear, therefore, that she had been anchored previously, that the crew had not given up hope, and that they were now trying to weather the rocky bay, and get into the nearest harbour.
Old Jonas turned away, and lent his glass to others. The vessel was not filling with water, it was true, but could such a battered hulk, rolling as it did, ever live through the "race" at the extremity of the bay? He doubted it, for his part–but he was disposed to doubt!
Others were more hopeful, and many a "Thank God for His goodness" relieved the anxious breasts of those who had hitherto looked on in trembling suspense.
The villagers were gradually dispersing to their different occupations, when a couple of boys, who had gone down by the cliffs to the shore, came running back with the news that the old sailor's (Mr. Bowman's) cottage, the only one near the shore, was shut up, the key gone, and nobody there. This new surprise was heartily welcome, coming as it did to enliven the natural reaction of dullness that follows the cessation of great excitement; and the good wives of the village, with their aprons over their heads, huddled together, more full of wonder and conjecture over the disappearance of the Bowmans than over the fate of the still peril-surrounded ship. It was then discovered, but quite by an accident, that some one else had disappeared–no other than Tomkins, the sexton. A neighbour, on her road home, accidentally dropping in at Mr. Tomkins's door to ask after the lady that had fainted, found the good woman sitting over the fire, rocking to and fro, and crying her heart out.
"Go away, woman!" cried she to her neighbour, as the door opened. "Get away wi' ye! I want none of ye! I want none of your talking! I'll not listen to any of ye till I know whether the ship's gone down or not!"
"The woman's beside herself!" cried the neighbour. "Why, you don't know what you are saying, surely. The ship isn't likely to go down now! There's a mast and

a sail up, woman!"
"Aye, aye, but the 'race'!" cried Mrs. Tomkins, rocking to and fro in despair.
"The 'race' will not hurt it, there's a many says. It was only old Jonas that shook his head over that. Eh, woman, but you've lost your head with watching them. Where's your good man?"
Mrs. Tomkins almost shrieked, "There! He's there–with them! I saw him through Jonas's glass."
The neighbour was thunderstruck. Here was news indeed. But she pressed the matter no further, thinking in truth that Mrs. Tomkins's head was unsettled, and so, after soothing her a bit in the best fashion she could, she left her to talk the matter over in the village.
Mrs. Tomkins was not unsettled in her head at all. She had been one of those who had had a peep through Jonas's glass, and, to her horror, had detected, by some peculiarity of dress, the form of her husband sitting in the boat behind the vessel. The terror and astonishment that seized her rendered her mute, and she had retired to her own cottage to think it out by herself–what it could mean, and how it could have happened–but she had caught Jonas's remark about the "race," and on reaching her own fireside, all thoughts merged in the one terrible idea that her husband might go down with the devoted ship.
The report of Mrs. Tomkins's hallucination soon spread, and there is no saying to what a pitch of mysterious belief in some supernatural visitation it might not have led, had not the arrival of Bowman's daughter in the village, and the account she gave, explained the whole affair.
Bowman and his sons had not gone regularly to bed at all on the night previous, but, true to their intention, had kept watch in turn, walking up and down along the front of their cottage, which stood upon ground slightly raised above the shore. It was the old man himself who happened to be watching when the first blue lights went up, and it was then considerably past midnight.
"What a mercy!" was his first exclamation, after hurrying to the cottage, and bidding his sons follow him to the Hall; "What a mercy!" and he threw up his right arm with a clenched fist into the air, his whole frame knit up by strong emotion. The boys, not knowing what he meant, had only stared at him in surprise for a moment, for there was no time for talking. But the mind of the old man had, with the first sight of the lights, gone back to his churchyard lounge, to his observations on the weather, to the startling inscription, and to his determination to watch and provide. It had gone, forward, too, as well as backward. Forward, with the elastic determination and hope, which comes like inspiration to a good cause; and for him, by anticipation, the daring deed had been done, and the perishing crew rescued. "–What a mercy!" The exclamation comprehended past, present, and future.
As by the position of the signals of distress, Bowman judged it would be best to put off the boat from the place where it usually lay, he locked up his cottage, (for the girl refused to be left there alone,) taking the key with him, and proceeded at once to the Hall; but recollecting that his friend, the sexton, had made an urgent request to be called up, should any disaster occur, one of the lads ran up the cliff

to the village, to give notice of what they were about.
But before he was halfway there he met poor Tomkins himself, who, rendered restless and uneasy by Bowman's fears and the terrible weather, had come out to inquire how matters were going on. Thus, therefore, he joined their expedition at once, while his wife remained as ignorant of his movements as the rest of the village.
The Captain, a fine old sailor, round the evening of whose days the glories of Trafalgar shed an undying halo, had made it clearly understood when applied to, that, in case of the boat being wanted, his own assistance, also, might be depended upon; and he was true to his word; so that as soon as the dawn had broken five men were to be seen on the beach under the Hall, up to their waists almost in water, struggling with the foaming breakers, and pushing off, with an energy which nothing but the most desperate resolution could have given them, a boat from the shore. Few words were spoken; the one gave orders, and the rest obeyed–promptly, implicitly, and willingly, as if they had worked for years in company; and thus, life and death at stake, they rowed over the waste of waters with mute courage, and a hope which never for an instant blinded them to the knowledge of the peril they incurred.
And thus it was that ere the full daylight had revealed to the villagers the disaster at sea, and even while they were shuddering for the fate of the supposed doomed vessel, help and comfort had reached the despairing hearts of the bewildered men on board.
There were plenty of people afterwards to say that anybody might have known–if they had only thought about it–that that man who was lashed to the wheel, and who had never changed his position for an instant, could have been nobody but the grand old Captain who had been so long in the wars!
There were plenty also to say that Bowman, old as he was, was constantly on the look out, and was sure to be the first to foresee a disaster, and suggest what ought to be done, even when he could not do it himself; and didn't everybody know, too, that Tomkins was always foremost to have a hand in a job, whatever it might be?
The vessel cleared the "race," and got safe to the harbour, and half the village went with Bowman's daughter and Mrs. Tomkins (now weeping as hard for joy as she had before done for terror), to meet them as they landed.
What a talking there was! And what bowing to the Captain, who, dripping wet and cold, had nevertheless a joke for everybody, and even made Mrs. Tomkins smile by saying her husband had come with them on the look-out for a job, but happily his professional services had not been required, though he had done his duty otherwise like a man.
But the wet fellow-labourers had to be dried and taken care of, and the half-exhausted crew had to be attended to and comforted; and the time for chatting comfortably over the events of that night did not come till people's minds and spirits had cooled down from the first excitement.
The weather cleared up wonderfully after that terrible storm had passed over, and the following Sunday shone out over village and sea, with all the brilliancy

of spring.
It was just as they were issuing from church after morning service, that the Captain observed Bowman standing by the porch, as if waiting till the crowd had passed. He looked far more upright than usual, and had more of a smile upon his face than was commonly seen there. The Captain beckoned to him to come and speak, and Bowman obeyed.
"This has made a young man of you, Bowman," was the Captain's observation, and he smiled.
"It has comforted me, Sir, I'll not deny," was Bowman's answer.
"I hope it will teach as well as comfort you," continued the Captain, with a half good-natured, half stern manner. "You've been very fond of talking of age and infirmity, and 'cumbering the ground,' and all that sort of thing. But what it means, is, quarrelling with your lot. We may not always know what we're wanted for, nor is it for us to inquire, but nobody is useless as long as he is permitted to live. You can't have a shipwreck every day to prove it, Bowman, but this shipwreck ought to teach you the lesson for the rest of your life."
"I hope it will, Sir," cried Bowman.
"Not that you've so much credit in that matter, after all, as I thought," observed the Captain with a sly smile. "By your own account, if it hadn't been for these comrades of yours in the churchyard here," and as he spoke the Captain pointed with his stick to the Dial and Weathercock, "you might have gone to bed and snored composedly all the night through, without thinking of whether the storm would last, or what it would do."
Bowman touched his hat in compliment to the joke, recollecting with a sort of confusion that, as they were bringing the vessel into port, he had told the Captain the whole story of his noticing the change of wind at the particular hour of three, harping nervously and minutely on the importance of each link in the little chain of events, and dwelling much on the half-effaced inscription, the words of which had never left his mind from the moment when he got into the Captain's boat, to that when they reached the shore in safety.
Scarcely knowing how to reply, Bowman began again–
"Well, your honour, it's really true, for if it hadn't been that–"
"I know, I know," interrupted the Captain, laughing. "And now let us see your friends. I must have a peep at the inscription myself."
The old sailor led the way over the grassy graves to the Dial, and pointed out to his companion the almost illegible words.
There was a silence of several minutes, after the Captain had bent his head to read; and when he raised it again, his look was very grave. Except for the mercy that had spared their lives in so great a risk, the hour might have been over for them.
"Bowman," cried the Captain at length, in his old good-natured way, "these comrades of yours shall not go unrewarded any more than yourself. Before another week is over, you must see that this plate is cleaned and burnished, so that all the parish may read the inscription; and as to the Weathercock, I must have him as bright as gilding can make him before another Sunday. Come, here's

work for you for the week, and the seeing that this is done will leave you no time for grumbling, eh, old fellow?"
Bowman bowed his lowest bow. It fell in with all his feelings to superintend such an improvement as this.
"And while you're looking after them, don't forget the lesson they teach," continued the Captain.
Bowman bowed again, and was attentive.
"I mean that everything, as well as everybody, is useful in its appointed place, at the appointed time. But neither we nor they can choose or foresee the time."
On the following Sunday, the sun himself scarcely exceeded in brilliancy the flashing Weathercock, which hovered gently between point and point on the old church-tower by the sea, as if to exhibit his splendour to the world. Not a creak did he make as he moved, for all grumbling was over, and he was suspended to a nicety on his well-oiled pole. Below, and freshly brightened up and cleaned, the Dial basked in the sunlight, telling one by one the fleeting hours, while the motto underneath it spoke its warning, in letters illuminated as if with fire. Many a villager hung about the once-neglected plate, and took to heart those words of divine wisdom,

"Watch, for ye know not the hour,"

and many an eye glanced up to the monitor of storms and weather, and echoed the "What a mercy!" of old Bowman the sailor.
"Are you silent, my sprightly comrade?" inquired the old Dial from below, of his shining friend above.
"Only a little confused and overpowered at first," was the answer of the Weathercock. "My responsibility is great, you know. I have a great deal to do, and all the world is observing me just now."
"That's true, certainly," continued the Dial. "Things are coming round in a singular manner. Everything's right, after all; but under such a cloud as we were a short time ago, it was not very easy to find it out."
"Undoubtedly not, and a more excusable mistake than ours could not well be imagined. People, with fifty times our advantages, are constantly falling into the same errors."
"Which is such a comfort," pursued the Dial, smiling as he glowed in the sunbeams. "However," added he, that' s a good idea of the old gentleman that was here just now, and I shall try and remember it for future occasions, for it really appears to be true. 'Everything is useful in its place at the appointed time.' That was it, wasn't it?"
"Exactly. And, conscious as I feel just now of my own responsibility, I could almost add (in confidence to you, of course, my ancient friend) that I have a kind of sensation that everything is useful in its place, always, and at all times, though people mayn't always find it out."
"Just my own impression," was the Dial's last remark.

DAILY BREAD

"I WISH your cheerfulness were a little better timed, my friend," remarked a Tortoise, who for many years had inhabited the garden of a suburban villa, to a Robin Redbreast, who was trilling a merry note from a thorn-tree in the shrubbery. "What in the world are you singing about at this time of year, when I, and everybody else of any sense, are trying to go to sleep, and forget ourselves?"

"I beg your pardon, I am sure," replied the Robin; "I did not know it would have disturbed you."

"You must be gifted with very small powers of observation then, my friend," rejoined the Tortoise. "Here have I been grubbing my head under the leaves and sticks half the morning, to make myself a comfortable hole to take a nap in; and always, just as I am dropping off, you set up one of your senseless pipes."

"You are not over-troubled with politeness, good sir, I think," observed the Robin; "to call my performance by such an offensive name, and to find fault with me for want of observation, is the most unreasonable thing in the world. This is the first season I have lived in the garden, and all through the spring and summer you have never objected to my singing at all. How was I to know you would dislike it now?"

"Your own sense might have told you as much, without my giving myself the trouble of explanation," persisted the Tortoise. "Of course, it's natural enough, and not disagreeable, to hear you little birds singing round the place, when there is something to sing about. It rather raises one's spirits than otherwise. For instance, when the weather becomes mild in the early year, and the plants begin to grow and get juicy, and it is about time for me to get up from my winter's sleep, I have no objection to be awakened by your voices. But now, in this miserable season, when the fruits and flowers are gone, and when even the leaves that are left are tough and dry, and there is not a dandelion that I care to eat; and when it gets colder and colder, and damper and damper every day, this affectation of merriment on your part is both ridiculous and hypocritical. It is impossible that you can feel happy yourself, and you have no business to pretend to it."

"But, begging your pardon once more, good sir, I do feel happy, whatever you may think to the contrary," answered the Robin.

"What, do you mean to say that you *like* cold, and damp, and bare trees, with scarcely a berry upon them?"

"I like warm sunny days the best, perhaps," replied the Robin, "if I am obliged to think about it and make comparisons. But why should I do so? I am quite comfortable as it is. If there is not so much variety of food as there has been, there is, at any rate, enough for every day, and everybody knows that enough is as good as a feast. For my part, I don't see how I can help being contented."

"Contented! What a dull idea, to be just contented! I am contented myself, after a fashion; but you are trying to seem happy, and that is a very different sort of thing."

"Well, but happy; I am happy, too," insisted the Robin.

"That must be then because you know nothing of what is coming," suggested the Tortoise. "As yet, while the open weather lasts, you can pick up your favourite worms, and satisfy your appetite. But, when the ground has become so hard that the worms cannot come through, or your beak get at them, what will you do?"
"Are you sure that will ever happen?" inquired the Robin.
"Oh! Certainly, in the course of the winter, at some time or another; and, indeed, it may happen any day now, which makes me anxious to be asleep and out of the way."
"Oh, well, if it happens now, I shall not mind a bit," cried the Robin; "there are plenty of berries left!"
"But supposing it should happen when all the berries are gone?" said the Tortoise, actually teased at not being able to frighten the Robin out of his singing propensities.
"Nay, but if it comes to supposing," exclaimed the Robin, "I shall suppose it won't, and so I shall be happy still."
"But I say it *may* happen," shouted the Tortoise.
"And I ask *will* it?" rejoined the Robin, in quite as determined a manner.
"Which you know I cannot answer," retorted the Tortoise again. "Nobody knows exactly about either the weather or the berries beforehand."
"Then let nobody trouble themselves beforehand," persisted the Robin. "If there was anything to be done to prevent or provide, it would be different. But as it is, we have nothing to do but to be happy in the comfort each day brings." Here the Robin trilled out a few of his favourite notes, but the Tortoise soon interrupted him.
"Allow other people to be happy, then, as well as yourself, and cease squalling out of that tree. I could have forgiven you, had the branches been full of haws; but as they are all withered or eaten, you have no particular excuse for singing in that particular bush, rather than elsewhere, so let me request you at once to go."
"Of course I will do so," answered the Robin, politely. "It is the same thing to me exactly, so I wish you a good morning, and, if you desire it, a refreshing sleep."
So saying, the Robin flew from the thorn-tree to another part of the grounds, where he could amuse himself without interruption; and the Tortoise began to hustle under the leaves and rubbish again, with a view to taking his nap.
But, by-and-by, as the morning wore away, the frosty feeling and autumnal mists cleared off; and when the sun came out, which it did for three or four hours in the early afternoon, the day became really fine.
The old Tortoise did not fail to discover the fact; and not having yet scratched himself a hole completely to his mind, he came out of the shrubbery and took a turn in the sunshine.
"This is quite a surprise, indeed," said he to himself. "It is very pleasant, but I am afraid it will not last. The more's the pity; but, however, I shall not go to bed just yet."
With these words, he waddled slowly along to the kitchen garden, where he was in the habit of occasionally basking under the brick wall; and now, tilting

himself up sideways against it, he passed an hour, much to his satisfaction, in exposing his horny coat to the rays of the sun; a feat which he never dared to perform during the heats of summer.

Meanwhile, the poor little Robin continued his songs in a retired corner of the grounds, where no one objected to his cheerful notes. A tiny grove it was, with a grassy circle in the middle of it, where a pretty fountain played night and day.

During the pauses of his music, and especially after the sun came out, he wondered much to himself about all the strange uncomfortable things the Tortoise had said. Oh, to think of his having wanted to go to sleep and be out of the way; and now here was the sunshine making all the grove as warm as spring itself. If he had not been afraid the Tortoise might consider him intrusive, he would have gone back and told him how warm and pleasant it was, but absolutely he durst not.

Still, he could not, on reflection, shut his eyes to the fact, that there were no other songsters in the grove just now beside himself, and he wondered what was the reason. Time was, when the nightingale was to be heard every night in this very spot; but, now he came to think of it, that beautiful pipe of his had ceased for months, and where the bird himself was, nobody seemed to know.

The Robin became thoughtful, and perhaps a little uneasy.

There was the Blackbird, too; what was he about that he also was silent? Was it possible that all the world was really as the Tortoise said, thinking it wise to go to sleep and be out of the way?

The Robin got almost alarmed. So much so, that he flew about, until he met with a Blackbird, whom he might question on the subject, and of him he made the inquiry, why he had left off singing?

The Blackbird glanced at him with astonishment.

"Who does sing in the dismal Autumn and Winter?" said he. "Really, I know of scarcely any who are bold and thoughtless enough to do so except yourself. The Larks may, to be sure, but they lead such strange lives in the sky, or in seclusion, that they are no rule for any one else. Your own persevering chirruping is (in my humble judgment) so out of character with a season, in which every wise creature must be apprehensive for the future, that I can only excuse it on the ground of an ignorance and levity, which you have had no opportunity of correcting."

"It would be kinder to attribute it to a cheerful contentment with whatever comes to pass," cried the Robin, ruffling his feathers as he spoke. "I rejoice in each day's blessing as it comes, and never wish for more than does come. You, who are wishing the present to be better than it is, and fearing that the future may be worse, are meanwhile losing all enjoyment of the hour that now is. You think this wise. To me it seems as foolish as it is ungrateful!"

With these words the Robin flew away as fast as he could, for, to say the truth, he felt conscious of having been a little impertinent in his last remark. He was rather a young bird to be setting other people right; but a Robin is always a bold fellow, and has moreover rather a hot temper of his own, though he is a kind creature at the bottom. He had been insulted, too, there was no doubt; but when

people feel themselves in the right, what need is there of ruffling feathers and being saucy?
And the Robin did honestly feel himself in the right but, oh! How hard it is to resist the influence of evil suggestions, even when one knows them to be such, and turns aside from them. They are so apt to steal back into the heart unawares, and undermine the principle that seemed so steady before. To a certain extent, this was the case with our poor little friend; and those who are disposed to judge harshly of his weakness, must remember that he was very young, and could not be expected to go on right always without a mistake.
Certain it is, that he drooped awhile in spirits, as the winter advanced. He sang every day, it is true, and would still have maintained his own opinions against any one who should have opposed them; but he was decidedly disturbed in mind, and thought sadly too much, for his own peace and comfort, of what both the Tortoise and Blackbird had said.
The colder the days became, the more he became depressed; not that there was any cold then that he really cared about, but he was fidgeting about the much greater cold which he had been told was coming; and, as he hopped about on the grass round the fountain, picking up worms and food, he was ready to drop a tear out of his bright black eye at the thought of the days when the ground was to be so hard that the worms could not come out, or his beak reach them.
Had this state of things gone on long, the Robin would have begun to wish to go to sleep, like the Tortoise; and no more singing would have been heard in the plantation of the suburban villa that year.
But Robins are brave-hearted little fellows, as well as bold and saucy; and one bright day our friend bethought himself that he would go and talk the matter over with an old Woodlark, whom he had heard frequented a thicket at a considerable distance off.
On his way thither, he heard several larks singing high up in the sky over the fields; and by the time he reached the thicket he was in excellent spirits himself, and seemed to have left all his megrims behind.
It was fortunate such was the case, for when, as he approached the thicket, he heard the Woodlark's note, it was so plaintive and low, that it would have made anybody cry to listen to it. And when the Robin congratulated him on his singing, the Woodlark did not seem to care much for the compliment, but confided to his new acquaintance, that although he thought it right to sing and be thankful, as long as there was a bit of comfort left, he was not so happy as he seemed to be, since in reality he was always expecting to die some day of having nothing at all to eat.
"For," said he, "when the snow is on the ground, it is a perfect chance if one finds a morsel of food all day long."
"But I thought you had lived here several seasons," suggested the Robin, who in his braced condition of mind was getting quite reasonable again.
"So I have," murmured the Woodlark, heaving his breast with a touching sigh.
"Yet you did not die of having nothing to eat, last winter?" observed the Robin.
"It appears not," ejaculated the Woodlark, as gravely as possible, and with

another sigh; whereat the Robin's eye actually twinkled with mirth, for he had a good deal of fun in his composition, and could not but smile to himself at the Woodlark's solemn way of admitting that he was alive.
"Nor the winter before?" asked he.
"No," murmured the Woodlark again.
"Nor the winter before that?" persisted the saucy Robin.
"Well, no; of course not," answered the Woodlark, somewhat impatiently, "because I am here, as you see."
"Then how did you manage when the snow came, and there was no food?" inquired the Robin.
"I never told you there was actually no food in those other winters," answered the Woodlark somewhat peevishly, for he did not want to be disturbed in his views. "Llittle bits of things did accidentally turn up always. But there is no proof that it will ever happen again. It was merely chance!"
"Ah, my venerable friend," cried the Robin; "have you no confidence in the kind chance that has befriended you so often before?"
"I can never be sure it will do so again," murmured the Woodlark despondingly.
"But when that kind chance brings you one comfortable day after another, why should you sadden them all by these fears for by and by?"
"It is a weakness, I believe," responded the Woodlark. "I will see what I can do towards enjoying myself more. You are very wise, little Robin; and it is a wisdom that will keep you happy all the year round."
Here the Woodlark rose into the air, and performed several circling flights, singing vigorously all the time. The old melancholy pervaded the tone, but that might be mere habit. The song was, at any rate, more earnest and strong.
"That is better already," cried the Robin gaily; "and for my part, if I am ever disposed to be dull myself, I shall think of what you told me just now of all the past winters; namely, that little bits of things did always accidentally turn up. What a comforting fact!"
"To think of my ever having been able to comfort anybody!" exclaimed the Woodlark. "I must try to take comfort myself."
"Ay, indeed," cried the Robin earnestly; "it is faithless work to give advice which you will not follow yourself."
So saying, the Robin trilled out a pleasant farewell, and returned to the shrubbery grounds, where, in an ivy-covered wall, he had found for himself a snug little winter's home.
It was during the ensuing week, and while the Robin was in his blithest mood, and singing away undisturbed by megrims of any kind, but rejoicing in the comforts of each day as it came, that the Tortoise once more accosted him.
When Robin first heard his voice he was startled, and feared another scolding, but he was quite mistaken. The old Tortoise was sitting by the side of an opening in the ground, which he had scratched out very cleverly with his claws. It was in a corner among some stones which had lain there for years; and there was one large one in particular overhung the entrance of the hole. The wind had drifted a vast quantity of leaves in that direction, and some of them had been blown into

the hole, so that it looked like a warm underground bed.
"Hop down to me, little bird!" was the Tortoise's address, in a quite friendly voice; an order with which the Robin at once complied. "Ah, you need not be afraid," continued he, as the Robin alighted by his side. " I am quite happy now. See what a comfortable place I have made myself here in the earth. There, there, put your head in and peep. Did you ever see anything so snug in your life?"
The Robin peered in with his sharp little eye, and really admired the Tortoise's ingenious labour very much.
"Hop in," cried the Tortoise gaily; "there's room enough and to spare, is there not?"
Robin hopped in, and looked round. He was surprised at the size and convenience of the place, and admitted that a more roomy and comfortable winter's bed could not be wished for.
"Who wouldn't go to sleep?" cried the Tortoise; "what say you, my little friend? But you need not say; I see it in your eye. You are not for sleep yourself. Well, well, we have all our different ways of life, and yours is a pleasant folly, after all, when it doesn't disturb other people. And you won't disturb me any more this year, for I have made my arrangements at last, and shall soon be so sound asleep, that I shall hear no more of your singing for the present. It's a nice bed, isn't it? Not so nice, perhaps, as the warm sands of my native land; but the ground, even here, is much warmer inside it than people think, who know nothing of it but the cold damp surface. Ah, if it wasn't, how would the snowdrop and crocus live through the winter? Well, I called you here to say good-bye, and show you where I am, and to ask you to remember me in the Spring; if–that is, of course–you survive the terrible weather that is coming. You don't mind my having been somewhat cross the other day, do you? I am apt to get testy now and then, and you disturbed me in my nap, which nobody can bear. But you will forgive and forget, won't you, little bird?"
The kind-hearted Robin protested his affectionate feeling in a thousand pretty ways.
"Then you won't forget me in the Spring," added the Tortoise; "but come here and sit on the laurel bush, and sing me awake. Not till the days are mild, and the plants get juicy, of course, but as soon as you please then. And now, good-bye. There's a strange feeling in the air today, and before many hours are over there will be snow and frost. Yours is a pleasant folly. I wish it may not cost you dear. Good-bye."
Hereupon the old Tortoise huddled away into the interior of his hole, where he actually disappeared from sight; and as soon afterwards the drifting leaves completely choked up the entrance of the place, no one could have suspected what was there, but those who knew the secret beforehand. He had been right in his prognostication of the weather. A thick, gloomy, raw evening was succeeded by a bitterly cold night, and towards the morning the over-weighted clouds began to discharge themselves of some of their snow; and as the day wore, the flakes got heavier and heavier; and as no sunshine came out to melt them, and a biting frost set in, the country was soon covered with a winding-sheet of white.

And now, indeed, began a severe trial of the Robin's patience and hope. It is easy to boast while the sun still shines, if ever so little; but it is not till the storm comes, that the mettle of principle is known.
"There are berries left yet," said he, with cheerful composure, as he went out to seek for food, and found a holly-tree by the little gate of the plantation, red with its beautiful fruit. And, after he had eaten, he poured out a song of joy and thankfulness into the cold wintry sky, and finally retreated under his ivy bush at night, happy and contented as before.
But that terrible storm lasted for weeks without intermission; or, if it did intermit, it was but to a partial thaw, which the night of frost soon bound up again, as firmly, or more firmly, than ever.
Many other birds besides himself came to the holly-tree for berries, and it was wonderful how they disappeared, first from one branch, and then from another; but still the Robin sang on. He poured out his little song of thanks after every meal. That was his rule. Other birds would jeer at him sometimes, but he could not be much moved by jeers. He had brought his bravery, and his patience, and his hope into the field against whatever troubles might arise, and a few foolish jests would not trouble a spirit so strung up to cheerful endurance.
"I will sing the old Tortoise awake yet," said he, many and many a time, when, after chanting his little thanksgiving in the holly-tree, he would hover about the spot where his friend lay asleep in the ground, and think of the spring that would one day come, bringing its mild days and its juicy plants, and its thousand pleasant delights.
I do not say, but what it was a great trial to our friend, when, after dreaming all these things in his day-dreams, he was roused up at last by feeling himself unusually cold and stiff; and was forced to hurry to his ivy home to recover himself at all.
The alternations, too, of winter, are very trying. The long storm of many weeks ceased at last, and a fortnight of open weather ensued, which, although wet and cold, gave much more liberty to the birds, and allowed of greater plenty of food. The Robin could now hop once more on the grass round the fountain, and get at a few worms, and pick up a few seeds. And he was so delighted with the change, that he half hoped the winter was over; and he sat in the laurel tree by the Tortoise's cave, and poured out long ditties of anticipative delight. But the bitterest storm of all was yet in store–the storm of disappointed hope.
Oh, heavy clouds, why did you hang so darkly over the earth just before the Christmas season? Oh, why did the fields become so white again, and the trees so laden with snow wreaths, and the waters so frozen and immovable, just when all human beings wanted to rejoice and be glad? Did you come–perhaps you did!–to rouse to tender pity and compassionate love, the hearts of all who wished to welcome their Saviour with hosannas of joy? But who cannot forget, if they read the gospel of love, that whosoever does a kindness to one of the least of His disciples, does it unto Him. Surely, thus may the bitter cold, and the trying weather of a biting, snowy Christmas, be read. Surely, it calls aloud to every one, that *now* is the moment for clothing the naked, for feeding the hungry, and

for comforting the afflicted.
Heavily, heavily, heavily, it came down. There were two days in which the Robin never left his ivy-covered hole, but hunger took him at last to the holly-tree by the little gate. Its prickly leaves were loaded with snow, and on one side the stem could not be seen at all. Was it his fancy, or was the tree really much less than before? He hopped from one white branch to another, and fancied that large pieces were gone. He peered under and over, picked at the leaves, and shook down little morsels of snow; but nowhere, nowhere, nowhere, could a single berry be found!
The Robin flew about in distress, and in so doing caught sight of a heap of holly, laurel, and bay branches that were laid aside together to be carried up to the house to decorate its walls. He picked two or three of the berries from them as they lay there–ripe, red berries, such as he had gathered but lately from the tree; and then came the gardener by, who carried the whole away. He flew after the man as he walked, and never left him until he disappeared with his load into the house. Its unfriendly doors closed against the little wanderer, and no one within knew of the wistful eyes which had watched the coveted food out of sight.
"I have eaten; let me be thankful," was the Robin's resolute remark, as he flew away from the house and returned to the holly tree, which had so lately been his storehouse of hope, and from its now stripped and barren branches, poured out, as before, his lay of glad thanksgiving for what he had had.
Not a breath of wind was blowing, not a leaf stirred; not a movement of any kind took place, save when some overloaded branch dropped part of its weight of snow on the ground below; as the sweet carol of the still hungry little bird rose through the air on that dark, still winter's afternoon.
What did it tell of? Oh, surely, that clear bell-like melody, that musical tone, that exquisite harmonious trill, told of something–of something, I mean, besides the tale of a poor little desolate bird, whose food had been snatched away before his eyes, and who might be thought to have eaten his last meal.
Surely those solitary notes of joy, poured into the midst of a gloom so profound, were as an angel's message, coming with a promise of peace and hope, at a moment when both seemed dead and departed.
Homeward from his day's work of business there passed by, at that moment, the owner and inhabitant of the little suburban villa. It had been a melancholy day to him, for it was saddened by painful recollections. It was the anniversary of the day on which his wife had been laid in her churchyard grave, and since that event two sons had sailed for the far-off land of promise, which puts a hemisphere between the loved and loving on earth. So that far-distant land held them whilst one, not so distant, perhaps, but more unattainable for the present, held the other. No wonder, therefore, that on that owner's face, as he approached his home, there hung a cloud of suffering and care, which not even the thought of the Christmas-day at hand, and the children yet spared to his hearth, could prevent or dispel.
Verily the autumn of man's life comes down upon him as the autumn season descends upon the earth. Clouds and tears mixed with whatever brightness may

remain.
All at once, however, the abstracted look of sorrow is startled. What is it that he hears? He is passing outside the little plantation which skirts the grounds. He is close to the little gate near which the holly-tree grows. He pauses–he stops–he lifts up those troubled eyes. Surely, a wholesome tear is stealing over the cheek. Beautiful, tender, affecting, as the voice of the cuckoo in spring, there swept over the listener's heart, the autumnal song of the Robin. Sing on; sing on, from the top of your desolate tree, oh, little bird of cheerfulness and hope! Pour out again that heaven-taught music of contentment with the hour that now is. Shalt thou be confident of protection, and man destitute of hope! Shalt thou, in the depth of thy winter's trial, have joy and peace, and man never look beyond the cloud?
Poor little innocent bird, he sang his pretty song to an end, and then he flew away. Quarrel not with him, if in painful recollection of the holly-berries that had been carried into the house, he hovered round its windows and doors, with anxious and curious stealth. Whether across the middle of one window he observed a tempting red cluster hanging down inside, no one can say. But the tantalising pain of such a sight, if he felt it, was soon over, for just then the window was opened, and along its outside ledge something was strewn by a careful hand. The window was closed again immediately, and, whoever it was within, retreated backwards into the room.
From a standard rosebush, whither he had flown, when the window was opened, our little friend watched the affair.
Presently a fragrant odour seemed to steal towards him, something unknown yet pleasant, something tempting and very nice. Was there any risk to be feared? All seemed quiet and still. Should he venture? Ah, that odour again! It was irresistible.
In another minute he was on the ledge, and boldly, as if a dozen invitations had bidden him welcome to the feast, he was devouring crumb after crumb of the scattered bread.
A burst of delighted laughter from within broke upon his elysium of joy for a moment, and sent him back with sudden flight to the rosebush. But no disaster ensued, and he was tempted again and again.
The children within might well laugh at the saucy bird whom their father had, by his gift of bread-crumbs, tempted to the place. They laughed at the bold hop, the eager pecking, the brilliant bead-like eye of their new guest, and at the bright red of his breast; but it was a laugh that told of nothing but kind delight.
"Little bits of things do accidentally, turn up always, indeed!" said the Robin to himself, as he crept into his ivy hole that evening to sleep; and he dreamt half the night of the wonderful place and the princely fare. And next morning, long before anybody was awake and up, he was off to the magical window ledge again, but neither children nor breadcrumbs were there. (How was he to know about breakfast hours, and the customs of social life?) So it almost seemed to him as if his evening meal had been a dream, too good a thing to be true, or if it had ever been true, too good to return. Yet a sweeter song was never heard on a

summer eve, than that with which the Robin greeted that early day, the Christmas morning of the year.

Perched in the laurel bush near the Tortoise's retreat, he told his sleeping friend a long, marvelous tale of his yesterday's adventures, and promised him more news against the time when he should return to wake him up in the spring.

Nor did he promise in vain; for whether the Tortoise would be patient enough to listen or not, there was no doubt the Robin had plenty to tell. He had to tell of the daily meal that was spread for him, by those suddenly raised up friends–that daily meal that had never failed; of the curious tiny house that was erected for him at the end of the ledge, which, carpeted as it was with cotton-wool and hay, formed almost too warm a roosting place for his hardy little frame.

But even to the Tortoise he could never tell all he had felt during that wonderful winter, for he could never explain to any one the mysterious friendship which grew up between himself and his protectors. He could never describe properly the friendly faces that sat round the breakfast-table on which at last he was allowed to hop about at will.

He told, however, how he used to sing on the rose-tree outside, every morning of every day, to welcome the waking of his friends, and how, in the late afternoons, the father would sometimes open the window, and sit there alone by himself, listening to his song.

"Come, come, my little friend," remarked the Tortoise, when he did awake at last, and had come out of his cavern-bed, and heard the account; "I have been asleep for a long time, and I dare say have been dreaming all manner of fine things myself, if I could but think of them. Now, I suspect you have had a nap, as well. However, I am very glad to see you alive, and not so half-starved looking as I expected. But as to your having sung every day, and had plenty to eat every day, and been so happy all the time–take my advice, don't try to cram older heads than your own with travelers' tales!"

NOT LOST, BUT GONE BEFORE

"—Will none of you in pity
To those you left behind, disclose the secret?"
BLAIR'S GRAVE.

"I WONDER what becomes of the Frog, when he climbs up out of this world, and disappears, so that we do not see even his shadow; till, plop! He is among us again, when we least expect him. Does anybody know where he goes to? Tell me, somebody, pray!"

Thus chattered the Grub of a Dragon-fly, as he darted about with his numerous companions, in and out among the plants at the bottom of the water, in search of prey.

The water formed a beautiful pond in the centre of a wood. Stately trees grew around it and reflected themselves on its surface, as on a polished mirror; and the bulrushes and forget-me-nots which fringed its sides seemed to have a twofold life, so perfect was their image below.

"Who cares what the Frog does?" answered one of those who overheard the Grub's inquiry; "what is it to us?"

"Look out for food for yourself," cried another, "and let other people's business alone."

"But I have a curiosity on the subject," expostulated the first speaker. "I can see all of you when you pass by me among the plants in the water here; and when I don't see you any longer, I know you have gone further on. But I followed a Frog just now as he went upwards, and all at once he went to the side of the water, and then began to disappear, and presently he was gone. Did he leave this world, do you think? And what can there be beyond?"

"You idle, talkative fellow," cried another, shooting by as he spoke, "attend to the world you are in, and leave the 'beyond,' if there is a 'beyond,' to those that are there. See what a morsel you have missed with your wonderings about nothing." So saying, the saucy speaker seized an insect which was flitting right in front of his friend.

The curiosity of the Grub was a little checked by these and similar remarks, and he resumed his employment of chasing prey for a time.

But, do what he would, he could not help thinking of the curious disappearance of the Frog, and presently began to tease his neighbors about it again, *What becomes of the Frog when he leaves this world?* being the burden of his inquiry.

The minnows eyed him askance and passed on without speaking, for they knew no more than he did of the matter, and yet were loath to proclaim their ignorance; and the eels wriggled away in the mud out of hearing, for they could not bear to be disturbed.

The Grub got impatient, but he succeeded in inspiring several of his tribe with some of his own curiosity, and then went scrambling about in all directions with his followers, asking the same unreasonable questions of all the creatures he met.

Suddenly there was a heavy splash in the water, and a large yellow Frog swam down to the bottom among the grubs.
"Ask the Frog himself," suggested a Minnow, as he darted by overhead, with a mischievous glance of his eye. And very good advice it seemed to be, only the thing was much easier said than done. For the Frog was a dignified sort of personage, of whom the smaller inhabitants of the water stood a good deal in awe. It required no common amount of assurance to ask a creature of his standing and gravity, where he had been to, and where he had come from. He might justly consider such an inquiry as a very impertinent piece of curiosity.
Still, such a chance of satisfying himself was not to be lost, and after taking two or three turns round the roots of a water lily, the Grub screwed up his courage, and approaching the Frog in the meekest manner he could assume, he asked–
"Is it permitted to a very unhappy creature to speak?"
The Frog turned his gold-edged eyes upon him in surprise, and answered–
"Very unhappy creatures had better be silent. I never talk but when I am happy."
"But I shall be happy if I may talk," interposed the Grub, as glibly as possible.
"Talk away then," cried the Frog; "what can it matter to me?"
"Respected Frog," replied the Grub, "but it is something I want to ask you."
"Ask away," exclaimed the Frog, not in a very encouraging tone, it must be confessed; but still the permission was given.
"What is there beyond the world?" inquired the Grub, in a voice scarcely audible from emotion.
"What world do you mean?" cried the Frog, rolling his goggle eyes round and round.
"This world, of course, our world," answered the Grub.
"This pond, you mean," remarked the Frog, with a contemptuous sneer.
"I mean the place we live in, whatever you may choose to call it," cried the Grub pertly. "I call it the world."
"Do you, sharp little fellow?" rejoined the Frog. "Then what is the place you don't live in, the 'beyond' the world, eh?"
And the Frog shook his sides with merriment as he spoke.
"That is just what I want you to tell me," replied the Grub briskly.
"Oh, indeed, little one!" exclaimed the Froggy, rolling his eyes this time with an amused twinkle. "Come, I shall tell you then. It is dry land."
There was a pause of several seconds, and then, "Can one swim about there?" inquired the Grub, in a subdued tone.
"I should think not," chuckled the Frog. "Dry land is not water, little fellow. That is just what it is *not*."
"But I want you to tell me what it *is*," persisted the Grub.
"Of all the inquisitive creatures I ever met, you certainly are the most troublesome," cried the Frog. "Well, then, dry land is something like the sludge at the bottom of this pond, only it is not wet, because there is no water."
"Really!" interrupted the grub, "what is there then?"
"That's the difficulty," exclaimed Froggy. "There is something, of course, and they call it air; but how to explain it I don't know. My own feeling about it is,

that it's the nearest approach to nothing, possible. Do you comprehend?"
"Not quite," replied the Grub, hesitating.
"Exactly; I was afraid not. Now just take my advice, and ask no more silly questions. No good can possibly come of it," urged the Frog.
"Honoured Frog," exclaimed the Grub, "I must differ from you there. Great good will, as I think, come of it, if my restless curiosity can be stilled by obtaining the knowledge I seek. If I learn to be contented where I am, it will be something. At present I am miserable and restless under my ignorance."
"You are a very silly fellow," cried the Frog, "who will not be satisfied with the experience of others. I tell you the thing is not worth your troubling yourself about. But, as I rather admire your spirit, (which, for so insignificant a creature, is astonishing,) I will make you an offer. If you choose to take a seat on my back, I will carry you up to dry land myself, and then you can judge for yourself what there is there, and how you like it. I consider it a foolish experiment, mind, but that is your own look out. I make my offer, to give you pleasure."
"And I accept it with a gratitude that knows no bounds," exclaimed the enthusiastic Grub.
"Drop yourself down on my back, then, and cling to me as well as you can. For, remember, if you go gliding off, you will be out of the way when I leave the water."
The Grub obeyed, and the Frog, swimming gently upwards, reached the bulrushes by the water's side.
"Hold fast," cried he, all at once, and then, raising his head out of the pond, he clambered up the bank, and got upon the grass.
"Now then, here we are," exclaimed he. "What do you think of dry land?"
But no one spoke in reply.
"Halloo! Gone?" he continued. "That's just what I was afraid of. He has floated off my back, stupid fellow, I declare. Dear, dear, how unlucky! But it cannot be helped. And, perhaps, he may make his way to the water's edge here after all, and then I can help him out. I will wait about and see."
And away went Froggy, with an occasional jaunty leap, along the grass by the edge of the pond, glancing every now and then among the bulrushes, to see if he could spy the dark, mailed figure of the dragon-fly Grub.
But the Grub, meanwhile? Ah, so far from having floated off the Frog's back through carelessness, he had clung to it with all the tenacity of hope, and the moment came when the mask of his face began to issue from the water.
But the same moment sent him reeling from his resting-place into the pond, panting and struggling for life. A shock seemed to have struck his frame, a deadly faintness succeeded, and it was several seconds before he could recover himself.
"Horrible!" cried he, as soon as he had rallied a little. "Beyond this world there is nothing but death. The Frog has deceived me. He cannot go there, at any rate."
And with these words, the Grub moved away to his old occupations, his ardour for inquiry grievously checked, though his spirit was unsubdued.
He contented himself for the present, therefore, with talking over what he had

done, and where he had been, with his friends. And who could listen unmoved to such a recital? The novelty, the mystery, the danger, the all but fatal result, and the still unexplained wonder of what became of the Frog–all invested the affair with a romantic interest, and the Grub had soon a host of followers of his own race, questioning, chattering, and conjecturing, at his heels.
By this time the day was declining, and the active pursuit of prey was gradually becoming suspended for a time; when, as the inquisitive Grub was returning from a somewhat protracted ramble among the water-plants, he suddenly encountered, sitting pensively on a stone at the bottom of the pond, his friend the yellow Frog.
"You here!" cried the startled Grub; "you never left this world at all, then, I suppose. What a deception you must have practised upon me! But this comes of trusting to strangers, as I was foolish enough to do."
"You perplex me by your offensive remarks," replied the Frog, gravely. "Nevertheless, I forgive you, because you are so clumsy and ignorant, that civility cannot reasonably be expected from you, little fellow. It never struck you, I suppose, to think what my sensations were, when I landed this morning on the grass, and discovered that you were no longer on my back. Why did you not sit fast as I told you? But this is always the way with you foolish fellows, who think you can fathom and investigate everything. You are thrown over by the first practical difficulty you meet."
"Your accusations are full of injustice," exclaimed the indignant Grub.
It was clear they were on the point of quarrelling, and would certainly have done so, had not the Frog, with unusual magnanimity, desired the Grub to tell his own story, and clear himself from the charge of clumsiness if he could.
It was soon told, the Frog staring at him in silence out of those great goggle eyes, while he went through the details of his terrible adventure.
"And now," said the Grub, in conclusion, "as it is clear that there is nothing beyond this world but death, all your stories of going there yourself must be mere inventions. Of course, therefore, if you do leave this world at all, you go to some other place you are unwilling to tell me of. You have a right to your secret, I admit; but as I have no wish to be fooled by any more travelers' tales, I will bid you a very good evening."
"You will do no such thing, till you have listened as patiently to my story as I have done to yours," exclaimed the Frog.
"That is but just, I allow," said the Grub, and stopped to listen.
Then the Frog told how he had lingered by the edge of the pond, in the vain hope of his approach, how he had hopped about in the grass, how he had peeped among the bulrushes. "And at last," continued he, "though I did not see you yourself, I saw a sight which has more interest for you, than for any other creature that lives," and there he paused.
"And that was?" asked the inquisitive Grub, his curiosity reviving, and his wrath becoming appeased.
"Up the polished green stalk of one of those bulrushes," continued the Frog, "I beheld one of your race slowly and gradually climbing, till he had left the water

behind him, and was clinging firmly to his chosen support, exposed to the full glare of the sun. Rather wondering at such a sight, considering the fondness you all of you show for the shady bottom of the pond, I continued to gaze, and observed presently–but I cannot tell you in what way the thing happened–that a rent seemed to come in your friend's body, and by degrees, gradually and after many struggles, there emerged from it one of those radiant creatures who float through the air I spoke to you of, and dazzle the eyes of all who catch glimpses of them as they pass, a glorious Dragon-fly!

"As if scarcely awakened from some perplexing dream, he lifted his wings out of the carcase he was forsaking; and though shriveled and damp at first, they stretched and expanded in the sunshine, till they glistened as if with fire.

"How long the strange process continued, I can scarcely tell, so fixed was I in astonishment and admiration; but I saw the beautiful creature at last poise himself for a second or two in the air before he took flight. I saw the four gauzy pinions flash back the sunshine that was poured on them. I heard the clash with which they struck upon the air; and I beheld his body give out rays of glittering blue and green as he darted along, and away, away, over the water in eddying circles that seemed to know no end. Then I plunged below to seek you out, rejoicing for your sake in the news I brought."

The Frog stopped short, and a long pause followed.

At last–"It is a wonderful story," observed the Grub, with less emotion than might have been expected.

"A wonderful story, indeed," repeated the Frog; "may I ask your opinion upon it?"

"It is for me to defer mine to yours," was the Grub's polite reply.

"Good! You are grown obliging, my little friend," remarked the Frog. "Well then, I incline to the belief, that what I have seen accounts for your otherwise unreasonable curiosity, your tiresome craving for information about the world beyond your own."

"That were possible, always provided your account can be depended upon," mused the Grub with a doubtful air.

"Little fellow," exclaimed the Frog, "Remember that your distrust cannot injure me, but may deprive yourself of a comfort."

"And you really think, then, that the glorious creature you describe, was once a–"

"Silence," cried the Frog; "I am not prepared with definitions. Adieu! The shades of night are falling on your world. I return to my grassy home on dry land. Go to rest, little fellow, and awake in hope."

The Frog swam close to the bank, and clambered up its sides, while the Grub returned to his tribe, who rested during the hours of darkness from their life of activity and pursuit.

"Promise," uttered an entreating voice.
"I promise," was the earnest answer.
"Faithfully?" urged the first speaker.
"Solemnly," ejaculated the second.
But the voice was languid and weak, for the dragon-fly Grub was sick and uneasy. His limbs had lost their old activity, and a strange oppression was upon him.
The creatures whom he had been accustomed to chase, passed by him unharmed; the water-plants, over which he used to scramble with so much agility, were distasteful to his feet; nay, the very water itself into which he had been born, and through which he was wont to propel himself with so much ingenuity, felt suffocating in its weight.
Upwards he must go now, upwards, upwards! That was the strong sensation which mastered every other, and to it he felt he must submit, as to some inevitable law. And then he thought of the Frog's account, and felt a trembling conviction that the time had come, when the riddle of his own fate must be solved.
His friends and relations were gathered around him, some of his own age, some a generation younger, who had only that year entered upon existence. All of them were followers and adherents, whom he had inspired with his own enthusiastic hopes; and they would fain have helped him, if they could, in this hour of weakness. But there was no help for him now, but hope, and of that he possessed, perhaps, even more than they did.
Then came an earnest request, and then a solemn promise, that, as surely as the great hopes proved true, so surely would he return and tell them so.
"But, oh! If you should forget!" exclaimed one of the younger generation, timid and uneasy.
"Forget the old home, my friend?" ejaculated the sick Grub, "forget our life of enjoyment here, the ardour of the chase, the ingenious stratagems, the triumph of success? Forget the emotions of hope and fear we have shared together, and which I am bound, if I can, to relieve? Impossible!"
"But if you should not be able to come back to us," suggested another.
"More unlikely still," murmured the half exhausted Grub. "To a condition so exalted as the one in store for us, what can be impossible? Adieu, my friends, adieu! I can tarry here no longer. Ere long you may expect to see me again in a new and more glorious form. Till then, farewell!"
Languid, indeed, was the voice, and languid were the movements of the Grub, as he rose upwards through the water to the reeds and bulrushes that fringed its bank. Two favourite brothers, and a few of his friends, more adventurous than the rest, accompanied him in his ascent, in the hope of witnessing whatever might take place above; but in this they were, of course, disappointed.
From the moment when, clinging with his feet to the stem of a bulrush, he emerged from his native element into the air, his companions saw him no more.
Eyes fitted only for the watery fluid, were incapable of the upward glance and power of vision which would have enabled them to pierce beyond it; and the

little coterie of discoverers descended, mortified and sorrowful, to the bed of the pond.
The sun was high in the heavens when the dragon-fly Grub parted from his friends, and they waited through the long hours of the day for his return; at first, in joyful hope, then in tremulous anxiety, and, as the shades of evening began to deepen around, in a gloomy fear, that bordered at last on despair. "He has forgotten us," cried some. "A death from which he never can awake, has overtaken him," said others. "He will return to us yet," maintained the few who clung to hope.
But in vain messenger after messenger shot upwards to the bulrushes, and to various parts of the pond, hoping to discover some trace of the lost one. All who went out, returned back dispirited from the vain and weary search, and even the most sanguine began to grow sick at heart.
Night closed at last upon them, bringing a temporary suspension of grief; but the beams of the next rising sun, while it filled all nature beside with joy and hopefulness, awakened them, alas, to a sense of the bitterest disappointment, and a feeling of indignation at the deception which had been practised upon them.
"We did very well without thinking of such things," said they, "but to have hopes like those held out, and to be deceived after all–it is more than we can be expected to bear in patience."
And bear it in patience they did not. With a fierceness which nothing could restrain, they hurried about in the destructive pursuit of prey, carrying a terrible vengeance in all directions.
And thus passed on the hours of the second day, and before night a sort of grim and savage silence was agreed upon among them, and they ceased to bewail either the loss of him they had loved, or their own uncertain destiny.
But on the morning of the third day, one of the Grub's favourite brothers came sailing into the midst of a group who were just rousing up from rest, ready to commence the daily business of their life.
There was an unnatural brilliancy about his eyes, which shone as they had never done before, and startled all who looked at them, so that even the least observant had their attention arrested as he spoke.
"My friends," said he, "I was, as you know, one of our lost relation's favourite brothers. I trusted him, as if he had been a second self, and would have pledged myself a thousand times for his word. Judge, then, what I have suffered from his promise remaining still unfulfilled. Alas! That he has not yet returned to us!"
The favourite brother paused, and a little set in a corner by themselves murmured out, "How could he? The story about that other world is false."
"He has not returned to us," recommenced the favourite brother. "But, my friends, I feel that I am going to him, wherever that may be, either to that new life he spoke about, or to that death from which there is no return. Dear ones! I go, as he did, upwards, upwards, upwards! An irresistible desire compels me to it; but before I go, I renew to you–for myself and him–the solemn promise he once made to you. Should the great hopes be true, we will come back and tell you so. If I return not–but rely on me; my word is more to me than life. Adieu!"

The Grub rose upwards through the water followed by the last of the three brothers, and one or two of the younger ones; but on reaching the brink of the pond, he seized on a plant of the forget-me-not, and clinging to its firm flower-stalk, clambered out of the water into the open air.

Those who accompanied him, watched him as he left the water; but, after that, they saw no more. The blank of his departure alone remained to them, and they sank down, sad and uneasy, to their home below.

As before, the hours of the day passed on, and not a trace of the departed one was seen. In vain they dwelt upon the consoling words he had spoken. The hope he had for a time re-awakened, died out with the declining sun, and many a voice was raised against his treachery and want of love. "He is faithless," said some. "He forgets us, like his brother, in his new fortune," cried others. "The story of that other world is false," muttered the little set in the corner by themselves. Only a very few murmured to each other, "We will not despair."

One thing along was certain, he did not return; and the disappointed crowds took refuge from thought as before, in the fiercest rapine and excitement, scattering destruction around them, wherever they moved.

Another day now elapsed, and then, in the early dawn following, the third and last brother crept slowly to a half-sleepy knot of his more particular friends, and roused them up.

"Look at my eyes," said he; "has not a sudden change come over them? They feel to me swelled and bursting, and yet I see with a clouded and imperfect vision. Doubtless it is with me now, as it was with our dear ones before they left us. I am oppressed, like them. Like them, an invisible power is driving me upwards, as they were driven. Listen, then; for on my parting words you may depend. Let the other world be what it will, gorgeous beyond all we can fancy of it, blissful beyond all we can hope of it, do not fear in me an altered or forgetful heart. I dare not promise more. Yet if it be possible, I will return. But, remember, there may well be that other world, and yet we, in ours, may misjudge its nature. Farewell, never part with hope. With your fears I know you never can part now. Farewell!"

And he too went upwards, through the cool water to the plants that bordered its side; and from the leaf of a golden king-cup he rose out of his native element into that aërial world, into which water-grub's eye never yet could pierce.

His companions lingered awhile near the spot where he had disappeared, but neither sign nor sound came to them. Only the dreary sense of bereavement reminded them that he once had been.

Then followed the hours of vain expectation, the renewed disappointment, the cruel doubts, the hope that struggled with despair.

And after this, others went upwards in succession; for the time came to all when the lustrous eyes of the perfect creature shone through the masked face of the Grub, and he must needs pass forward to the fulfillment of his destiny.

But the result among those who were left was always the same. There were ever some that doubted and feared, ever some that disbelieved and ridiculed, ever some that hoped and looked forward.

Ah! If they could but have known, poor things! If those eyes, fitted for the narrow bounds of their water world, could have been endued with a power of vision into the purer element beyond, what a lifetime of anxiety would they not have been spared! What ease, what rest would have been theirs!
But belief would, in that case, have been an irresistible necessity, and hope must have changed her name.
And the Dragon-fly, meanwhile, was he really faithless, as they thought? When he burst his prison-house by the waterside, and rose on glittering wings into the summer air, had he indeed no memory for the dear ones he had so lately left? No tender concern for their griefs and fears? No recollection of the promise he had made?
Ah! So far from it, he thought of them amidst the transports of his wildest flights, and returned ever and ever to the precincts of that world which had once been the only world to him. But in that region also, a power was over him superior to his own, and to it his will must submit. To the world of waters he could never more return.
The least touch upon its surface, as he skimmed over it with the purpose of descent, brought on a deadly shock, like that which, as a water-grub, he had experienced from emerging into air, and his wings involuntarily bore him instantly back from the unnatural contact.
"Alas! For the promise made in ignorance and presumption, miserable Grub that I was," was his bitter, constantly-repeated cry.
And thus, divided and yet near, parted yet united by love, he hovered about the barrier that lay between them, never quite, perhaps, without a hope that some accident might bring his dear ones into sight.
Nor was his constancy unrewarded, for as, after even his longest roamings, he never failed to return to the old spot, he was there to welcome the emancipated brother, who so soon followed him.
And often, after that, the breezy air by the forest pond would resound in the bright summer afternoons, with the clashing of Dragon-flies' wings, as, now backwards, now forwards, now to one side, now to another, without turn or intermission, they darted over the crystal water, in the rapture of the new life.
It might be, on those occasions, that some fresh arrival of kindred from below, added a keener joy to their already joyous existence. Sweet assuredly it was to each new-comer, when the riddle of his fate was solved, to find in the new region, not a strange and friendless abode, but a home rich with the welcomes of those who had gone before.
Sweet also it was, and strange as sweet, to know that even while they had been trembling and fearing in their ignorant life below, gleams from the wings of those they lamented, were dropping like star-rays on their home, reflected hither and thither from the sun that shone above. Oh! If they could but have known!
Beautiful forest pond, crowded with mysterious life, of whose secrets we know so little, who would not willingly linger by your banks for study and for thought? There, where the beech-tree throws out her graceful arms, glorying in the loveliness that is reflected beneath. There, where in the nominal silence the

innocent birds pour out their music of joy. There, where the blue forget-me-not tells its tale of old romance, and the long grasses bend over their pictured shadows. There, where the Dragon-flies still hover on the surface of the water, longing to reassure the hearts of the trembling race, who are still hoping and fearing below.

MOTES IN THE SUNBEAM

IT was a bright, sunshiny day at Christmas-tide, when, once upon a time, two little girls were sitting on their mamma's sickbed. One was a very little thing, who could only just talk, and she was leaning her curly head against the bed-post. The other, some two or three years older, was sitting on a pillow near her mother. The children were not talking much, for there was a new baby in the house, and everybody was very quiet, though very happy; and these two little sisters of the new-comer had only been admitted to see poor mamma, on condition that they would be very good and make no noise.

But the active spirits of young animals cannot be long kept under; and so it happened that a strong gleam of winter sunshine, entering into the room through a half-opened shutter, shot right across the middle of the bed, and attracted the eyes and attention of both the children; for up and down in this narrow strip of light danced innumerable sparkling motes. The elder child, the Kate of our story, had a little open box in her hand, and she stretched it out, up and down, into the beam, and whispered in a half-giggle of delight, "I'll catch the stars." Her mamma looked on and smiled, for the merry Kate made the play very amusing to herself. She pretended to catch the shining motes in. the empty box; and then put on a face of mock surprise and disappointment at finding nothing inside when she peeped to see. Moreover, she kept up a little talk all the time: "There's one–oh, he's such a beauty–I must have him!" and then she dashed the box once more into the streak of light.

But this sport and the smiles on mamma's face soon became irresistible to the little Undine child by the bedpost, and she said, very gently, "Give me some, too."

"Some 'what?', my little Undine?" asked mamma: "what are they?"

Undine glanced at her mother, and then at the motes, and then she said, "Stars;"–but there was a misgiving look on her face as she spoke.

"No, they're not stars, are they, Mamma?" observed the wiser Kate: "They're nothing but dust"–and the box danced about quicker than ever.

"They're not dust," pouted the offended little one: "they're stars!"

"Well then, here, you shall have a boxful," cried Kate, thrusting the box on to Undine's lap, and covering it over with her pinafore: "Take care of them–take care of them–or they'll all go out."

Very carefully and slowly did Undine uncover the box, and with a very grave and inquiring face did she examine it both inside and out, in search of the stars; and then, in one of those freaks of change so common to children, she burst into a gay laugh, tossed the box up like a ball, and cried out, "They're nothing but dust–nothing but nasty, dirty dust! There they go!"

And, "There they go!" echoed Kate; and forthwith the children commenced a jumping and noise, which quickly brought the nurse to the room, and an order for the removal of the riotous little damsels.

"But, Mamma," inquired Kate, in a grave whisper, before she went away, "why does the dust look so like stars?"

"Because the sun sent his light upon it," answered mamma. "Sunshine is like love, Kate–it makes everything shine with its own beauty. You and Undine," added she, kissing her little girl's fat cheek, "are stars in my eyes, because I see you in the sunshine of love."
"But we're not 'nothing but nasty, dirty dust,' in reality," observed Kate, shaking her head very knowingly, as she led her little sister from the room.

* * * * * *

Those of my young readers who have lived in the north of England will remember the fine old Christmas hymn that is sung in that part of the country. They will remember the many happy snowy Christmas-eves on which they went to bed, delighted at the thought of hearing it in the night; and how a curious thrill of pleasure came over them when they really were roused from sleep by the solemn and beautiful sounds sung by the village waits, usually the church singers of the place. As I think of these things myself, I almost hear the grand old melody; and can just fancy some little urchin, more hardy than the rest of his companions, creeping out of his snug bed to peep behind the blind at the well-known old men and girls, all wrapped up in great coats and cloaks, to protect them from the stormy December night. I can fancy, too, how, after feeling very chilly as he stood at the window, he would go back to the warm bed, and say how cold the poor waits must be! And how, between whispering about the waits and listening to the music, those children would while away one of the happiest hours of merry Christmas; and then, after hearing the sounds revive and die away in other more distant parts of the village, would drop asleep as easily as tired labourers at night.
Well! You wonder what this Christmas hymn has to do with my story of Kate and Undine? Merely this, that one of the verses begins thus:

"Oh may we keep and ponder in our mind,
God's wondrous love in saving lost mankind."

Most people talked about them, and made a fuss about them, and then very likely forgot them; but "*ponder them*"--this is a practice which has, alas, gone sadly too much out of fashion; for everybody now-a-days is so busy either learning or talking, that for "pondering things in the heart" there seems to be neither time nor inclination.
Nevertheless, mothers are still more apt to do it than anybody else. Indeed, they are constantly pondering in their minds the things that their children say, or the things that people say of them. Sometimes they may ponder foolishly, but I hope not often, especially if they ponder in their hearts, and not in their heads only.
Now the mother of Kate and Undine was a great ponderer; and as she had, especially just then, nothing else to do, you may be sure how she pondered over the pretty scene of her two little ones and the motes in the sunbeam. And the dust *did* look very like stars, she confessed to herself, as she lay looking up at

the light.

"But how wise," thought she, "the sober Kate felt at her own superior knowledge! How proud to recognise dust for dust, even under its most sunny aspect! And yet how often, before life is ended, may she not make Undine's mistake herself, and take even dust for stars, merely because the sun shines upon it!"

And here the poor mamma uttered a short prayer that she might be enabled to instill good principles into her children's minds, that so Kate, and Undine too, might know dust for dust whenever they saw it, let the outward world shine upon it never so brightly.

And then she looked up at the sunbeam, as it streamed across her sick-bed, till she thought it was like so many things, she felt her head becoming quite confused.

It was like love, as she had said–yes; but it was like cheerfulness–like good-temper–like the Gospel charity: for do not the commonest things of life, and the dullest duties of life, shine, star-like, under their rays? Yes; but it was most of all like "the peace of God, which passeth all understanding;" for that lightens up the dark career of earthly existence, and leads the soul upward along the bright path of its rays, till it reaches the everlasting home of light itself.

"Ay, ay," thought the mother, as she looked once more: "Motes in the sunbeam as we are–miserable dust and ashes in ourselves–the light streams down upon us and transfigures us: we follow the light upwards, and become the children of light ourselves."

Her head had indeed become confused amidst similes, and fancies, and half-waking dreams; but before she could think the matter over, clearly and distinctly, she had fallen fast asleep.

RED SNOW

"Or tu chi se', che vuoi sedere a scranna,
Per giudicar da lungi mille miglia
Con la veduta corta d'una spanna?"
DANTE.

"And who art thou, that on the stool wouldst sit
To judge at distance of a thousand miles,
With the short-sighted vision of a span?"
CARY'S Translation.

LITTLE Siegfried, the widow's son, climbed day by day up the hill which overlooked his mother's cottage, and rambled about on the top, running after birds and insects, and gathering the beautiful wild-flowers that grow on the Swiss Alps.

There were the dark blue gentians and the Alpine rose, as it is called, and campanulas and salvias, are almost as common as the cowslips and daisies of English fields, and, from the brightness of their colours, make the hillsides look like gardens, instead of uncultivated ground.

Little Siegfried's father had been killed in battle some months before his child's birth, and so, when he came into the world, he was cradled in tears instead of smiles; and what wonder if he grew up less thoughtless and gay than other boys of his age?

It was his mother who had first shown Siegfried where to climb the hill, and where to find the finest flowers; and had made him look at the hills still higher than their own, by which their valley was enclosed, and had pointed out to him Mont Blanc in the distance, looming like a shadowy giant in the sky.

For thus and thus had her husband shown her all these things, during the few happy months of their marriage, before he was called away to the wars; and on the same heights where the child now roamed after flowers, his parents had sat together among them, in quiet summer evenings, sometimes talking, sometimes reading, always praising God for the happiness He was permitting them to enjoy. But having thus led her child to the spot so fondly endeared to herself, and bidden him rejoice in the sights and scenes of Nature, and told him of the protecting God of goodness who ruled over all, the widowed mother went back alone to her cottage, to weep out in secret her re-awakened grief. Siegfried, meanwhile, amused himself on the flowery heights, his new play-ground; and after he had gathered for his mother the nosegay she had asked him to bring, he lay down on the soft turf, and looked round at the hills, and up to the snowy sides of the huge Mont Blanc, (of which he could see so much more here than down in the valley below,) till it took possession of his fancy as something wonderful and grand; something far beyond the flowers, bright and lovely as they were.

And ever afterwards, day-by-day, when he had had enough of chasing and rambling, he used to lie down in the same place, and look at the hills in the same way, that he might feel again what he had felt at first.

Yet he found no sameness in the sight. The clouds that sometimes lifted themselves up from, and at other times came down over, the mountain, were never quite alike. The shadows that flitted across it varied from day to day in their shape and size and course; and the sunshine that broke over it was of many different tints, and lit it up in a thousand different ways. At one time it was wrapt in a silvery haze; at another the air became so clear, that the child could see the glittering of the snow atoms, as they seemed to dance in and out, like the stars in the sky.

So Siegfried never wearied of watching the huge mountain, but got to love it more and more, with a love mixed with respectful awe, and a feeling as if it had some sort of life and consciousness.

At last, one day, when his mother was putting his little basket in his hand, that he might go on the hill as usual to play, he asked her if he might go to the top of Mont Blanc instead, and if she would show him the way.

It was no wonder that the good widow smiled, as she told him that neither he nor she were able to climb up such a terrible mountain. But she did smile; and although she noticed how the little face flushed over as she spoke, she thought, naturally enough, that this was because of his disappointment. So, kissing him lovingly, she said, "You must be a great strong man, Siegfried, before you can scramble up the heights of Mont Blanc; and even for great strong men the way is very dangerous. And even if you were there, you would find nothing but cold and snow and misery; neither life nor flowers; our own hills are as pleasant again."

So Siegfried went away with his basket; but instead of running about and picking flowers, he threw himself at once upon the ground, and looked at the mountain, and cried, for he felt very sorry at what his mother had said. Presently, however, he wiped his eyes, and looked again; then sprang up and stared before him as if surprised. All the distance was bathed in bright sunshine, and the air was more transparent than usual, and, lo! a round rosy-coloured patch was visible on the far-off snows. He had never seen it before. What could it be? He thought he knew; and running hastily down to the cottage, threw open the door, and shouted in delight, "Mother! There is a rose on Mont Blanc!"

Siegfried's mother did not laugh now, for she saw the child was excited; and she was grieved for him. Ah! He had only half the love that should have been his; she must console him as best she could; he was not like other boys, she knew–and thinking this, she took him on her knee, and tried to explain to him that it must be only some accidental light from the sky that caused the rosy patch, for that no vegetation of any kind grew on the sides of the snowy mountain; there could be no roses there; and she knew that it often looked pink in the evening sun–only now it was not evening.

Siegfried was silent for a few seconds, and hung down his head; but presently he murmured out, "Why?"

"Ah, Siegfried!" cried his mother, "is it not enough that God chooses it to be so?

It is He who sends the everlasting snows there, and the flowery herbage here."
"I am very sorry for the mountain," persisted little Siegfried, sadly; so sadly that his mother grieved for the fanciful child, and asked should she go up with him again to the hill, and see the rosy patch on the snow herself? On which the smiles came back to Siegfried's face, and they went away together very happily, and with the basket as usual; for, said the mother, "You came back empty-handed today, Siegfried, and brought me no flowers."
But, by the time they reached the spot, heavy mists had come down over the landscape, and neither Mont Blanc nor its rosy patch could be seen. Even Siegfried laughed at the journey they had had for nothing, and, after filling his basket, was contented to return home; but in doing so, he began to talk again.
"If we had fewer flowers, Mother, we should be quite as happy, and then the great mountain could have some too. I wish God would make things equal."
"Hush, little Siegfried, hush!" cried his mother, in a half whisper; "God has a right to do what He pleases, and we must not dispute about it, nor wish it otherwise. He chooses that there shall be desolate places as well as pretty ones in the world; outcast ends of the earth, as it were, which nobody seems to care for, as well as happy valleys. I am afraid it is the same with human beings–men and women, I mean–which is much worse. I am afraid there are many outcast, God-deserted men, as well as desolate mountains. But you are too young to understand such things."
The mother sighed as she spoke. Verily, she did not understand such things herself.
And so they walked on a few steps farther, and then the boy began again–
"At any rate, the top of the mountain is nearer Heaven than our hill, Mother. It goes right into the blue."
"No, no," cried the widow, passionately; "it only looks to be so. It is no nearer the real Heaven than we are. If it were, oh! Would I not have gone there long ago, at the risk of life itself!"
The child looked very surprised at his mother; for she spoke in tones very unusual to her; and seeing how sad her face, he wondered to himself if she, also, were fretting that Mont Blanc was so miserable and forlorn.
And, snatching the nosegay from the basket, he flung the flowers as far into the air as he could, exclaiming, "There! I wish you had wings, and would fly away to the mountain, and make it look beautiful, too!"
Nothing more was spoken between them, but after little Siegfried had said his evening prayers, and gone to bed, and while the mother was sitting alone in the chamber below, she heard a sound of crying; and, going up-stairs, found the boy in tears, the only account he could give of which was that he could not help thinking about the poor outcast, God-deserted mountain.
Now, she had not called the mountain God-deserted. That was his own disturbed idea, a confusion he had got into from what his mother had said. But how hard this was to explain! How painful to touch the chords of a subject which jarred so cruelly against the natural hopes and faith of a gentle heart!
How difficult also for one who had known the stern realities of sorrow, to "feel

along" the more delicate "line" of an infant's dreamy griefs!
He was soothed by degrees, however, and after she left him, her thoughts soon wandered away from what she felt to be his fanciful troubles about the desolate mountain, to her own struggles with her desolate heart.
The next day was Sunday, and Siegfried was able to walk to the somewhat distant church, and even to repeat a few of the prayers, and listen, now and then, to bits of the sermon, when his mother thought there was something he could understand, and drew his attention to it.
But on this particular day there was no need for her to call his attention to the preacher; nay, had she been able, she would have been very glad to have prevented his hearing him at all. But how could he help hearing, when the pastor, addressing his flock, asked if there was a single one, young or old, among them, who had not gazed hundreds and hundreds of times at the giant mountain of their land–the snow-covered, inaccessible heights of Mont Blanc?
Siegfried and his mother looked at each other, and his heart leapt within him, to think that now, at last, he should hear something about his mysterious friend; and, clasping his mother's hand tightly in his own, he listened for every word.
But alas for what he heard. The pastor, after describing the mountain in all the magnificence of its size and form, painted it as being, nevertheless, the region of hopeless desolation; the abode of everlasting lifelessness and despair. Cold, hard, insensible, what could rouse it from its death-like torpor? The life-giving sun shone upon it from day to day, from age to age; but no influence from its rays ever penetrated that frozen bosom. The dews fell upon it, the storms burst over it, equally in vain. Unmoved, it lifted up its gloomy crest to Heaven, as if defying its very Maker to touch the stony depths and bid the waters flow, or warm and soften them into life and gladness!
Siegfried was already in tears, but what followed was still worse, for the pastor now called upon his congregation to consider whether there was not something in the moral world of which the insensible mountain was but the too faithful type? And then he answered himself. Yes! The hardened human heart, the wicked natural heart, the Pharaoh-heart of the multitude on which the sunshine of Divine Grace and the storms of Divine wrath were equally poured out in vain. Yet, that "offences must needs come," he was well aware; that such God-deserted beings as he had spoken of, must come up and be cut down, he knew: "vessels of wrath appointed to destruction." But, oh! Might none of the congregation now before him be of the number of those lost ones! Might all there present take warning henceforth, as they turned their eyes to the stiff-necked hill of their native country, and flee from the wrath of the Lamb!
Siegfried's sobs had by this time become so uncontrollable that the neighbours were disturbed; and the widow thought the best thing she could do, was to rise up and leave the church with her child.
There was no use arguing with him; he was both too young and too much distressed, added to which his mother was scarcely less pained by the stern words than he was.
She, too, could have wept to think of "vessels of wrath appointed to destruction,"

and longed to hope against hope for the world of her fellow-creatures. In the material world she had but little interest, for she knew but little about it, and had not sufficiently considered the text which says that "God's mercy is over *all* His works;" not limited to one class of creatures, or even to one sort of life.

Feeling as she did, therefore, she entered into no discussion with her boy, but through the home evening contrived to divert his mind, by reading him pleasant stories of good people who had lived in favour with God, and had died full of hope and peace.

Nevertheless, Siegfried's last thought, as he fell asleep, was not of comfort and joy in the righteous, but of pity and almost love for all the wretched things for whom there seemed no hope.

The next day, his mother would fain have persuaded him to remain below in the valley, and seek some new amusement, but finding she could not reconcile him to the idea of forsaking his favourite haunt, she gave way, though with a sigh; and so, after his little daily tasks and helps to her were ended, he climbed up the heights as usual.

It was well that he had promised his mother to tease her no more about the matter. Otherwise, on that day, he would have made more fuss than ever, for, when the sun was at the highest, the rosy flush re-appeared on the distant snow, only not now confined to one small patch, but spread in broad tracts of delicate colour, which threatened to cover the whole mountain with its Aurora-like tint.

Once or twice Siegfried's resolution to keep his promise nearly gave way, but he held out manfully even to the last, contenting himself, on his return into the valley, with inquiring of a neighbour's son, whom he met driving home his father's cattle, why some of the snow on the hills looked pink? At first the boy said he didn't know, but presently he recollected that he had heard it said, that red snow fell sometimes out of the sky. Very likely that was it; but what it was, or what became of it, he had no notion. Only it went away as it came. Nothing ever stopped on the hill but the snow that was always there.

Hearing this, Siegfried had no longer even a wish to speak to his mother about it. She would say it was because the mountain was so cold and hard, no good thing, even from Heaven, could stay upon it!

And thus a day or two passed, and the tracts of rosy colour grew fainter, and finally disappeared, as the farmer's son had said was always the case; and Siegfried never spoke about it again, but sat on the hillside daily, wondering and dreaming to himself.

But he was interrupted at last. One morning, when the snow looked colder and whiter than ever against the blue sky, and he had been sitting for a while, with his face hidden by his hands, a voice he did not know called to him, asking what he was doing. And when he lifted up his eyes, a stranger stood between him and Mont Blanc.

A child always answers "Nothing" to such a question, for children never feel thinking to be doing anything.

But the stranger would not be so easily satisfied, and smiling, persisted in his inquiries.

"What are you thinking of, then, little boy? One must be either doing or thinking while one is awake. And I want you to talk to me. I have come from such a long way off, and am so weary."
Here the stranger seated himself by Siegfried's side on the grass.
"First," continued he, "I want you to tell me, if you can, whether I can get to the town of —, through the pretty valley here at the bottom of this hill? Then, I want you to tell me for whom you have picked this basket of flowers? Then, why you are on this wild hillside alone? Then, what you think about when you cover up your face with your hands? Now, then, can I get to the town through the valley?"
The voice that asked was so good-natured, and the smile on the stranger's face so kind, that Siegfried was won at once, and looking full at his new friend, and smiling himself, nodded ascent to this first question.
"Does your nod always mean yes, little boy?" asked the stranger, amused.
Siegfried nodded again.
"Very good. Now we understand each other. Will you answer my other questions?"
Siegfried gave another nod, and then they both laughed, and the stranger went on.
"For whom have you gathered the flowers?"
"For my mother."
"And why are you here alone?"
"To play."
"What, alone? Why?"
"I have nobody else to play with."
"And what is it you think of when you sit with your face covered up?"
Siegfried's heart melted within him, and, pointing by a sorrowful nod to the giant mountain, he answered, "I think of it."
"Of *it?*" What can you find in it to think about?"
"I am so sorry for it!" cried little Siegfried, passionately; "so sorry it is so miserable and outcast, and that God will let nothing grow there, while we have all these flowers!"
And once more he tossed the flowers contemptuously out of the basket.
"Ah, little boy," said the stranger, putting his arm kindly around the child, and drawing himself nearer to him. "You must answer another question now. Who put such strange fancies into your heard? Who told you this about the poor mountain?"
"They all say so," murmured Siegfried. "The pastor preached about it on Sunday, and mother says so, too, and the farmer's son, and everybody; and I am so sorry, so very sorry!"
The young voice died away, as it were, in regret.
"And why do you care so much about the mountain, little boy?"
Siegfried looked up, puzzled, for a moment, but very soon out came the simple, child-like answer, "I look at it so much when I come up here to play."
It was the stranger's turn now to feel his eyes moisten, as he thought of the solitary child sending out his heart into the inanimate creation around him.

Extremely interested, therefore, he made a few more inquiries, and, by degrees, brought out a part, at any rate, of what Siegfried's mother and the pastor between them had told and taught of outcast countries and God-deserted men. All was confusion in the child's account, but the drift of it could easily be discovered.
Without making a single remark, however, the stranger smiled again, and said, quite cheerfully, "I will tell you a secret, little boy. Neither the pastor, nor your mother, nor the farmer's son were ever up the mountain, I suspect, so they cannot know very much about it."
"I wanted to go, but they would not let me," interposed Siegfried. "They said I was not able to get up."
"They said right," replied the stranger. "But I, you see, am older and stronger, and could go; and I have been."
Quietly as he purposely spoke, the effect of what he said was, as he expected, very great. Siegfried jumped up; then sat down; then once more started from his seat, and was far more anxious to run down the hill and tell his mother the news, than to remain quietly where he was, and hear what more the stranger had to tell. He allowed himself to be controlled, however, and his friend went on talking as if he had not been interrupted.
"And the place is neither lifeless nor deserted. God sends it the beautiful red snow plant instead of flowers. I have been gathering it for days."
As he spoke, he unfastened from the leathern strap that went across his shoulders a small tin box, and, opening it for a moment, let Siegfried peep at a bright carmine-coloured mass of something within.
The child was speechless at first, overpowered by admiration and delight, but presently exclaimed, "Then that was what I saw!" adding gently, "And it really came down from Heaven, then?" He was thinking of what the farmer's son had said.
"All good things come from Heaven, that is, from the God of Heaven," answered the stranger. "But this is as much a plant as the Alpine rose by your side. It did not drop down from the sky, but grows in the very snow itself, and covers over miles and miles of the hill you thought so desolate. God sends good things everywhere, though not everywhere alike."
Oh, the joy of such a doctrine! The simplest child could understand it, and be glad! All was explained now, too; the rosy patch and the broad tracts of colour were both accounted for, and Siegfried was as happy as he now believed the mountain to be. And, embracing his new friend, he forthwith began such a blundering account of what he, and his mother, and the farmer's boy, had thought about the rosy patch, that the stranger could do nothing but laugh, and at last stopped him by exclaiming, "Then you see you were all wrong; but never mind. Take me to your mother's cottage, and we will tell her all about it, too, and I will show it to you both, for even you have not really seen it yet."
Siegfried's mother welcomed the friendly stranger whom her son brought to her door with all the heartiness of a Swiss welcome; and not the less when she found he was an English traveler, on his way to a neighbouring town to visit a well-known officer there, who had been deprived of a limb in the same action in

which Siegfried's father had lost his life.
And as the town was but a few miles off, and the summer evenings so long, the stranger was easily persuaded to rest for a few hours in the Swiss cottage, and tell the widow and her son the history of his adventures on Mont Blanc, and of the red snow plant he had brought from it. Not that telling its history only would have been enough; nor was there anything either beautiful or wonderful-looking in the red, jelly-like mass in the tin box, when looked at with the naked eye. The stranger had far more in store for them than that.
"I am going to show you," he began, at last, and after busying himself in unpacking that revealer of secrets, a microscope, "that God has sent many more gracious things into the world than our natural eyes are able to see. Do you like to know this, little Siegfried?" he added, turning purposely to the child.
Siegfried nodded his heartiest nod of assent, and the widow said, with a smile, "You should have asked that question, Sir, of me. It is I who have not believed, because I did not see. He has had the instinct of the truth all along."
"Well, then, good Mother," replied the stranger, "you shall see and believe what will, I think, comfort you for life–namely, that God makes the very wilderness to burst forth and blossom like a rose: that there are no outcast ends of the earth uncared for by Him; no desolate corners where His goodness is not shown forth."
As he spoke he finished the last adjustment of the microscope, and touching the red jelly in the tin box with the fine point of a porcupine's quill, he placed the tiny morsal so obtained in a glass, to be looked at, and called to Siegfried to have the first peep.
The widow, struck as she had been with the stranger's words, had her own doubts as to what there could be to be seen, for she had not been able to detect anything on the porcupine's quill, but she said nothing, and very soon Siegfried's shouts of delight announced that *some*thing, at any rate, was there.
And, truly, what there was, was a very pretty sight. Four or five bright little red balls, and two or three colourless ones among them, were lying like gems in the few drops of water which had been put in to keep them separate.
The child believed at once, but at the first moment the mother could scarcely credit what she saw. That this should be a bit of the shapeless stuff she had looked at in the tin box–it was marvelous indeed.
The stranger now proceeded to explain. He told them that each of the red balls was a perfect plant in itself. That is was a little colourless bag, finer than gold-beater's skin, filled with a red substance, which shone through. That, as soon as it was full grown, the red substance within divided into four, eight, and sometimes sixteen separate red balls, of course of the tiniest size possible, all which immediately began to grow very fast, and grew, and grew, and grew, till the little bag in which they lived could hold them no longer, but burst, and dropt them out.
"These," said he, "are the young plants; and when each of them is full grown, the same thing happens again. The red substance in each divides into other tiny balls, and, as these grow, they burst out from the parent bag, (called a *cell*,

properly,) and begin life for themselves. And thus comes another generation of the ball-like plants, and so another and another; and all this so quickly, that, in a few hours, millions of them have sprung from a few single cells. So now, little Siegfried, you know why, when you looked the second time at the rosy patch, it has spread into those great broad tracts of colour which, in fact, covered over miles of the poor snow with its beauty. It was no wonder, was it?"

No, that was no wonder; but that such things were, of which so many people did not know, was a wonder from which the good widow could not easily recover. Besides, she was thinking of the pastor having made such a mistake.

As for Siegfried, he had not lived long enough to know why he should be so much surprised about the red snow plant; was it a bit more really strange than the growth of the Alpine rose, which astonished nobody? So his chief feeling was extreme delight at there being something on the mountain to make amends for its want of flowers.

"And now," said the stranger, "is there anything more you would like to ask?"

The mother was about to speak at once, but hesitated and drew back. She knew so little; she feared to seem so ignorant and foolish.

Reassured, however, she begged to be told how the marvelous plant could live amidst nothing but snow; could come up, and bring forth a thousand fold, with nothing to nourish and support it?

The stranger repeated the word "*nothing*" with a smile.

"Nothing, because we see nothing!"

"Ah, see what a bad habit is!" cried the mother. "I had forgotten already. Then you think there may be things I do not know of, in what we call the cold, barren snow?"

"Ay, ay," was the answer; "germs of life, hidden and buried, perhaps, for years; seeds scattered no one can tell how or when; and salts and chemical properties, needing only some accident of a sunbeam, or dew, or state of the very air, to make all work together, and the frozen surface to become moist, and the red snow plant to spring up by millions."

Here he paused, and seeing little Siegfried looking wistfully at him, as if trying to understand, he took him on his knee caressingly, and said, "That microscope is a very curious thing, is it not?"

The child nodded his "yes" as heartily as ever, and then laid his head, contentedly, on his friend's shoulder, while he went on talking.

"Yes; it is very curious, for it shows us quantities of things we could not see without it; but the best lesson it teaches is, how much more there may be of which, even with its help, we can see and know nothing; for, although there is a limit to our power of seeing God's works, no naturalist dares to think he has reached the limits of the works themselves. In this life we cannot hope to know a hundredth part of the creations which surround us. You can believe this now, good Mother?"

"With all my heart," was her answer.

"And, further," he added, "you can judge now for yourself, that even of the things we do what we call see with the naked eye, there are a great many of which we can never know anything like the real truth, without such aid as this (pointing to the microscope). What was the red snow plant to you at first? A piece of shapeless jelly. What did it become to your more enlightened eye? A living organism, unmistakably from Almighty hands, endowed with a system of life, if not of life-enjoyment, peculiarly its own. This is something to have discovered, certainly, but is it all? Ah! As I tell it, I feel how imperfect the account is–how much remains behind. All we have done is but to have made a step or two out of complete ignorance. *'The rest remaineth unrevealed.'* Yet a glory comes into our hearts from the thought of the worlds beyond reach of our present senses, like the reflection from lightning below our own horizon, and both faith and hope ought to be strengthened."

The widow did not speak.

"I have one more word to say," continued the stranger guest, "if you will allow me to say it, and can forgive the old traveler for preaching as well as teaching. I have taught you something of God's doings in the natural world, which has given you comfort and hope. What then, you believe of His works, believe also of His mercies. If you cannot find a limit to the one, suspect and hope that the other, too, may be infinite–far beyond our comprehension. Will you try and take this last lesson to heart?"

The poor mother's eyes filled with tears. She had passed tremblingly through life, and sadly needed the good counsel.

After a short pause, her counselor went on, firmly, but very kindly–

"You have seen how weak and short-sighted the natural eye is; can you for a moment suppose that the spiritual eye is more far-seeing and better able to acquaint you with God's purposes and doings? Are His works to be infinite, and His mercies bounded, so that a man can point to the limit, and say, Here God's mercy ceases; here there is no hope–but only everlasting lifelessness and despair? Oh, good Mother, to whom is entrusted the rearing of a very tender plant, take heed what you teach, and foster in it, above all other virtues, the charity which hopeth all things,' and then can both believe and endure."

The lesson was not spoken in vain even then, and it was never forgotten. And Siegfried grew on, and the stranger revisited the cottage many times, and by and by aided in the education of the child whose acquaintance he had made in so singular a manner. And, after many years, the young man, Siegfried, became a teacher himself–a pastor–though not in his own country.

But never, through a long life, did he forget his early hopes, and fears, and fancies, about the desolate mountain, nor the lesson he learnt from the stranger traveler. And into whatever scenes of darkness and ignorance he forced his way; whatever he met of sin and sorrow; however often baffled, thrown back, and disappointed, he never despaired; for he used to recall the past, and take comfort to himself by thinking, "It may be God's will yet, that the red snow plant may one day burst into life on the cold hillside."

WHEREUNTO?

"I see in part
That all, as in some piece of art,
Is toil cöoperant to an end."
TENNYSON.

"THIS is dreadful! What can I do?"
"Why, follow me, to be sure! Here! Quick! Sideways! To the left! Into this crevice of the rock! There! All's right!"
"Oh, it's easy to talk, when people can trip away as lightly as you do. But look at me with the ground slipping away wherever I try to lay hold."
"Come along; all's right," repeated the Crab (for such was the speaker) from his crevice in the rock.
And all was right certainly, as far as he was concerned; but as for the poor Starfish, who was left on the sand, all was as wrong as possible, for he was much too hot; and no wonder.
It was a low tide–a spring tide–and even for a spring tide, a particularly low one; for there was very little wind astir, and what there was, blew off the shore.
So the rocks were uncovered now, which seldom tasted the air, and the stems of the great oarweed, or tangle, which grew from them, were bent into a half-circle by the weight of their broad leathery fronds, as, no longer buoyed up by the sea, they lay trailing on the sands.
What a day it was, to be sure! One of those rare, serene ones, when there is not a cloud in the delicate blue sky, and when the sea lies so calm and peaceful under it, that one might almost be persuaded to believe nothing would ever again ruffle its surface. The white-sailed vessels in the distance, too, looked as if they had nothing in the world to do for ever, but to float from one beautiful end of the world to the other, in security and joy. Yet delicious–unspeakably delicious–as the day was, it brought discomfort to some who lived under it. The numberless star-fishes, for instance, who had been unexpectedly left stranded on the shore by the all-too-gently-retreating waves, how could they rejoice in the beautiful sunshine, when it was streaming so pitilessly on their helpless limbs, and scorching them by its dry cruel heat? And as for the jellyfishes, who had shared a similar fate, they had died almost at once from the shock, as the wave cast them ashore; so of the merits of the delicious day they knew nothing at all.
All creatures did not suffer, of course. The Crab, for instance, who had given such good advice to his friend (if he could but have followed it), did very well. In the first place, he liked the air nearly as well as the water, so that being left high and dry on the shore now and then was quite to his taste. Moreover, he could scuttle off and hide in a crevice of the rocks whenever he chose. Or he could shelter under the large sea-weeds, and because of his hard coat was even able to take a short walk from time to time, to see how matters went on, and observe how far the tide had gone down; and if the sun did happen to bake him a little too much, he had only to run off to a pool and take a bath, and then was as

fresh as ever in a minute.

And now, just as the tide was at the lowest, where it was likely to beat about for some time without much change, two other creatures appeared on the sands, and approached the very spot where the Starfish lay in his distress, and near which the Crab was hid. Now there was a ledge of rocks here, which would have furnished seats for dozens of human beings, and from the front of it grew almost a forest of oarweed plants.

What the creatures were who came up to this place and stopped to observe it, I shall not say; but one of them remarked to the other, "Here again, you see; the same old story as before. Wasted life and wasted death, and all within a few inches of each other! Useless, lumbering plants, not seen half-a-dozen times in the year; and helpless, miserable sea-creatures, dying in health and strength, one doesn't know why."

As the creature who spoke, said this, it lifted up two or three tangle fronds with a stick it carried in its hand, and then let them flop suddenly down on the sand; after which it used the end of the same stick to chuck the unhappy Starfish into the air, who, tumbling by a lucky accident under the shelter of the tangle, was hid for a time from sight.

"And so we go up, and so we go down, ourselves," continued the creature; "a good many of us, with no more end in life, and of no more use that one can see than these vile useless seaweeds; coming into the world, in fact, for no earthly purpose but to go out of it, in some such wretched manner as this!"

And here the creature kicked three or four more stranded star-fishes across the narrow sands, till he had fairly kicked them into the sea; muttering as he did so, "What did you come into the world for, I wonder, and you, and you, and you? Purposeless life and purposeless death–the fate of thousands. And I for one as useless as any of them, but at any rate having the grace to acknowledge that the world would get on quite as cleverly without me as with! Whereunto, whereunto, whereunto? Answer it if you can!" As the creature finished speaking, the two moved on together; but what the companion answered was never exactly known; for though the voice sounded as if in dispute, what was said was not heard by those who were left behind, for they began at once to chatter among themselves.

And first out popped the head of the Crab from the crevice he had taken shelter in; and he cocked his eyes knowingly, first to one side, and then to the other, and began to talk; for he had always plenty to say for himself, and was remarkably bold when there was no danger. "Miserable sea-creatures!" was his first exclamation, repeating what the land-creature had said. "I suppose I am included in that elegant compliment. I say! Where are you, old Lilac-legs? Have you contrived to crawl away after all? Come out of your corner, or wherever you are, for a bit. Who was the creature that was talking such nonsense just now? Only let me come across him, that's all! Helpless sea-creatures, indeed! I should like to have seen him hiding in a crevice as nimbly as I can do! He'd better not come within reach of me any more, I can tell him!"

It was all very well for the Crab to sit outside the rock looking so fierce, and

brushing his mouth so boldly with his whisker-like feelers, now that there was nobody to fight with. How he would have scuttled away sideways into his hole, if the creature had re-appeared, everybody can guess.
"You happy fellow!" answered the meek voice of the Starfish, Lilac-legs; "you can afford to joke about everything, and can do whatever you please. You have so many things in your favour–your stiff coat, and your jointed legs, and your claws with pincers at their ends; and your large eyes. Dear me, what advantages! And yet I have an advantage too, and that a very great one, over you all, so I shall not grumble, especially not now that I am in the shade. That sun was very unpleasant, certainly; I felt something between scalded and baked. Horrible! But I am sheltered now. And how did that come to pass, do you think?"
The Starfish paused for an answer; but the Crab declared he couldn't think–had no time for thinking; it was too slow work to suit him. So Lilac-legs told him how she had been chucked into the air by the stick, and how she had come down in the midst of the tangle, and fallen under shelter. "So you see," added she in conclusion, "that you were quite right in saying what nonsense the creature talked. Why, he said he was as useless as these vile useless sea-weeds, and had come into the world, like them, for nothing; whereas, don't you see, he was born to save me, which was something to be born for, at any rate, that's quite clear; and so was the vile useless sea-weed, as he called it, too. I, with my advantages, can tell them both that!"
"You go in and out, and in and out, over people's remarks, till you make me quite giddy, I get so puzzled," replied the Crab; "and then you are always talking of your advantages," he continued, whisking his feelers backwards and forwards conceitedly as he spoke, "and I can't make out what they are. I wish you would say at once what you mean."
"Oh, my advantages, you want to know about?" answered Lilac-legs. "Well, I certainly have one in each leg, near the end, with which I–but I don't think I can describe it exactly. You have several advantages yourself, as I told you just now, and we have one or two in common; for instance, the loss of a leg or two is nothing to either of us; they grow again so quickly; but still I am very helpless now and then, I must admit! On the sand, for instance–it is so soft–and the more I try to lay hold, the more it slips away. Still these advantages in my legs make amends for a good deal, for at any rate I know my own superiority, and there's a great comfort in that; I can't explain, but you may safely take it for granted, that with my advantages, I know a good deal more than you give me credit for. I know, for instance, that the poor ignorant creature need not consider himself useless, since he was the means of chucking me here, and that this fine old tangle hasn't lived for nothing, since it is sheltering me."
"How conceited some people are with their advantages!" murmured a silver voice from one of the tangle fronds. "If the tangle had come into the world for nothing but to shelter you, there would have been a fuss to very little purpose indeed! Can't your advantages tell you there are other creatures in the world quite as important as yourself, if not more so, you poor helpless Lilac-legs? Do you know who is speaking? It is the blue-eyed limpet, I beg to say–the Patella

pellucida, if you please. I have an advantage or two myself! My coat is harder even than the crab's, and it is studded with a row of azure spots, as bright as the turquoise itself. That is something to reflect upon in one's solitude, I can assure you! And the tangle plants are the natural home and food of our lovely race. The creature was ignorant enough in calling them useless, therefore, of course; but you were not much wiser in thinking they were put into the world to shelter you. I flatter myself I have said enough! To be the home and the food of beings like us is cause sufficient–almost more than sufficient, I venture to think–for the existence of any vegetable that fringes these shores. And while they live for us, our turquoise-gemmed backs are, in return, their highest ornament and pride. The whole thing is perfect and complete. Anybody with half an eye, and a grain of understanding, may see that!"

"Oh, the narrow-mindedness of people who live under a shell!" murmured a score of whispers, in unison, from another tangle frond close by. "Oh, the assurance of you poor moveable limpets in talking about your home, when you do but stick to first one part of these vast leaves and then another, moving from place to place, and never fairly settling anywhere! Home, indeed, you call it? What sort of a home is it when an unlucky chance can force you off at any moment, or some passing creature pick you from your hold? The pretension would be disgusting, if it were not so absurd. Think of mere travelers, as one may say, talking of their lodging-house as if it were their own, and belonged to them by a natural right! How ridiculous, if not wrong! We can afford to speak–we, of whose dwelling-places it is the foundation and support. Talk of the useless tangle, indeed! Yes, the creature was ignorant indeed who said so. Little he knew that it was the basis of the lives of millions. Little he knew of the silver net-work we spread over it from year to year, or of the countless inhabitants of the beautiful web–a fairy-land of beings, so small, that the crab can scarcely see us, yet spreading so far and wide, and accomplishing so much; but that is because we work in unison, of course. We never quarrel among ourselves, as some folks do–not altogether unlike the crab in the crevice yonder. We work to one end, so that we are sure to continue strong. Useless tangles, forsooth, when they have been the foundations of colonies like ours from the beginning of the world! Of course the thing is clear enough to those who choose to look into it; any one who knows us, can tell people what the tangle is in the world for, I should think!"

"Hear how they talk," murmured another shell-fish, no distant relation of the blue-eyed limpet who had spoken before, and who lay hidden in the midst of the twisted roots by which the tangle stem held fast to the rock; "Hear how the poor scurfy creatures talk, to be sure, as if there was nobody in the world but themselves. But anything can talk, which has so many mouths to talk with. I could say a good deal myself, if I chose to try, with only one; but I don't care to let out my secrets into everybody's foolish ears. Much better hold my tongue, than let certain people, not a hundred miles off know I am here. I don't fancy being sucked at by starfishes, or picked out of my place by crab's claws. Of course I know what the tangle is in the world for, as well as anybody else. For

while they are fighting merely about his flapping leathery ends, here I sit in the very heart of the matter, safe in the roots themselves, knowing what's what with the cleverest of them. Useless tangle, the creature said–useless enough, perhaps, as far as he could tell, who only looked at the long, loose, rubbishy leaves; but those who want to know the truth of the matter, must use their eyes to a little more purpose, and find out what's going on at the roots. Ah, they'd soon see then what the tangle is for! I don't speak of myself alone, though of course I know one very sufficient reason why the tangle is in the world, if I chose to say. Am I right, little Silver-tuft, in the corner there, with the elegant doors to your house?"
Now, little Silver-tuft, the coralline, piqued herself particularly on the carving of the curious doors which guarded the front of every one of the numberless cells in which her family lived; so she was flattered by the compliment, and owned that the limpet was right in the main. She was, nevertheless, rather cool in her manner, for, thought she to herself, "The rough fellow forgets that he is but a lodger here, as the sea-mat said of his blue-eyed cousin; whereas everybody knows that I am a *bonâfide* inhabitant, though with a little more freedom of movement than people who stick to their friends so closely as to cover them up! No offence to the sea-mat, or anybody who can't help himself. Nevertheless, my fibres being firmly interlaced with the roots, I am here by right forever. These limpets may talk as they please, but nobody in their senses can suppose the tangle came into the world merely to accommodate chance travelers like them, even though they may now and then spend their lives in the place. But vanity blinds the judgment, that's very clear. Roots and plants have to grow for such as myself and my silver-tuft cousins, however; but that's quite another affair. There's a reason in that–a necessity, I may say; we want them, and of course, therefore, they are here. The thing is as straightforward and plain to anybody of sense, as–"
But, unfortunately, the simile was lost; for a wave of the now-returning tide interrupted Silver-tuft's speech, by breaking suddenly over the tangle with a noisy splash. It drew back again for a bit immediately after; but, meantime, both plants and animals were reveling in the delicious moisture, and for a few moments thought of nothing else. And just then, hurrying along the narrow strip of sand that yet remained exposed, as fast as their legs could carry them, came the land-creature and its companion.
Before, however, they had passed the spot where they had stopped to talk when the tide was low, another wave was seen coming; to avoid which, the friends sprang together on the ledge of rock, and from thence watched the gathering water, as it fell tumbling over the forest of tangle plants. And again and again this happened, and they remained to observe it, and see how the huge fronds surged up like struggling giants as the waves rushed in below; and how by degrees, as the tide rose higher and higher, their curved stems unbent so that they resumed their natural position, till at last they were bending and bowing in graceful undulations to the swell of the water, as was their wont.
And, "Look at them!" cried the creature's companion. "For the existence of even these poor plants in the world, I could give you a hundred reasons, and believe

that as many more might be found. Of their use, I could tell you a hundred instances in proof; there is not one of them but what gives shelter to the helpless, food to the hungry, a happy home to as many as desire it, and vigour and health to the element in which it lives. Purposeless life you talk of! Such a thing exists nowhere. Come, I will explain. To begin–but see, we must move on, for the wind as well as the tide is rising, and we might chance to be caught. Follow me quick, for even we might be missed; and, besides, it is cowardly to shirk one's appointed share of work and well-doing before one's time. For if the vile seaweeds are able to do good in the world, how much more–"

But here, too, the discourse was cut short by the roar of a breaking wave, which carried the conclusion out of hearing.

People talk of the angry sea; was he angry now at what he had heard? No, he was only loud and in earnest, after all. But undoubtedly he and the risen wind between them contrived to make a great noise over the tangle beds. And he gave his opinion pretty strongly on the subject in hand. For, cried he, "You foolish creatures, one and all! What is all this nonsense about? Who dares to talk of useless seaweeds while I am here to throw their folly in their face? And you, poor little worms and wretches, who have been talking your small talk together, as if it was in your power to form the least idea of anything an inch beyond your own noses–well, well, well, I won't undeceive you! There, there! Believe what you like about yourselves and your trumpery little comforts and lives; but if any really philosophical inquirer wants to know what seaweeds are in the world for, and what good they do, I will roar them the true answer all day long, if they please–to keep me, the great sea, pure, and sweet, and healthy! There, now, that's the reply! They suck in my foul vapours as food, and give me back life-supporting vapours in return. Vile and useless! What fool has called anything so? Only let me catch him–thus–"

Bang! With what a roar that wave came down! And yet it did no harm–didn't even dislodge the Crab from the new crevice he had squeezed himself into for the present. And as to Starfish Lilac-legs, she was spreading herself out in the rocking water, rejoicing in her regained freedom, and telling all her friends of her wonderful escape, and of the creature who had been born into the world on purpose to save her from an untimely death.

It was a very fine story indeed; and the longer she told it, the more pathetic she made it, till at last there was not a creature in the sea who could listen to it with dry eyes.

PURRING WHEN YOU'RE PLEASED

THEY had been licked over hundreds of times by the same mother, had been brought up on the same food, lived in the same house, learnt the same lessons, heard the same advice, and yet how different they were! Never were there two kittens more thoroughly unlike than those two! The one, with an open, loving heart, which never could contain itself in its joy, but purred it out at once to all the world; the other, who scarcely ever purred at all, and that never above its breath, let him be as happy or as fond as he would.

It was partly his mother's fault, perhaps, for she always set the children the example of reserve; rarely purring herself, and then only in a low tone. But, poor thing, there were excuses to be made for her; she had had so many troubles. Cats generally have. Their kittens are taken away from them so often, and they get so hissed about the house when people are busy, and the children pull them about so heedlessly, and make the dogs run after them–which is so irritating–that really the wonder is they ever purr at all.

Nevertheless, her not feeling inclined to purr much herself was no good reason for her thinking it silly or wrong in other people to purr when they were pleased; but she did, and she and her purring daughter were always having small tiffs on the subject.

Every morning, for instance, when the nice curly-headed little boy brought the kittens a saucer of milk from his breakfast, there was sure to be a disturbance over the purring question; for, even before the saucer had reached the floor, Puss Missy was sure to be there, tail and head erect and eager, singing her loudest and best, her whole throat vibrating visibly; while Puss Master, on the contrary, took his food, but said very little about it, or, if ever tempted to express his natural delight, did it in so low a tone that nobody could hear without putting their ears close down to him to listen.

Now this was what the mother cat called keeping up one's dignity and self-respect, so it can easily be imagined how angry she used to get with the other child. "Wretched little creature!" she would say to poor Puss Missy, who, even after the meal was over, would lie purring with pleasure in front of the fire; "what in the world are you making all that noise and fuss about? Why are you to be always letting yourself down by thanking people for what they do for you, as if you did not deserve it, and had not a right to expect it? Isn't it quite right of them to feed you and keep you warm? What a shame it would be if they left you without food or fire! I am ashamed to see you make yourself so cheap, by showing gratitude for every trifle. For goodness' sake have a little proper pride, and leave off such fawning ways! Look at your brother, and see how differently he behaves–takes everything as a matter of course; and has the sense to keep his feelings to himself; and people are sure to respect him all the more. It keeps up one's friends' interest when they are not too sure that one is pleased. But you, with your everlasting acknowledgments, will be seen through, and despised very soon. Have a little more esteem for your own character, I do beg! What is to become of self-respect if people are to purr whenever they are pleased?"

Puss Missy had not the least notion what would become of it in such a case, but she supposed something dreadful; so she felt quite horrified at herself for having done anything to bring it about, and made a thousand resolutions to keep up her dignity, save self-respect from the terrible unknown fate in store, and purr no more.

But it was all in vain. As soon as ever anything happened to make her feel happy and comfortable, throb went the little throat, as naturally as flowers come out in spring, and there she was in a fresh scrape again! And the temptations were endless. The little boy's cousin, pale, and quiet, and silent as she was, would often take Puss Missy on her knee, and nurse her for half-an-hour at a time, stroking her so gently and kindly–how could any one help purring?

Or the boy would tie a string, with a cork at the end of it, to the drawer-handle of a table, so that the kittens could paw it, and pat it, and spring at it, as they pleased–how was it possible not to give vent to one's delight in the intervals of such a game, when the thing was swinging from side to side before their very eyes, inviting the next bound?

And when there was nothing else to be pleased about, there were always their own tails to run after, and the fun was surely irresistible, and well deserved a song.

Yet the brother very seldom committed himself in that way–that was the great puzzle, and Puss Missy grew more perplexed as time went on. Nay, once, when they were alone together, and her spirits had quite got the better of her judgment, she boldly asked him, in as many words, "Why do you not purr when you are pleased?" as if it was quite the natural and proper thing to do. Whereat he seemed quite taken by surprise, but answered at last: "It's so weak-minded, mother says; I should be ashamed. Besides," added he, after a short pause, "to tell you the truth–but don't say anything about it–when I begin there's something that chokes a little in my throat. Mind you don't tell–it would let me down so in mother's eyes. She likes one to keep up one's dignity, you know."

Had Mother Puss overheard these words, she might have been a little startled by such a result of her teaching: but, as it was, she remained in happy ignorance that her son was influenced by anything but her advice . . . Yet, strange to say, she had that choking in the throat sometimes herself!

But, at last, a change came in their lives. One day their friend, the curly-headed boy, came bounding into the kitchen where Puss and her kittens were asleep, in raptures of delight, followed by the pale, quiet, silent cousin, as quiet and silent as ever. The boy rushed to the kittens at once, took up both together in his hands, laid one over the other for fun, and then said to the girl, "Cousin, now they're going to give us the kittens for our very own, just tell me which you like best, really? I'm so afraid you won't choose for yourself when they ask you, and then, if I have to choose instead, I shan't know which you would rather have! And I want you to have the one you like most–so do tell me beforehand!"

"Oh, I like them both!" answered the girl, in the same unmoved, indifferent tone, in which she generally spoke.

"So do I," replied her cousin; "but I know which I like best for all that; and so must you, only you won't say. I wonder whether you like to have the kittens at all?" added he, looking at the pale child a little doubtfully; then whispering, as he put them both to her face to be kissed, "Cousin, dear, I wish I could see when you were pleased by your face! See! Give a smile when the one you like best goes by. Do–won't you–this once–just for once?"

It was in vain! He passed the kittens before her in succession, that she might see the markings of their fur, but she still only said she liked both, and, of course, was glad to have a kitten, and so on; till, at last, he was disheartened, and asked no more.

It is a great distress to some people when their friends will not purr when they are pleased; and as the children went back together to the drawing room, the little boy was the sadder of the two, though he could not have explained why.

And then, just what he expected happened–the choice between the two kittens was offered first to the girl; but, instead of accepting it as a favour, and saying "Thank you" for it, and being pleased, as she ought to have been, she would say nothing but that she liked both, and it could not matter which she had; nay, to look at her as she spoke, nobody would have thought she cared for having either at all!

How was it that she did not observe how sorrowfully her aunt was gazing at her as she spoke; aye, and with a sorrow far beyond anything the kittens could occasion?

But she did not; and presently her aunt said, "Well, then, as she did not care, the boy should choose." On which the poor boy coloured with vexation; but when he had sought his cousin's eyes again and again in vain for some token of her feelings, he laid sudden hold on Puss Missy, and cuddled her against his cheek, exclaiming–

"Then I will have this one! I like her much the best, mother, because she purrs when she is pleased!"

And then the little girl took up Puss Master, and kissed him very kindly, but went away without saying another word.

And so a week passed; and though the children nursed their kittens, they never discussed the question of which was liked best again, for a shyness had sprung up about it ever since the day the choice had been made.

But at the end of the week, one sunshiny morning, when the boy was riding his father's pony, and only the little girl was in the house, her aunt, coming suddenly into the school-room, discovered her kneeling by the sofa, weeping a silent rain of tears over the fur-coat of Puss Missy, who was purring loudly all the time; while her own kitten, Puss Master, was lying asleep unnoticed by the fire.

* * * * * *

Now, the pale, silent little girl had been an orphan nearly two years–father and mother having died within a few weeks of each other; and she had been ever since, till quite lately, under the care of a guardian, who, though married, had no children, and was more strict and well-intentioned than kind and

comprehending; so that, between sorrow at first and fear afterwards, joined to a timid, shrinking nature, she had, without knowing anything about it, shut herself up in a sort of defensive armor of self-restraint, which, till now, neither aunt, nor uncle, nor even loving cousin, had been able to break through.
But they had gently bided their time, and the time had come at last, and Puss Missy pointed the moral; for, with her aunt's arms folded round her, and a sense of her comforting tenderness creeping into the long-lonely heart, she owned that she had fretted all the week in secret because–actually because–*it was so miserable to nurse a kitten who would not purr when he was pleased!*

* * * * * *

Anybody may guess how nice it was, ten minutes afterwards, to see the little girl, with the roused colour of warm feeling on her cheeks, smiling through her tears at the thought of how like the unpurring kitten she had been herself! Anybody may guess, too, with what riotous joy the loving boy-cousin insisted on her changing kittens at once, and having Puss Missy for her very own. And now, on the other hand, he set to work himself, with a resolute heart, to make Puss Master so fond of him that purr he must, whether he would or no; and how that, now and then, by dint of delicate attentions, such as choice morsels of food and judicious rubbing under the ears, he worked the creature up to such a pitch of complacency, that the vibrations of his throat became, at any rate, visible to sight, and perceptible to touch.
Truly, they were a very happy party; for after Puss Master took Puss Missy for friend, confidante, and adviser, he grew so loving and fond, that he could not help showing his feelings in a thousand pretty pleasant ways: and the mother-cat herself relaxed by degrees; perhaps because she found her kittens were not taken away–partly, perhaps, because Puss Missy's open-heartedness stole into her heart at last, with a sense of comfort–who knows? Certainly she left off scolding and lecturing, and would not only watch their gambols, but join in them at times herself. And if neither she nor her son ever purred quite so much, or so loudly as their neighbours, the reason, no doubt, was only that tiresome choking in the throat!
Why, the pale little girl herself complained of having felt something very like it, during the sad two years before her kind aunt made her happy again! It always used to come on when she wanted to say what she felt.
And, perhaps, there is always something that chokes in the throat when people do not purr when they are pleased.
Let us hope so!

THE VOICES OF THE EARTH

"Let everything that hath breath, praise the Lord."–Ps. cl. 6.

"WOULD that I could pass away, and cease to be!" murmured the Wind, as it performed its circuits round the earth, long ages ago. "Would that I could cease to be! Since the creation of man, existence has become insupportable."

"Thou art mad!" cried the Mountains and Valleys, over whom the wind was passing, with its outcry of lamentation. "Is not man the glory of the world, the favourite of Heaven? Surely thou art mad, or else jealous of the greatness of others–jealous of the masterpiece of creation. Oh thou, ungrateful and unwise, to whom is committed the privilege of refreshing the earth and its inhabitants, why turn aside to hold judgment and condemn? Enough that thou fulfill thine own appointed work, and, in so doing, exist to the glory of the Creator."

"Yet, hear me in patience," wailed the Wind. "It is for the honour of man, and the glory of his Creator, that I am so troubled. Hence comes all my misery. I, who know no rest but in His will, and once went on my way rejoicing–I now am, of all creatures, the most miserable. Oh earth, with thy mountains and valleys, and forests, and fast-flowing rivers and seas, do me justice! Thou knowest it was not so with me of old, when I was first called into being. Thou knowest with what joy I roamed over thy confines, and beheld the universal beauty that then was spread around; how tenderly I whispered through thy flowers, how joyfully I carried up their fragrant odours as a thank-offering to heaven; how merrily I sported on the hills, or taught the branches of thy lofty trees to bow, as in obeisance to Him who made them! Thou knowest that I even failed not in due obedient love, when storms were needed, whether to drive the sluggish vapours through the sky, or rouse the sea itself to healthy action. When have I ever failed? Have I not always fulfilled His word? For even now, in these my days of misery, I carry out unwearyingly the great decree. Still I bear aloft from tropical seas, in ceaseless revolution round the world, those vapours which must descend in northern latitudes as dew, or rain, or snow. Still I labour–still I love to labour in the way ordained. But woe for me! Another burden than labour is upon me now! Woe for the pollution I have suffered, since the earth was overspread by the wretched race of men! Woe for their civilised lands, which I must needs pass through! Woe for the cities, and towns, and villages, their haunts and habitations, which I cannot avoid! Woe! For I bear thence in my bosom the blasphemies of the multitudes, and am laden with the burden of ingratitude, denial, and doubt. Woe that I must spread these black results of misguided reason from pole to pole! Woe that I must carry up the jests of the scorner and the oaths of the intemperate, as incense from man to his Maker: from man formed in His image, and boasting in his faculties of sense! Oh that I could pass away, and cease from being! And that with me might perish these fruits of an evil heart of unbelief!"

"Thou hast numbered curses," breathed the Mountains and Valleys in reply; "and alas! That such should ever defile thee, thou messenger of blessing. But this is not all thou bearest upon thy wings. Other outpourings stream into thy bosom; other voices are wafted upon thee to the skies; other sounds are spread by thee from pole to pole. Hast thou weighed in the balance, against the utterances of the rebellious, the prayers of the faithful, the childlike, and the pure; the steadfast avowal of martyrs; the daily thanksgiving of saints; the songs of holy praise and joy?"

"Yet what are these but what are due, and more than due, ten hundred thousand fold?" exclaimed the angry Wind. "What merit can you find in these? How strike a balance between them and the unnatural sin which says, 'There is no God'? All His works everywhere have praised Him from the beginning: only among men is there silence and doubt. And shall the remnant take credit for not joining in their sin? Inanimate creation and the beasts have never swerved from their allegiance. What room is there for boasting in man? Has he done more than these, from the foundation of the world?"

"But he alone of all creation, with a free, intelligent will." The words came up in soft response from the Earth, and spread like harmony upon the air. "He alone of all creation, with a free, intelligent will. Merit there can be none, indeed; but acceptability–where can it ever be found, but in the free-will worship of a spirit which has choice? And if choice, then of necessity, liberty to err. And with liberty to err, comes, alas! The everlasting contest between right and wrong. Yet why do I say, 'alas'? Obedience to a law which cannot be resisted is not the service of the heart–not the highest tribute to the Creator's glory. Far dearer to Him may be the struggle by which the human will is subdued to unison with the will Divine, in anticipation of that day when all its wisdom shall be made known. Have patience, then, with the contest between good and evil, so long as the good is accepted of Heaven; and while this is so, be contented to labour and to be!"

"Yet listen once again," sighed the Wind. "I have been jealous for the glory of the Maker, it is true, and troubled for the honour of man. But I am also wretched for myself. Oh Earth, Earth, Earth! The Creator has made His human favourite mortal! The mountains stand fast for ever, the hills cannot be moved, the very trees survive from generation to generation; but man–the chosen–passes away like a shadow; he cometh up and is cut down as the grass; I go over him, and his place knows him no more. Alas for the misery I am doomed to share! The breath of the dying has passed into my soul for ages; it is borne upon every breeze; it has tainted every air. I am filled with those bitter agonies, and loathe my very being. Would that I could pass away into nothing, and be as though I had never been, that so I might taste no more the vile dishonour of death."

"Thou judgest with the judgment of those who see and know but in part," came up the soothing answer from the Hills. "What, if the dying breath, which falls so sadly on thy breast, releases from its prison-house of clay some spirit more ethereal than thine own, some essence subtler far than thine, which thou must bear before the mercy-seat? Shall not the Judge of all the earth do right? Canst thou not trust the Almighty with His own? Why grieve for the last sigh of perishing flesh, if it be also the first breathing of a freed immortal soul? How rail

at death, if it is He who strikes the chord of everlasting life?"
"Yet once more hear me, and be just," persisted the Wind. "Not the breath of the dying only overwhelms me with this wild desire to be at rest. The breath of the living who suffer on is even worse. The sigh of natural grief, which none can blame; the moanings of the afflicted in mind, body, or estate; the outcries of the oppressed and desperate; the shrieks of madness and of pain, the groanings of despair; all, all are outpoured on me! Those dreadful voices haunt me from all sides. This mass of human woe corrodes my soul. I meet it in the cottage, and pass through to find it in the palace; I rush from the battlefield to the cloister, but in vain! For no seclusion can shut out man from sorrow. Wherever the chosen creature is found, there must I gather up the voices of grief; for lo! As the sparks fly upwards, so man is born to trouble. Oh that I might pass away for ever, and cease to know the wretchedness I have no power to avert!"
"Yet wait, wait, wait," implored another whisperer from the Earth. "What, if in human sorrow may be found an answer to the riddle of human guilt? What, if amidst its saddest cries, thou carriest up the voice of heartfelt penitence on high? Wilt thou not weigh against the transient earthly grief the joy in heaven for one repenting sinner? Or, if amidst the mortal agony of the righteous, the triumph-songs of faith grow loud as those the angels sing round the throne, 'Thy will, Thy will, Thy will–doing or suffering–Thy will be done; 'Wouldst thou not fear to take away the one, lest the other perchance should fail from off the earth? Watch well the balance between suffering and its fruits; but while these rise acceptable on thee to Heaven, well mayst thou rest contented in thy work, and rejoice both to labour and to be."
"Yet is man–the favourite–of all creatures the most wretched," moaned the Wind, "since he alone must purchase happiness with pain."
"Unjust! Unjust!" expostulated the Earth. "Thou keepest record of men's sighs, hast thou no consciousness of the unceasing breathings of simple, natural joys? Yet, number the one by thousands, and by tens of thousands of the other will I answer and refute thy words. The peaceful respirations of health, unnoticed and, alas! How often unthankfully enjoyed through years, count them if thou canst! Count them as they float to thee, while the night hours pass over the sleeper's head: count them when he wakes with the young daylight to a fresh existence. Count the laughs of frolic childhood. Count the murmurs of happy love. Count the stars if thou wilt, but thou canst never count the daily outpourings of common earthly joys. Alas for those who judge of life only by startling periods, and are deaf to the still small voices, which tell of hourly mercies, hour by hour!"
"Yet once more listen," cried the Wind, "for more and worse remains behind. The utterances of vice–oh innocent Earth, in whom the glory of the Creator is yet left visible to all! I sicken at the thought of what I know of what I bear unwillingly about. The loathsome words of sin–the lies of the deceiver–the prating of the fool–the seductions of the dissolute–the shouts of drunken revelry–the songs of the profane–the gifts of speech and thought misused to evil: those voices horrible to God and man..."

"Be they as dust before thee, and thou as the angel of the Lord scattering them!" shouted a cry of indignation from the Earth. "Yet wait, wait, wait! For thyself, be thou still contented to labour and to be. Wouldst thou be wiser than the Judge? Wilt thou lose patience, while He yet forbears? No! Watch the balance as before, and weigh the evil and the good. And so long as the prayers which the faithful pour on thy bosom out-value the words of the scorner; so long as the blessings of the righteous float above the curses of the blasphemer; so long as the voice of penitence follows close upon the utterances of sin; so long as pious submission makes harmony of the cries of grief; so long as thou carriest up daily thanksgiving for unnumbered daily mercies; so long as souls of saints are breathed up to Heaven by death–so long be thou contented to have patience, and labour and be."

"But should the day ever come," shouted the Wind in return, "when the balance is reversed; when vice, only tolerated now, becomes triumphant; when sin reigns on the altars, and no man pulls it down; when the voice of the good man's worship is drowned in the bad man's scorn, and I cannot lift it to the skies; when the wretched curse God and die, and men have forgotten to be thankful; then, then at last wilt thou acknowledge the justice of my complaints, and help me to pass away in peace? Promise this, and till then I will watch the struggle, and be contented to labour and to be."

And the Earth paused and consented, and the Wind fled satisfied away.

L'envoi to the Reader:

And he is still careering round the world; still gathering "the Voices of the Earth;" still watching the struggle between good and evil. In our public walks he meets us face to face. In our private chambers he is with us still. There is no secret corner where he cannot come; no whisper which is not breathed into his ear. It behooves us well, then, to be careful, lest, by thoughtlessness or sin, we add weight to the wrong side of the scales. For if the balance should ever incline to evil, and the wind cease to blow, what would become of the world?

THE MASTER OF THE HARVEST

"That which thou dost not understand when thou readest, thou shalt understand in the day of thy visitation; for there are many secrets of religion which are not perceived till they be felt, and are not felt but in the day of a great calamity."–JEREMY TAYLOR.

THE Master of the Harvest walked by the side of his cornfields in the early year, and a cloud was over his face, for there had been no rain for several weeks, and the earth was hard from the parching of the cold east winds, and the young wheat had not been able to spring up.

So, as he looked over the long ridges that lay stretched in rows before him, he was vexed, and began to grumble, and say, "The harvest would be backward, and all things would go wrong." At the mere thought of which he frowned more and more, and uttered words of complaint against the heavens, because there was no rain against the earth, because it was so dry and unyielding; against the corn, because it had not sprung up.

And the man's discontent was whispered all over the field, and all along the long ridges where the corn seeds lay; and when it reached them they murmured out, "How cruel to complain! Are we not doing our best? Have we let one drop of moisture pass by unused, one moment of warmth come to us in vain? Have we not seized on every chance, and striven every day to be ready for the hour of breaking forth? Are we idle? Are we obstinate? Are we indifferent? Shall we not be found waiting and watching? How cruel to complain!"

Of all this, however, the Master of the Harvest heard nothing, so the gloom did not pass away from his face. On the contrary, he took it with him into his comfortable home, and repeated to his wife the dark words, that all things were going wrong; that the drought would ruin the harvest, for the corn was not yet sprung.

And still thinking thus, he laid his head on his pillow, and presently fell asleep.

But his wife sat up for a while by the bedside and opened her Bible, and read, "The harvest is the end of the world, and the reapers are the angels."

Then she wrote this text in pencil, on the fly-leaf at the end of the book, and after it the date of the day, and after the date the words, "Oh, Lord, the husbandman, Thou waitest for the precious fruit Thou hast sown, and hast long patience for it! Amen, O Lord, amen!"

After which the good woman knelt down to pray, and as she prayed she wept, for she knew that she was very ill.

But what she prayed that night was heard only in heaven.

And so a few days passed on as before, and the house was gloomy with the discontent of its master, but at evening, the wind changed, the sky became heavy with clouds and before midnight there was rain all over the land; and when the Master of the Harvest came in next morning, wet from his early walk by the cornfields, he said it was well it had came up at last, and that, at last, the corn had sprung up.

On which his wife looked at him with a smile, and said. "How often things came right, about which one had been anxious and disturbed." To which her husband made no answer, but turned away and spoke of something else.
Meantime, the corn seeds had been found ready and waiting when the hour came, and the young sprouts burst out at once; and very soon all along the ridges were to be seen rows of tender blades, tinting the whole field with a delicate green. And day-by-day the Master of the Harvest saw them and was satisfied; but because he was satisfied, and his anxiety was gone, he spoke of other things, and forgot to rejoice.
And a murmur arose among them, "Should not the Master have welcomed us to life? He was angry but lately, because the seed he had sown had not yet brought forth; now that it has brought forth, why is he not glad? What more does he want? Have we not done our best? Are we not doing it minute-by-minute, hour-by-hour, day-by-day? From the morning and evening dews, from the glow of the midday sun, from the juices of the earth, from the breezes which freshen the air, even from clouds and rain, are we not taking in food and strength, warmth and life, refreshment and joy; so that one day the valleys may laugh and sing, because the good seed hath brought forth abundantly? Why does he not rejoice?"
As before, however, of all they said the Master of the Harvest heard nothing; and it never struck him to think of the young corn-blades' struggling life. Nay, once, when his wife asked him if the wheat was doing well, he answered, "Very fairly," and nothing more. But she then, because the evening was fine, and the fairer weather had revived her failing powers, said she would walk out by the cornfields herself.
And so it came to pass that they went out together.
And together they looked all along the long green ridges of wheat, and watched the blades as they quivered and glistened in the breeze, which sprang up with the setting sun. Together they walked, together they looked; looking at the same things, and with the same human eyes; even as they had walked, and looked, and lived together for years, but with a world dividing their hearts; and what was ever to unite them?
Even then, as they moved along, she murmured half-aloud, half to herself, thinking of the anxiety that had passed away–"Thou visitest the earth, and blessest it; Thou makest it very plenteous."
To which he answered, if answer it may be called–"Why are you always so gloomy? Why should Scripture be quoted about such common things?"
And she looked in his face and smiled, but did not speak and he could not read the smile, for the life of her heart was as hidden to him as the life of the corn-blades in the field.
And so they went home together, no more being said by either; for, as he turned round, the sight of the setting sun, and of the young freshly-growing wheat-blades, brought tears into her eyes.
She might never see the harvest upon earth again–for her that other was at hand, whereof the reapers were to be angels.
And when she opened her Bible that night she wrote on the fly-leaf the text she

had quoted to her husband, and after the text the date of the day, and after the date the words, "Bless me, even me also, oh my Father, that I may bring forth fruit with patience!"

Very peaceful were the next few weeks that followed, for all nature seemed to rejoice in the weather, and the corn-blades shot up till they were nearly two feet high, and about them the Master of the Harvest had no complaints to make.

But at the end of that time, behold, the earth began to be hard and dry again, for once more rain was wanted; and by degrees the growing plants failed for want of moisture and nourishment, and lost power and colour, and became weak and yellow in hue. And once more the husbandmen began to fear and tremble, and once more the brow of the Master of the Harvest was over-clouded with angry apprehension.

And as the man got more and more anxious about the fate of his crops, he grew more and more irritable and distrustful, and railed as before, only louder now, against the heavens, because there was no rain; against the earth, because it lacked moisture; against the corn-plants, because they had waxed feeble.

Nay, once, when his sick wife reproved him gently, praying him to remember how his fears had been turned to joy before, he reproached her in his turn for sitting in the house and pretending to judge of what she could know nothing about, and bade her come out and see for herself how all things were working together for ill.

And although he spoke it in bitter jest, and she was very ill, she said she would go, and went.

So once more they walked out together, and once more looked over the cornfields; but when he stretched out his arm, and pointed to the long ridges of blades, and she saw them shrunken and faded in hue, her heart was grieved within her, and she turned aside and wept over them.

Nevertheless she said she durst not cease from hope, since an hour might renew the face of the earth, if God so willed; neither should she dare to complain, even if the harvest were to fail.

At which words the Master of the Harvest turned round, amazed, to look at his wife, for her soul was growing stronger, as her body grew weaker, and she dared to say now things she would have had no courage to utter before.

But of all this he knew nothing, and what he thought, as he listened, was, that she was as weak in mind as in body; and what he said was, that a man must be an idiot who would not complain when he saw the bread taken from under his very eyes!

And his murmurings and her tears sent a shudder all along the long ridges of sickly corn-blades, and they asked one another, "Why does he murmur and why does she weep? Are we not doing all we can? Do we slumber or sleep, and let opportunities pass by unused? Are we not watching and waiting against the times of refreshing? Shall we not be found ready at last? Why does he murmur and why does she weep? Is she, too, fading and waiting? Has she, too, a master who has lost patience?"

Meantime, when she opened her Bible that night, she wrote on the fly-leaf the text, "Wherefore should a man complain, a man for the punishment of his sins?" and after the text the date of the day, and after the date the words, "Thou dost turn Thy face from us, and we are troubled: but, Lord, how long, how long?"

And by and by came on the long-delayed times of refreshing, but so slowly and imperfectly, that the change in the corn could scarcely be detected for a while. Nevertheless it told at last, and stems struggled up among the blades, and burst forth into flowers, which gradually ripened into ears of grain. But a struggle it had been, and continued to be, for the measure of moisture was scant, and the due amount of warmth in the air was wanting. Nevertheless, by struggling and effort the young wheat advanced, little by little, in growth; preparing itself, minute by minute–hour by hour–day by day, as best it could, for the great day of the harvest–as best it could! Would the Master of the Harvest ask more? Alas! He had still something to find fault with, for when he looked at the ears and saw that they were small and poor, he grumbled, and said the yield would be less than it ought to be, and the harvest would be bad.

And as more weeks went on, and the same weather continued, and the progress was very, very slow, he spoke out his vexation, to his wife at home, to his friends at the market, and to the husbandmen who passed by and talked with him about the crops.

And the voice of his discontent was breathed over the cornfield, all along the long ridges where the plants were labouring, and waiting, and watching. And they shuddered and murmured, "How cruel to complain! Had we been idle, had we been negligent, had we been indifferent, we might have passed away without bearing fruit at all. How cruel to complain!"

But of all this the Master of the Harvest heard nothing, so he did not cease to complain.

Meantime another week or two went on, and people, as they glanced over the land, wished that a few good rainy days would come and do their work decidedly, so that the corn-ears might fill. And behold, while the wish was yet on their lips, the sky became charged with clouds, darkness spread over the country, a wild wind arose, and the growling of thunder announced a storm. And such a storm! People hid from it in cellars, and closets, and dark corners, as if now, for the first time, they believed in a God, and were trembling at the newfound fact; as if they could never discover Him in His sunshine and blessings, but only thus in His tempests and wrath.

And all along the long ridges of wheat-plants drove the rain-laden blast, and they bent down before it and rose up again, like the waves of a labouring sea. Ears over ears they bowed down; ears above ears they rose up. They bowed down, as if they knew that to resist was destruction: they rose up, as if they had a hope beyond the storm. Only here and there, where the whirlwinds were strongest, they fell down and could not lift themselves again. So the damage done was but little, and the general good was great. But when the Master of the Harvest saw here and there patches of over-weighted corn yet dripping from the thundershowers, he grew angry for them, and forgot to think of the long ridges that stretched over his fields, where the corn-ears were swelling and rejoicing.

And he came in gloomy to his home, when his wife was hoping that now, at last, all would be well; and when she looked at him the tumult of her soul grew beyond control, and she knelt down before him as he sat moody in his chair, and threw her arms round him, and cried out, "It is of the Lord's mercies that we are not utterly consumed. Oh, husband! Pray for the corn and for me that it may go well with us at the last! Carry me upstairs!" And his anger was checked by fear, and he carried her upstairs and laid her on the bed, and said it must be the storm which had shaken her nerves. But whether he prayed for either the corn or her that night, she never knew.

And presently came a new distress, for when the days of rain had accomplished their gracious work, and every one was satisfied, behold, they did not cease. And as hitherto the cry had gone up for water on the furrows, so now men's hearts failed them for fear lest it should continue to overflowing, and lest mildew should set in upon the full, rich ears, and the glorious crops should be lost.

And the Master of the Harvest walked out by his cornfields, his face darker than ever. And he railed against the rain, because it would not cease; against the sun, because it would not shine; against the wheat, because it might perish before the harvest.

"But why does he always and only complain?" moaned the corn-plants, as the new terror was breathed over the field. "Have we not done our best from the first? And has not mercy been with us, sooner or later, all along? When moisture was scant, and we throve but little, why did he not rejoice over that little, and wait, as we did, for more? Now that abundance has come, and we swell, triumphant in strength and in hope, why does he not share our joy in the present, and wait, in trust, as we do, for the future ripening change? Why does he always complain? Has he himself some master, who would fain reap where he has not sown and gather where he has not strawed, and who has no pity for his servants who strive?"

But all of this the Master of the Harvest heard nothing. And when the days of rain had rolled into weeks, and the weeks into months, and the autumn set in, and the corn still stood up green in the ridges, as if it never meant to ripen at all, the boldest and most hopeful became uneasy, and the Master of the Harvest despaired.

But his wife had risen no more from her bed, where she lay in sickness and suffering, yet in patient trust; watching the sky through the window that faced her pillow; looking for the relief that came at last. For even at the eleventh hour, when hope seemed almost over, and men had half learned to submit to their expected trial, the dark days began to be varied by a few hours of sunshine; and though these passed away, and the gloom and rain returned again, yet they also passed away in their turn, and the sun shone out once more.

And the poor sick wife, as she watched, said to those around her that the weather was gradually changing; and that all would come right at last; and sighing a prayer that it might be so with herself also, she had her Bible brought to the bed, and wrote in the fly-leaf the text, "Some thirty, some sixty, some an hundredfold;" and after the text the date of the day, for on that day the sun had been shining steadily for many hours. And after the date the words, "Unto whom much is given; of him shall much be required; yet if Thou, Lord, be extreme to mark iniquity, O Lord, who may stand?"

And day by day the hours of sunshine were more in number, and the hours of rain and darkness fewer, and by degrees the green corn-ears ripened into yellow, and the yellow turned into gold, and the harvest was ready, and the labourers not wanting. And the bursting corn broke out into songs of rejoicing, and cried, "At least we have not waited and watched in vain! Surely goodness and mercy have followed us all the days of our life, and we are crowned with glory and honour. Where is the Master of the Harvest, that he may claim his own with joy?"

But the Master of the Harvest was bending over the bed of his dying wife.

And she whispered that her Bible should be brought. And he brought it, and she said, "Open it at the fly-leaf at the end, and write, 'It is sown in corruption, it is raised in incorruption: it is sown in dishonour, it is raised in glory: it is sown in weakness, it is raised in power: it is sown a natural body, it is raised a spiritual body.'" And she bade him add the date of the day, and after the date of the day the words, "O Lord, in Thy mercy say of me–She hath done what she could!" And then she laid her hand in his; and so fell asleep in hope.

And the harvest of the earth was gathered into barns, and the gathering-day of rejoicing was over, and the Master of it all sat alone by his fireside with his wife's Bible on his knee. And he read the texts, and the dates, and the prayers, from the first day when the corn-seeds were held back by drought; and as he read, a new heart seemed to burst out within him from the old one–a heart which the Lord of the other Harvest was making soft, and the springing whereof He would bless.

And henceforth, in his going out and coming in from watching the fruits of the earth, the texts, and the dates, and the prayers were ever present in his mind, often rising to his lips; and he murmured and complained no more, let the seasons be what they would, and his fears however great; for the thought of the late-sprung in his own dry, cold heart, and of the long-suffering of Him who was Lord and Master of all, was with him night and day. And more and more as he prayed for help, that the weary struggle might be blessed, and the new-born watching and waiting not be in vain; so more and more there came over his spirit a yearning for that other harvest, where he, and she who had gone before, might be gathered in together.

And thus, in one hope of their calling, the long-divided hearts were united at last.

INFERIOR ANIMALS

"How? When? And I whence? The gods give no reply.
Let so it is suffice, and cease to question why."
GOETHE.

WHAT do they say? What do they say? What do they say?

What can they have to say, those noisy, cawing rooks, as they sail along the sky over our heads, gathering more and more friends as they go on to the appointed place of meeting?

What have they to say? What have we to say? they may equally ask. They have life, and labour, and food, and children to say their say about; and if they do not say it in what we are pleased to call language, they say it in a way intelligible to each other, which is all that is wanted.

That they do understand each other's say is clear, for they are collecting from far and near in large numbers for a definite object–viz. that of assembling in some field, or open pasturage, or park, where they will settle down together for upwards of an hour, and walk or hop about, as if they had serious thoughts of giving up flying altogether, and taking to an earthly life; saying a say, all the while, whereof we are altogether as ignorant as they would be of ours round a large dinner-table, if they had the opportunity of hearing it.

We call their say noisy cawing; what they would call ours round the large dinner-table one cannot guess; but, if they concluded it had no meaning, because they did not happen to understand it, their judgment would not be worth much.

As to the noises, there is not much to choose between them in the matter of agreeableness. Nay, of the two, perhaps the din produced by human voices is the more discordant and confused.

If you never thought of this before, O reader, think of it now, and take an early opportunity of listening and judging for yourself. Listen, not as listening to the meaning of what is uttered, but to the mass of noise as mere noise. Listen to it, as you might imagine a rook to do, ignorant of human speech, and judging only of the hubbub of sounds; and then own to yourself–for conscience will force you so to do–that there is neither sweetness nor sublimity, neither melody or majesty, in the shouting, and piping, and whistling, and hissing, and barking, of closely intermixed human voices and laughter.

Alas, for the barriers which lie so mysteriously between us and the other creatures among whom we are born, and pass our short existence upon earth! Alas! For a desire for intercommunion is one of the strong instincts of our nature, and yet it is one which, as regards all the rest of creation but our human fellow-beings, we have to unlearn from babyhood.

See the little child as she babbles to her cat on the rug, and would fain be friends with the soft plaything. Observe in every action how she expects it to understand her, and return her love. Look at the angry disappointment if a vicious bite or scratch disturb the security of the affectionate dream. It is not pain alone the child feels, let the matter-of-fact observer say what he will; there is the vexation

of hurt feelings as well. Puss should not have behaved so to her; puss, with whom she had so gladly shared her breakfast of milk; puss, whom she had nursed on her knee; puss, who must have known how much she loved her!
And then follows the lesson: it may have been given before, but it has to be given again; and while mamma tells her little one that poor pussy does not know what she means, cannot hear what she says, cannot talk as she can, has no sense to know how much she loves her, and therefore is not to blame for biting, although she must be slapped when she does it, to make her remember not to do it again–behold! How the wistful eyes of the listening child haze over with a dull dreaminess as she becomes more and more perplexed. It is all far too puzzling for her to understand, and when she turns again to puss–as if by looking at her to make it out–lo! The veil between the two natures remains as thick as before; neither the bite, nor anything else, has been explained.
But, practically, the unlearning of the instinct has begun, and so, practically, the lesson goes on, until we get so used to it, we forget it was ever a lesson at all; and only a few of us, here and there in grown-up life, are haunted, as we stand among the lower forms of creation, by a painful wonder at the gulf which lies between.
That the lower should not fully understand the higher; that they should not understand us, is comprehensible enough; nay, is a necessity involved in the very idea of a lower and higher; let the philosophers rave as they will at the chains thereby hung around their own necks. But that the higher should not fully understand the lower, that we should not fully understand them, is a mystery indeed, and one of which no solution has been offered.
What more natural than that the dog should not know much about his master? What more strange than that the master should know so little of his dog? In one sense, of course, he knows all about him, i.e., the uses he can put him to, and what he may expect from him; but of the inner world of the dog's life, his feelings and motives of action, he knows almost nothing. Nay, even of his physical capabilities he has no complete idea. Who has ever explained by what power a dog will take a short cut across the country to the house where his master is, although he has never been the road before? or why he never, even by any accident or mistake, brings back any but the stone his master threw–thrown, perhaps, with a gloved hand, and into wet meadow grass, and not found for several minutes?
Verily, in more than one sense, we are "strangers and pilgrims upon earth;" for, from the first moment of waking to conscious thought, we find ourselves in a country where all utterances but our own are to us a blank; all the creatures strange; all life unintelligible, both in its beginning and its end: all the present, as well as the past and future, a mystery.
"Only children, or child-like men," says Novalis, "have any chance of breaking through the charm which holds nature thus as it were frozen around us, like a petrified magic city." Oh, if this be true, who would not be a child again? Reader, can you hear this and remain unmoved, or shall you and I become children in heart once more? Come! Own with me how hateful were the lessons

which undeceived us from our earlier instincts of faith and sweet companionship with all created things: and let us go forth together, and for a while forget such teaching.
Hand in hand, in the dear confiding way in which only children use, let us go forth into the fields, and read the hidden secrets of the world. Clasp mine firmly as I clasp yours. See, there is magic in the action itself! So we placed our hands in those of our parents; so our children love to place theirs in our own. So, then, even so, let us two walk trustingly and lovingly together for a while, and join again the broken threads of old feelings, wishes, friendships, and hopes. }

* * * * * *

Hush! Is it a parliament, or a congregation, or what, that darkens over yonder field? Are rook-politics, or rook-faith, or rook domestic hopes and fears, the subjects of that everlasting cawing, those restless movements, those hoppings and peckings, and changes of position?
Cower down here with me by this hole in the hedge;–let us lean against this old elm-root and look through. See! The honeysuckle is twined in the thorn above our heads, and is giving out its scent around us, as if to bid us we1come
Oh, dear companion, do you see the dark glossy creatures at their play? Their play? Am I not bold to do so? They have come here for some object ith some distinct intention and purpose. Yonder, in the tall oak that overlooks the field in the opposite corner, I see the sentinel guard, who will never stir from his post until the assembly has dispersed, unless he hears or sees symptoms of danger or interruption, and then he will dash out and fly among them, making his warning cry, so different from all others, that any one who has once heard it will recognize it again. We must whisper our remarks very softly then, or he may give notice of our presence here, and all the flock may forsake the field.
How solemn and grave, yet how keen and attentive he looks! How patient and observant! Contented not to join the fun himself so that he may but promote it. Unselfish, dark watchman, are you paid for your trouble, and if so, how? Or do you do it out of love and affection for your brethren, expecting love and affection from them in return, on some future occasion, when one of them will watch, and you be allowed to play? Play, I still say; but can this be only play indeed? Surely something graver and more important than play must have brought these different companies and families from their often distant homes to this spot?
Alas! How vain are my questionings! Nature remains mute around me, and man is ignorant and unable to answer. Yes! Ignorant and unable to answer, let him say what he will. Hear this, oh you philosophers, you lights of the world, with your books and papers and diagrams, and collected facts, and self-confidence unlimited! You who turn the bull's-eye of your miserable lanthorns upon isolated corners of the universe, and fancy you are sitting in the supreme light of creative knowledge! Hear this; you are ignorant and unable to answer; or disprove it if you can, by showing me that you do know this one simple thing which puzzles

me now! Tell me what the rooks are doing and saying; those inferior animals about whom you, in your wisdom, ought to know everything. Tell me that, and I will own that your eyes have been opened indeed, and that you are as gods knowing good and evil.

Tell me what these grand assemblies are for; tell me how they are called; tell me how they are conducted; tell me by what message the distant colonies are warned of the particular spot and hour of meeting. Tell me by what rules the place is chosen. Tell me how the messenger is instructed. Tell me by what means he delivers his message. Tell me why they meet on level ground and walk like men, and not rather in their own deep woods, where they might fly and roost on branches, and run no danger, and need no guard?

Tell me what do they say, what do they say, what do they say, when they meet at last, and whether they are here for business or for play. Tell me these things, and then I will listen to you when you point out to me the counsels and the workings of the Creator of rooks and of men.

But, miserable guides, miserable comforters are ye all! Better a thousand times to be a child as I am now, lying under this twining honeysuckle, and listening reverently to the unknown murmurs in the field! But oh! Twining honeysuckle, why do you breathe out only scent around me? Stoop, stoop, stoop! I know you know! Why not whisper in my ear, then, what they say?

Tell me, what do they say? Childlike, I ask, childlike must I always ask in vain?

But hush for a moment! Someone speaks; some stranger interrupts us already! Calls,"gentlemen!" as if gentlemen were here. Oh! go, go, go, whoever you may be. There are no gentlemen here–only children: children for one brief hour of weary grown-up life. Leave us; let us dream our dream in peace.

But how is this? I see no one near, yet the voice is louder than before. Companion, where are you? Look! There is no disturbance in the field; the sentry sits firm at his post; the rest are hopping, pecking, jumping as before; and yet I hear–oh, what do I hear? A voice–and from among the rooks themselves! Have my senses left me, or have I received another? Anyhow the spell is broken at last, and language, language, language, resounds on every side! Quick, then, my tablets! Let me record what I see and hear.

One among them comes forward–a crowd surrounds him–he is congratulated–he inclines his head–he thanks his friends for a reception so far beyond his merits or his hopes. Oh, folly! Are they aping the mockeries of men? Wait! He is serious once more, and here on my tablets I record,

WHAT THE ROOK SAYS.

"The origin, therefore, of these creatures–these men–whom we equally fear and dislike, is decidedly the most useful of all subjects of study. How can it be otherwise? Their treatment of us, and our feelings to them, can never be placed on a proper footing, until we know something of the nature of the people themselves. In fact, my friends, I base my whole inquiry upon these two assumptions; first, that it is *desirable* to ascertain the exact truth on the subject; secondly, that it is *possible* to ascertain the exact truth upon any subject, if one chooses to try.

"Whoever goes along with me on these points, will be so good as to rise from the ground by a hop, and give a caw. . .
. . . "Thank you, thank you, gentlemen, for your applause! My recognition of our common capabilities is acceptable to you I perceive. Unlimited faith in them is indeed the keystone of all knowledge. . . . Thank you, thank you, once more!"
–But I–the transcriber of this arrogant nonsense–am ready, as I listen to their senseless caws, to throw down my tablets in despair. Oh! To think of finding the false musings of philosophical conceit among the birds of the air, and as welcome as . . . but hush! He speaks again.
"*How, when, whence*, and *why*, then, are the questions we must put and learn to answer. *How* came this creature in the land, and *whence*? *When* was he first our foe, and *why*? *Why* also is he here at all?
"These are difficult questions indeed, and before we answer them, let us look at the facts of the case. Unhappily they are too well known to need much description. It is, and has been from time immemorial (I have made inquiry of our oldest relations), a system of encroachment on one side, and retreat on the other. He comes near us and we fly; he pursues us again, and again we retire before him. Old solitudes and woodland homes are invaded, and made public; and we seek fresh retreats, only to be driven out afresh. It is a terrible position, and a time will certainly come when we must seek a new world, or cease to exist, unless some remedy for the threatened evil can be found.
"Now, the WHY of our yielding our place to man is *fear*. We can none of us deny it: a cowardly terror which seems to have possessed our race as far back as our oldest grandsires can recollect.
"But the WHY of this fear? What is that? Well! I am told on all sides that it is our sense of man's superiority to ourselves. Hence we give way, overawed by his presence. And here I will at once confess, that I was for a long time myself as firm a believer in this old tradition as any of you can be at the present moment. When I beheld ancient woods deserted, ancient homes forsaken, how could I fail to tremble before him who, I was told, was the mighty cause of such disturbance? But thanks to the awakened spirit of inquiry, I emerged at last from the labyrinth of what I now believe to be an old wife's tale.
"The *why* of our giving way was *fear:* that was obvious enough; the *why* of the fear, man's superiority. So it was said, at least; but of this, *what proofs,* was my next demand; and no one could give me an answer! Here was a position for an intelligent creature! Everything mysterious, unknown, and taken for granted; nothing proved. I shouted for proofs till I was hoarse, but every one turned away silent. Who can wonder, then, that my next inquiry was a doubt. Is man superior to ourselves after all? No one can show me the fact by proofs. May not this old tradition then be a mere myth? The delusion of timid minds imposed upon weak ones for truth? My friends! The moment when I asked myself these questions was the turning point of my life. Henceforth I resolved to inquire and investigate for myself, and the result of my labours I am going to place before you.
"Yet, lest you should accuse me also of mere assertion-making, let me guide you into examining the facts of the matter fairly for yourselves.

"Now all common observation is against the superiority of man. While we fly swiftly through the sky, behold him creeping slowly along the ground. While we soar to the very clouds, a brief jump and come down again is all his utmost efforts can accomplish, though I have seen him practising to get higher and higher, in his leaps, as if at a game. And at all times, if one of his legs is up, the other is obliged to be down, or the superior creature would be apt to tumble on his nose. Yet it is in this miserable lop-sided manner he moves from place to place, unless he can get some other being, more skilful than himself, to carry him along.

"Again, while we are clothed in a natural thick, glossy plumage, available equally for summer or winter, behold man, not possessing in himself the means of protection against any sort of weather whatever! Neither the warmth of summer nor the cold of winter suits his uncomfortable skin. In all seasons he must wear clothes. Clumsy incumbrances, with which he is driven by a sad necessity to supply the place of the feathers or fur with which every other creature on earth but himself is blessed. What sort of superiority is this?

"One more instance out of many, and I shall have said enough for the present. It is one, the force of which every philosophical mind will appreciate. While *we* are satisfied with ourselves and all around us, man is ever discontented and uneasy, seeking rest in everlasting change, but neither finding it himself, nor allowing it to others, as we know to our bitter cost.

"Ah, my friends, if restless dissatisfaction be a proof of superiority, who would not be glad to be an inferior animal?

"Now then, have I shaken the old faith in the old tradition? If so, you will be better disposed to accept the new one. Whoever is satisfied of this, let him soar from the ground and give a caw!"

–What a rising of dark forms in the air; what an outburst of caws! Verily 'tis a beautiful language after all, and beautiful creatures they are themselves! Only I am not sure I do not like them better so, than in the would-be wisdom of men. Yes! If they had but the sense not to sit in judgment upon things beyond their power! But hush! He speaks again.

"One objection remains to be answered. It was suggested by a keen-sighted friend, now, I am proud to say, a warm supporter of my views. In some of the unmannerly invasions of our premises already alluded to, painful events occur. While standing under our roosting trees, these creatures, men, will occasionally level at us sticks, of the most contemptible size, but which, owing to some contrivance which I have not at present had the time to investigate, make suddenly an abominable banging noise and a very unpleasant smoke. And no sooner do our youngsters see and hear all this, than some of them are pretty sure to fall down upon the ground, as if crouching at the very feet of our foe. All fathers of families here present will admit the truth of this description, and know the terrible result. The prostrate young ones are carried away unresisting, and are never heard of more.

"Now this has actually been brought forward as a proof of the superiority of man; though in what way wanton cruelty proves superiority, I confess I am

unable to see. But what cannot we flatter ourselves we have proved when our minds are warped by a theory! I, looking at the fact with an unprejudiced eye, see in it nothing but the miserable fruits of a delusion encouraged through so long a succession of ages, that we have transmitted to our very offspring an inheritance of paralysing fear! For, observe, it is rarely–very rarely–the grownup bird who is the victim of this terror. Only the tender and susceptible young ones, with no experience of life to counteract the insane cowardice which our obstinate adherence to the old wife's tale has bequeathed to their constitutions.
"Enough of this. I pass now to the pleasanter part of my task! The statement of a theory respecting the origin of men, which affords a beautiful and consistent explanation of all the puzzling facts we have been considering, and opens up a vista of triumph to the whole rook race!"
–Mercy! What thunders of applause! I am deafened, but curiosity is awakened at last. What folly! Yet if ingenuity were wisdom. . . . Well, well, if it were, judges would be overruled by barristers, and a thousand unjust verdicts become law. Again he opens his bill. . . .
"My friends, man is not our superior, was never so, for he is neither more nor less than a degenerated brother of our own race! Yes, I venture confidently to look back thousands on thousands of generations, and I see that men were once rooks! Like us they were covered with feathers, like us lived in trees, flew instead of walking, roosted instead of squatting in stone boxes, and were happy and contented as we are now!
"This is a bold proposition, and I do not ask you to assent to it at once. But if on testing it in various ways, you are forced to admit that by it you are able to explain things hitherto inexplicable, and to account for things otherwise unaccountable, though ocular proof cannot be had, then I insist that you cannot reasonably reject my solution, without offering me a better one in exchange. *If things are not so, how are they?* is the ground I stand upon. For remember we have already laid down the maxim, that everything *ought* to be and *can* be explained.
"Well! Here then I advance another step forward. I give an explanation (supported of course by facts), and I challenge you either to accept it, or to answer the searching inquiry, '*If things are not so, how are they?*' Gentlemen who see the justice of this remark, will, perhaps, afford me a congratulatory caw.
"Almost unanimous, I declare! And my venerable friends who hesitate–well, well–it is from the young I look for support. A natural distaste to disturbance of ideas comes on with declining years. Thank you, gentlemen, again; the voices of my young supporters are loud and impressive.
–Oh, birds of the air, the world and the vanities and follies of it are as deep in your hearts as in ours! But again he resumes–
"The test I begin with is this. Supposing that my theory be true, and that men are degenerated rooks, what would be the condition of their minds, what their feeling and conduct towards us, the original race? Would not the painful sense of degradation, in the first place, cause them to be restless and uneasy with their present condition, as in fact we see they are? And would it not, in the second

place, stimulate them to an incessant craving for re-association–a desire to be with us, among us, of us, and like us, once more? What more natural, then, than that they should pursue us with almost tiresome pertinacity (a fact inexplicable on the theory of man's superiority), and that when we retreat before them in fear, they should still follow us; not, however, as we have for so long imagined, with evil intent, but with the outstretched arms of love?

"My friends, I feel the moisture tremble in my eyes at the thought of the gross misconceptions we have cherished with respect to this much-maligned human race. How cruel, how cold we must have appeared to them! How heartless–pardon my emotion! Give me encouragement by an approving caw." . . .

–Louder than ever, only hoarse with suppressed emotion. The dream of nonsense is becoming real and exciting! He speaks–

"And now, even for the terrible loss of our young ones, an explanation dawns, and their probable fate becomes clear; and happily it is one, of which, in the midst of parental regrets, we cannot but be proud. Yes! I boldly picture to myself those lost young ones, carried away to become the friends and instructors of the race we have dreaded as enemies. I do not hesitate to imagine them tenderly nursed and watched in the stone boxes into which we cannot see, but which they inhabit as homes–every movement an object of interest to their captors, every action creating admiration, and made a subject of imitation–and I see no improbability in the picture! For if, as I shall presently show by unanswerable proofs, men are imitating not only our appearance, but our very customs and manners, their being able to do so can only be attributed to the instructions imparted to them, whether by example or precept, by our own offspring, for who else can have taught them? Ages may pass away before the reunion of the two races takes place, but when it does (and I look forward to it in confident faith), it will be our own children who will have been the means of bringing the long-parted brethren together: those children who once fell down in fear at the feet of men, and over whose fate, hitherto, the veil of an impenetrable mystery has been thrown. My friends, it is my proud delight at this moment to lift that veil, and reveal to the affectionate mourners the bright and pleasurable reality!

"And thus the mysteries of man's pursuit, and apparent ill-usage of us, become in the light of my theory natural and intelligible facts. But you have a right to reply. 'Clear as all this would be if the thing itself could be, that still remains to be shown. By what possible means could birds ever degenerate into men?'

"Nothing can be more reasonable than the inquiry; nothing more conclusive, I believe, than the explanation I am able to give.

"At this very moment, then, my friends, we are ourselves living examples of a first step in the same direction! Here we are assembled from all quarters of the country, having deserted our trees and woods, to meet in an open field, as men meet; walk lop-sided as they walk, with one leg up and the other down; or jump in short hops instead of using our wings. What account can we give of this? To descend to the earth for a few moments for food, sticks, or wool as they are needed, is one thing; to prolong our stay upon it, as we do now, is a matter of dangerous choice. Alas! Indolence and a fatal tendency to yield to the ease of the moment are the causes of our own conduct; and so they were, I can have no doubt whatever, of the degradation of our ancestors. Ages indeed may pass away without any perceptible effect being produced upon the individuals of a race by the bad habits in which all are indulging. In fact, where a gradual change is creeping over all, it attracts the attention of none. But heap ages upon ages, and other ages upon them, in a succession to which the century-lives of our grandfathers are a tiny fraction of time, and what then? Anything is possible in the course of such a period. Can any one disprove what I say? If so, let him caw it publicly out; if not, let him hold his tongue. You are silent: I perceive that you assent.

"Now, then, let us imagine a race of bygone rooks, less energetic even than ourselves; nay, we will, if you please, imagine them with some temporary weakness in their wings (such deviations from a general standard are quite possible), and indulging gradually more and more in the relief afforded to the evil by this pernicious habit of ground-walking. There seems to me to be no great difficulty in believing that a weakness so indulged should gain ground in proportion to the extent of the indulgence, until, in the course of the long ages alluded to, and by many inheritances of increased want of power, the mischief, once trifling, became insurmountable, and a race incapable of using their wings at all, arose.

"Now, it is well known to you all, by observation of our young ones, that wings grow by use. After the young brood make efforts at flying, those necessary appendages increase. Thus much therefore is clear. Practice brings power, and power brings on growth and enlargement. And, in a similar manner, want of practice brings a falling away of strength and diminution in size. Why then should there be any insuperable difficulty in further believing it possible that the never-used and consequently constantly diminishing wings of generation after generation, should disappear at last entirely as wings, leaving only the outer bone remaining, as a sort of claw whereby to lay hold on what was wanted–bared of all its beauty and ornament–in fact, the long uncouth arm of the present man?

"And I can hardly doubt that in a similar manner, the other unused feathers on back and breast and legs, would also gradually fail. No air blowing through them, no freedom of action, no battling with the breeze. On the contrary, a stuffy life in close stone boxes, enclosed on all sides. Well might wings diminish in size, and feathers decrease in quantity, until at length, in the naked, claw-armed, bare-legged creature, not a trace of them could be found!

"Every probability is in favour of such a result, provided you only allow time enough for the imperceptible action of the change.

"And now reflect upon the miserable creature presented to your imagination! Enlarged, it is true, in length, for his lazy habits encourage that sort of feeble growth; and the power which once produced feathers, must needs develop in some other form! But behold him–a featherless, thin-skinned biped–neither beast, nor bird, nor fish; wandering, shivering over the face of the earth, needing help from every other creature around him, yet never satisfied with anything he

gets! Need I fill up the picture further, or will not every one recognise at once in this miserable animal the portrait of the superior being, MAN!
–Well may the listeners caw! well may they wheel round and round in exulting flight. I myself grow giddy and confused. Am I then half convinced?–Yet for an imperfect being to hope to fathom the higher nature? Bah! what balderdash of folly! But hark, he has begun afresh. –
"That such a degeneration is possible is therefore clear; and of the thousand difficulties cleared away by the establishment of this fact, I will offer you one more.
"You must all admit that one of the most puzzling *whys* in connexion with man is, *why he wears clothes*? A habit which, viewing him as a perfect animal, it would be impossible to account for, but which, on the contrary, considering him as a degenerated one, is just what might be expected. He had his natural clothes once, like the rest of the animals of the earth; he has lost them now, through the disease of his deterioration, and must supply himself with the miserable make-shifts of dress.
"My friends, time does not allow me to give you now more than a few examples of my collection of proofs, the extent of which is enormous; for even after my own convictions were fixed for ever by the discoveries I have already named, I never relaxed in my researches; but being unable to be personally in more places than one at a time, I employed in active investigations several distinguished friends; I will mention particularly Mr. Raven-wing, Mr. Yellow-beak, and Mr. Grey-legs. Furnished with a complete understanding of what I believed and wished to be proved, these gentlemen have been unremitting in their efforts to procure corroborative facts; of which, therefore, I will, before I conclude, mention a few of the most striking.
"Mr. Raven-wing's particular line was to find evidence of attempts on the part of man to recover the colour of the original race, namely black; and to this end he did not shrink even from the distasteful task of approaching those vast masses of men's stone boxes, which they call cities, towns, or villages, in order that he might observe the proceedings of their inhabitants. And he came back to me absolutely overwhelmed with what he had met with. Black in all the streets struggling to overpower every other hue. Black quiescent on the pavements and walls. Black rising triumphantly into the air from the mouths of those smaller boxes, which are placed on the summit of the larger ones, apparently to raise their height–of which singular fact I shall have more to say by and by.
"Black also the usual colour of the coverings with which men protect their heads from the outer air. Black even the clumsy boots which cover their feet. Black pretty nearly everything, everywhere, Mr. Raven-wing positively declared.
"And on another occasion, in some parts of the country, he came upon whole races of men who left their homes every morning at an early hour, white, but returned to them every evening black, having accomplished this transformation during the course of the day. But by what means this significant change was effected he could not precisely ascertain; for the places to which these creatures resorted for the purpose were either deep holes in the earth, into which they

descended, and soon disappeared from sight, or large dark enclosures, full of fire and heat and smoke, into which no bird could follow them and live; so that all he knew of them was that everything there being black, people became blackened who remained there long enough. Alas! What sufferings men endure in their struggles to become like ourselves, it is pitiful to reflect upon! And the repetition of the endurance is not the least remarkable fact of the case. For, unhappily, the desired result appears to last for only the period of one day. These men emerge from their stone boxes next morning, pallid as before, again to go forth to similar haunts, and undergo the same tortures, to bring back for the same short time the coveted colour to their cheeks!

"All these circumstances, gentlemen, fell under Mr. Raven-wing's personal observation, and of them, therefore, no doubt can be entertained. But it is fair to tell you also that he did, in the course of his travels, hear of another class of facts, highly corroborative of these, but of which, as depending upon hearsay evidence, I cannot so positively speak. That hearsay evidence went to show that there are, already existing in the world, a class of men whose black colour remains with them for life–nay, who transmit it to their offspring, so effectual have been the means used by their ancestors in acquiring it! Singular and interesting as this circumstance is, if true, I do not wish to dwell upon it. Imperfect evidence is the one thing in the world on which no fair inquirer likes to build.

"On the other hand, Mr. Yellow-beak's mission was to obtain proofs of man's endeavour to resume his life in trees; and of this some very interesting instances were adduced. In the same cities or towns which were the seat of Mr. Raven-wing's investigations. Mr. Yellow-beak discovered narrow, upright, and very much elongated brick boxes, no thicker than the stems of our large trees, and in many cases strongly resembling them in formation, only destitute altogether of branches and leaves. And out of the tops of these Mr. Yellow-beak noticed to issue those same columns of black *smoke*, as he was told it was called, which Mr. Raven-wing had observed before, and which is evidently one of the many contrivances by which man is endeavouring after a restoration to the appearance of his lost primeval state.

"Indeed, my esteemed and acute friend satisfied himself that there was, at the present day, going on among men, a series of systematic and unremitting efforts for a return to the lost forests and the original condition; of which efforts these stem-like buildings furnish a notable example. Let some ingenious plan be devised for the construction of branches on each side, and there can be no possible reason why men should not, in the course of time–but, mark me–I do say in the course of time–roost in these brick trees, as they did of yore in the natural ones. In fact, that this will eventually take place, and that men will make their homes in the branched chimneys of cities, I see no difficulty in supposing; nor that this will be one most powerful step towards a return to the common interests and hopes between ourselves and them.

"Mr. Grey-leg's information was of a miscellaneous character. He was out early one morning, near a large village, and having fixed his attention on one of those smaller boxes usually placed on the others to raise the height of the building, he all at once observed emerging from its mouth a living creature. My friends, it is a solemn and important fact that this creature was black all over. Black as a black feather coat could have made him black in his skin, black in his clothes, black in the arm which lifted itself up and waved round and round, triumphantly, something also black, and more like a bird's feather than anything else. The gesture was triumphant, and the voice scarcely less so–Sweep-o-oh! Sweep-oh! Sweep-oh! Some feeble attempt, we may suppose, at a return to the caw of their better days, yet, in its monotony, indicating a common origin of language.

"Mr. Grey-leg's observations were especially valuable, however, in his discovery of more than one place near great towns, in which attempts are frequently made, on the part of our poor degenerate brothers, towards bringing to perfection a substitute for the lost power of soaring in the air. Clumsy as the machine or balloon used for this purpose is, the mere fact of its invention forms one of the most invaluable links in the chain of evidence of man's determination to return as soon as possible to the habits and manners of his forefathers. Weary of his degradation, he is, no doubt, at the very moment we are avoiding and fearing him, longing to make known to us his sense of his misery, and to obtain assistance and hope for the future. But, among other things, the total loss of our language, consequent upon a long cessation of intercourse, remains as an almost insuperable difficulty between us. The sounds he emits now from his bill-less mouth are, in truth, an unmeaning jargon, to which it is absolutely painful to listen. It serves his present necessities, we may presume, as orders seem to be given and taken between one individual and another; but beyond this it is mere jaw, and jaw, with as little music in it as meaning.

"There is, in fact, '*neither sweetness nor sublimity, neither melody nor majesty, in the shouting, and piping, and whistling, and hissing, and barking of closely intermixed human voices and laughter.*'"

–Where am I?–where am I?–what am I about? Is some mocking echo repeating my former words? But, hush once more, for the voice is speaking again:

"This is but the faintest outline of what will be laid before you hereafter, if, indeed, we ever meet again as now. These points meanwhile are established as facts which admit of no dispute:–man's degradation from his original brotherhood with ourselves; his yearnings for re-association; his constant efforts in that direction. And for my own part, I am equally satisfied of the probability of his success in those efforts. I venture confidently to anticipate futurity, and I see him mounted in his brick-roosting home, growing wings and feathers, because they have become a necessity; while, as the long ages pass over, and his present vile habits die out from want of use, he will gradually lay aside the unmeaning jargon which he has fallen into since he ceased to be one of us, and return to the original caw of his happier state.

"Alas! My friends, that for us, personally, these bright visions cannot be realized! We shall none of us behold that glorious day! I speak it with regret. As long as we can hope to last, men will probably remain the thin-skinned, clothes-wearing creatures our grandsires remember them; still hop lop-sided on the ground, and only occasionally, and by very clumsy machines, soar into the sky. But I find no difficulty in looking forward through innumerable successions of ages to a time when men will again, through gradual successive developments of down and feathers, become swift-flying birds of the air; our friends, companions, brothers–rooks, in fact, like ourselves. All observations tend to show that a change in this direction is already at work, nay, has been so for a considerable length of time, and with increasing symptoms of success, as the observations of Mr. Raven-wing, Mr. Yellow-beak, and Mr. Grey-legs must have convinced you. All probability therefore is in favour of that success becoming one day complete.

"But, in the meantime, knowing the peculiar relations between their race and ours, and anticipating the day when they shall become one, should it not be our endeavour to . . . " . . .

–What silence is this, which has cut short the sentence, and which neither their caws nor the voice of the speaker break again? How is this?–Where am I?–Do I wake or dream?

I peep through the hedge once more, but see nothing but a bare, deserted field. Gone, gone, all gone. The green pasture lies void and empty under the setting sun. A deathlike silence is around, or so it seems to me. Only the constant honeysuckle wearies not of breathing out its sweetness round my head. Companion, where are you? Alas! No hand is clasped in mine. Alone, then, have I been dreaming some foolish dream, or is some one in secret sympathising with me still?

–Ah! Memory re-awakens by degrees. I recall the book that was lying upon my desk when I issued forth into these fields; and the thought of the first temptation of man flashes from another book upon my soul.

Woe upon us! The world grows old, and life is repeated from age to age, and the same sins are sinned. Still we desire to be as God in knowledge; still the hand writes in fire upon our walls, "Except ye become as little children, ye shall not enter into the kingdom of Heaven."

THE GENERAL THAW

"Ah! When shall all men's good
Be each man's rule, and universal Peace
Lie like a shaft of light across the land."

TENNYSON.

ICE, Snow, and Water–only think of such near neighbours–blood relations, so to speak, from the creation–squabbling about their rights and dignities, and which was best of the three; instead of living pleasantly together, giving and taking in turn, as the case might be.

But so it was, and the facts were these. It was a very, very hard winter that year, and the ice on the mill-dam grew so thick and strong, and was, besides, so remarkably smooth and fine, that it forgot its origin, and fancied itself a crystal floor.

Only think what nonsense! But there is no nonsense people will not be ready to believe when they once begin to meditate upon their own perfections.

And so, fancying himself a crystal floor, the Ice got to look down upon the Water which flowed underneath him, as an impertinent intruder; and considered it a piece of great familiarity, on the part of the Snow, to come dropping upon him from the sky.

In fact, his head was so full of his own importance in the world that it seemed to him, everybody else ought to be full of it too, and keep at a respectful distance, and admire him. And he made some very unpleasant remarks to that effect.

For instance: "I should be much obliged to you," observed he one day to the water which ran into the dam from the stream, "if you would have the goodness to turn yourself in some other direction, when you find yourself coming near me. Over the fields to the right hand, or to the left; or into the ditches, if you please; anywhere, in fact, but just under me. You fidget me to death with your everlasting trickling and movement. Pray amuse yourself in some other way, than by disturbing people in such a position as mine. I dare say you have no notion of how disagreeable you make yourself to others; you are so used to your own ways, yourself. But the truth is, I can bear it no longer, and you must carry your restlessness somewhere else–it distracts my attention from my friends!"

Now the "friends" he spoke of were the skaters and sliders, who did nothing but praise his beauty as they darted along on his surface, making beautiful figures as they went.

"But *I* wish," answered the Water, as it kept running in, "that you would not talk nonsense, but leave me a little more elbow-room, instead of pressing so close upon me that I get thinner and thinner every day. If you don't, I shall certainly break out if I can, and be at the top myself. I've no notion of being kept down by my neighbours, however grand and polished they may be. Just take care of yourself, and look out. If the springs on the moors should get loose, and the streams fill and come in here with a rush, I should lift you up like nothing, and

silly enough you would look. Turn in another direction, indeed–into the ditches if I please–many thanks for the pleasant suggestion–and all to accommodate you! Why, I should as soon think of sinking into the ground, and I hope I know my own level better than that! Meantime, I give you notice. If you won't be obliging yourself, you must expect no favour from me, and it will be good-bye to your beauty and grandeur if I can only squeeze through!"
"*If!* " shouted the Ice, in a mocking tone.
"If? Well, if!" echoed the Water in a rage. "Stiff and strong as you are, it only wants a thaw in the hills to send a torrent your way, and the whole thing's done. But what do you know about thaws, and hills, and torrents, and the force of pent-up water, fixed in one place as you are, and never getting any information?
"Now if you were to ask my advice…who know so much more than you do… and could give you a hint or two…upon yielding gracefully to necessity…it would be greatly to your advantage…But…"
But the *but* died away, and was lost; for, even while the Water was talking, some of it was freezing; and as it froze, its voice got thinner and thinner, till at last it could not be heard at all!
Meantime, the Ice got thicker and thicker, and more conceited every minute. And said he, "It cannot be worth my while to trouble myself with what is happening underneath me! There the water is, and there he must remain, let him brag and chatter as he will, he at the bottom, and I at the top. As to making out what he means by his long talk, that's hopeless. He stuck fast in the middle of the story himself. I wish he would get out of the way; but as he won't–well–there he must stay, I suppose–he at the bottom, and I at the top. He's all in a muddle with his *ifs* and his threats. But one cannot expect firmness of mind from anything so restless as he is. It needs some solidity of character to maintain one's position in life. Rolling stones gather no moss. I sit firm. And here come my friends to do me honour, I declare!"
And come they did; and in such quantities, that the mill-dam Ice had never felt half so grand before.
It was really the prettiest sight in the world! Here, were beautiful ladies in chairs, pushed along from behind by gay young men. There, other young men were skating or sliding; sometimes shooting by like stars, sometimes stooping to hit balls, which flew half across the large expanse of ice by the effort of one blow; sometimes cutting figures, which the eye could scarcely follow, so rapid and brilliant were the movements. While, in a separate corner, children were sliding and shouting, tumbling down, laughing, and getting up again, as happy as any of the others.
Really the Ice, on whom this pretty scene took place, must be excused for feeling a little vain. It seemed to him as if it was all done in compliment to himself; for, you see, he had never been at school to learn any better, and find out how insignificant everybody is to his neighbour. "That I should be treated with such honour and distinction! That I should be the supporter of such a brilliant assembly! That I should be necessary to the happiness of such crowds!"
Such were the Ice's reflections from time to time, as his friends continued their

sports. Talk he could not, for he was lost in a rapture of delight; and he felt that, as life could have nothing more to give he wished it might last on in this way for ever. Poor Ice! He thought only of himself! As to the trickling of the Water underneath him, it fidgeted him no longer. "What can I or my friends care for such trifles?" was his consolatory reflection.

So it trickled away unattended to, and presently the day closed in, and the company went away home. And then, as night drew on, the wind veered to the south, and a drizzle of snow began to fall. It was very light at first, mere snow-dust, in fact, and in the darkness the Ice knew nothing of what was happening, for feel it he could not. But by degrees the drizzle turned into flakes, which dropped with graceful delay through the air, and said to themselves as they did so, "How we shall be admired by the world when it awakes! It isn't every day in the year it's so beautifully dressed. It's only now and then it has visitors from the skies. Do let us cover it well over, so that it may find itself white altogether for once!"

Which they did; and when the morning came, not a bit of the mill-dam Ice was to be seen. Indeed, he might have gone on all day, fancying it was night (for everything was dark to him, as he lay underneath in the shade of the snow-fall), but that one or two luckless urchins, who wanted to slide, came and kicked some of it away with their feet.

And then he found out the truth. There he was, covered up with a great white sheet, and couldn't see out! His beauty, his friends, his glories, where were they now? He thought of yesterday, and his heart almost broke! Oh! Who had dared to send those miserable Snow-flakes to disfigure him thus? Never was insolence like this! The trickling of the water below was a trifle, a mere nothing by comparison!

The Snow-flakes were amazed. "We come of ourselves, nobody sent us," murmured they, as they still kept falling gently from the sky, and dropping like eider-down on the ice; "and we have the right to come where we please. Who can hinder us, I wonder? The clouds are too heavy to carry us all, so some of us come down. My sisters and I were nearest, so here we are. We don't understand your rudeness. You ought to be flattered that we choose to come–we, who are used to be carried about by the breezes, and live in the clouds! But such a reception as this, why, it hurts the feelings, of course!"

"*The feelings* " shouted the Ice, half-ready to crack with vexation; "you to talk of feelings, who have flung yourselves uninvited on my face; beggarly wanderers as you are, without house or home; and have spoilt my beauty and happiness at once!"

He couldn't go on; the words stuck fast as he tried.

"Beggarly wanderers!" echoed the Snow-flakes, almost losing their temper as they repeated the words: "Now see what comes of being low-born, and envious, and vile. See what it is to live in the dirty hole of an earthly world! You don't know the good when it comes to you, you dreary, motionless lump of ignorant matter! Beggarly wanderers, indeed! This to us, who are carried about by the breezes, and live in the clouds of the sky! Dear us! Who would lower themselves to your level by choice? And beauty–you talk of beauty, as if we could find any here but what we bring ourselves. Fancy the beauty of dingy, dirty stuff like this earth of yours! But, of course, you know no better; and, what is worse, you won't learn when you might. Oh dear, what it is to be low-born, and envious, and vile! Oh dear, what it is to belong to the winds and the skies, and to find one's self in an alien land!"

"If the winds and the skies are so fond of you, let them come and take you away," cried the Ice. "I ask only one thing–Be gone! Be gone with your mincing conceit and your beauty, you are not worthy that I should hold you up."

"You braggart! We should like to hide you and cover you over forever," muttered the Snow-flakes. "And we don't intend to go for your pleasure and whim. Here we are, and here we shall stay, let you squall and bawl as you will. We at the top, and you at the bottom; and there you may remain!"

And such seemed likely to be the case; but by and by, when all the clouds had passed over, and no more snow was falling, and the sun had begun to shine, a party of skaters and sliders came and stood on the bank of the dam.

And said they one to another, first, "What a pity!" and then, "But the snow is not very thick;" and then, "It surely might be shoveled away if we had but two or three men with shovels and brooms." So they sent for two or three men with shovels and brooms, and these swept and shoveled, and shoveled and swept, till a great space of the ice was left clear, and the snow was laid in heaps on the sides.

It was a very hard case for the snow! Such a poor, soft, delicate thing to be so ill-used–it was really cruel work! Pushed, and flung, and dirtied, and shoveled about till she was ready to melt with self-pity.

But there is no helping one's fate, so she lay along the sides of the mill-dam, grumbling and groaning–the only satisfaction she could get.

"So inhospitable to visitors, anyhow," cried she; "and so stupid to visitors like us! But this comes of leaving one's station to mix with things below. And to soil my lovely colour with their hateful besoms and brooms! And to squeeze me, and throw me about with their odious shovels, as if I was dirt! Ah! We who belong to the sky should never come near the earth, that's very clear. People here don't know what it is to be delicate and refined. Oh, mercy! What comes next?"

She might well exclaim. The party of sliding boys had quarreled–a sort of fun-quarrel among themselves. So there was just now a rush to the side of the dam, a seizing and pommelling, and squeezing of snow into lumps by a dozen active little hands; and then the balls were let fly in every direction; and some hit necks, and others faces, and others jackets, and others caps: and all got messed and broken, and thrown about. There is no knowing when the fight would have ended, if the skaters had not interfered.

The scattered, begrimed morsels could not utter a single word. But the Ice talked fast enough. "Now you have got your deserts," cried he, gaily. "Now you see what it is to come and boast over your betters. Oh, you're too delicate and refined for earth, are you? Well, then, keep in the sky. Nobody wants you here–I told you that before. See, now, you have to sit in a corner, and watch how the world admires me! You wanted to hide me forever, did you, you poor, soft, foolish thing? But my friends knew better than that, and now you've got your deserts. I shall have you all in order one of these days. You and the water below, with his fidgety spite. What a droll idea it is! Why, you *both* want to be at the top, if–poor dears–you only could. And you can't see–poor blind things–that *I 'm* the only one fit to stand alone!"

"We will soon see to that," growled the Water from below, and surely rather louder than usual. "I feel what I feel, and you'll feel it presently, too. If I can't stand alone, I can bide my time. We both want to be at top, do you say? And who are both, if you please? Are you classing me, with my strength, and that flimsy snow together? What a judge you must be!"

"As if strength was the only merit!" murmured what still remained of flaky snow on the ice. "What a coarse, earthy notion! But it 's just what one might expect; they're all alike down here, Water and Ice and all. No fit companions for us; but we've found that out too late. We lowered ourselves to come down–the more 's the pity, I'm sure!"

Were there ever three creatures so silly as the Water, the Snow, and the Ice? I dare not answer, No.

Well, before the day was over, the skaters had asked each other, as they passed and repassed, "Was there not a softness on the ice?" "Was not the snow less crisp?" But all was perfectly safe, so people did not stop to talk then: only, as they went home, they agreed that a thaw was coming.

Which remark, the Ice, not hearing, knew nothing about. So he never suspected why the water underneath was more fussy than ever, but thought it was all out of spite to himself; so he raved and scolded away; boasting that his friends should one day help him to get rid of it, as they had done just now of the snow. "It's a great thing to have powerful friends!" cried he, triumphantly.

But the water gurgled and giggled, and made no answer.

The truth was, that one or two springs in the hills had got loose from a few hours' thaw; and a strong stream, though not a torrent, was pouring into the dam. And presently there was a cry for room.

"More room! More room! Make much more room? You stiff-necked Ice, do you hear?"

And now the contest began. "I shall not give way an inch, you noisy vagabond Water!"

–"If you don't, I shall wash you away!"

–"You shall wash the world away first. *I* shall maintain my position."

–"We shall see about that in a minute."

And so they went on, while the Snow-heaps whimpered at the sides: "What a coarse-minded couple they are! What it is to be low-born and vile! We are quite unfit to be here!"

Meantime, the water poured in, and kept swelling more and more; till at last there was a heaving upward–in spite of all he could do–of the crystal floor; and by and by a sharp crack rang along its surface, from one end to the other.

He could not maintain his position after all!

And now came another, and another, and these were along the sides, as the lift-up came; and at one corner in oozed the water itself. It had no chance of bragging, however: for as fast as it touched the surface it froze, and was turned to ice.

So this was all the Water could do then, for the thaw in the hills had stopped. But the Ice never rallied again, because of those horrible cracks. He was laughed at on every side–he, who had boasted so much! For the Water below and the Snow above, who were ready enough to tease each other at other times, were willing to join together now in spiting a common foe. Such is the way of the world!

And when a real general thaw came in the air, and all over the country, as it soon did, and the sliders and skaters withdrew–oh, dear, those were dismal days for the poor deserted Ice! "My friends forsake me," cried he, "and my foes rejoice! Those cracks have broken my heart! I believe it is melting away."

And it was; but the Snow-flakes were the first to disappear, and then the Ice became wet outside. And said he: "The water has squeezed through, I declare! This comes of keeping bad company; but, anyhow, the Snow-flakes are gone, and that's civil at least. They did what they were asked, and that's something."

Now the Water had not squeezed through, and the Snow-flakes had not been civil; but the cleverest people make mistakes sometimes.

And presently the Water below found the pressure upon him not quite so great. There was a little more room to move in. So said he: "Dear me! This is good. My friend the Ice is giving way. 'Better late than never,' we'll say. He's coming to reason at last."

But the Ice was not coming to reason–he was only melting away. And as he got thinner and thinner, he struggled less and less with the Water; and said he, "We shall all live to be friends and neighbours at last, I believe."

But they lived to be far more than that, for one day they found themselves brothers! For when the Ice got so thin that the water poured over the sides, it broke into a thousand fragments, and went rolling and tumbling about, dissolving away every minute. And the snow-heaps which had stuck on the sides fell in too, and they all rolled about together, Ice and Snow and Water in one. And they wept, and rolled, and tumbled, and tumbled, and rolled, and wept; and cried they, "What have we been doing? What folly have we been talking? Scolding, and thwarting, and boasting, when, my friends–my dear, dear friends–we are all of us brothers together!"

It was a long and happy embrace: it is going on still! But, oh! What a pity they did not find the truth out sooner! Let those who are brothers by nature think of this, and not wait for *The General Thaw*–Death.

THE LIGHT OF LIFE

"Except the Lord build the house, their labour is but lost that build it."–PSALM cxxvii. I.

"WHAT more could have been done for it than I have done!" The cry came from an afflicted heart.

It was uttered by Hans Jansen, the Hamburgh printer's only son, as he sat moaning over a dying rose-tree in the corner of a little back-yard behind his father's house.

Hans Jansen was what is commonly called *not all there;* that is, he could not see and comprehend the things of this life as his neighbours did. More than half of what passed around him was hidden from his eyes. He was in part, though not altogether, an idiot.

It was a great distress to his parents that this should be the case–it had been so once, however. But being good Christians, they had reconciled themselves to it, and learned by degrees, to see comfort through the cloud. If Hans was below the rest of the world in some ways, he was above them in others. The fear of God and the love of his neighbour had come to him almost as an instinct; at any rate, without the struggles some people have to go through before their hearts are touched by either one or the other. He wouldn't have missed saying his prayers night and morning, or grace at meals, to please an emperor; and an unkind word about any one could never be got out of him. Truly their Hans was ripening for a better state of existence, whether he had any book-learning or not. He had nothing to fear, but everything to hope for, from death.

And he had one passion–one special cause of enjoyment and delight. He doted on flowers, and was seldom seen without one in his button-hole all the summer through. But this was because his good nature had made him many friends, who took a pleasure in seeing him pleased, and gave him a nosegay when they could. It was very well known that he had no garden of his own.

Mr. Jansen's house was a red brick one, in a row, with a square enclosure in front, covered with pebbles, and a square yard at the back, which had a pump in the middle, and a dog-kennel on one side. It is true this yard was covered with soil, and there were scrubby patches of grass upon it here and there; but it was used for a drying-ground, and had never once been brightened by flowers since the day it was first parceled out and the walls were built round it, across which were now stretched the lines on which the linen was hung to dry.

The fact was, Mr. Jansen had not wished for a garden. He was busy from morning to night at his printing business in the town; his wife had quite enough on her hands in household cares; and no effectual work could be expected from an idiot child.

How Hans came to be so fond of flowers was a mystery; but there are many mysteries of this sort in the world. It had been so from his baby-days, and many were the hours he had spent, unnoticed, in a corner of that back-yard, grubbing in the old black soil, "making believe" to have a garden with beds and walks like those he had seen elsewhere. Nay, once or twice he had tried to grow mustard and cress, and even sweet-peas, a few seeds of which were given him by a neighbour's child; but somehow or other, nothing ever came of these real attempts, and he had to make himself happy with the make-believe garden at the end.

But it was no make-believe plant he was wailing over now, but a real Géant de Batailles rose-tree, which had been given him many weeks before. It was thus: A good-natured nursery gardener, who knew his father, had let him walk through his grounds one flower-show day, before the company came; and having, by chance, noticed poor Hans sobbing from excitement at sight of the glories round him, his own heart melted; for he had an only and clever son himself, and he felt sorry for the darkness over his friend's child. So when Hans was going away, he gave him, not only a nosegay of the tulips and hyacinths, but a fine young rose-tree in a pot; "as fine a Géant de Batailles as had ever been raised," said he to Hans, as he offered it; adding that it would flower in six or eight weeks, and brighten all the place up by its rich blaze of colour.

Hans trembled as he received it, and he stood with his mouth half open, irresolute and abashed, wanting to speak, yet not daring.

"What is it, boy?" asked the nursery gardener. "Speak out."

"How do you make your flowers so beautiful?" gasped Hans, half afraid of what he had said.

"Well, well," returned the nursery gardener, with a smile, "some in one way and some in another; but we don't tell our secrets to everybody. Nevertheless, I'll tell you how to make your rose beautiful, for you'll make no bad use of anything, I'll be bound. You've a yard or a court, or some place with soil in it, eh?"

"Yes, yes," cried Hans.

"Then I'll tell you what you must do," pursued the nursery gardener. "Dig a hole in a sheltered place, pretty deep, you know, and put in a bone or two, and some hair (my son shall give you a handful) at the bottom. Then turn the plant out of the pot, not disturbing the ball of earth for the world, remember; and set it right down upon the hair. Then fill up the hole neatly with soil, and say nothing about what you've done to anybody, and there's an end. Keep it sheltered, mind, and water it at first, or if you see it get very dry; and with soapsuds whenever you can get them. Soapsuds and bones and hair are the main things. There 's nothing like them for bringing roses to perfection. You'll have flowers as big as a hat, and as bright as cherries before the summer's over, if you do as I say, and look well after the plant. There! Good luck to you and it! Good-bye."

And this was the plant–this, poor wizened thing–over which Hans was moaning. But how had it come to this? That was the difficulty. The gardener's son had given Hans the hair, and he had found the bones–there were plenty by the dog-kennel; and he had dug the hole and put them at the bottom; and he had turned the plant out of the pot, and not broken the ball of earth; and he had placed it upon the hair, and filled up the hole; and watered it at first, and whenever he saw it get very dry, and with soap-suds on a wash-day; for he had only to ask and have, without question or trouble. He had done everything, in short–surely everything! For he had put it in the most sheltered spot he could find–in the self-same corner where he had played at make-believe gardens as a child; and it seemed as if an old dream were suddenly come true. And as to looking well after it, could a miser have watched his gold with more jealous care? And no one had interfered; for he had told nobody, partly from some indefinite idea that the nursery gardener had ordered him not; partly because he thought it would be so nice to surprise his mother, some day before the summer was over, by the rich blaze of colour that was to brighten all the place.

The very maid who hung out the clothes in the yard didn't know of it; for to keep the secret, and make the shelter of the tree more complete, he had set up boards across the corner where it was planted, from wall to wall, and no one could see what was there. They looked upon the boards as some idle freak of the idiot mind.

It was the buds that failed first; those buds which ought to have swollen and grown larger day by day. Even his eye, sharpened now by anxious care, could detect that they rather dwindled than increased in size; and, observing this more and more as time went on, he one day summoned courage to walk to the Nursery Gardens, and tell his fears to the giver of the plant.

But he, when he found that all he had ordered had been done, only smiled.

"I tell you again," said he, "and from long experience, there's nothing like bones and hair for bringing roses to perfection. You can't go wrong with them. Give it a little more water or soapsuds. You've perhaps a light soil in your place. Give it more water. The buds will swell fast enough, I'll be bound. Indeed, I fancy you're watching it so closely you can't see true. It's easy enough to do that, I can tell you. The buds are grown, I suspect, though you don't think so. Leave it to itself. Don't fancy anything wrong. It's sure to be right with bones and hair and soapsuds. They're the finest rose-manure in the world."

Hans listened with his mouth open, nodded his head, with a "Thank you!" at the end, and went away, hoping he had not "seen true." And he did not take the boards down nearly so often afterwards, lest his watching too closely should do harm. But every time he did take them down, he grew more and more unhappy. The healthy green of the leaves was no longer to be seen; as for the buds, they shriveled gradually more and more. Growth anywhere there was none. Inch by inch the plant was dying–or Hans thought so, and he rubbed his eyes for further light in vain. And one day, when the last leaves which remained had crinkled up and turned brown, he sat down on the ground, and wailed, as I have said:

"What more could I have done for it than I have done?"

The dream of a dream come true at last, was over. The make-believe garden was still the only one he had ever enjoyed. He must go back to it again.

He replaced the boards, for he shrank from the very sight of the dying plant, and sat down on the ground again, though he scarcely knew why.

But presently there was a barking of the dog, and an opening of the door, and a shouting of "Hans!" by his mother. The nursery gardener was passing that way, and had called to admire the roses he expected to see. Hans could not speak, but led the way to the corner of the yard, and, when they were there, he pointed to

the boards before he took them down, and exclaimed, trying to smile through his tears:
"I couldn't have sheltered it more, could I? It's never been scorched, or chilled, or blown upon, even. It's had bones, and hair, and water, and all you ordered, and I've looked well after it, and yet it's dead, I know!"
As he spoke, Hans lifted down the boards, and exposed the withered tree.
The nursery gardener stared at it, and then at Hans, in genuine amazement.
"You don't mean to say you ye kept it *so* all the time?" cried he. "Why, what have you been thinking about, man? How could you expect it to live? Why, it's had no light!"
"You said nothing about that," replied Hans, his face distorted with bewilderment and grief. "You said you made roses beautiful with bones, and hair, and soapsuds, and that I should make mine beautiful with them too."
"But not without sunshine," shouted the nursery gardener, quite excited at the idea of such a mistake.
Hans made no answer. He could not utter another word. He sat down on the ground again and hid his face in his hands.
"I must have spoken like a fool," exclaimed the nursery gardener, half to himself. "But who'd have thought of anybody fancying a plant could get on without light? Well, perhaps I ought to have thought though," added he, as his eye fell on poor Hans' doubled-up figure. Then, laying his hand on the lad's shoulder, it came into his heart to try and explain matters.
"Look up, Hans," said he. "It's not your fault at all–it's mine. There was something I forgot to tell you. I spoke like a fool when I talked of making roses beautiful with manure and things like that, as if they could do it themselves. I didn't mean that. It is God who makes the roses, you know, and He makes them so that they can't do without the light He chooses them to live in, and that's the light from heaven–do you see?"
Here the nursery gardener paused to consider how he must go on, and Hans shuffled a bit, and then looked up at his friend. And his friend saw the light from heaven streaming on that sad, half-intelligent face, with the red eyes straining upwards for comprehension; and he proceeded.
"So they can't do without God's light, let you give them what manure you will. They're only helps, Hans, such things as those."
"A man may help or hinder what God intends, by good or bad management, it's true; but that's all, and that's all I meant. Bones, and hair, and soapsuds are the finest rose manure in the world, that's true too, and it's a great secret; but they're all nothing–nothing, lad!–without God's secret–the light from heaven. Do you see what I mean, Hans?"
"I'm trying," said Hans.
"Hans," continued the nursery gardener, "it's been my fault, not yours; and you shall have another rose-tree, or we'll save this one yet, for if there's a bit of life left in it, God's light may bring it round. But tell me, now. You are a very good lad, you know, at times–indeed, I fancy always; but no matter, we'll call it at times. What makes you ever good?"

Hans' catechism had been short, but sound; and he answered at once, "God's grace."
"Now that's just it!" shouted the nursery gardener, in delight. "That's just what I meant. And all the schooling, and teaching, and trying in the world won't do without God's grace, will they, Hans?"
Hans nodded his negative assent.
"No, they're only manures and helps," pursued the nursery gardener, "and very good things, no doubt, the same as bones, and hair, and soapsuds for roses, and there's nobody can dispute about them. But all the helps in the world can do nothing without the main thing God chooses them to thrive by, and that's God's grace for a man, and God's light for a plant; and what one is for one, that the other is for the other, and it's my opinion it's the light of Heaven for both."
If Hans did not quite follow the thread of the nursery gardener's argument he must be excused. The nursery gardener understood what he meant himself, and that was something; and Hans added to his small stock of observations the useful truth he had bought so dearly, viz., that plants cannot live without light.
Those who are interested further in his fate will be glad to hear that the nursery gardener soon after turned one side of the old printer's back-yard into a garden, at his own expense, and gave Hans such plants and help that both mother and son had a few bright flowers of their own the next year to delight their eyes.
But more than this. The poor lad proved so watchful and attentive; so obedient, too, to advice in his own small matters; and the rational occupation to an end seemed so evidently to clear something from the confusion of his mind, that it struck the nursery gardener one day to trust him with some little employment on his more important premises. And the experiment was not unsuccessful. On the one subject of flowers Hans became not only trustworthy but intelligent.
And so it came to pass, that it was in the nursery garden, among the flowers–his only idea of an earthly paradise–that the poor idiot ended his days. There, guileless as the beautiful creatures which surrounded him, and trustful as the Highest Wisdom could have made him, he lived; and thence did the spirit, so long pent in an imperfect earthly tabernacle, return to the great Lord of life and light and intelligence, without whom "nothing is strong, nothing is holy."

GIFTS

ONE–two–three–four–five; five neatly-raked kitchen-garden beds, four of them side by side, with a pathway between; the fifth a narrow slip, heading the others, and close to the gravel walk, as it was for succession-crops of mustard and cress, which are often wanted in a hurry for breakfast or tea.

Most people have stood by such beds in their own kitchen-gardens on soft spring mornings and evenings, and looked for the coming up of the seeds which either they or the gardener had sown.

Radishes in one, for instance, and of all three sorts–white-turnip, red-turnip, and long-tailed.

Carrots in another; and this bed had been dug very deep indeed–subsoil digging, as it were; two spades' depth that the roots might strike freely down.

Onions in another. Beet in the fourth; both the golden and red varieties; while the narrow slip was half mustard and half cress.

Such was the plan here, however; and here, for a time, all the seeds lay sleeping, as it seemed. For, as the long smooth-raked beds stretched out dark and bare under the stars, they betrayed no symptoms of anything going on within.

Nevertheless, there was no sleeping in the case. The little seed-grains were fulfilling the law of their being, each after its kind; the grains, all but their inner germs, decaying; the germs swelling and growing, till they rose out of their cradles, and made their way, through their earthen coverlid, to the light of day.

They did not all come up quite together, of course, nor all quite alike. But as to the time, the gardener had made all his arrangements so cleverly, that none was very far behind his neighbour. And as to the difference of shape in the first young leaves, what could it signify? It is true the young mustards were round and thick; the cresses oval and pointed; the carrots mere green threads; the onions sharp little blades; while the beet had an odd, stainy look. But they all woke up to the same life and enjoyment, and were all greeted with friendly welcome, as they appeared, by the dew, and light, and sunshine, and breezes, so necessary to them all, children of one mother, dependent on the same influences to bring them to perfection.

What could put comparisons, and envyings, and heart-burnings into their heads, so filling them either with conceit or melancholy misgivings? As if there was but one way of being right or doing right; as if every creature was not good after its kind, but must needs be good after somebody else's kind, or not be good at all!

It must have been some strolling half-informed grub, one would think, who had not yet come to his full senses, who started such foolish ideas.

It began with an inquiry at first, for no actual unkindness was meant.

"I find I get deeper and deeper into the soil every day," remarked the Carrot. "I shall be I don't know how long, at last. I have been going down regularly, quite straight, for weeks. Then I am tapering off to a long point at the end, in the most beautiful proportions possible. A traveler told me, the other day, this was perfection, and I believe he was right."

(That mischievous vagabond grub, you see!)

"I know what it was to live near the surface in my young days," the Carrot went on; "but never felt solid enjoyment till I struck deeply down, where all is so rich and warm. This is really being firmly established and satisfactory to one's self, though still progressing, I hope, for I don't see why there should be a limit. Pray tell me, neighbours," added he, good-naturedly enough, "how it fares with all the rest of you. I should like to know that your roots are as long, and slim, and orange-coloured as mine; doing as well, in fact, and sinking as far down. I wish us to be all perfect alike. Perfection is the great thing to try for."

"When you are sure you are trying in the right way," sneered a voice from the neighbouring radish bed (the red and white turnip variety were always satirical). "But if the long, slim, orange-roots, striking deep into the earth, are your idea of perfection, I advise you to begin life over again. Dear me! I wish you had consulted us before. Why, we stopped going down long ago, and have been spreading out sideways and all ways, into stout, round solid balls ever since, close white flesh throughout, inside; and not orange, but red without."

"White, he means," shouted another.

"Red I call it," repeated the first. "But no matter; certainly not orange!"

And "Certainly not orange!" cried they all.

"So," continued the first speaker, "we are quite concerned to hear you ramble on about growing longer and longer, and strongly advise you to keep your own counsel, and not mention it to any one else. We are friends, you know, and can be trusted; but you really must leave off wasting your powers and energy in the dark inside of the ground, out of everybody's sight and knowledge. Come to the surface, and make the most of it, as we do, and then you'll be a credit to your friends. Never mind what travelers say. They've nothing else to do but to walk about and talk, and they tell us we are perfection too. Don't trust to them, but to what we tell you now, and alter your course at once. Roll yourself up into a firm round ball as fast as you can. You won't find it hard if you once begin. You have only to–"

"Let me put in a word first," interrupted one of the long-tailed Radishes in the same bed; "for it is of no use to go out of one extreme into another, which you are on the high road to do if you are disposed to take Mr. Roundhead's advice; who, by the way, ought to be ashamed of forcing his very peculiar views upon his neighbours. Just look at us. We always strike moderately down, so we know it's the right thing to do, and that solid round balls are the most unnatural and useless things in the world. But, on the other hand, my dear friend, we have learnt where to stop, and a great secret it is, but one I fear you know nothing about at present; so the sooner you make yourself acquainted with it the better. There's a limit to everything but folly–even to striking deep into the soil. And as to the soil being better so very far down, nobody can believe it; for why should it be? The great art is to make the most of what is at hand, as we do. Time enough to go into the depths when you have used up what is so much easier got at. The man who gathered some of us yesterday called out, 'These are just right.' So I leave you to judge whether some other people we know of must not be wrong."

"You rather overwhelm me, I own," mused the Carrot; "though it's remarkable you counselors should not agree among yourselves. Is it possible, however, that I have been making a great mistake all my life? What lost time to look back upon! Yet a ball; no, no, not a ball! I don't think I could grow into a solid round ball were I to try for ever!"

"Not having tried, how can you tell?" whispered the Turnip-Radish persuasively. "But you never will if you listen to our old-fashioned friend next door, who has been halting between two opinions all his life: will neither make an honest fat lump of it, as I do, nor plunge down and taper with you. But nothing can be done without an effort; certainly no change."

"That is true," murmured the Carrot, rather sadly; "but I am too old for further efforts myself. Mistake or no mistake, my fate is fixed. I am too far down to get up again, that's certain; but some of the young ones may try. Do you hear, dears? Some of you stop short, if you can, and grow out sideways and all ways, into stout, round, solid balls."

"Oh, nonsense about round balls!" cried the long-tailed Radish in disgust; "what will the world come to, if this folly goes on! Listen to me, youngsters, I beg. Go to a moderate depth, and be content; and if you want something to do, throw out a few fibres for amusement. You're firm enough without them, I know, but the employment will pass away time."

"There are strange delusions abroad just now," remarked the Onions to each other; "do you hear all this talk about shape and way of growth? And everybody in the dark on the subject, though they seem to be quite unconscious of the fact themselves. That fellow chattered about solid balls, as if there was no such thing as bulbs, growing layer upon layer, and coat over coat, at all. Of course the very long orange gentleman, with his tapering root, is the most wrong of the whole party; but I doubt if Mr. Roundhead is much wiser when he speaks of close white flesh inside, and red (of all ridiculous nonsense) without. Where are their flaky skins, I should like to know? Who is ever to peel them, I wonder? Poor things! I can't think how they got into such ways. How tough and obstinate they must be! I wish we lived nearer. We would teach them a little better than that and show them what to do."

"I have lived near you long enough," grumbled a deep-red Beet in the next bed; "and you have never taught me; neither shall you, if I can help it. A pretty instructor you would be, who think it ridiculous to be red! I suppose you can't grow red yourself, and so abuse the colour out of spite. Now I flatter myself I am red inside as well as out, so I suppose I am more ridiculous than your friend who contrives to keep himself white within, according to his own account; but I doubt the fact. There, there! It is a folly to be angry; so I say no more, except this: get red as fast as you can. You live in the same soil that I do, and ought to be able."

"Oh, don't call it red!" exclaimed a golden Beet, who was of a gentle turn of mind; "it is but a pale tint after all, and surely rather amber than red; and perhaps that was what the long-tailed orange gentleman meant."

"Perhaps it was; for perhaps he calls red orange, as you call it amber," answered the redder Beet; "anyhow he has rather more sense than our neighbour here, with his layer upon layer, and coat over coat, and flaky skin over all. Think of wasting time in such fiddle-faddle proceedings! Grow a good honest fleshy substance, and have done with it, and let people see you know what life is capable of. I always look at results. It is something to get such a body as I do out of the surrounding soil. That is living to some purpose, I consider. Nobody makes more of their opportunities than I do, I flatter myself, or has more to show for their pains; and a great future must be in store."

"Do you hear them? Oh! Do you hear them?" whispered the Cress to her neighbour the Mustard (there had been several crops, and this was one of the last); "do you hear how they all talk together of their growth, and their roots, and their bulbs, and size, and colour, and shape? It makes me quite unhappy, for I am doing nothing like that myself–nothing, nothing, though I live in the same soil! What is to be done? What do you do? Do you grow great white solid balls, or long, orange tapering roots, or thick red flesh, or bulbs with layer upon layer, and coat over coat? Some of them talked of just throwing out a few fibres as a mere amusement to pass away time; and this is all I ever do for business. There will never be a great future in store for me. Do speak to me, but whisper what you say, for I shame to be heard or thought of."

"I grow only fibres too," groaned the Mustard in reply; "but I would spread every way and all ways if I could–downwards and upwards, and side ways and all ways, like the rest. I wish I had never been sown. Better never sown and grown, than sown and grown to such trifling purpose! We are wretched indeed. But there must be injustice somewhere. The soil must give them what it refuses to us."

"Or we are weak and helpless, and cannot take in what it offers," suggested the Cress. "Alas! That we should have been sown only to be useless and unhappy!"

And they wept the evening through. But they alone were not unhappy. The Carrot had become uneasy, and could follow his natural tastes no longer in comfort, for thinking that he ought to be a solid round ball, white inside, and red without. The Onion had sore misgivings that the Beet might be right after all, and a good honest mass of red flesh be more worth labouring for, than the pale coat-within-coat growth in which he had indulged. It did seem a waste of trouble, a fiddle-faddle plan of life, he feared. Perhaps he had not gone down far enough in the soil. Some one talked of growing fibres for amusement–he had certainly not come to that; they were necessary to his support; he couldn't hold fast without them. Other people were more independent than he was, then; perhaps wiser–alas!

And yet the Beet himself was not quite easy; for talk as he would, what he had called fiddle-faddle seemed ingenious when he thought it over, and he would like to have persuaded himself that he grew layer upon layer too. But it wouldn't do.

Perhaps, in fact, the bold little Turnip-Radishes alone, from their solid, substantial growth, were the only ones free from misgivings, and believed that everybody ought to do as they did themselves.

What a disturbance there was, to be sure! And it got worse and worse, and they called on the winds and fleeting clouds, the sun, and moon, and stars above their heads, to stay their course awhile, and declare who was right and who was wrong; who was using, who abusing his gifts and powers; who was making most, who least, of the life and opportunities they all enjoyed; whose system was the one the rest must all strive to follow–the one only right.

But they called and asked in vain; till one evening, the clouds which had been gathering over the garden for days began to come down in rain, and sank swiftly into the ground, where it had been needed for long. Whereupon there was a general cry, "Here comes a messenger; now we shall hear!" as if they thought no one could have any business in the world but to settle their disputes.

So out came all the old inquiries again: who was right–who was wrong–who had got hold of the true secret? But the Cress made no inquiry at all, only shook with fright under the rain; for, thought she, the hour of my shame and degradation is come; poor useless creature that I am, I shall never more hold up my head!

As to the Carrot, into whose well-dug bed the rain found easiest entrance, and sank deepest, he held forth in most eloquent style upon the whole affair; how it was started, and what he had said; how much he had once hoped; how much he now feared.

Now, the Raindrops did not care to answer in a hurry; but as they came dropping gently down, they murmured, "Peace, peace, peace!" all over the beds. And truly they seemed to bring peace with them as they fell, so that a calm sank all around, and then the murmur proceeded: "Poor little atoms in a boundless kingdom–each one of you bearing a part towards its fullness of perfection, each one of you endowed with gifts and powers especially your own, each one of you good after its kind–how came these cruel misgivings and heart-burnings among you? Are the tops of the mountains wrong because they cannot grow corn like valleys? Are the valleys wrong because they cannot soar into the skies? Does the brook flow in vain because it cannot spread out like the sea? Is the sea only right because its waters only are salt? Each good after its kind, each bearing a part in the full perfection of the kingdom which is boundless, the plan which is harmony–peace, peace, peace, upon all!"

And peace seemed to fall more soothingly than ever upon the ground as the shower continued to descend.

"How much more, then," resumed the murmur, "among you, to whose inner natures gifts and powers are given, each different from each; each good in its kind; each, if rightly carried out, doing service in that kingdom, which needs for its full perfection, that there shall be mountains to rise into the skies, valleys to lie low at their feet; some natures to go deep into the soil, others to rejoice on its surface; some to lie lightly upon the earth, as if scarcely claiming a home, others to grasp at it by wide-spread roots, and stretch out branches to the rivers; all good in their kind, all bearing a part in the glory of that universe whose children are countless as their natures are various–none useless, none in vain.

"Upon one, then, upon all–each wanted, each useful, each good after its kind–peace, peace, peace, peace, peace!" . . .

The murmur subsided to a whisper, the whisper into silence; and by the time the

moon-shadows lay upon the garden there was peace everywhere.
Nor was it broken again, for henceforth even the Cress held up her head–she, also, good after her kind.
Only once or twice that year, when the Carrots were gathered, there came up the strangest growths–thick, distorted lumps, that had never struck properly down.
The gardener wondered, and was vexed, for he prided himself on the digging of the carrot-bed. "Anything that had had any sense might have gone down into it, he was sure," he said. And he was not far wrong; but you see the Carrot had had no sense when he began to speculate, and tried to be something he was not intended to be.
Yet the poor clumsy thing was not quite useless after all. For, just as the gardener was about to fling it angrily away, he recollected that the cook might use it for soup, though it could not be served up at table–such a shape as it was!
And this was exactly what she did.

NIGHT AND DAY

IN old times, long long ago, when Night and Day were young and foolish, and had not discovered how necessary they were to each other's happiness and well-being, they chased each other round the world in a state of angry disdain; each thinking that he alone was doing good, and that therefore the other, so totally unlike himself in all respects, must be doing harm, and ought to be got rid of, altogether if possible.

Old northern tales say that they rode, each of them in a car with a horse to it; but the horse of Night had a frosty mane, while that of Day had a shiny one. Moreover, foam fell from Frosty-mane's bit as he went along, which dropped on the earth as dew, and Shiny-mane's mane was so radiant that it scattered light through the air at every step. And thus they drove on, bringing darkness and light over the earth in turn–each pursuing and pursued; but knowing so little of this simple fact, that one of their chief causes of dispute was, which was going first. For of course if they had been able to settle that, it would have been known which was the more important of the two. But as they drove in a circle the point could not be decided, since what was first on one side was sure to be last on the other; as anybody may see who tries to draw their journey. They never gave this a thought, however, and there were no schoolmasters about just then to teach them. So round and round the world they went, without even knowing that it was round, still less that there is no such thing as first and last in a circle. And they never succeeded in overtaking, so as to pass each other, though they sometimes came up very close, and then there was twilight.

Of the two, one grumbled and the other scolded the most, and it is easy to guess which did which. Night was gloomy by nature, especially when clouds hid the moon and stars, so her complaints took a serious, melancholy tone. She was really broken-hearted at the exhaustion produced all over the world by the labours and pleasures which were carried on under the light of day, and used to receive the earth back as if it was a sick child and she a nurse, who had a right to be angry with what had been done to it. Day, on the contrary, was amazingly cheerful, particularly when the sun shone; never troubled his head about what was to happen when his fun was over: on the contrary, thought his fun ought to last for ever because it was pleasant, was quite vexed when it was put a stop to, and had no scruple in railing at his rival; whose only object, as it seemed to him, was to overshadow and put an end to all the happiness that was to be found.

"Cruel Night," he exclaimed, "what a life you lead me! How you thwart me at every turn! What trouble I have to take to keep your mischief in check. Look at the mists and shadows I must drive on one side, before I can make the world bright with my beautiful light! And no sooner have I done so than I feel your cold unwholesome breath trying to come up to me behind! But you shall never overtake me if I can help it: though I know that is what you want. You want to throw your hateful black shadow over my bright and pleasant world."

"*I* doing mischief which *you* have to keep in check!" groaned Night, quite confused by the accusation. "I, whose whole time is spent in trying to repair the mischief other people do: *your* mischief, in fact, you wasteful consumer of life and power! Every twelve hours I get back from you a half worn-out world, and this I am expected to restore and make as good as new again, but how is it possible? Something I can do, I know. Some wear and tear I can renew and refresh, but some, alas! I cannot; and thus creep in destruction and death."

"Hear her," cried Day, in contempt, "taunting me with the damage I do, and the death and destruction I cause! I, the life-giver, at whose touch the whole world awakes which else might lie asleep for ever. She, the grim likeness of the death she talks about, and bringing death's twin-sister in her bosom."

"You are Day the destroyer, I Night, the restorer," persisted Night, evading the argument.

"I am Day the life-giver, you Night the desolator," replied Day, bitterly.

"I am Night the restorer, you Day the destroyer," repeated Night.

"You are to me what death is to life," shouted Day.

"Then death is a restorer as I am," exclaimed Night.

And so they went on, like all other ignorant and obstinate arguers, each full of his own one idea, and taking no heed of what the other might say. How could the truth be got at by such means? Of course it could not, and of course, therefore, they persisted in their rudeness. And there were certain seasons particularly when they became more impertinent to each other than ever. For instance, whenever it was summer, Day's horse, Shiny-mane, got so strong and frisky that Night had much ado to keep her place at all, so closely was she pressed in the chase. Indeed, sometimes there was so little of her to be seen, that people might have doubted whether she had passed by at all, had it not been for the dew Frosty-mane scattered, and which those saw who got up early enough in the morning.

Oh, the boasting of Day at these times! And really he believed what he said. He really thought it would be the greatest possible blessing if he were to go on forever, and there were to be no Night. Perhaps he had the excuse of having heard a whisper of some old tradition to that effect: but the principal cause of the mistake was, that he thought too much about himself, and too little about his neighbour. "Fortunate world," cried he; "it must be clear to every one, now, who it is that brings blessings, and does good to you and your inhabitants. Good old earth, you become more and more lovely and fruitful, the more and more I shorten the hours of Night and lengthen my own. We can do tolerably well without her restoring power it would seem! If we could be rid of her altogether, therefore, what a Paradise there would be! Then the foliage, the flowers, the fruits, the precious crops of this my special season would last forever. Would that it could remain uninterrupted!"

"He is praying for a curse. Were it granted no life could exist," murmured Night; and Frosty-mane's dew fell in tears as she spoke. No one heard her, however, but the dew was very acceptable, for the weather was very hot.

And she had her revenge; for when it was summer on one side the globe it was winter on the other; and then it was her turn to boast, as it was in winter that Frosty-mane came out in all his glory; every now and then running his car so nearly side by side with that of Day, that he squeezed him up into the smallest possible compass, besides putting out half his light. On which Night kept up a sort of murmuring triumph: "Good, good, very good; this is something like rest at last; now worn-out Nature is recruiting herself to some purpose. Now weary muscles may gather strength instead of giving it out. Now strained eyes may recover brightness, and worn brains energy. Now all the secret forces of Nature are at work, and exhaustion is being repaired on every side. Now trees and plants may keep their gases for themselves, and earth hold her own. Now waste and consumption cease, for the wear and tear of life have stopped. Ah, if it could but cease forever! Then the world would be renewed, indeed, and giant races of man and beast and plant arise!"

"But never glow with the light of active life, or be seen but in the pale unmeaning moonlight," sneered the mortified Day, but he struggled in vain to make himself heard. The truth is he was in the background just then, and nobody cared to listen. Yet he made his presence known from time to time at midday, by the light of Shiny-mane's hair. Nothing could quite put that out, even in winter when the weather was fine; and sometimes it shone over the ice and snow so brightly that they glittered like diamonds or might almost have been taken for fireworks.

And so things went on till a check came, and it came in a very odd way. It is not always very easy to tell the exact causes of change even in one's own mind, much less in other people's, so I do not pretend to trace the whole process out in this case. But Night and Day did grow wiser as time went on, for, as every one knows, there is no squabbling or boasting going on between them now. On the contrary, they glide after each other as gently and sweetly as possible, without any kicking of horses or rumbling of chariot wheels. And one may conclude that after the first flush of feeling cooled down, they were better able to look round them and judge dispassionately of each other. And, lo and behold! They discovered at last that there were just two portions of the globe, where each had in turn his own way as nearly as possible for six whole months at a time; viz., at the Poles; and that yet, nevertheless, the brilliant consequences which they had insisted would occur under these circumstances, never took place. On the contrary, those were the dreariest and most desolate portions of the whole globe–barren wastes of ice and rock, where both animal and vegetable life were at the lowest possible ebb. Nothing could be more mortifying, it must be owned. In vain did Shiny-mane drive round and round that frozen horizon with a light that was never interrupted: where was the promised Paradise which was to follow? The foliage, the flowers, the fruits, the precious crops which should have adorned this unchecked reign of Day, where were they? The dove would have sought in vain here for even a shrub on which to rest her foot. Scarcely a wandering seagull ever disturbed the death-like stillness of the air. Day, the life-giver, looked down upon a kingdom without life! What wonder if he began at last to distrust himself! What wonder if he went on to suspect that there might be some truth in what Night had said after all! That she might in some way or other be Night the restorer; in some way, however mysterious and unaccountable, be

necessary to his own prosperity.
And it was the same with Night, when her turn came round. In vain did Frostymane distil his dews. They were useful–at least Night thought so–everywhere else; but here, what did they avail? Here was the unbroken rest which was to recruit and refresh all Nature: now her secret powers might work as they pleased: there was no waste of power now either from labour or heat, or any other destructive cause: but where were the giant races of man and beast and plant that were to arise in consequence? The wear and tear of life had stopped, but what was the Earth advantaged? Night, the restorer, ruled, but over a kingdom where there was nothing to restore! Well might tears mingle with her dews. Well might she call to the morning stars to bring back that Day whom once she had dreaded as a rival, but now longed for as a friend. Day the life-giver, he had called himself, and Day the life-giver perhaps he was. Certainly without him she could do nothing; at any rate here, where he was not, the whole world was a blank!
They had made a terrible mistake, that was clear; and if they did not at first see that there must be other and more important powers at work, besides theirs, or the good old earth would not be what it is in most places, they must be excused. People cannot grow quite wise all at once, and they had made a very good beginning by learning to distrust themselves, that being always the first step towards doing justice to a neighbour.
"I called you Day the destroyer, bright and beautiful friend," murmured Night, in her softest tones; "you who bring light over my shadows, and make my good deeds known to all men. Day, the life-giver, forgive me, and return at the seasons appointed. Touch the earth with your glory from time to time, lest all things perish from its face, and it and I are forgotten together."
"But I mistook your friendly shadow for that of death," answered Day, with his sweetest smile, though tears trembled in his eyes as he thought of the injustice, causing the brightest of rainbows to span the landscape below; "and that was a thousand times worse! You, in whose silence and rest the very fountains of life are renewed. Ah, while earth remains what it is, an everlasting day–a day without night–would be destruction! Dear friend, forgive me, and ever and ever return."
"There is nothing to forgive," whispered Night, as she came round once more. "And death also may restore as I do," added she, tenderly; for the harvest moon was shining upon long fields of golden corn, some waving still, some gathered into sheaves; and she felt particularly hopeful about everything.
"Any how we are friends–loving, helpful friends," sang Day.
"Friends–comforting and abiding friends," echoed Night, in return, as the weary world sank on her bosom; eyes closing, limbs relaxing, and flowers folding, as if the angel of rest had come down from heaven.
And friends they were and remain, though long ages have passed away since the time the old northern tales tell of; and though now the wise men will not allow that Night and Day drive round the world in cars with horses to them. Well, perhaps they don't. Perhaps it is really true that the earth is a dark ball, hanging

in the open space which we call the firmament of heaven, moving slowly round the shining sun, but spinning like a top all the time itself, so that first one side and then the other faces the brightness; and thus there is a constant change from light to darkness and darkness to light going on all over the world; and this makes Day and Night. But no matter which way the changes come, Night and Day are the work of the Lord; and, like all the other "works of the Lord" which the three children in the fiery furnace called upon to praise Him, have a voice, and say many things worth listening to, especially now that they are no longer young and foolish. And from time to time, according as we keep our ears open or shut, little streams of melody do float round us from the natural world, as musical sounds break out from the strings of an old-fashioned harp when the wind blows over it; or sweep along the wires of the electric telegraph on breezy days. Listen only, and you will hear. And which speaks you can surely guess, for they praise each other now and not themselves. One sings–

"Dear Night, whom once I dreaded as the dark end of life and enjoyment. Dear Night, whom now I know as the forerunner of life renewed. Welcome, blessed restorer; take our worn-out child to your bosom. Drop over her striving and straining your mantle of repose. All her day-labourers grow weary, for a portion of life goes from them, in the toil of limb and of muscle, in the working of eye and of brain; in all the changes that circle round an ever-changing world. Restore what thou canst and mayst, let the rest remain in hope; for the mercy thou bringest now, foreshadows a greater in store. Oh, type of the mighty change which must one day pass upon all; of the deep, mysterious rest in which all things shall be renewed; of the needful, hopeful death which quickens unto life! Dear Night, my sister and friend, the twilight shades approach, and I see in thankful peace your darker shadows beyond."

And the other answers in turn.

"Dark and secret my mission; men call me Night the gloomy; but I hold in my bosom the germs of a glory full of hope: hiddenly working within, till thou, the life-giver, returnest, to break through the mists and shadows, and touch my nurslings with light. So, at the first creation, at the touch of the first young dawn, lo! Gleams of life universal were lit all over the world, and nature, amazed, awoke in songs of thanksgiving and joy.

"So come, then, Day the life-giver, ever and ever reviving the slumbering germs I nourish, the hidden life I feel. Welcome for this, but thrice welcome as type of a dayspring eternal, that shall dawn at last on the night of sin and sorrow and death; when, our secret missions accomplished, our secret workings completed, thou and I, oh, life-giving Day, shall merge our blessings in one: when the light that never wastes, and the life that never wearies, shall be one with the rest eternal, that remaineth evermore!"

KICKING

"Rebellion is as the sin of witchcraft."–I SAM. xv. 23.

THREE years of complete liberty, and then to have to learn in three short weeks to submit entirely to the will of other people!

This sounds a hard plan of education, and perhaps is not the very best one possible. Still, thousands of young colts have turned into good horses upon it; and if there is to be a reform, it must come from above, not from below. Reforms from below savour of rebellion, and that is sure to lead to a reaction the wrong way again.

Yet people ought not to blind themselves–those above, I mean, any more than those below. Every man, therefore, ought to sit from time to time in his neighbour's chair, and look with his neighbour's eyes, from his neighbour's position, at what he himself is about. It is wonderful how much wiser, as well as kinder, people grow if they do this.

And among a man's neighbours he should not be ashamed to reckon the creatures he collects round him for his own convenience and amusement, and calls his "domestic animals." Why "domestic," but that he has taken them from their own natural homes, and brought them to his? And if so, surely it is not too much to ask that he should give them, each in his degree, the comforts of a home-citizenship, in return for the duties he exacts. If he does this honestly, a few errors of judgment on his part will not matter more than a few errors of conduct on theirs; for imperfection has not only to be struggled against, but borne in this world.

Sitting in neighbour Firefly the spirited young chestnut colt's chair, then, it is but fair to own that he may well have felt it queer, after three years' luxury of doing as he liked in large grassy pastures, to find himself suddenly cooped up in a small square stuffy place, ceiled in instead of open to the air, and surrounded by walls, to one particular part of which he was fastened by a horrible contrivance that went round his head and neck, and gave him a most unpleasant pull whenever he tried to get away. But yesterday he was free as the wind, so far as the hedges extended–could gallop from one to the other while his breath lasted; might snort at the passengers in the road which skirted the field as much as he pleased; throw out his legs at everything and everybody; kick, plunge, bound, jump, till he was tired; whinny at his companions, whether he had anything worth saying or not; and all this at will: while now–but the contrast is too painful to dwell upon, for Firefly was now in a horse-breaker's stable, with a halter round his neck.

He had one consolation, however, and it is not a small one to most people–indeed it ought always to be a matter of thankfulness to all–he was extremely well fed. It is true the very delicious grain he had now been champing at three separate meals to his heart's content, with his nose bent over the manger, had been very dearly purchased by the loss of his freedom the morning before. The wild driving he had undergone from the field to the stable-yard, with the treacherous capture at the end, still rankled in his mind, and the cruel outrage to his young heart's nervous shyness, when hands of violent men overcame him, and the fatal noose was slipped over his head, was not to be forgotten. Still taste is taste; the food remained delicious all the same, and he was so young, he could enjoy the present, irrespective of the past or future.

But all feeds of corn come to an end at last; and at the end of the first he began to fidget, after the second he grew angrily impatient, and when he had swallowed the third, he became what is called (archaically) *rampageous*, for in point of fact the good corn had begun to warm his blood. It was very high living compared to the cold grass he had been used to.

Now, as was natural, one of the first things he did was to call out for his old companions of the field, and this he did in colt's fashion of course; but what colt's fashion really is will not be known till men become good linguists, and have learnt other languages besides those of their own race. At present they are miserably backward in that branch of learning, and have no idea even of what flies talk about, though they hear them murmuring away in the air, as soon as they themselves awake every summer morning, and for nearly all day after.

Well, in colt's fashion Firefly shouted for his companions, and after two or three attempts, each of them louder than the one before, must have made himself heard; for at last he was answered, though from what seemed a great distance, so smothered were the sounds. But this was only because they came through stonewalls. In point of fact, his young friends, Whitefoot and Silverstar by name, were very near–namely, in the very next adjoining stable–both of them captives like himself; both of them with halters round their necks, one in one stall, one in another.

Conversation was difficult under such circumstances, and could not be carried on for long. What they did say, when they discovered they were near each other, amounted to about this:

"So you are somewhere hereabouts, too, Whitefoot and Silverstar. Why don't you come where I am? Where are you?"

"We don't know where we are. Where are you? Why don't you come to us?"

"Because something twitches my head if I try to move away; so I can't."

"That's just what happens to us; so we can't."

"It's abominable!"

"It's very distressing."

"I wonder what it means! I am very angry."

"We wonder too, but it can't be helped."

Here the dialogue ended, for the colts were not the only inhabitants of the two stables. In the one, with Whitefoot and Silverstar, was a good-tempered, middle-aged, Welsh pony, known all over the countryside as good old Taffy. In the other, with Firefly, was an old, half-bred white Arabian mare, whose mother had been brought from the East.

Old people who talk to young ones should think of the young ones more than themselves. If they want to gossip and grumble, and let off vexed feelings, let them do it to each other. Life is very trying sometimes as age comes on, and

those of the same age can understand the feelings of the age, and make allowance for the groanings of the natural man. But young creatures may easily be led away by a few sad or passionate words, into believing all sorts of nonsense. I say, then, let old people unburden their personal feelings to each other, but never talk anything but useful sense, or pleasant nonsense, to a child.
Had the old white mare in the stable thought of this, it would have been better for Firefly; perhaps, at least, he would not have had the same encouragement to turn out unmanageable which she now gave him. For no sooner had he uttered the words, "I wonder what it means! I am very angry," to his companion next door, than she shook her own halter till the rattle roused his attention, and then observed, in a tone of melancholy which was of itself quite impressive: "I can tell you what it means, but I am afraid when you know you will not be less angry than now, but rather more."
Firefly's quick blood ran quicker at the startling announcement.
"Oh, dear, what makes you say so? Who can you be?" cried he in excitement.
"One who ought to know something, if age and experience can instruct," answered the sorrowful old mare, adding in a lower tone still, "or if unusual opportunities in early life have not been lost upon her."
"I am almost afraid of hearing, yet suspense is intolerable," cried Firefly. "Where am I? What is going to happen?"
"You are a prisoner, at the mercy of those who shut you up," answered the old mare, to whose monotonous existence the power of lashing a young colt up to indignation was rather an amusing novelty. "It is the first time this has happened to you, I suppose?"
"It is the first time I was ever made fast in this way," groaned Firefly. "If I was ever in an enclosure before, it was loose by my mother's side. My memory is confused so far back."
"I, too, had a mother once," murmured the old mare, Egeria; and her grief in thinking how long ago made her pause.
"Tell me about her," exclaimed Firefly; "what became of her? I want to know."
"What a tone you speak in," answered Egeria. "You want to know! You forget you are a prisoner, and must learn to want nothing but what is given you."
"I shall never learn that," cried he; "and why am I a prisoner? Tell me that."
"Because the people you belong to want to make you useful–useful to them, that is."
"And why must I be useful to them? Why may I not please myself as I have done before? What are they to me?"
"Ask them," said Egeria coldly. "They will tell you–masters, superiors."
"You provoke me," cried Firefly, stamping into the straw at his feet. "Tell me why I am here, as you promised. My former history is short enough, as you shall hear. I–"
"Spare yourself the trouble," interrupted Egeria. "Our histories in this country are all alike. We are left to ourselves for nearly three years, and are taught nothing; then our superiors get hold of us, by fright and force, and in three weeks make us learn everything they want."

"And then?" gasped Firefly.
"And then it depends upon the people into whose hands one falls, whether one is well or ill-used."
"And you have borne all this in patience?" asked Firefly.
"I had no heart to act otherwise," sighed Egeria. "I felt no spirit to resist."
"But I feel plenty of spirit, and shall resist," cried the young chestnut, straining against the halter as hard as he could bear, and dashing his legs against the sides of the stall, first on one side, then on the other.
"But what can you do?" whined Egeria, a little startled by his violence.
"Do?" shouted Firefly; "why, I shall kick, kick, kick!" And each time he uttered the words he struck out against the wooden partition between the stalls. Egeria began to be alarmed.
"I do not advise it," she said; "I assure you it will do no good. You had better bear it all as well as you can."
"Oh, that is all very well for those who can receive it, old lady," exclaimed Firefly: "I can't. I can't stand injustice; and what's more, I won't. Why, my blood is boiling already. Only to think of the way they drove us along before they got us here. Of course, if I had known, I should never have left the field. And the still worse fright those men gave me when they all laid hold of me and threw this horrible thing over my head! It's all treachery and injustice from beginning to end."
"Ah! If we were but in my mother's country!" sighed Egeria.
"Why, what then?" inquired Firefly.
"Oh, my poor young friend, I'm afraid it will do more harm than good to tell you," said Egeria, "yet, if you wish it so very much, I hardly know how to refuse."
The old goose, to consent to tell what she felt might do harm! But she was vain of knowing more than other people on the subject, which she really did. Besides which, she wanted to stop Firefly's kicking and plunging, by holding his attention. So said she–
"The people there–in the East, I mean–treat young colts quite differently from the people here. As soon as ever they can leave their mothers, they are brought among the tents, where the men, women, and children live, and the women take care of them, and feed them, and pet them. So they get used to their masters from the first, and there is not the fright and horror and startling change to go through which we suffer so much from at the end of our first three years; and so the halter, and teaching, and all that sort of thing, come much easier–though, of course, restraint is restraint everywhere. But, for pity's sake, don't begin to kick again," concluded Egeria, interrupting herself at the sound of renewed struggles on Firefly's part. "I have been telling you my mother's story to keep you quiet."
"Quiet!" shouted the miserable colt. "I won't be quiet, to please anybody. How can I be quiet, when I want to get away from this savage country, and go to that other one–that East you talk of–where colts are properly managed?"
"But my dear young friend, consider–it's too late," expostulated Egeria. "You can't begin life over again. You really mustn't let your feelings run away with

you in this foolish way. People here don't mean badly, altogether. They are tolerably kind, on the whole; at least, some of them are. They feed you well, as you see; and after you have learnt what they teach, you will be glad, though you won't like it while it's going on."

"Then it shan't go on!" shouted Firefly. "They shan't teach me! I won't learn! I won't have their food, or their kindness! If they had brought me up properly, I could have submitted as well as anybody; but they have been unjust, and now I won't! I'll do something–I'll go to the East; and if I can't go to the East, I'll kick!"

"Oh, hush–do, pray, hush!" said Egeria, who, to do her justice, had merely wanted to excite a sympathetic grumble, not to rouse a storm. "You go much too far, I assure you."

"You say that because you have no spirit, you poor old creature!" exclaimed Firefly. "You know you haven't–you said so yourself, just now; but that's no rule for me."

"If I have not much spirit," remarked Egeria, "I may have some sense, and I want you to have some too. You can't get away, to begin with–so the East is out of the question; and you cannot resist these people to any purpose–so, take my advice, submit and have done with it. I can tell you from long experience, that kicking is never of any use."

"Then I shall go on kicking, out of spite, because it's of no use," cried Firefly; and as he announced this grand resolution, he broke out all over into a profuse sweat from excitement.

At which moment the stable-door opened, and the horse-breaker stepped in, just to have a look at the colt; and after doing so, and observing his irritable and uneasy condition, said he to himself, "I shall have a good deal of trouble with this one, I'm afraid."

Now, in saying this, he was making a sort of comparison between Firefly and the other two; for he had just been in the next stable, and seen Whitefoot and Silverstar unusually placid and quiet–for fresh-caught colts, that is to say; nobody expects from a kitten the gravity of a cat. But what wonder? Besides that they were greys, and therefore easier-tempered by nature than was to be expected from a chestnut (for in horses, colour and disposition are apt to go together), they had been hearing nothing but good advice ever since they were shut up–and, what is more, they had actually been attending to it!

But then, good old Taffy gave his good advice in such a very pleasant way! "My dear friends," cried he, when he heard them plunging about in their stalls at first, "I do feel so sorry for you–so very, very sorry–because I know so well what you suffer. Just the same was done with me when I was your age."

"Oh, how did you bear it?" asked the colts.

"Well, well, I was very impatient just at the beginning," answered Taffy; "for my Welsh blood made me chafe at the confinement, and I was alone, and had nobody to explain the meaning of it all to me, so it was hard work; and this makes me particularly glad to be here just now to help you. I can tell you a great deal that will comfort you, and plenty more that will surprise and amuse you very much. There are two sides to everything, even to things that vex one, I

assure you! But, quiet! Quiet! Dear friends, I do beg," continued he, as he heard more plunging and shaking of halters, "or I shall not be able to say another word!"
"We will be quiet," cried the colts, for they liked the idea of being surprised and amused, as who does not?
Then Taffy told them they were not brought here to be teased to death, as they had perhaps supposed, but to prepare them for being taught a thousand nice things which they would never be able to do if they were not taught, and which it was immensely jolly to be able to do, when the teaching was once over; and he proceeded to hold forth on the pleasures of trotting, cantering, and galloping over the country, with a good feed of corn, a comfortable stable, and a valet to rub one down at the end; as also the delightful excitements of racing and hunting, which even he had enjoyed, though only as a looker on; but he added that they couldn't have a share in all this, without first learning to obey their masters, and love them a little bit too.
Whereupon both colts shuddered all over, for the fright of the men who had shut them up was very great, and love seemed perfectly impossible.
"Ah! You can't bear the thought of this, I see," cried Taffy. "Well, of course, if it could be, one would like to have no master but oneself–eh, my friends?"
To which both Whitefoot and Silverstar agreed, with a whinny of satisfaction.
"But what is the use of fretting oneself, by wishing for what can't be," pursued Taffy. "These men and women are, though I don't know how, or why, our masters and superiors, and I know from my own experience, that we are happiest when we submit to their wishes with a good grace; when we struggle and resist we are miserable."
"But suppose they wish something cruel and unjust?" sighed Silverstar.
"But who is to decide what is so?" asked Taffy in return. "Many things seem so that are not; your being here against your will for instance–you will be so glad about it by and by, when the teaching is finished."
"It is comfortable to hear that," murmured Silverstar. "Is the teaching itself very unpleasant?" asked Whitefoot.
"Very," cried Taffy at once, at the mere recollection of it, and the colts shuddered again. "But here I am," he continued, "none the worse, and all the better, and as happy as possible, with a man or woman, or a little child on my back three or four times a week, and a pet with all the family. Oh! You have no notion how good-natured these men very often are–bringing one tit-bits both in the stable and field–bread, or apples, or carrots, or clover, which one takes out of their hands. But for pity's sake don't begin kicking again," cried he, as he heard them flinging wildly about, at the notion of men coming so near. "Why, you surely wouldn't kick at kindness? You must meet it half way, when it's offered, you foolish fellows, or you may live to want it before you die! But, don't alarm yourselves! You won't be able to be on these intimate terms with masters and superiors, till you've learnt to be well mannered and obedient. But my experience tells me they are kind when we are good; and where they seem otherwise, I try to believe it is because we don't understand the meaning of what

they are doing–with superiors one can't expect that one should."
A word spoken in season, how good it is! The colts grew calmer and calmer as Taffy went on, and when, in conclusion, he told them a story about a good-natured lady, who used to bring him handfuls of oats in reward of a pretty trick he learnt of opening the stable door with his nose, they half began to believe that these men and women were not, after all, such dreadful creatures as they had supposed.
And as it was just then that the horse-breaker entered the stable to look at them, it is not to be wondered at that they bore his presence with only about half the horror they would otherwise have felt, and so kept tolerably quiet.
And thus a week went on, Taffy encouraging them by his own example and experience, to bear what was coming with patience and in hope.
And he could but speak from his own experience, poor Taffy! Let us trust, then, that in these "days of advance," there are fewer and fewer exceptions to the rule that a docile horse makes a kind master. Shame on the master if it does not!
It was at the end of the first week that the real trial began for all three colts, and a trial indeed it was! They have hard hearts who would deny it. Those heavy iron bits forced into the young, tender mouths; so stiff against their teeth, so cold against their flesh, how horrible they were! And the bridles that pulled at them, forcing the poor heads to turn hither and thither, for mere whim's sake, as it seemed (for whatever reason there was for it, they could not find it out)–what a cruel contrivance! Then the long whips, which kept them at one distance all the time, so that, as they were forced to move on continually, they had no choice but to go round and round in a circle forever–how irritating! My heart bleeds when I think of it and imagine the two long hours of struggle on that first dreadful day. How severe the trial must have been to them–must ever be to all!
Worse still, however, when in the course of a few days, the corners of the mouths became sore from the pressure of the iron, and there was, for a time, the pain of a raw wound, as well as a day-by-day longer time of restraint to endure. Masters and superiors, verily, there is a great responsibility in your hands! Nevertheless, it is not for the colts to sit in judgment.
Now, then, how fared the three colts under the terrible but, at present, in some way or other, necessary training? (For even Egeria could not answer Firefly's maddened inquiries, by saying that in the East the bit and bridle and whip can be dispensed with.) Well, Whitefoot and Silverstar set out by intending to submit if possible, and therefore, though more or less cheerfully at some times than others, and with more or less pain to themselves, they contrived to manage it at last.
Firefly, on the contrary, started by a sort of 'resistance-on-principle' plan. Wishing to resist, in fact, he always found a reason for resisting. If people treated him properly he could submit as well as any one else, he was sure; but if they ill-used him, what could they expect but that he should kick–kick–kick? And as to what proper treatment was, he made himself the sole judge. Certainly the training process just described was not proper, but on the contrary cruel and unjust, and accordingly kick, kick, kick he went, whenever it was possible.
In vain Egeria begged him to forbear, seeing too late how much mischief her

folly had done.
"It is so senseless to resist when you can't help yourself," said she.
"It is so mean to yield to an unjust necessity!" cried he.
And she dared not contradict herself so far as to suggest, that it might not be so unjust as it seemed.
"Will you listen to me once more?" asked she, one day.
"If you talk sense, yes," replied Firefly, "not otherwise, old lady."
Egeria sighed; for his pert folly was but a stretched-out shadow of her own. Imperfect judgments; judgments formed on half-known grounds; judgments formed by the lesser intelligence concerning a greater which it cannot comprehend–what rebellion and ruin have they not caused!
"It is sense, if you have sense to find it out," cried Egeria, sharply; "It is downright wisdom. What I am going to say is truth and fact."
"I hear you; go on," said Firefly, impatiently.
"Well, if you go on kicking in this manner, every time you think you have–I beg your pardon–every time you have a reason for kicking, you know, you will get into such a habit of kicking, that you will do it whether you have a reason or not."
"Shall I!" shouted Firefly, with contempt.
"Yes, you *will* though!" persisted Egeria, vexed alike by his obstinacy and ridicule. "If you kick every time you can find or make an excuse, you will be very apt to kick on when you have none."
"I have never yet kicked without a reason, old lady, and I don't intend to do so," answered Firefly.
"I know, I know," replied Egeria, "so far you have always proved yourself right *to yourself:* what the horsebreaker thinks is another matter. But, dear friend, try and believe me–habits are such tremendous things! If you don't get into a habit of giving way, you mayn't be able to give way when you want, that's what I am afraid of. Those who indulge themselves in kicking at all, will sometimes kick when they would give worlds to forbear."
"How can that happen to me, when I never kick without a reason?" cried Firefly.
At which moment he was fetched from the stable for a morning's lesson, and Egeria was left to fret alone. For fret she did, not being a bad creature on the whole, but such an inconsiderate old simpleton, both in her way of viewing life and talking about it to others!
And alas! There was but too much cause for fretting, when at the end of five weeks Firefly remained still untamed–still in the horse-breaker's hands! A fortnight ago both Whitefoot and Silverstar had taken leave of the place, had finished their education with respectability, and gone out into the world on their own account. There are plenty of good masters to be found for docile, well-taught creatures, and they had been picked up at once by two neighbouring families, and often met in their rides, and talked over old times. Egeria heard this from Taffy, who, from being constantly out, learnt all the news of the countryside, and had once or twice met his friends himself; and it must be owned she regretted Firefly's conduct all the more, that she feared she had had some

share in it herself.
When Firefly was led out of the stable after Egeria had spoken, he had, for a few minutes, a misgiving that there might be some truth in what she had said. But the first crack of the horse-breaker's whip made his heart as hard as ever. He had accustomed himself for so long to look upon it and him and the whole affair as a system of barbarous injustice, that he could not have rid himself of the notion without a strong effort, and there was one great difficulty to his making it– namely, that he must acknowledge himself to have been in the wrong before. And alas! Hhe did not make it; and so another week went on, at the end of which the horse-breaker lost patience, and told Firefly's owner he was a hopeless kicker, and a very ill-conditioned animal as to temper, though otherwise with many good points, and a valuable beast.
It was not very pleasant news to the owner, but Firefly was so handsome in appearance, and moreover, so strong and able to work, that he was undertaken at last by a very fearless young squire, who cared for little but pace and beauty, had a seat like a rock, put his faith in a strong curb, and had no scruple in using his spurs.
What Firefly underwent in his hands I do not wish to describe, though, even there, if he would but have submitted, his fate would not have been bad, for if the master loved his galloping, so did Firefly himself. But again and again he would refuse to obey the curb if it checked or turned him suddenly when his face was set elsewhere; and then like an instinct came the impulse to kick, kick, kick! and he followed it. For an hour sometimes the two would battle together–the spur and the whip and the curb, against that insane determination to kick, kick, kick! And as to be conquered by main force and exhaustion is not to be reformed, Firefly was led away bleeding and foam-covered to his stable, as savage as when he left it, and still repeating the old strain, "If people treat me properly, I can submit as well as any one else; but if they don't, what can they expect but that I shall kick, kick, kick?" Like the horse-breaker's whim of driving him round in an everlasting circle, seemed the young squire's whim of checking him, and turning him round when he didn't expect it, and wanted to go straight on. He kicked, therefore, strictly on principle, and all the more when the injustice was enforced by the spur and the lash. So the squire got tired of his purchase, and Firefly was sold again.
But this time to a very knowing hand, a country doctor, who after trying different plans in turn–low feed and good feed, kindness and severity, and finding both unsuccessful, took him back to the horse-breaker. "He seems very hopeless at present," remarked he; "he kicks for nothing. But there is one more chance. Break him in for harness. Kicking-straps will perhaps bring him to his senses. At any rate, try; he has many good qualities, and is a fine fellow. I hope he'll do well."
The horse-breaker shook his head, and led Firefly back to his old stable. Another colt occupied his former stall, but there were still two vacant. He was led into the middle one, and before nightfall Egeria was brought into the third.
Firefly told his story at length, and was too eager to hear Egeria's shuffles of

impatience. "How unfortunate some people are!" observed she, when he ended; but there was a slight mockery in her tone.

"I have been so all along," said he; "I believe I am fated to ill-usage."

"People always are who will go nobody's way but their own," was Egeria's answer; "why don't you do what is wanted? Go the way your master pulls you, and give up fighting for your own."

"If people treat me properly, I can submit–"

"Oh, do stop!" cried Egeria, "I've heard that much too often. You never do submit."

"Because they never–"

"Oh, they, they, they! Would they be masters, if you, and not they, were to lead the way?"

"Oh, as to masters, perhaps I have my own opinion," cried Firefly; "I wonder who has been master of the two I have had! But no matter about that. I could have borne leading, but I wouldn't be dragged. It was the curb and spurs and whip of that young squire I kicked against."

"And of your last master, the doctor, when he was kind?" asked Egeria.

"He wasn't always kind," muttered Firefly.

"But when he was?" insisted the old mare.

"Fool!" murmured Firefly, between his teeth; "was I likely to go his fidgetty way–stopping at one house then at another; no sooner started than having to stop; twisted down one lane and up another, never having a good run all the time; I, who had galloped over half a countryside in a morning with the squire? Kick? Why who wouldn't kick at a life like that?"

"It is as I feared," exclaimed Egeria. "Anybody who wants to kick, can find a reason for it, of course." And she spoke not another word, for she did not understand the matter to the bottom, as Taffy did, and her way of argument was, therefore, not convincing.

The first thing in the morning, however, Firefly spoke to her. He had a question to ask. Did she know what *kicking-straps* were? Perfectly; what made him want to know?

He repeated what the doctor had said.

"Capital!" said Egeria. "If you are put into those you will never be able to kick again."

"We shall see about that," groaned Firefly, grinding his teeth as if he were champing oats. "Masters–masters–masters indeed!"

In which state of mind he was taken out, two hours afterwards, put into kicking-straps, and had his first lesson of going into harness. The plan answered at first; but this was only while the shock of surprise and helplessness lasted. Still, being rather less wild, the horse-breaker returned him as "fit for harness, if driven in kicking-straps;" and Egeria twitted him when he left her, as being "fairly caught at last." "We shall see about that," muttered Firefly, fuming to himself, as the doctor drove him home. But the kicking-straps were amazingly strong, and he restrained himself. Nevertheless, the first principles of submission had not entered his head, and Egeria's folly and ridicule had done all that an unwise friend could do to confuse the truth.

The truth? Ah, we can only get at that by sitting in our neighbour's chair, and looking with his eyes. Had Firefly done this, he would have known why the kicking-straps were added to his harness, and have laid the blame on the right shoulders. As it was, he laid the blame on the doctor, and considered himself the victim of injustice.

So, one unlucky day, after a round of rather tiresome visiting, a very slight correction for impatience set his blood working; and, without thinking either of kicking-straps or consequences, he took the bit between his teeth, laid his ears down, close to his head, muttering; "Masters indeed!" to himself, and pulling madly at the reins, dashed at full speed down the narrow country lane. They stopped him at last at a turnpike-gate, and as the kicking-straps had given way soon after he started, he concluded the day's work by smashing the splashboard to pieces, his master escaping with difficulty.

So he was sent back to the market town, and resold.

It is impossible to pursue him through all his adventures; they were all, so to speak, variations upon the same set of notes–the battle of authority with one who refused to acknowledge its claims. A miserable struggle, whether of man or beast; whether against the powers ordained of God, or the God of power Himself; whether breaking out into open contest, or indulged in by inward repining.

At last, poor Firefly fell into the hands of a regular horse dealer, who forwarded him to a neighbourhood where his tricks were not known, and after some weeks of low diet and constant work, sold him (more shame for the fact) to a quiet country clergyman, for a birthday present for his daughter, just bursting into the beauty of girlhood.

Now, by this time, our friend Firefly had had experience enough to discover that his habit of opposition was constantly bringing him into trouble. And though he was not sick of the bad habit, he was decidedly sick of the trouble, and every now and then was vexed with himself for giving way to it. And now and then he recalled Egeria's words, "Those who indulge themselves in kicking at all, will sometimes kick when they would give worlds to forbear." Still, he could not remember a single case in which he had kicked without a very good reason–as it seemed to him–so he assured himself at least, and tried to forget that Egeria had also said, "Anybody who wants to kick can find a reason for kicking, of course!"

Now at last, however, came Firefly's halcyon days. What more could heart of horse desire than to belong to a gentle young girl, who was ready to love him, not only as her servant but companion and friend? Egeria's tales of Eastern kindness came back to his mind again and again, as his new mistress brought him delicate morsels which she would fain have had him eat from her hand; and when, as was generally the case, he could not overcome his repugnance, but started back from her caresses, all she said was, the poor fellow was nervous and shy; perhaps–who knew?–he had at some time or other been harshly treated.

"This is as it should be," remarked Firefly; and he began to think better than ever of himself. The few misgivings he had lately had went to sleep. "*I* was right, and not Egeria," thought he, as he bore his light burden over her favourite haunt, the Downs. "I was right, and Egeria wrong. I told her I had never kicked without a reason, and never should. It was nonsense about not being able to leave off."

And so he really believed, till, alas! The renewed good living brought back the impatience as well as fire into his blood, and what had he to restrain them with, who had not got the law in his heart? There followed one other week of self-confidence and enjoyment, and then…

She was not in the least to blame–that beautiful young girl who had been so kind to him. He admitted this even to himself, when he saw her stretched at his feet; the eyes that had looked so kindly at him, closed; the rich black hair surrounding the white cheeks and forehead like a pall–the groom so horror-struck when he came up, that he never thought of even laying hold on Firefly's bridle.

They had been out for a morning ride on the Downs, and she had wished to canter. For a day or two past, some evil spirit (evil spirits are so ingenious) had been whispering in his ear, that to be patronised was all very well, if it were not another form of unjust restraint. Masters? Had he not proved himself the master in every case yet? And so he had done here–here, where, as Egeria had prophesied, he would have given worlds to forbear. Now rose before him the only half-valued tenderness, the anxiety for his daily comfort, the little personal sacrifices in his favour, and this as the conclusion; that because the canter had been prolonged, and she had wished to rest, and so checked him with the bridle, the old habit had proved too strong for him, and prompted him to kick, kick, kick–and he had kicked until she was stretched at his feet.

More than an hour passed, and Firefly stood by her still. Stood in the same spot, seeing the same sight, without care to go his own way, now that he might have done it at will.

And then came the trampling of feet, horses and other men, and among them all a father in the first agony of despair. But no one noticed Firefly–he was nothing to his masters then, and so he stood on there like a horse of marble, in the same old place, looking at what he had done.

But presently some one who had been touching her wrist and had sprinkled her with water whispered, "She is coming to herself!"

And it was true. Firefly's mistress had been stunned and one arm was hurt, but she awoke again to life; and when the poor father had wept out his joy on her neck, and she had looked up, she smiled to see so near them the creature who had caused this evil. Yes, there he stood, and his eye watched hers, as it first glanced at him, and then fixed on her father's face anxiously, while she murmured, "Promise me one thing, dear father. Let poor Firefly go to Rarey to be cured."

Masters? They may well be masters and superiors, in whom the abiding spirit of forgiveness and love is triumphant! So Firefly was taken to Rarey; but what then happens to horses must be looked for in other books. This does not contain an argument on the merits of the different methods of horse-breaking; only thus much as regards Rarey's process is the turning point of the tale. The object aimed at is the subjection of the will, not merely the control of the body–the full

and complete recognition of the mastership and superiority of man. This, and this only, is what is wanted when the legs are tied up, and struggles rendered powerless by force, so that the indignant animal is brought through exhaustion of body to submission of feeling. He has plunged, he has kicked, he has reared, for hours together, if he will have it so; but the man stands by him unscathed, unruffled, and still kind–his master and superior–the terrible discipline proves it, but still kind–and the kindness proves it too.
All this Firefly went through; and when the Rarey-breaker "gentled" him all over his miserable frame, as he lay panting and overpowered on the sawdust, conquered and convinced at last, all his mistakes and misconceptions of other people came before him, as plainly as if Taffy himself had spoken them; so plainly, that he wondered at himself. But remembering his old and all-too-firmly-adhered-to resolution to kick, kick, kick, whenever he was vexed, a fresh outbreak of perspiration astonished the breaker so much, that he "gentled" and soothed the troubled spirit more and more tenderly, till Firefly could think of nothing like it but the father and daughter comforting each other on the Downs, that terrible day of his guilt.
And thus at last, he learnt that it was possible for submission and love and happiness to go hand in hand together. Firefly was cured.
And then he was taken back to a home which he helped in his degree, however humble, to make what a home should be–a circle in which animals, superior and inferior, should all work together, each after its measure and kind, for the comfort and pleasure of all.
At last, therefore, he gave a willing obedience to every touch of his dear young lady's rein: and yet he feared her no longer as before; and yet he loved her more! Which is a great mystery, but the world repeats it in a thousand forms.
Animals under man–servants under masters–children under parents–wives under husbands–men under authorities–nations under rulers–all under God; it is the same with all–in obedience of will is the only true peace.
Happy the colts who learn submission without a lifetime of personal struggle! Happy the men and women who find in the lesser obediences a practise-field of the greater; for assuredly the words of Egeria are true: "Those who indulge themselves in kicking at all, will sometimes kick when they would give worlds to forbear."

IMPERFECT INSTRUMENTS

"And others' follies teach us not,
Nor much their wisdom teaches,
And most, of sterling worth, is what
Our own experience preaches."

TENNYSON.

OVER the old church-tower passed the rooks, on their way from the neighboring trees, cawing into the fresh morning air as they went. Dew hung yet upon every stone of the building, on the bits of moss and grass which time had suffered to creep over or between them, here and there, on the edges of the tombs below. There was no one astir at this early hour of an autumn day to speak to or interrupt the dark-eyed Geronimo, as he strode hurriedly up the pathway to the porch, the church keys dangling from his hand, and slightly clanking against each other as he stepped.

Behind him followed a rough-haired country lad, but at a little distance, and silent. He had a stick in his hand, however, with which he began to whisk off the wet from the grass-blades of the graves on each side of the path; but at one turn and glance from Geronimo, he desisted. Soon the key was in the lock, the bolt had turned, grating, back; the heavy door was pushed open, the shock echoing through the building; and Geronimo and little Roger, the mason's son, his companion, were walking up the aisle; on one side of which, at the upper end, in a small transept, stood the organ and choir-seats.

Let me recall that lonely village, nestling in a narrow valley on the borders of Southern Wales, traversed by a rapid streamlet, which ran through it like a silver thread; rich in orchards, embosomed in ancient trees, where rooks had built their nests for generations; where the cuckoo's voice reverberated from surrounding hills. At one extremity was the church, at the other the quiet vicarage; so that the flock were wont to watch about their doorways for the passing by of the Pastor to his sacred office, that they might follow and enter with him into the ark of the visible church on earth, he leading them on their way. It was a pretty custom and a pleasant sight; there was a tone of loyal respect and trust about it, which social progress has, it is to be feared, some tendency to disturb.

Let me recall the old Pastor himself, in his happy, scholarly simplicity; the serenity of submission on his face, for he had undergone a life's long grief. Let me recall him in the days when the time was drawing hear for the silver chord to be broken, and when his visions brought him closer and closer to the day of re-union with his dearly-loved Italian wife, who had died when their only child, Geronimo, was but five years old. And Geronimo was now his father's curate, a youth fresh from the schools; energetic, enthusiastic, determined even to self-will, a worshipper of system and order.

The father, on the other hand, past middle-age, was old for his years, for the fire of his spirit had died out; but the power of his intellect remained unaltered, as is often the case in fine natures; and an originally widely educated judgment grew wider and gentler as the river of his life widened out to the everlasting sea. He doubted about his son's motto, therefore, as a universal rule of life. It had to be considered, said he, whether the "right" you followed, or the "consequence" you scorned, was of the greater vital importance. There was a right and a wrong–he once added as a homely illustration–in the way of cutting a pencil; but if you have to deal with a weak-leaded one, which would not bear long shoulders without breaking, it was better to cut it with short shoulders than waste it altogether. If he had to choose a motto himself, it must be from the broader teaching of St. Paul.

Geronimo listened in impatience. He thought his father's argument a letting down of principle, the homely illustration trivial, and with regard to St. Paul, everybody knew that texts could be found to support most anything.

It stood thus, then, that the father admired the son for his strength of purpose and purity of intention, yet sometimes wondered what his future would be; but that the son never properly appreciated the father, except for his amiability to himself. He thought him a kind but feeble old man, behindhand in the lights of day.

And it was true that while Geronimo had passed from school to college, his father had remained in the narrow valley; and while the kaleidoscope of public opinion was presenting fresh combinations of thought and feeling to the gaze and admiration of the ardent young, the old man was out of the circle of their influence, and judged of them afar off with the mind of a philosopher.

It was, perhaps, a rash arrangement that Geronimo should have come to be his father's Curate; but he had made the offer, and the old man had accepted it with tears of joy. There was, in fact, between them a strong natural affection, overruling all theoretical differences of opinion, as well as a strong sense of parental and filial duty. There was also, perhaps, some hope on both sides of influencing each other for good; and there was, moreover, the unspoken bond of common interest in one grave.

The triangular white marble slab on the chancel wall of the church bore upon it a name which to both father and son was still the dearest name upon earth, "Maria Maddalena:"–to the old man naturally so, who through so many years had lifted up weary, loving eyes to the golden letters in which it was traced, travelling in spirit to that heaven of heavens whither the taper central angle of the tablet continually pointed.

And the son had his own recollections–dim ones of old embraces from that mother who had so soon passed away–vivid ones of looking upwards to that tablet from his seat in church ever since he was a child–of gazing on the shining words, and the shining emblems above them, the palm branches, the cross, and the star, until their glitter first dazzled and then brought tears to his eyes. Had he tried, by gazing, to get nearer to the bearer of that golden name–the mother, whom every motherless child feels to want so much? Had he hoped to charm her back, he knew not whence, to comfort him, he knew not how?

He could not have answered himself. Children do and feel many things of which

they can give no account, and the why, matters so little in comparison with the fact.
Enough that the long-cherished habit of love to the pure white marble slab remained as firm in Geronimo's heart, as if he had been able to reason about its propriety, and justify it by argument.
Judge, then, what he must have suffered, when, on his first coming to the place as curate, he felt it his duty to ask permission of his father to have that tablet removed to some other part of the church!
Let us go back to that time, some nine months before the opening of my story, for it was the beginning of Geronimo's practical troubles.
It was a painful scene that took place; Geronimo's voice trembled as he made the request, and his father's heart-wrung "Never!" was followed by a silence equally distressing to both. Then the old man asked for reasons, and the young one gave them. The kaleidoscope had brought certain proprieties into full observation which had for some time been unnoticed–there was no doubt about that. The tablet was on a wall within the communion rails; it would have been better elsewhere. Private memorials were inappropriate there. Geronimo thought them inappropriate in the church anywhere–the father disputed this–it was the ark of the dead as well as of the living; but were the matter to be done over again, he would place the stone without the rails in preference; as it was, there was no vital principle involved–no sufficient reason, therefore, for the desecrating act of removal.
The son returned to the argument. His father had admitted the objection; was it not then clearly an act of duty to sacrifice personal feeling to the example of right–whether the right were small or great?
"Measure me the measure of right," cried the troubled father, "as compared with the impressions it will cause. You cannot drive straight lines through life without knocking over good feelings as well as bad ones, and woe to those who knock down what little there is of good in the world!"
"The right way is a narrow way," replied the son; "to trim to the prejudices of the ignorant is to sacrifice principle to man-pleasing." There was more said in the shape of argument than needs to be repeated here–let every one fight the matter out as he will. On the following day, the father had come to a resolution.
"When I am gone," said he to his son, "and my name is added to hers on the tablet, you may remove it to where you will; and even now, if, on hearing this, you remain offended, you may remove it at once. I warn you, however, that it is my belief your doing so will cause evil rather than good among those whose souls' health you are bound to consider. You cannot get them to understand your motives, and they will abominate the act. What you lose will be far more, therefore, than what you will gain. Of my personal feelings I say nothing. On that point I suspect we suffer together. Now, then, do as you please."
If the father hoped, by yielding a point so trying to himself, to set Geronimo an example of giving way, he deceived himself. Geronimo did not accept what he said as an example, but as an acknowledgment of an error that needed rectifying. About any consequences to other people he refused to think at all. Consequences

were nothing in matters of duty and principle.
So he went to Roger, the village-mason, explained what he wanted, and gave his orders, announcing his intention of coming himself to assist. But the man stared in astonishment. "You ben't in earnest surely, sir?" said he. "Surely you're never going to pull down your own mother's tombstone? Why, it'll break the old gentleman's heart–and she such a woman as she was!"
"My father has given his consent," said Geronimo, annoyed, but not betraying the smallest impatience.
Roger the mason shook his head, and took up a tool he had laid down, as if intending to return to his work.
"You'll excuse me, Mr. Geronimo; you've, maybe, persuaded him to it. Young people will be young people, I know," remarked Roger; "though it's a downright miracle to me why *you* should want to do it–you, the lady's only son; and such a lady as she was!"
"It's out of no disrespect to my mother, I assure you," expostulated Geronimo.
"I should think not, indeed!" interrupted the mason.
"But," continued Geronimo, "we have all to sacrifice personal feelings, you know, in matters of right and wrong."
Geronimo paused; but the mason was silent–he had no idea what was meant.
"Or where there is a question of propriety in the treatment of holy places," continued the youth; but still the mason stared at him in silence.
"You don't understand me, I think," said Geronimo
"I'm free to own I don't," answered the mason.
"Will you let me come in and explain myself?" asked the young man.
"Your father's son is welcome in *my* house at any time!" cried Roger, who had at last got hold of an idea he could fully understand; and leading the way along a narrow passage, he ushered his guest into a small parlour, to which he presently called his wife down, having asked permission for her to share in what Mr. Geronimo was going to say.
But let Mr. Geronimo say what he would, neither of his hearers succeeded in comprehending him, though, to do them justice, they tried. There they sat, the mason holding his cap in both hands between his knees, slightly stooping, but looking up at Geronimo from time to time; his wife bolt upright, and never taking her eyes off him for a second. And still they didn't understand! They had two or three ideas of their own in their heads, it is true, which were adverse to Mr. Geronimo's arguments, and perhaps darkened their powers of comprehension. "The Mrs.," as they called her, had been an angel on earth, if ever there was one, and no place could be too good for her stone, they were sure, for wasn't she herself in heaven? At least, who would ever get there if she wasn't there? And the poor dear gentleman had stood under it every Sunday ever since she was taken, and who'd have the heart to deprive him of the comfort of feeling her so near? If that stone were to be taken away, they shouldn't have him there much longer–Mr. Geronimo might depend upon that! Roger's good woman declared she wouldn't see the poor gentleman standing there alone, as if he'd never had a wife, for all the world, if she could help it. Take down his own

mother's tombstone! As if her name wasn't a credit anywhere, and a good example into the bargain–Mr. Geronimo couldn't be thinking of what he was saying! And Roger protested that if he never had another job in all his life, he wouldn't have this. But Mr. Geronimo was young, put in the wife, and hadn't come to his feelings; he would think better of it presently. They wished him a very good morning, and hoped he would call again.
Mr. Geronimo bit his lips as he left the house. Learning! Authority! What had become of them? What had he done with them? What could he have done with them against such stolid country heads? Entirely spoilt into the bargain, thought he–the fruit of taking things easy. There was but one hope of cure–to go the way you thought right, and leave such people to get reconciled to it as they could. Explanation and reasoning! He was ashamed of having tried them. The people had treated him like a child.
So he crossed the hills next morning, and rode ten miles, to the nearest town, where he engaged a marble-mason to come over and remove the tablet. But Sunday intervened, and as it chanced, his father was ill, and he had to stand in his place under the tablet in the chancel. And all at once, while there, there flashed into his mind one, at any rate, of the words which Roger the mason had spoken–quite an unreasonable word, be it granted, but reason, even in the most reasoning men, is not always a match for feeling, and Geronimo was suddenly unnerved.
His resolution had received a shock, and he was up betimes next morning to meet the marble-mason on his way. He had altered his intentions, he told him, with respect to the tablet, but there was another little matter of restoration in the church which he wished him to undertake. And now Geronimo breathed freely again, and met his father at breakfast with an easy mind. He therefore spoke quite cheerfully of the proposed restoration of a Knight Templar's tomb, which had long been in disorder, and alluded to the marble-mason from the town as being there.
A cry from his father interrupted him.
"Geronimo! That marble-mason! Have you really had the heart to–" Here breath failed the old man, and he turned very pale.
"No, no!" cried Geronimo, passionately, for he knew what was meant.
"It is well," murmured the father. "I gave you leave, I know; but, Geronimo, I doubt if I could have borne it. One gets weaker as one gets older; and, with weak people as with ignorant ones, the grasshopper is sometimes a burden."
If Geronimo could but have recollected this! But he had seen so little of life and the world himself, that he could scarcely help being one-sided and narrow-minded; and as he would not avail himself of his father's wider knowledge, what remained but to make mistakes?
So, priding himself on an inflexible firmness in matters of "principle," however small, he confounded together things indifferent and important; did even wise ones foolishly, and attempted others which were neither wise, nor worth a hundredth part of the offence they created.
"We are to 'be hated of all men for His name's sake,'" quoted he, in justification

of the course he was pursuing.
"His name's sake!" I dare not record the trivialities he dignified upon that sacred ground.
But on one or two points the father interfered authoritatively, and then domestic disagreement arose. Now Geronimo had thought scorn of Roger the mason for not yielding to his better knowledge and authoritative position, as a matter of course. Yet here, where to the counselor was added father as well as priest, and to the knowledge of the schools the broader experiences of a long and varied life, it came quite natural to this mere lad by comparison, to think, and betray the thought, that he knew a thousand times the better of the two. Verily, if a little of the old heathen respect for the wisdom of grey hairs had been added to his theological dogmas, Geronimo's Christianity would not have suffered.
"And a man's foes shall be they of his own household," murmured the old man to himself in the bitterness of his heart, as he wondered whether it would not soon be his duty to send this his only son from his side. For how could he be justified in letting the clouds of miserable parties and party feelings gather into a storm?
But now Geronimo, too, awoke to the fact that such a storm threatened. The gossip spread on every side that father and son did not always agree, and the flock were not likely to be unanimous. The wicked natural man loves contest; the weak natural man loves excitement. An expression of partizanship to himself, coupled with disrespect for his father, awoke Geronimo to a sense of his position, if it did not explain his mistake. And on looking further round, his tender conscience was grieved. The old confidence was broken up, the old love was failing–whether with or without a reason was not the question now. What could be the cause? What was the remedy? Perhaps he had been too busy with his plans and changes to have made himself as much a personal friend as was desirable. He redoubled his exertions and visits, endeavoured to conciliate on all sides; but, somehow, something was wanting. If from long habit a good many still came out to follow himself and his father to church, they did so at a greater and greater distance. Only a few came up now to claim the friendly greeting, which he remembered as part of the Sunday's intercourse in the days of his childhood. Geronimo was puzzled.
An idea at once bright and kind struck him, and he lost no time in carrying it out with zeal.
Geronimo was musical–he had been so from childhood upwards–had introduced better music as well as greater beauty into the venerable old church; and for both these things the people were grateful, as they ought to be.
He would make use of this happily universal feeling; he would give a treat to high and low–would have a festival; they should keep holiday with singing and gladness and feasting; and the day should be his father's birthday. He would dispel the dreadful and mischievous idea that the house to which all the parish looked for example was divided against itself!
Never was a happier thought struck out! It furnished occupation for hearts, and minds, and hands; and the old folks, who could do nothing but talk, had a

harmless subject of conversation. "Eh dear, then, Mr. Geronimo and his father were as friendly as ever! It had all been a mistake about their not agreeing. Eh, how pleased the old gentleman looked, to be sure, when he called, here and there, to ask them if they were going to get ready! Why, he was helping everybody to trim themselves up in their best for the grand supper there was to be at the end. And on the old gentleman's birthday, and all! It *was* something to think of! They *were* glad!"

And so they were; but so also, only more deeply so, were father and son, for they felt reunited.

And now the time drew near, and only one small contradiction had arisen. The organ was not so perfectly in tune as to please Geronimo's delicate ear; and when, nearly at the last moment, he wrote over for the one organ-builder of the distant town, he found, to his dismay, that the man was absent, and would be so till the day after the festival.

The evil was slight, and the father entreated Geronimo to be satisfied so few would discover the imperfection. But Geronimo could not rest; his passionate love of order was offended; and it must be owned that the instinct is a good one. "In the beginning," the will of God brought an organised world out of elemental confusion. In the end, we hope He will bring harmony into the discordant world of spirits. And in the present life men may, each one in his degree, labour to the same good end. It is both their privilege and their duty to do so. Lawyers, physicians, statesmen, men of science, and, above all, divines, undertake to do it by their very professions. Entangled claims, diseased bodies, disturbed nations, complicated physical laws and distressed souls, all need the peace that comes with being ordered aright. In Geronimo the instinct was almost a passion; but of the judicious application of means to the blessed end, he did not know a great deal more than of how to bring the organ of the village church into the desired perfection of tune.

Nevertheless less, he knew something of that, for he had been present when the organ-builder had tuned the instrument before, had observed the process of widening or narrowing the mouths of the pipes in order to change their tone, and had since ventured on correcting a defective note or two himself. What was to hinder him from tuning the whole of them now, if he could but ascertain the order in which the guiding scale of notes was made perfect? To bring all the rest into unison with that would be no difficulty, for he could perfectly trust his ear. The difficulty was, to get at the first principles of the matter. The youth who played the organ when Geronimos's duties precluded his assistance, knew nothing of the subject.

But Geronimo would not be baffled. The day before the festival he crossed the hills to the town, and called at a musical-instrument maker's shop. Could they give him, he asked, the succession of notes by which organs were tuned?

Mr. Somebody asked Mr. Somebody else, and there was a reference to an authority through a door. The shopman, who was left behind, eyed Geronimo askance. Was he in their line of business? he wondered. Presently the other man returned, and presented him with a bit of music-paper, on which twenty notes

were marked down.
"These are the notes, sir," said he, rather coolly, as if he, too, half suspected a rival; "the same as for a pianoforte–as, of course, you know," he added, with a half-inquiring look.
Geronimo disliked familiarity, and gave a half-impatient nod.
"Mr. — desired me to say, with his compliments, sir," continued the messenger, "he supposed you're aware it's a difficult business, organ-tuning, to any one that hasn't practised it."
"Has your master practised it?" inquired Geronimo, with a new hope.
"Oh, no, sir," replied the man, who himself did duty as master on the other side of the door; "we're pianoforte-tuners only, sir."
"What does the fool mean?" thought Geronimo, as he walked away. "A difficult business it may be to the man without an ear, but easy enough otherwise, with the clue in his hand. Thank Heaven, there is the comfort of certainty in dealing with material things! Fixed laws, and fixed results! Not that everlasting trimming and yielding, which leave every work one undertakes imperfect at last!"
As Geronimo mused thus, and read over the clearly-defined system by which his organ was to be brought into that harmonious order which we call "being in tune," he almost felt that an organ-builder's business was more satisfactory than a clergyman's.
There was still the little brass cone, used for widening or contracting the pipes, to be obtained; but this he asked for at the organ-builder's establishment–no remark passing there on what it was wanted for; and then Geronimo hurried home.
And now it will be understood what took the young curate to the church so early, on the morning of that autumn festival-day. He had begun, but not nearly completed, the tuning of the organ the evening before, having gone to it as soon as he could make an excuse to leave his father again; for the bold feat was to be kept secret till its successful accomplishment proved how wisely it had been undertaken. And now it must be finished before breakfast; for the decorations were to be brought in afterwards, and he himself had a thousand other things to do.
For two hours and upwards therefore, did he persevere in his anxious work; his greatest trouble being the special care required in the mechanical part, inasmuch as a hasty or too heavy insertion of the cone into the mouths of the pipes was liable to split the metal and do mischief. But Geronimo kept every faculty on the full stretch of attention, and his perfect ear made the bringing of the notes into correct harmony a matter of no trouble at all, but, on the contrary, of the keenest pleasure. And the instrument was more glaringly out of order than he supposed. His father had fancied it was only a little out of tune, and he himself had not thought the disorder very great. But now that he tested it by the scale, almost every note was wrong, and must be altered. A few of the octaves harmonised together, it is true; but all the fifths were either too flat or too sharp. That not one should have remained perfect by accident, as several of the octaves had done,

puzzled him not a little; but the fact of their all being imperfect, more or less, was undeniable. What a blessing he had it in his power to remedy the evil!
Yes; for two hours and upwards did the work go on; the occasional drone of the pipes vibrating drearily through the aisles, and causing little Roger to fall asleep at his post of the blower. At last, however, every octave had been gone through, had been brought into perfect unison with the perfected scale of the twenty notes, and Geronimo's labours were over!
"Roger," cried he to the child, whose blowing efforts were perceptibly failing.
"Yes, sir!"
"Blow steadily and strongly now, for ten minutes more, and you shall go home to breakfast. Fill the bellows, there's a good lad."
Roger worked his arms vigorously, and the bellows were soon full.
"It's all right now, please, sir," said he.
Geronimo had his eyes on a piece of music open on the desk before him. It was Haydn's Mass in five flats–his dream of beauty among all the classical music of the world. As Roger spoke, the young curate bent forward, and struck down the full magnificent chords of the key.
But almost as he struck them, he uttered a cry, which it was well the louder organ sounds drowned, or Roger would have thought Geronimo mad–a cry of both despair and physical distress. As it was, something startled the lad, and he let go the blowing handle with a jerk. It ran up at once, and the organ notes died out in a mournful squeal.
As to Geronimo, it would be difficult to describe what he did. He was off the stool in an instant, shouting to Roger to know if he had broken the bellows; then back again to retouch the expiring notes, and see if he had been under a delusion, or if he had struck the instrument at random. But no, no, no! Then how–by what miracle–could he account for the fact that his touch upon that chord had filled the air with dissonant vibrations–horrible to the most untutored ear, but to his refined one absolutely insufferable? Chord indeed! The very word was a mockery; what he had struck was a clash of discords.
Human nature itself had never puzzled Geronimo half as much!
After the first agony was over, he examined the matter with all the calmness and care he could command–made Roger blow again–tried other chords in succession–but in all cases with the same result, in a greater or less degree. Once more, then, he got out the tuning-scale–once more ran over the guiding twenty notes: there was not a single flaw, not one; not a varying vibration could be heard; and all the others were in unison with those. And then again he struck a chord, and the chord was no chord at all. He next examined the pipes: perhaps he had cracked all their mouths with his cone. But no, there was not a split in any one of them; he had been far too careful for that. And now time was getting on, and Roger was half starved. A knocking had already been heard at one of the doors. The decorators must be let in, and he must go home to his breakfast and his father. Geronimo's face, as he locked up the organ and put the keys in his pocket, looked ten years older than it had done before he had begun his work. He gave Roger half-a-crown, as a treat for the day, and hastened home.

It is difficult to reckon on the conduct of any one under the trial of having made a great mistake. Some people fight meanly to get out of a little fault, as if self-conceit was the leading principle of their lives, but humble themselves nobly under a great one; and this was the case with Geronimo. He went at once to his father, and told him all he had done, blaming himself more bitterly than his father would allow he deserved. But he did more than that; he stepped into many houses that morning, both of farmers and shopkeepers, and told them they must forgive him for being the cause of what he feared would be a great disappointment. He had wanted to make the organ better, and he had, unfortunately, done something to it which had made it worse; and as he could not find out what was amiss, it couldn't be remedied. He would get the choir to make amends by singing their very best, and he would help them all he could himself. He begged that the blunder might not be allowed to spoil the pleasure of the day.

Unaccountable human race! We ought indeed to be patient, one with the other! Geronimo had not received so many smiles in all the time he had been curate, as now, when he was carrying round the painful message of his own defeat.

It was wonderful! Kind words were on every lip; not a reproach was heard. It had been so good of Mr. Geronimo to try. They were sure it couldn't have been his fault, but something had gone wrong of itself. Anyhow, they didn't mind at all, and hoped he wouldn't trouble himself. They should hear him sing all the plainer for there being no music besides; and, as for that piece the old Master had talked about so much, they hoped he'd be so good as to play it to them some other day. They begged he wouldn't mind–that was all!

Geronimo felt crowned with roses, for his frankness, if not for the error he had committed; and service, feast, and festival were kept with unclouded comfort, bringing a promise of further comfort in store–a better understanding of what was meant on all sides.

And now for the explanation. Neither father nor son could unravel the mystery. The only guess even that they could make was that the man at the music-shop might have given them a wrong scale to work by. It was not a bad idea, and it served to keep them quiet till the organ-builder, whom they sent for at once, came over. He was an odd, sententious old man, with a good deal of dry humour. So when he got into the church, and touched the fatal organ, he first chuckled and then laughed outright.

Were the bellows out of order? Were the pipes injured? Was the scale incorrect? Was the tuning imperfect? Geronimo's questions fell thick and fast.

"Nothing of the sort, young gentleman," said the organ-builder to every suggestion. "There's only one thing the matter–but it's everything–the tuning's *too perfect by half*!"

Both Geronimo and his father stared, to the organ-builder's great delight.

"You don't seem to have heard of this before, gentlemen," observed he; "but it's a fact, nevertheless. The scale's all right; the system's perfect; but if you stick too close to it, it sets you wrong. The organ won't bear it, that's the fact."

"Not bear being put into perfect tune?" asked Geronimo, really astonished. "How

is that possible?"
"It's an imperfect instrument, sir," answered the organ-builder: "and that being the case, you have to make the best you can of it, and not expect to get it perfect, for that's not possible."
Here he took up the scale paper, and went on to explain that most of the fifths must be left somewhat flat, and the few others made somewhat sharp; the octaves alone being tuned in perfect unison. And this was the best plan, he assured them, of getting a harmonious whole–"not perfect, I grant, even then," added he, "but pretty fair for this present life, gentlemen, you see."
Geronimo listened in silence. A system of expediency in the material world, and in music especially, seemed to him monstrous. He sat silently by, too, while the organ-builder made his preparations for repairing the mischief that had been done. He father slipped away, as silent as himself, though possibly he made his own reflections before he went.
But Geronimo sat silently on, till at last the organ-builder began to tune the fifths, leaving each one flat in succession; and them he could contain himself no longer. He got up, but only to sit down again, and then rose once more.
"This is most trying!" he exclaimed. "As unsatisfactory to the mind as the ear! To have a perfect system to go by" (here he pointed to the scale of twenty notes), " and not be allowed to carry it perfectly out, though ear and heart rebel against the disorder! To have an evil under your very hand to be remedied, and be obliged to suffer it still. I call this dreadful!"
The organ-builder stopped his work, to listen and reply:
"It's not very pleasant, I admit," said he, "but there's one thing worse–to find you've worked so hard for the system, that you've missed the end it was made for."
"A perfect system ought to work out a perfect end," murmured Geronimo.
But the organ-builder shook his head. "Not if the instrument isn't perfect too," persisted he; "there's sure to be a cross somewhere."
Drone went another pipe, another imperfect fifth was tuned, and the organ-builder made another pause. He was a very sententious man and liked to explain all round his subject.
"It's the same all through life," observed he; "the best rules, even, short of Gospel rules, of course, mustn't be pressed too close; neither man nor organ can bear it. If we were all up in heaven it might be different."
In spite of himself Geronimo smiled, and the smile did him good. "What a choice of evils!" said he.
"Can't be otherwise," remarked his companion, "so long as things are all imperfect together–men and organs–and perhaps even rules too, sometimes."
Geronimo shook his head, but the organ-builder did not notice it, and went back to his tuning as cheerful as if no such thing as a sad necessity existed in the world. And Geronimo went on listening to the unsatisfactory sounds, musing the while thereupon.
Irregularity–inconsistency–contradictions even–were as rife then in the material world as in the spiritual–must be borne with–allowed for–made the best of–in

the one case as in the other, in order to compass the great object at last. The organ-builder's business was not so much more satisfactory than a clergyman's after all!
"Now, sir, you may play Haydn's Mass in five flats for as long as you please," observed the organ-builder, as he concluded the tuning, striking down the full chord of the key in proof of the fact: "The organ goes sweetly enough now."
And so it did–"sweetly enough," if not as perfectly as Geronimo could have desired; but he had had his lesson, and must henceforth be contented with something short of his ideal.

"That type of Perfect in his mind, In Nature can he nowhere find."

Nowhere in the lower nature, at least, and for the full development of the higher, he must wait in patience. But patience is the philosophy of experience; and even Geronimo attained it at last.

COBWEBS

"I cannot make this matter plain,
But I would shoot, howe'er in vain
A random arrow from the brain."

TENNYSON.

TWINETTE the Spider was young, hungry, and industrious. "Weave yourself a web, my dear," said her mother, "as you know how without teaching, and catch flies for yourself; only don't weave near me in the corner here. I am old and stay in the corners; but you are young and needn't. Besides you would be in my way. Scramble along the rafters to a little distance off, and spin. But mind! Just see there's nothing there–below you, I mean–before you begin. You won't catch anything to eat, if there isn't empty space about you for the flies to fly in."

Twinette was dutiful, and obeyed. She scrambled along the woodwork of the groined roof of the church–for it was there her mother lived–till she had gone what she thought might fairly be called a little distance off, and then she stopped to look round, which, considering that she had eight eyes to do it with, was not difficult. But she was not so sure of what there might be below.

"I wonder whether mother would say there was nothing here–below me, I mean–but empty space for flies to fly in?" said she.

But she might have stood wondering there forever. So she went back to her mother, and asked what she thought.

"Oh dear, oh dear!" said her mother, "how can I think about what I don't see? There usen't to be anything there in my young days, I'm sure. But everybody must find out things for themselves. Let yourself down by the family rope, as you know how, without teaching, and see for yourself if there's anything there or not."

Twinette was a very intelligent young spider, quite worthy of the age she was born in; so she thanked her mother for her advice, and was just starting afresh, when another thought struck her. "How shall I know if there's anything there when I get there?" asked she.

"Dear me, if there's anything there, how can you help seeing it?" cried the mother, rather teased by her daughter's inquiring spirit, "you with at least eight eyes in your head!"

"Thank you. Now I quite understand," said Twinette; and scuttling back to the end of the rafter, she began to prepare for the family rope.

It was the most exquisite thing in the world–so fine you could scarcely see it; so elastic, it could be blown about without breaking; such a perfect grey that it looked white against black things, and black against white; so manageable that Twinette could both make it, and slide down it at once; and when she wished to get back, could slip up by it, and roll it up at the same time!

It was a wonderful rope for anybody to make without teaching. But Twinette was not conceited. Rope-making came as natural to her as eating and fighting do

to intelligent little boys, so she thought no more about it than we do of chewing our food.
How she did it is another question, and not one easily answered, however intelligent we may be. Thus much may be hinted: out of four little spinning machines near the tail came four little threads, and the rope was a four-twist of these. But as each separate thread was itself a many-twist of a great many others, still finer, I do not pretend to tell the number of strands (as rope-threads are called) in Twinette's family rope. Enough, that as she made it now, it has been made from generation to generation, and there seems to be no immediate prospect of a change.
The plan was for the spinner to glue the ends to the rafter, and then start off. Then out came the threads from the spinning machines, and twist went the rope; and the further the spinner traveled, the longer the rope became.
And Twinette made ready accordingly, and turning on her back, let herself fairly off.
The glued ends held fast, the four stands twined closely together, and down went the family rope, with Twinette at the end, guiding it. Down into the middle of the chancel, where there were carved oaken screens on three sides, and carved oaken seats below, with carved oaken figures at each end of each.
Twinette was about halfway down to the stone-flagged floor, when she shut up the spinning machines, and stopped to rest and look round. Then, balancing herself at the end of her rope, with her legs crumpled up round her, she made her remarks.
"This is charming!" cried she. "One had need to travel and see the world. And all's so nice in the middle here. Nice empty space for the flies to fly about in and a very pleasant time they must have of it! Dear me, how hungry I feel–I must go back and weave at once."
But just as she was preparing to roll up the rope and be off, a ray of sunshine, streaming through one of the chancel windows, struck in a direct line upon her suspended body, quite startling her with the dazzle of its brightness. Everything seemed in a blaze all around her, and she turned round and round in terror.
"Oh dear, oh dear, oh dear!" cried she, for she didn't know what to say, and still couldn't help calling out. Then, making a great effort, she gave one hearty spring, and, blinded though she was, shot up to the groined roof, as fast as spider could go, rolling the rope into a ball as she went. After which she stopped to complain.
But it is dull work complaining to oneself, so she ran back to her mother in the corner.
"Back again so soon, my dear?" asked the old lady, not over-pleased at the fresh disturbance.
"Back again at all is the wonder," whimpered Twinette. "There's something down there, after all, besides empty space."
"Why, what did you see?" asked her mother.
"Nothing; that was just it," answered Twinette, "I could see nothing for dazzle and blaze: but I did see dazzle and blaze."

"Young people of the present day are very troublesome with their observations," remarked the mother; "however, if one rule will not do, here is another. Did dazzle and blaze shove you out of your place, my dear?"
Twinette said, "Certainly not–she had come away of herself."
"Then how could they be anything?" asked her mother. "Two things could not be in one place at the same time. Let Twinette try to get into her place, while she was there herself, and see if she could."
Twinette did not try, because she knew she couldn't, but she sat very silent, wondering what dazzle and blaze could be, if they were nothing at all! a puzzle which might have lasted her for ever. Fortunately her mother interrupted her, by advising her to go and get something to do. She really couldn't afford to feed her out of her web any longer, she said.
"If dazzle and blaze kill me, you'll be sorry, mother," said Twinette, in a pet.
"Nonsense, about dazzle and blaze," cried the old spider, now thoroughly aroused. "I dare say they're only a little more light than usual. There's more or less light up here in the corners even, at times. You talk nonsense, my dear."
So Twinette scuttled off in silence; for she dared not ask what light was, though she wanted to know.
But she felt too cross to begin to spin. She preferred a search after truth to her dinner, which showed she was no commonplace spider. So she resolved to go down below in another place and see if she could find a really empty space; and accordingly prepared the family rope.
When she came down, it was about a half a foot further east in the chancel, and a very prosperous journey she made. "Come! All's safe so far," said she, her good humour returning. "I do believe I've found nothing at last. How jolly it is!" As she spoke, she hung dangling at the end of her rope, back downwards, her legs tucked up round her as before, in perfect enjoyment, when, suddenly, the south door of the church was thrown open, and a strong gust set in. It was a windy evening, and the draught that poured into the chancel blew the family rope, with Twinette at the end of it, backwards and forwards through the air, till she turned quite giddy.
"Oh dear, oh dear!" cried she, puffing, "what shall I do? How could they say there was nothing here–oh dear–but empty space for flies–oh dear–to fly in?" But at last, in despair, she made an effort of resistance, and, in the very teeth of the wind, succeeded in coiling up the family rope, and so got back to the rafter.
It was a piece of rare good fortune for her that a lazy, half-alive fly happened to be creeping along it just at the moment. As she landed from her air-dive she pounced on the stroller, killed him, and sucked his juices before he knew where he was, as people say. Then, throwing down his carcass, she scrambled back to her mother, and told her what she thought, though not in plain words. For what she thought was that the old lady didn't know what she was saying, when she talked about empty space with nothing in it.
"Dazzle and blaze were nothing," cried she at last, "though they blinded me, because they and I were in one place together, which couldn't be if they'd been anything; and now this is nothing, though it blows me out of my place twenty

times in a minute, because I can't see it. What's the use of rules one can't go by, mother? I don't believe you know a quarter of what's down below there."
The old spider's head turned as giddy with Twinette's arguments as Twinette's had done while swinging in the wind.
"I don't see what it can matter what's there," whimpered she, "if there's room for flies to fly about in. I wish you'd go back and spin."
"That's another part of the question," remarked Twinette, in answer to the first half of her mother's sentence. In answer to the second she scuttled back to the rafter, intending to be obedient and spin. But she dawdled and thought, and thought and dawdled, till the day was nearly over.
"I will take one more turn down below," said she to herself at last, "and look round me again."
And so she did, but went further down than before; then stopped to rest as usual. Presently, as she hung dangling in the air by her line, she grew venturesome. "I will sift the matter to the bottom," thought she. "I will see how far empty space goes." So saying she reopened her spinning-machines and started afresh.
It was a wonderful rope, certainly, or it would not have gone on to such a length without breaking. In a few seconds Twinette was on the cold stone pavement. But she didn't like the feel of it at all, so took to running as fast as she could go, and luckily met with a step of woodwork on one side. Up this she hurried at once, and crept into a corner close by, where she stopped to take a breath. "One doesn't know what to expect in such queer outlandish places," observed she; "when I've rested I'll go back, but I must wait till I can see a little better."
Seeing a little better was out of the question, however, for night was coming on, and when, weary of waiting, she stepped out of her hiding-place to look round, the whole church was in darkness.
Now it is one thing to be snug in bed when it is dark, and another to be a long way from home and have lost your way, and not know what may happen to you next minute. Twinette had often been in the dark corner with her mother, and thought nothing of it. Now she shook all over with fright, and wondered what dreadful thing darkness could be.
Then she thought of her mother's rules and felt quite angry.
"I can't see anything and I don't feel anything," murmured she, "and yet here's something that frightens me out of my wits."
At last her very fright made her bold. She felt about for the family rope; it was there safe and sound, and she made a spring. Roll went the rope, and up went the owner; higher, higher, higher, through the dark night air; seeing nothing, hearing nothing, feeling nothing but the desperate fear within. By the time she touched the rafter, she was half-exhausted; and as soon as she was safely landed upon it, she fell asleep.
It must have been late next morning when she woke, for the sound of organ music was pealing through the church, and the air-vibrations swept pleasantly over her frame; rising and falling like gusts of wind, swelling and sinking like waves of the sea, gathering and dispersing like vapours of the sky.
She went down by the family rope to observe, but nothing was to be seen to

account for her sensations. Fresh ones, however, stole round her, as she hung suspended, for it was a harvest-festival, and large white lilies were grouped with evergreens round the slender pillars of the screens, and filled the air with their powerful odour. Still, nothing disturbed her from her place. Sunshine streamed in through the windows–she even felt it warm on her body–but it interfered with nothing else; and, meanwhile, in such sort as spiders hear, she heard music and prayer–whether as music and prayer come to us, or as deaf men enjoy sound by touch, let those say who can! A door opened and a breeze caught her rope; but still she held fast. So music and prayer and sunshine and breeze and scent were all there together; and Twinette was among them, and saw flies flying about overhead.

This was enough; she went back to the rafter, chose a home and began to spin. Before evening, her web was completed, and her first prey caught and feasted on. Then she cleared the remains out of her chamber, and sat down in state to think; for Twinette was now a philosopher. It came to her while she was spinning her web. As she crossed and twisted the threads her ideas grew clearer and clearer, or she fancied so, which did almost as well. Each line she fastened brought its own reflection; and this was the way they went on:

"Empty space is an old wife's tale:"–she fixed that very tight. "Sight and touch are very imperfect guides"–this crossed the other at an angle. "Two or three things can easily be in one place at the very same time"–this seemed very loose till she tightened it by a second. "Sunshine and wind and scent and sound don't drive each other out of their places"–that held firm. "When one has sensations there is something to cause them, whether one sees it, or feels it, or finds it out, or not"–this was a wonderful thread, it went right round the web and was fastened down in several places. "Light and darkness, and sunshine and wind, and sound and sensation, and fright and pleasure, don't keep away flies"–the little interlacing threads looked quite pretty as she placed them. "How many things I know of that I don't know much about"–the web got thicker every minute. "And perhaps there may be ever so much more beyond–ever so much more–ever so much more–beyond." Those were her very last words. She kept repeating them till she finished her web: and when she sat up in state, after supper, to think, she began to repeat them again; for she could think of nothing better or wiser to say. But this was no wonder, for all her thoughts put together made nothing but a cobweb, after all!

And when the Turk's-head broom swept it, with others, from the roof, Twinette was no longer in the little chamber below. She had died and bequeathed her cobweb-wisdom to another generation. But as it was only cobweb-wisdom, spiders remain spiders still, and still weave their webs in the roofs of churches without fathoming the mystery of unseen presences below.

BIRDS IN THE NEST

"Safe in the hand of one disposing power,
Or in the natal, or the mortal hour,
All Nature is but art, unknown to thee;
All chance, direction, which thou canst not see."

POPE'S ESSAY ON MAN.

ONCE upon a time there was in a wood a nest which held eight of the dearest little eggs a hen-mother ever looked upon with joy. At least this particular hen-mother thought so, and her mate rather agreed with her when they talked the matter over together. And his opinion had weight, for in his flights he sometimes saw other eggs, and would tell her about them on his return. But what could they be to her own? Nothing could be better than what was perfect, and her own were perfect in her eyes. What a fine shape they had! How beautifully rounded! How soft their tint! How tasteful the arrangement of spots! All others must needs be too light or too dark, or too something or other, to suit her particular taste. The seagull who ate snails in the garden boasted of his family egg as twenty times larger and twenty times more beautiful. "But if it be more beautiful, what can that matter to us," said the hen-mother, in conclusion, "when ours are perfect in our eyes, and we are so very happy?"

"And shall be so much happier yet," pursued her mate, who, as a traveled bird, had had experience, and knew what was in store; "when the little ones awake to a life and enjoyment of their own, and can feed and sing, and know and love us both."

"Ah, to be sure, to be sure, that will be rapture, indeed," cried the hen-mother. "Thank you so much for telling me! How silly I was, thinking I was as happy as I could possibly be! Of course I shall be happier by and by; and how very happy that will be, for I am happy enough now. I wish the day were come!"

Yes she was very happy, but most so when she forgot she was to be happier still. And by and by the time came; and when the little ones were all hatched, and could peer about and see their father bringing food, and open their mouths and swallow it very fast, and cry for more.

"Now then, at last the happiness is perfect," said the hen-mother; "I have nothing further to wish for."

And she watched them being fed and satisfied, and never felt hungry herself, till they had had plenty and were at ease.

"Eight darlings in one nest! What a sight to fill one's heart! There may be trouble enough, it's true, and very little room to rest; but one's own eight beautiful creatures round one, under one's wing, all chirping and alive–this is perfection of happiness indeed!"

"You cannot say so just yet," sang the mate; but he did not tell her this quite at first. He waited for a soft evening in early summer before he piped about what was in store.

"You cannot say so just yet. Our darlings are very sweet, but they are poor helpless things at present. Wait till they have grown more feathers, have learnt to take care of themselves, and fly and sing. They cannot be perfect, nor can your happiness be perfect, till then. Some of our neighbours are beforehand with us. There were fine young birds among the boughs yesterday, twitting our youngsters in their songs with being behindhand altogether."

"They will not have to twit long, I suppose," exclaimed the hen-mother rather angrily. "Of course you will bring ours forward as fast as you can. Of course they must not be behind their neighbours. Of course they must learn to take care of themselves, and fly and sing, like the rest. Dear, dear! How silly I was! But thank you so much for telling me. It's very well to be easily pleased, and the poor helpless things are very sweet, as you say; but of course it will be a much grander thing when they have grown to be fine young birds like those others; able to take care of themselves and to twit their neighbours who can't. And of course I shall be as happy again. I wish the time were come."

And it did come; but there was a great deal of trouble to be taken first. The little ones had to be nursed and fed till their feathers had grown, and then they had to be trained, by slow degrees and with much care, to use their young wings in flight. Now the hen-mother had left her mate no rest till he began to teach; for, first, she was jealous for her children's credit; and secondly, she wanted to feel what it was to be as happy as it was possible to be. Happy enough she was, but for this wish.

But alas! For the trouble and fear that came over her when the teaching really began. The eight darlings must come out of their nest, from under her wing; she could help them no longer–they could scarcely help themselves. Yet they must spread the feeble pinion, and strain the unpractised muscle, and run a risk of failure and even life, to insure success.

Oh, poor hen-mother, what a trying change was this, though brought about by her own especial desire! No wonder that, while the teaching was going on, she would sit and shake with fright, and wish all manner of foolish things: that they were back in the nest, of course; but far more than that–even that they were back in the old baby days again, in the egg-shells of their first existence, unconscious of life and of them. "They were all under my wing then, at any rate," said she; "my own dear little ones with me, and I with them: what more could I want?"

And, oh dear, when the youngsters were safe in the nest once more at night, how she used to gather them under her wings with joy!

"I am getting to like night better than day," said she at last to her mate, "for then my birds are in the nest again. You are training them very cleverly, I know and I was the first to want them to be clever like other young birds, and they are getting cleverer day by day, I dare say, so I ought to be happier; but the happiness is not as pleasant as it was. How can it be, when they are away so much, and the empty nest stares me in the face? The risks are so many too, till they can really fly well, and I tremble with fear. But all is right at night, when you all come back and sing. Yes, if it wasn't for thinking of the morrow, the happiness would be perfect indeed then: if it were always evening, I mean, and

they and you were always here."
"It is natural you should feel as you do," replied the mate; "but you mistake the cause. If you are not quite happy yet, it is merely because things are not quite perfect, that is all. When the young ones can fly really well, for instance, there will no longer be any risk; and when they can sing better still, our music will be pleasanter than ever; and when they are able and independent, all your cares and anxieties will be at an end. Wait a little longer, and you will be happy indeed."
The hen-mother sighed. "I suppose you must be right," said she; "I will wait. But if I could sing myself, I would sing a mother's song about the birds in the nest. It may not have been perfection, but it was a very happy time."
So she waited and did her best to be pleased. But for longer and longer intervals the empty nest stared her in the face, and she thought many things she did not dare to say–even the old foolish wish that they were all in their eggshells again. Still, every evening, when they came back and perched in the boughs, if not in the nest, and the singing grew sweeter and sweeter, she cheered up and rejoiced once more.
And now at last the nestlings were full-grown birds, and could fly and sing as well as their parents. Perfection had come; they were independent; nobody's young birds could twit them now. "But now, of course," said their father, "they must go out and seek their fortunes, as we did, and choose mates, and settle in life for themselves. You see the justice of this?"
The hen-mother, to whom he was speaking, answered, "Yes;" but her heart was half broken. And when he added, "This is the real perfection of happiness to parents," she made no answer at all.
"It ought to be, perhaps," thought she to herself, "but it isn't so with me. I wonder why?" She sat on the edge of the empty nest and wondered still; but she couldn't find out the secret there.
Then the young ones piped to her from the woods; and at last said she, "Things are altered, I see; I will go to them!" and the very thought comforted her as she flew away. And when she had found them, and watched them in the full enjoyment of their own young life–listened to them as they warbled merrily to each other among the trees, or sported with friends here and there, she began to understand the whole matter. She was rejoicing in their joy rather than in her own.
And time went on; and one day as she sat, so listening, on a branch in the centre of the wood, her mate by her side, said she, "It is all becoming quite clear, and I can see that you were right on the whole. This is nearer the perfection of happiness than anything else could be, but the quite perfect is not to be had. Still, this is nearest and best; whether sweetest or not, I scarcely know. But thank you for telling me! I was selfish before: wanted my own darlings to myself, under my own wing, in my own particular nest–safe, as I called it–foolish that I was! Oh, narrow, narrow thought! As if one place was safer than another, when the sun looks down everywhere, streaming warmth and comfort upon all! I see things differently now. The wood is but a larger nest, and those that live in it but a larger family. I spread out my love a little wider, and behold my happiness

spreads out too! Though each in turn, for a time, must form his own little circle of joy, the whole must form one larger circle together; and who knows where it is to end?"

She ceased, and then listened again, and truly the wood was ringing with melodies: her mate by her side; her children now here, now there with the dear ones they loved. The circle grew wider and wider as time went further on.

But by and by, when age had crept over both, the mate had tender thoughts himself of old times, and tenderer still for her. She had not been wrong altogether, he whispered softly and kindly. It was not selfishness only that had filled her heart. He would sing her the song she used to wish she could have sung herself–a mother's song about the birds in the nest.

And it went to the hearts of both.

* * * * * *

Other mothers in other nests, lift up your souls, as the circle widens from your feet. "One God and Father of all, who is above all, and through all, and in you all," has all together now in the circle of His care; yea, even though a world, or the change we call death, may seem to divide them: and He will bring His own together at last into one home–the "Father's House"–one home, be the mansions never so many!

THE END.

CPSIA information can be obtained
at www.ICGtesting.com
Printed in the USA
LVHW020803270523
748233LV00029B/440

SpringerBriefs in Education

For further volumes:
http://www.springer.com/series/8914

Amy Cutter-Mackenzie
Susan Edwards · Deborah Moore
Wendy Boyd

Young Children's Play and Environmental Education in Early Childhood Education

Amy Cutter-Mackenzie
School of Education
Southern Cross University
Coolangatta, QLD
Australia

Wendy Boyd
School of Education
Southern Cross University
Lismore, NSW
Australia

Susan Edwards
Deborah Moore
Faculty of Education
Australian Catholic University
Fitzroy, Melbourne, VIC
Australia

ISSN 2211-1921 ISSN 2211-193X (electronic)
ISBN 978-3-319-03739-4 ISBN 978-3-319-03740-0 (eBook)
DOI 10.1007/978-3-319-03740-0
Springer Cham Heidelberg New York Dordrecht London

Library of Congress Control Number: 2013958138

Printed on acid-free paper

Springer is part of Springer Science+Business Media (www.springer.com)

Acknowledgments

The work presented in this book was supported by funding from the Australian Research Council under the Discovery Projects Scheme (2010–2012). Fieldwork for this project was conducted in Victoria, Australia with ethical approval from the Department of Education and Early Childhood Development and the Monash University Human Research Ethics Committee. The authors wish to thank the participating children, families and teachers for their contribution to the project. The authors also wish to acknowledge support with fieldwork and data management provided by Deb Moore, Tracy Young and Tiffany Cutter.

Material presented in this book is informed by previously published work, including:

- Cutter-Mackenzie, A., Edwards, S., & Widdop Quinton, H. (in press). Child-Framed Video Research Methodologies: Issues, Possibilities and Challenges for Researching with Children. *Children's Geographies.*
- Edwards, S., & Cutter-Mackenzie, A. (2013). 'Next time we can be penguins': expanding the concept of 'learning play' to support learning and teaching about sustainability in early childhood education. Chapter in O. Lillemyr, S. Dockett., & B. Perry (Eds.), *International perspectives on play and early childhood education.* New York: Information Age Publishing.
- Cutter-Mackenzie, A., & Edwards, S. (2013). Towards a model for early childhood environmental education: Foregrounding, developing and connecting knowledge through play-based learning. *The Journal of Environmental Education, 44*(3), 195–213.
- Edwards, S. & Cutter-Mackenzie, A. (2013). Pedagogical play-types: what do they suggest for learning about sustainability in early childhood education? *International Journal of Early Childhood.*
- Edwards, S., Moore, D., & Cutter-Mackenzie, A. (2012). Beyond 'killing, screaming and being scared of insects': learning and teaching about biodiversity in early childhood education. *EC Folio, 16*(2), 12–16.
- Edwards, S., & Cutter-Mackenzie, A. (2011). Environmentalising early childhood education curriculum through pedagogies of play. *Australasian Journal of Early Childhood, 36*(1), 51–59.

Contents

Figures

Tables

Chapter 1
A Challenge for Early Childhood Environmental Education?

Abstract This chapter orients the reader by introducing the underlying premise of the book, in addition to outlining the remaining six chapters. The book's foundation lies squarely in an era in which environmental education has been described as one of the most pressing educational concerns of our time, leading to the critical need for further insights in understanding how best to approach the learning and teaching of environmental education in early childhood education. In this chapter and indeed this book more broadly we address this concern by identifying two principles for applying play-based learning in early childhood environmental education. The principles we identify are the result of research conducted with teachers and children using three different types of play-based learning, namely open-ended play, modelled-play and purposefully framed play. Such play types connect with the historical use of play-based learning in early childhood education as a basis for pedagogy.

1.1 Introduction

Four children assembled around a wading pool at a preschool are intently engaged in play. Samples collected during a recent excursion to their local beach are the focus of attention. Seaweeds and sponges have been combined with plastic sea animals and placed in the wading pool with a small amount of water to help the children learn aspects of biodiversity. The children introduce well-known characters from a Nickelodeon™ cartoon, and one of the sponges becomes SpongeBob Squarepants™, whilst a plastic sea star morphs into his sidekick Patrick. Seaweed is heaped upon both SpongeBob and Patrick by two of the children. The remaining children swirl the water vigorously with sticks gathered from a nearby tree, creating whirlpools that lift seaweed from SpongeBob and Patrick. Seth (the teacher) observed the children at play, noting the appropriateness of their social interactions and the sophisticated articulation of the cartoon genre to their SpongeBob SquarePants dramatisation.

A. Cutter-Mackenzie et al., *Young Children's Play and Environmental Education in Early Childhood Education*, SpringerBriefs in Education,
DOI: 10.1007/978-3-319-03740-0_1,

This typical approach to science education in the early years (Howitt et al. 2011) seems to capture what one might think early childhood environmental education should entail. Four young children are happily engaged in playing outside and experiencing nature whilst participating in an open-ended play-based activity. Elements of traditionally valued early childhood education are evident, including access to outdoor play, opportunities for freely experimenting with materials and participation in pretend play. Many early childhood teachers may have considered not much more would be needed to help these children acquire the conceptual underpinnings of the biodiversity to be found on their local beach. They may have also hoped that these children would learn to respect other living creatures and possibly embrace 'biophilic' dispositions or express an 'affinity with nature' rather than being 'biophobic' or 'afraid of nature' (Wilson 1992; Orr 1992). Now, and later, as they grow into adulthood these four children might also carry such knowledge and attitudes into their understandings about the environment and develop a commitment to living a sustainable life.

Children developing conceptual knowledge about biodiversity, understanding the importance of sustainability, and avoiding or disrupting the development of biophobic attitudes towards nature are laudable outcomes for early childhood education to achieve. However, recent research has expressed concern regarding the extent to which such exploratory play facilitates children's conceptual learning (Fleer 2010) in environmental education. In this regard, outdoor play alone has been labelled by some researchers (Davis 2010; Waller et al. 2010) as insufficient for supporting children's developing environmental attitudes and dispositions towards sustainability (Davis 2010). Experiences such as those described in the opening vignette may no longer be enough to ensure young children are having meaningful engagements with environmental education in early childhood settings. In an era in which environmental education has been described as one of the most pressing educational concerns of our time (UNESCO-UNEP 1976), further insights are needed to understand how best to approach the learning and teaching of environmental education in early childhood education. In the context of early childhood education, this is a particularly interesting concern, because the question of 'how' to approach the learning and teaching of environmental education necessarily relates to the use of play-based learning as a basis for pedagogy.

1.2 Play-Based Learning in Early Childhood Environmental Education

In this book we address this concern by identifying two principles for using play-based learning in early childhood environmental education. The principles we identify are the result of research conducted with teachers and children using different types of play-based learning whilst engaged in environmental education. The play-types used in the research connect with the historical use of play-based learning in early childhood education as a basis for pedagogy. This history is examined in Chap. 2 of the book. The principles are also informed by consideration of the environmental education literature. Here, we consider the extent to which environmental education expresses different epistemological and ontological perspectives regarding the purpose of environmental learning. In Chap. 3 we reflect on these differing viewpoints and canvass how they have been expressed to date in early childhood education, including the well-known 'Education for Sustainability' (EfS) approach.

Chapters 4–6 of the book are dedicated to showcasing the pedagogical work of teachers and children using different types of play-based learning to engage in environmental education. The final chapter, Chap. 7, reflects on this work and articulates two guiding principles for using play-based learning in early childhood environmental education. These principles are:

1. Valuing different play-types according to their pedagogical potential for engaging with aspects of environmental education; and
2. Creating combinations of play-types that support engagement with different aspects of environmental education.

The pedagogical work showcased in Chaps. 4–6 is derived from a research project conducted in Victoria, Australia over a 2-year period. The focus of the project was on examining approaches to play-based learning and how these relate to environmental education in the early years. The project involved sixteen early childhood educators and 114 children. The children were all aged 3–5 years and were attending early childhood education in formal prior-to-school settings. All sixteen of the participating educators held university level qualifications in early childhood education at the Bachelor degree (4 years) or higher level. The early childhood settings included a mixture of inner city and suburban locations, as well as a range of socio-economic levels. All settings included a culturally diverse mixture of children and families. In this book we share the pedagogical work and subsequent reflections of three of the participating teachers, including Jeanette, Josh and Robyn. At the start of each chapter we introduce the teachers and provide some background information about their interests in environmental education, their teaching and learning philosophies, and the social and educational context associated with their centres. Each chapter concludes with a brief summary of the approach undertaken by Jeanette, Josh and Robyn which highlights how the two principles of play-based learning were used in their work with the children.

1.3 Project Overview

During the course of the project teachers were invited to a professional learning session and provided with a summarised history of the role of play-based learning in early childhood education (Chap. 2). The teachers were then introduced to three 'types' of pedagogical play-based learning evident in the literature including those described by Trawick-Smith (2012) as the 'trust in play', 'facilitate play' and 'learn and teach play' approaches. The three play-types also included reference to Wood and Attfield's (2005) work describing pedagogical play along a continuum of activity in which children's self-selected play is located towards the left of the continuum and adult-framed activity towards the right (see Chap. 3). In previous work we aligned these play-types with the teaching and learning of biodiversity with young children in early childhood settings (Edwards et al. 2010), describing them as 'open-ended play', 'modelled play' and 'purposefully-framed play'. We selected biodiversity as an important environmental education concept for engaging teachers and children via these play-types because it focuses children's attention on the natural world, exposes children to opportunities for thinking about habitat, and promotes opportunities for learning to respect other living beings (Edwards and Cutter-Mackenzie 2013; Shaffer et al. 2009). The three play-types the teachers used in their engagements with the children therefore included explicit reference to biodiversity as an environmental education concept:

1. *Open-ended play*: located towards the left of the continuum and involving play experiences where the teacher provides children with materials suggestive of a biodiversity concept, and with minimal engagement and interaction allows them to examine and explore the materials as a basis for learning about the concept.
2. *Modelled-play*: located in the middle of the continuum and involving play experiences where the teacher illustrates, explains and/or demonstrates the use of materials suggestive of a biodiversity concept prior to allowing children to use the materials with minimal adult interaction as basis for learning about the concept.
3. *Purposefully-framed play*: located across the entire spectrum of the continuum and involving play experiences in which the teacher provides children with materials suggestive of a biodiversity concept and provides opportunities for open-ended play, followed by modelled-play and then teacher-child interaction/ engagement.

The teachers were invited to use these three play-types to engage children in learning about biodiversity in their own settings. Each teacher was provided with a concept map outlining what topics might be associated with biodiversity as an environmental education concept. This included animal habitats, habitat destruction and plant life as relevant areas of investigation (Fig. 1.1).

The play-types were clustered into several different iterations so that of the 16 participating teachers there were small groups of teachers implementing the play-types in different orders. This meant that some teachers implemented open-ended play experiences with the children, then a modelled-play experience and finally a purposefully-framed play experience. Other educators commenced with purposefully-framed play, then modelled-play and finished with open-ended play. As we

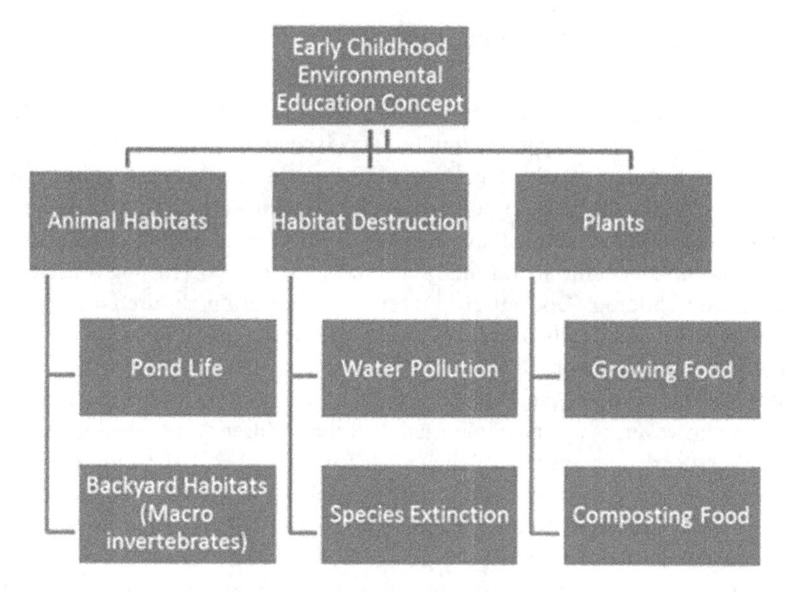

Fig. 1.1 Concept map provided to teachers—what topics might be associated with biodiversity as an early childhood environmental education concept?

discuss in Chaps. 4–6, the order of play-types implemented by Jeanette, Josh and Robyn influenced their thinking about the children's engagement with environmental education. This included how the children were acquiring conceptual knowledge about biodiversity and the provision of opportunities to directly engage children in challenging biophobic (fear of nature) dispositions.

At each setting the teachers progressively implemented a planned play-type experience with the participating children focusing on their selected biodiversity topic. The biodiversity topic was selected by the teachers in collaboration with the children's interests shown at the time. Jeanette selected pond life (Chap. 4), Josh focused on macroinvertebrates (Chap. 5) and Robyn on worms and worm habitat (Chap. 6). The implementation of these experiences were video-taped by the research team and later re-played to the children who were invited to comment on their play and any learning about biodiversity they recalled from their participation. These child video-stimulated recall interviews were also video-taped and the 'second level' video footage was later shown to the teachers during a post play-type implementation interview (Cutter-Mackenzie et al. 2013). During these interviews the teachers reflected on their use of the play-types, including what they believed the children were learning, and how different combinations of play-types appeared to support different aspects of environmental learning. In Chap. 7 we consider how these teacher reflections inform the identification of the two principles for using play-based learning in early childhood environmental education.

1.4 Children as Active Participants

Although the research was specifically about pedagogical strategies implemented by the educators, the participating children's perspectives were critical to understanding the learning involved in each play type. As such, these children were equally involved in the study as active participants who were considered competent to express an opinion about their learning (Lundy et al. 2011). Child focused researchers have become increasingly aware of the ethical tensions raised when working with children (Dockett 2011), especially ensuring children are given the opportunity to authentically decide if they are willing to participate and/or withdraw their assent at any stage of the study (Phelan and Kinsella 2013). All of the children involved in this project participated with the full consent of their parents and guardians; however, it was also important that the children were asked to give their 'written' and verbal assent to participate (McTavish et al. 2012). Consequently, the children were provided with a child-friendly explanatory letter about the research, and invited to read this with their parents/guardians. Children interested in participating indicated their agreement by 'signing' (coloring, making a mark, writing their name) an assent form. At the actual time of each data collection session, the children were verbally re-invited to participate and asked 'would you like to do this today?' and, 'can we make a video of you playing?' Children who said 'no' were able to participate in the activity at a later time if they chose to and were not filmed.

As becomes evident when reading the descriptions of the play-types in Chaps. 4–6, the children's participation varied even throughout the implementation of the experiences once the filming had commenced. Some of the children started the experiences and then left. Others came in and out of the experiences and were supported to do so by the teachers and the researchers. A child leaving the experience was deemed to have withdrawn 'assent' for that period of time and so was not filmed. In this way, the researchers can be seen to be respecting the children's ethical right to withdraw participation without overt or subtle coercion by adults focused on the collection of data (Sumsion 2003). Instead, this process demonstrates the value placed on the children's meta-narratives as they 'analysed and reported' their own learning witnessed through the video recall of biodiversity focused play experiences (Lundy et al. 2011, p. 716). Children and parents/guardians were invited to either select a pseudonym or indicate a preference for using the child's first name only in the reporting of the research. In all cases except one, children and families elected to use the child's first name.

1.5 Conclusion

The opening vignette for this chapter presents a challenge for early childhood environmental education. This is because swirling some seaweed and playing with some plastic sea animals is simply not enough to help children engage with the range of knowledge, skills and dispositions needed to support their active participation in society as environmentally engaged citizens. In this book, we draw on the early childhood education and environmental education literature, in addition to our own research with teachers and children, to identify two principles for using play-based learning in early childhood environmental education to address this challenge. As the examples in Chaps. 4–6 highlight, these principles enable educators to value the pedagogical potential of different play-types and to combine the play-types in ways that enable them to realise particular environmental learning goals for young children. These goals could include engaging with content knowledge, developing biophilic dispositions towards nature, or learning to value the environment for its own sake. In the last chapter of the book we use the two principles to illustrate how Seth's engagement with the children's learning about biodiversity (opening vignette) could be reconsidered, and in doing so allow him to realise environmental learning experiences that move beyond noting only the social and pretend play value associated with the children's play in the wading pool.

References

Cutter-Mackenzie, A., Edwards, S., & Widdop Quinton, H. (2013). Child-framed video research methodologies: Issues, possibilities and challenges for researching with children. *Children's Geographies.*

Davis, J. (2010). What is early childhood education for sustainability? In J. Davis (Ed.), *Young children and the environment: Early education for sustainability* (pp. 21–43). Cambridge: Cambridge University Press.

Dockett, S., Einarsdottir, J., & Perry, B. (2011). Balancing methodologies and methods in researching with young children (Chap. 5). In D. Harcourt, B. Perry, & T. Waller, (Eds.) *Researching young children's perspectives: Debating the ethics and dilemmas of educational research with children.* Oxon: Routledge.

Edwards, S., Cutter-Mackenzie, A., & Hunt, E. (2010). Framing play for learning: Professional reflections on the role of open-ended play in early childhood education. In L. Brooker & S. Edwards (Eds.), *Engaging Play* (pp. 136–151). London: Open University Press.

Edwards, S., & Cutter-Mackenzie, A. (2013). Pedagogical play-types: what do they suggest for learning about sustainability in early childhood education? *International Journal of Early Childhood, 45*(3), 327–346.

Fleer, M. (2010). *Early learning and development: Cultural-historical concepts in play.* Melbourne: Cambridge University Press.

Howitt, C., Lewis, S., & Upson, E. (2011). 'It's a mystery!' A case study of implementing forensic science in preschool as scientific inquiry. *Australasian Journal of Early Childhood, 36*(3), 45–55.

Lundy, L., McEvoy, L., & Byrne, B. (2011). Working with young children as co-researchers: An approach informed by the United Nations convention on the rights of the child. *Early Education and Development, 22*(5), 714–735.

McTavish, M., Streelasky, J., & Coles, L. (2012). Listening to children's voices: Children as participants in research. *International Journal of Early Childhood, 44*, 249–267.

Orr, D. W. (1992). *Ecological literacy: Education and the transition to a postmodern world.* Albany: State University of New York.

Phelan, S. K., & Kinsella, E. A. (2013). Picture this…Safety, dignity, and voice—ethical research with children: Practical considerations for the reflexive researcher. *Qualitative Inquiry, 19*(2), 81–90.

Shaffer, L., Hall, E., & Lynch, M. (2009). Toddlers' scientific explorations. Encounters with insects. *Young Children, 64*(6), 18–41.

Sumsion, J. (2003). Researching with children: Lessons in humility, reciprocity and community. *Australian Journal of Early Childhood, 28*(1), 1–9.

Trawick-Smith, J. (2012). Teacher-child play interactions to achieve learning outcomes: Risks and opportunities. In R. C. Pianta, W. S. Barnett, L. M. Justice, & S. M. Sheridan (Eds.), *Handbook of early childhood education*. New York: Giuldford Publications.

UNESCO-UNEP. (1976). The Belgrade Charter: A global framework for environmental education. *Connect: UNESCO-UNEP Environmental Education Newsletter, 1,* 1–2.

Waller, T., Sandseter, E., Wyver, S., Arlemalm-Hagser, E., & Maynard, T. (2010). The dynamics of early childhood spaces: Opportunities for outdoor play? *European Early Childhood Education Research Journal, 18*(4), 437–445.

Wilson, E. O. (1992). *The diversity of life*. Cambridge: Harvard University Press.

Wood, E., & Attfield, J. (2005). *Play, learning and the early childhood curriculum* (2nd ed.). London: Paul Chapman.

Chapter 2
Play-Based Learning in Early Childhood Education

Abstract This chapter problematises play in the twenty-first century and begins with a review of the work of Rousseau, Froebel and Dewey highlighting their enduring influence on play-based practices in early childhood education. The chapter reviews the influence of Piaget's theory on the construction of knowledge via active exploration through play. Working under a Piagetian approach, which has significantly influenced Developmentally Appropriate Practice, the perspective that children learn 'naturally' through play, with the teacher facilitating opportunities for play in the environment, is apparent. However, the authors question whether these views are still current in the twenty-first century, and further question the notion that children learn 'naturally' through play. Applying Vygotsky's understanding about the social mediation of knowledge and learning, and play as a context for adult interaction, the role of the teacher during play to support children's learning is apparent. The authors further question through this reconceptualisation of play: How do teachers know that children are learning? And what is the role of the teacher in children's play? Attention to these questions leads to a more critical consideration of the role of pedagogical play, and the role of the teacher, in early childhood education. This chapter explores such considerations in-depth.

2.1 Introduction

"Recently, I made some profound discoveries that have provided a pivotal moment in my long career within the early childhood profession. The first discovery, which I found in a secret compartment of an old jewellery box, was a yellowed but neatly folded clipping from an early Australian newspaper from the turn of the last century (Fig. 2.1). It detailed the opening of a new kindergarten for the 'small wee ones' in the local Parish Hall. The newspaper spoke in effusive terms of the pencils, paper and dolls provided for the children who were 'seated on wee chairs at little wee tables' under the loving care of the teacher. The second discovery, I realised with a shock, was that nothing much has changed since the

A. Cutter-Mackenzie et al., *Young Children's Play and Environmental Education in Early Childhood Education*, SpringerBriefs in Education,
DOI: 10.1007/978-3-319-03740-0_2,

Fig. 2.1 Australian newspaper clipping about the opening of Pingelly Kindergarten in Western Australia from the early 1900s (unknown newspaper and date)

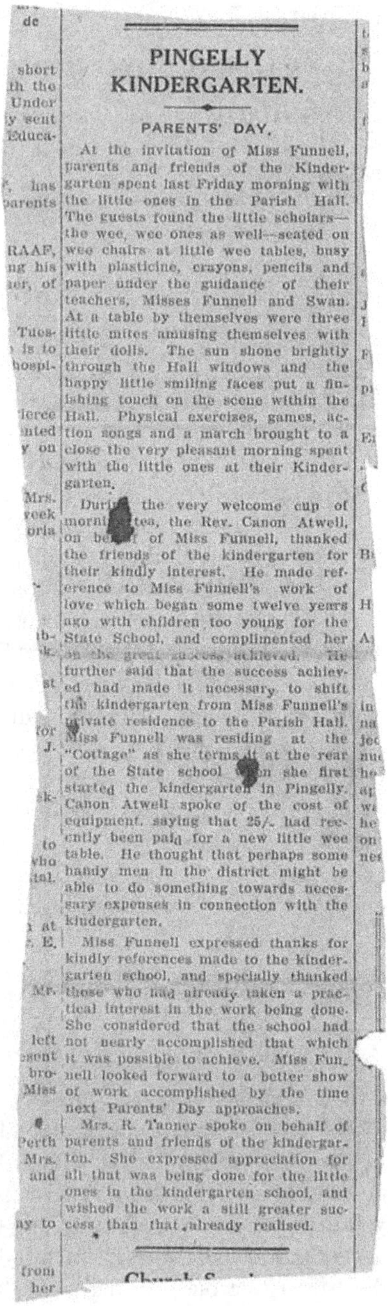

PINGELLY KINDERGARTEN.

PARENTS' DAY.

At the invitation of Miss Funnell, parents and friends of the Kindergarten spent last Friday morning with the little ones in the Parish Hall. The guests found the little scholars—the wee, wee ones as well—seated on wee chairs at little wee tables, busy with plasticine, crayons, pencils and paper under the guidance of their teachers, Misses Funnell and Swan. At a table by themselves were three little mites amusing themselves with their dolls. The sun shone brightly through the Hall windows and the happy little smiling faces put a finishing touch on the scene within the Hall. Physical exercises, games, action songs and a march brought to a close the very pleasant morning spent with the little ones at their Kindergarten.

During the very welcome cup of morning tea, the Rev. Canon Atwell, on behalf of Miss Funnell, thanked the friends of the kindergarten for their kindly interest. He made reference to Miss Funnell's work of love which began some twelve years ago with children too young for the State School, and complimented her on the great success achieved. He further said that the success achieved had made it necessary to shift the kindergarten from Miss Funnell's private residence to the Parish Hall. Miss Funnell was residing at the "Cottage" as she terms it at the rear of the State school when she first started the kindergarten in Pingelly. Canon Atwell spoke of the cost of equipment, saying that 25/- had recently been paid for a new little wee table. He thought that perhaps some handy men in the district might be able to do something towards necessary expenses in connection with the kindergarten.

Miss Funnell expressed thanks for kindly references made to the kindergarten school, and specially thanked those who had already taken a practical interest in the work being done. She considered that the school had not nearly accomplished that which it was possible to achieve. Miss Funnell looked forward to a better show of work accomplished by the time next Parents' Day approaches.

Mrs. R. Tanner spoke on behalf of parents and friends of the kindergarten. She expressed appreciation for all that was being done for the little ones in the kindergarten school, and wished the work a still greater success than that already realised.

early 1900s in the contemporary early childhood settings and provisions of the twenty-first century. This seems true I realised, despite more than 100 years of intense investigation and research into children's play, learning and education. Why, I wondered with this concrete evidence in my hand, is the early childhood community so resistant to change?" (Moore, personal communication, 20th June, 2012)

A kindergarten established over 100 years ago is filled with small chairs, paper, pencils and dolls. Many years later, this very description remains a familiar account of typical early childhood provision. In this chapter we examine the concept of 'pedagogical play' and how this concept has informed the use of materials such as those celebrated in the opening of the Pingelly Kindergarten in Western Australia in the early 1900s—and continues to inform approaches to learning and teaching in early childhood education today. Pedagogical play refers to the use of play in early childhood education to promote the learning of young children (Wood 2010). Pedagogical play has a long and contentious history in early childhood education, beginning with the argument that children learn most 'naturally' from play, and focussing more recently on problematising what and how children learn through play. In this chapter we consider this history and outline where ideas about the naturalness of children's play came from and how these ideas have more recently been challenged by 'postdevelopmental' perspectives on pedagogical play.

2.2 Historical Theoretical and Philosophical Informants to Early Childhood Education

Deeply entrenched within the historical roots of early childhood education, play has long been a dominant feature of Western-European pedagogy (Rogers 2011). Over many centuries, philosophers, theorists, educationalists and more recently, policy makers have worked hard to define the nature of childhood, play and the purposes of education (Fisher 2008). In particular, researchers have become increasingly interested in how traditional and contemporary theories on play and childhood have informed conceptualisations of childhood (Grieshaber and McArdle 2010), the 'image of the child' (Malaguzzi 1994), and the development of early childhood curriculum (Graue 2008). Wood and Attfield (2005) claim that until the nineteenth century, "childhood was seen as an immature form of adulthood and children from all social classes had little status in society" (p. 29). Wood and Attfield suggest that it was the studies of classical play theorists, such as Rousseau, Froebel and Dewey, that dramatically changed societal views and attitudes towards children, to the extent that "freedom to learn could be combined with appropriate nurturing and guidance" (p. 29), through the strongly held belief that play was critical to children's learning and development (Platz and Arellano 2011).

These early theorists were strong advocates for children learning in, and from, nature as active learners, suggesting that "children learned best when they were allowed to observe and interact with nature and life" (Platz and Arellano 2011, pp. 56–57). Integral to their beliefs, was the view that children were naturally good, and so educational and social goals for young children should be orientated towards nurturing this natural innocence. Platz and Arellano (2011) suggest that "the origins of many early childhood education theories and practices today can be traced back in time to early educators and philosophers who had a passion for the development and education of young children" (p. 54). However, despite the fact that the philosophies of these theorists were not always endorsed during their lifetimes (due to various political and moral stances of the time), their work has clearly impacted on European-Western ideologies regarding the importance of play as a primary mode of learning for young children in early childhood education (Lillemyr 2009).

Jean Jacques Rousseau (1712–1778), as one of the first notable philosophers, was attributed with many idealistic views about children and childhood. Notions associated with child-centred education where "nature requires children to be children first" are believed to have initiated from Rousseau's theories on education (Platz and Arellano 2011, p. 56). Rousseau is known for his romantic views on children's innocence and the 'golden age of childhood' together with other significant shifts in the concept of childhood, as James et al. (1998) suggest:

> Rather than just instilling a sense of childhood innocence, Rousseau, more significantly, opened up the question of the child's particularity, a question that remains central in the status of person, a specific class of being with needs and desires and even rights. And it is this personification which has paved the way for our contemporary concern about children as individuals (p. 13).

While the issue of children's rights appears to have foundations in Rousseau's pioneering work, it has only become a "special safeguard for children" with the *United Nations Convention on the Rights of the Child* (1989) in more recent times (Lee 2001). Rousseau's projection of childhood innocence also paved the way for an image of the innocent child needing protection, and a tendency for adults to feel the need to "shelter children from the corrupt surrounding world … by constructing a form of environment in which the young child will be offered protection, continuity and security" (Dahlberg et al. 1999, p. 45). Early childhood settings have been perceived as providing this protective role, especially in relation to environmental education which has been viewed as a potentially overwhelming topic for the developmental capacity of young children (see for example Duhn 2012). Graue (2008) argues that this situation is a misplaced function of early childhood education's concern with children's development, and the sense that very young children in their innocence may not be ready to engage with complex conceptual or socially-based ideas.

Oelkers (2002) in his study of *Rousseau and the image of 'modern education'*, claims that Rousseau "took for granted that the self-development of the child is driven by immediate interests, i.e., not by instruction or by formal education" (p. 683), and continues this line of Rousseau's thinking by stating, "If educators let the child always be himself, attending to only what touches him immediately, then and only then will they find the child learning, capable of perceiving, memorizing, and even reasoning" (p. 683). The underlying premise intrinsic to many early childhood philosophies and policies of 'taking the child's interest' clearly has its roots in this theory of Rousseau's approach to early education (Hedges et al. 2011).

It is generally agreed that the theories espoused by the German theorist, Fredrich Froebel (1782–1852) as the creator of the first 'kindergarten' or 'children's garden', were not only the most significant during his time, but still have an enduring influence on current early childhood practices (Ailwood 2007). Sherwood and Reifel (2010) comment on the "central element" of United States kindergartens initially holding "tightly to its Froebelian roots" (p. 323). These roots can likewise be viewed across many Western-European orientated approaches to early childhood curriculum, including in the New Zealand *Te Whariki* (Ministry of Education 1996) early childhood guidelines, the Australian *Early Years Learning Framework* (Department of Education, Employment and Workforce Relations 2009), the Singaporean Curriculum Framework for Kindergartens *Nurturing Early Learners* (Ministry of Education 2012), the framework for the *Early Years Foundation Stage* in the United Kingdom (Department for Education 2012), the *National Curriculum Guidelines on Early Childhood Education and Care in Finland* (Ministry of Social Affairs and Health 2004) and in the American National Association for the Education of Young Children's (NAEYC) *Developmentally Appropriate Practice Guidelines* (2009). In each of these documents reference is commonly made to children's play and their play-based interests as an initial site for learning and development. For example, the Singaporean curriculum document suggests:

> Play is the primary mechanism through which children encounter and explore their immediate environment. As such, play becomes a natural way to motivate children to learn about themselves and the world around them (Ministry of Education 2012, p. 34).

Likewise the Developmentally Appropriate Practice Guidelines say of play:

> Children of all ages love to play, and it gives them opportunities to develop physical competence and enjoyment of the outdoors, understand and make sense of their world, interact with others, express and control emotions, develop their symbolic and problem-solving abilities, and practice emerging skills (NAEYC 2009, p. 14).

Froebel believed that children would learn through their play, and therefore, "learn to live in harmony with others and nature" (Platz and Arellano 2011, p. 60). Edwards and Hammer (2006) suggest that:

> Froebel devised curriculum materials and a methodology of education that would foster a blossoming of concepts and understanding in young children's thinking. His approach to early childhood teaching emphasized the inherent nature of children's learning that unfolds through their play; the structure of developing concepts that were drawn from nature and the role of the teacher. Froebel's understanding of children's play was extrapolated as 'serious work' and he developed a sequence of 'Gifts' and 'Occupations' to harness what he described as a natural energy that could be directed towards learning concepts (p. 195).

The importance Froebel placed on the concepts of "first hand experiences and self-chosen activities" were manifestations of his belief that adults should "begin where the learner is" and only "sensitively intervene" in children's play (Wood and Attfield 2005, p. 29). Many of these ideas are still evident in the philosophies and teaching techniques associated with early childhood education today (Krogh and Slentz 2010). For example, Liebschner (1993) highlights Froebel's theories around the importance of meaningful play embedded in his gifts, occupations and practical 'work in the garden' by quoting Froebel's actual tenet as:

> Play must always be in agreement with the total life of the child as well as with his environment, and cannot stand in isolation or be divorced from it; play will then be educative, serious and meaningful. Through it, life becomes more relevant (p. 54).

Interestingly, Froebel's appeal for play to be in agreement with the child's life could be viewed as a harbinger of the cultural historical argument regarding the significance of context in children's learning. For example, Vygotsky (1997) also talked of the need for educational experience to connect strongly with children's life experiences, saying that "Ultimately only life educates, and the deeper that life, the real world, burrows into the school, the more dynamic and the more robust will be the educational process" (p. 345). Froebel however, was especially interested in implementing his kindergarten ideas and practices for young children in the "space between home and school" as a "half day educational service" (Ailwood 2007, p. 53).

May (2006) argues that since Froebel's times, early childhood advocates have been attempting to "persuade society in general and politicians in particular as to the benefits of early childhood care and education for children prior to school entry" (pp. 245–246). May also suggests early childhood has "always been a site for experiment" (p. 262), and that indeed, to be considered "Froebelian, is about being an advocate for children, for women and for social justice" (p. 262). For Froebel, the image of the child, was one that focused on understanding "the young child as nature" where children's learning and "inherent capabilities" unfolded naturally when given the opportunity to do so (Dahlberg et al. 1999, p. 46).

John Dewey (1859–1952), an American philosopher and educational reformist, believed it was important to provide many different experiences to enable children's learning through play "as a lifelong process in which children grew and learned along the way" (Platz and Arellano 2011, p. 56). Dewey, similar to the philosophers before him, strongly believed in connecting with the natural interests and activities of young children, such that the "question of education is the question of taking hold of his [sic] activities, of giving them direction" (Dewey 1956, p. 36). Interests, play experiences and opportunities for exploring the outdoors arguably placed the child at the centre of education and emphasised learning in social and meaningful contexts (Dewey 1956, p. 33). Wood and Attfield (2005) argue that Dewey viewed children as "co-constructors of their learning; he saw them as active agents and active participants in shaping their learning environments and experiences" (p. 30). Years later these same ideas were to become visible in the Reggio Emilia early childhood education practices, particularly in the focus on the competent and capable child "as an architect of their own learning" (Dodd-Nufrio 2011, p. 236). Interestingly, the concept of the socially agentive child reflects many of the newly emerging ideas from the sociology of childhood (Bass 2010; Corsaro 2011) and the late 1990s positioning of the child as "the child as a co-constructor of knowledge, identity and culture" (Dahlberg et al. 1999, p. 48).

Further changes in societal attitudes towards children and childhood were influenced by increasing childhood studies during the early to mid-twentieth century. Wood (2007) describes the historical trend of increasingly combining theory and practice in early child development and education, providing the prime example of E.R. Boyce (1946) in the "child-centred educational experiment" she set up in London, and states:

> Child-centred education incorporated care, rescue and correction of 'defects' alongside a commitment to free choice and free play within a richly resourced learning environment. There was no distinction between work and play … Content knowledge was embedded in play activities that reflected their everyday lives, and promoted fantasy and imagination (p. 121).

Although, the educational reforms and curriculum created and implemented by the early theorists are relevant to the time and contexts in which they were developed it is clear that much of their early beliefs and images of childhood have had a powerful impact on our current early childhood education systems and practices (Lim and Genishi 2010). In the latter part of the twentieth century political, social and economic changes and pressures became progressively more controlling in how early childhood curriculum was approached, with increasing demands to produce children who would be a "well prepared workforce for the future" (Dahlberg et al. 1999, p. 45). The French historian, Aries in his work on *Centuries of Childhood* (1962) may have "rediscovered the lost childhood from the past" (Frijhoff 2012, p. 24), however the society of the mid-twentieth century also discovered "the child as labour market supply factor" (Dahlberg et al. 1999, p. 46).

Jean Piaget (1896–1980), a Swiss developmental psychologist, was particularly interested in young children's cognitive development. Many aspects of Piaget's theory became associated with early childhood education during the 1960s. This is possibly because of the extent to which his ideas regarding the children's construction of knowledge aligned with existing ideas about the naturalness of children's learning through play already in place due to the influence of Frobel and Rousseau (Krogh and Slentz 2010). Piaget's emphasis on the explorative capacities of young children combined with the suggestion that learning experiences were most appropriately matched with children's play-based stages of development had significant implications for the pedagogical strategies associated with many early childhood programs over the past 50 years (Hatch 2010). Dahlberg et al. (1999) argue that the image of "Piaget's child" as progressing biologically through stages towards maturity was preferred by the scientific and psychological disciplines, suggesting that "the dominant developmental approach to childhood provided by psychology, is based on the idea of natural growth… childhood therefore is a biologically determined stage on the path to full human status" (p. 46).

2.3 Developmentally Appropriate Practice in Early Childhood Education

Piagetian theory and philosophical ideas about children and childhood subsequently informed the influence of the Developmentally Appropriate Practice (DAP) guidelines for early childhood education. Initially published in 1987 by the American National Association for the Education of Young Children (Bredekamp 1987), the guidelines were intended to respond to pressures to make the early childhood curriculum overly academic and provide a theoretical and research evidence base for protecting children's opportunity to learn and develop through the provision of traditionally valued play-based experiences. There was an early emphasis on the provision of play experiences that would support children's active engagement in play and the matching of children's developmental capacities to play activities (Edwards 2003).

Later, significant critique of the DAP guidelines (Kessler 1991; Silin 1987) saw them modified in 1997 (Bredekamp and Copple 1997), and again in 2009, to include greater focus on the role of social and cultural interactions on children's learning, play and development. Nonetheless, many of the Piagetian ideals about early learning and development associated with the DAP guidelines have become firmly entrenched in understandings about appropriate early childhood education. Hatch (2010) attempts to explain why the early childhood field has been hesitant to leave the security of a Piagetian theoretical framework behind:

> It feels heretical to challenge the Piagetian orthodoxy of the early childhood field... [it is] difficult to say why Piaget's core ideas and assumptions of developmental approaches have endured... perhaps early childhood educators have associated the precepts of Piagetian developmentalism so closely with a 'child centred' approach that to abandon them would feel tantamount to abandoning their concern for children (pp. 266–267).

Hatch's view is possibly accurate given the particularly close links established between child-centred practice, the images of the child and the underlying premise for developmental theories. However, emerging pedagogical practices and research interests from outside Piagetian ideas saw increased interest in alternative viewpoints on young children's play and its role in early childhood education. In particular, research began to be directed towards questions such as 'what do young children learn through play?' And 'are children able to learn through free play alone?' (Gibbons 2007; Hedges 2010).

These concerns have recently been summarised by Yelland (2011) who suggested that learning through play can be "problematic and misleading" (p. 5) because whilst children may be having "fun participating in such free play sessions" the type of learning taking place may not necessarily be obvious. The opening vignette to this book in which Seth observed the children swirling seaweed is a case in point. In such situations it is possible to ask "what connections are being made to the child's lived experiences and knowledge building and how are these articulated and extended in supporting activities?" (Yelland 2011, p. 5). The 'problem' with play became highly debated as researchers emphasised the need for adult interaction during children's play to support learning (Winsler and Carlton 2003). Others criticised adult intervention in play as damaging to children's self-agency (O'Brien 2010), and still others worked to promote an understanding of balanced or integrated play that provided opportunities for both child-centred activity and adult interaction (Wood 2013). Meanwhile, the updated Singaporean Curriculum Framework for Kindergartens directly referenced a continuum perspective on children's play, emphasising the role of teacher interactions during play to support children's learning:

> Play can range from being unstructured with free choice by children and no/little active adult support to being highly structured with teacher-led instruction and direction. While recognising the benefits of child-initiated and free play-choice play, this framework highlights the critical role of the teacher in purposeful play (Ministry of Education, Singapore 2012, p. 34)

In part, the problem can be attributed to what was hinted at in the beginning of this chapter—somewhat unchanged materials and practices in the provision of early years pedagogy that mean it can be difficult to change what actually happens in terms of using play as the basis for supporting learning. Krieg (2010) taps neatly into this problem discussing the influence the 'technologies' (i.e., pencils, paper and dolls) of traditional kindergartens have on taken-for-granted pedagogies—that is, the assumption that the provision of stimulating materials will be sufficient for promoting the type of play that will allow children to learn and construct their own understandings of the world. This is the very basis of the play provision offered by Seth in the opening chapter. The plastic sea animals, seaweed and sponges supposedly embed concepts about biodiversity into the play experience—by making these materials available Seth may well believe the children will learn what characterises the different creatures. Meanwhile, recent arguments continue to suggest that, whilst challenging, the "time is ripe for a critical empirical and theoretical look at the contribution of play and an examination of what is perceived as play from the perspectives of all the stakeholders" (Stephen 2010, p. 19). This movement towards a more critical consideration of the role of pedagogical play in early childhood education has commenced within the context of postdevelopmental perspectives on early childhood education.

2.4 Postdevelopmental Perspectives on Early Childhood Education

Continued engagement with ideas associated with Developmentally Appropriate Practice in early childhood education were supported by a range of contemporary perspectives on early learning, development and play, including post-modernism, post-structural, sociocultural and sociology of childhood viewpoints (Nolan and Kilderry 2010). Collectively, these perspectives increasingly captured the notion of being 'postdevelopmental' (Blaise 2009), whilst individually they are understood to hold quite significant theoretical and philosophical lines of thought that distinguish each from the other.

Amongst the most significant of the postdevelopmental perspectives has been the work of the Russian psychologist Lev Vygotsky (1896–1934). Vygotsky developed his theory during the early part of the twentieth Century through periods of great social upheaval and war. Nonetheless, his work has had far reaching implications for early childhood education and contemporary childhood studies in terms of his explanation of children's mastery of play, the development of imagination and the increasingly significant role of the teacher in children's learning (Kozulin 2001; Bodrova 2008). Kozulin et al. (2003) describe Vygotsky's work as:

> At the heart of Vygtosky's theory lies the understanding of human cognition and learning as social and cultural rather than individual phenomena... Vygotsky strongly believed in the close relationship between learning and development and in the sociocultural nature of both. He proposed that a child's development depends on the interaction between a child's individual maturation and a system of symbolic tools and activities that the child appropriates from his or her sociocultural environment. Learning in its systematic, organized, and intentional form appears in sociocultural theory as a driving force of development, as a consequence rather than a premise of learning experiences (p. 1).

Corsaro (2011) supports Vygotsky's ideas about children's interpretation of their culture through the acquisition of language and other cultural "tools or signs" (such as, drawing, objects) which are "created over the course of history and change with cultural development" (p. 15). According to Vygotsky, children "through their acquisition and use of language, come to reproduce a culture that contains knowledge of generations" (Corsaro 2011, p. 15). Corsaro (2011) continues stating "Vygotsky saw practical activities developing from the child's attempts to deal with everyday problems. Furthermore, in dealing with these problems, the child always develops strategies collectively—that is, in interaction with others" (p. 16).

From a sociocultural perspective, the teachers' role is much more proactive and engaged than previous understandings of pedagogical play which tended to highlight the role of the child's freely-chosen investigation in learning. From this perspective, Seth's approach, in which he stood and watched as the children played in the wading pool, would be considered insufficient for supporting learning. The increased role of the adult in children's learning therefore challenged conventional ideas about the child being the 'centre' of learning (Graue 2008), and resulted instead in arguments about pedagogical play that increasingly emphasised adult interactions to support children's conceptual learning and the acquisition of content knowledge (Eun 2010; Fleer 2010). Göncü and Gaskins (2011) argued that this movement represented a feasible reading of Vygotsky's ideas about the social orientation of play, however, noted that the adult "harnessing" of play for educative purposes shifted children's play from a focus on symbolic exploration to an intentional focus on learning (p. 55).

This shift was seen in the uptake of the idea of 'intentional teaching' (Duncan 2009; Epstein 2007) and in the use of the term 'sustained shared thinking' (Siraj-Blatchford 2009), where the educator and child engage in conversation to further promote learning. Questions about how to best balance the role of intentional teaching with children, as opposed to setting up environments for open-ended play and acting as a facilitator to children's learning are becoming increasingly evident in research with educators (Thomas et al. 2011). This is particularly so where educators are concerned with the content associated with young children's learning and how such content learning can be best supported in early childhood contexts. Increasingly it is understood that content knowledge is constructed by children in concert with educators who already hold some degree of knowledge themselves. As Hedges and Cullen (2005) suggest:

> The kinds of informal, everyday knowledge children construct are mediated by teachers' domain knowledge in the context of responsive pedagogical approaches and can be a foundation for the co-construction of more formal knowledge (p. 5).

How children access content through pedagogical play is an area of research that increasingly highlights the relationship between children and teachers as a basis for learning (Hatch 2010). Whilst play and opportunities for freely-chosen play are historically valued and important, content knowledge and how this is co-constructed between children and teachers, is also considered increasingly significant in early childhood education. As Pramling-Samuelsson and Carlsson (2008) argued, if play is to be considered educative in basis it would have to teach children 'something'. This representation of the 'something' sums up the tensions associated with contemporary perspectives on pedagogical play in early childhood education and illustrates the need for principles of play-based learning to inform early childhood environmental education. Otherwise, the situation can be very like the opening vignette in this book in which Seth observed the children at play, but there was little sense of what they learning about biodiversity that was going to contribute to their environmental education.

A shifting emphasis on the nature of interactions between children and adults in early childhood settings suggests instead that content needs to be more explicitly engaged by teachers for the pedagogical potential of play to be realised as environmental learning. Pedagogical play (encompassing the idea that play can be used in early childhood education to support learning) therefore centres on the debate regarding the extent to which the play should be relatively open-ended and exploratory, and the extent to which it should involve focussed interactions between children and adults in relation to particular content (Fleer 2011).

Another area of postdevelopmental research that has contributed to perspectives on pedagogical play is associated with the emergence of ideas from the sociology of childhood perspective (Dahlberg and Moss 2005; Moran-Ellis 2010; Shanahan 2007). James et al. (1998) describe a "new paradigm of the sociology of childhood" where children are no longer merely a "category" but "social actors shaping as well as shaped by their circumstances" (p. 6). James et al. (1998) claim that "the discovery of children as agents" (p. 6) is of prime importance in this new way of thinking about children because it opens opportunities for thinking about how children construct perspectives, experiences and knowledge in relational ways. Dahlberg (2009) also established this perspective, suggesting that knowledge is socially co-constructed by children as social actors capable of creatively influencing their own lives within "their everyday lives in the preschool" (p. 235). Pedagogically, Nolan and Kilderry (2010) argue that:

> Postdevelopmental orientations are inspired by theories and practices located outside child development theory, and suggest that play, and the pedagogical use of play, are not governed by individual children's 'needs'. Instead children are viewed as competent, socially active learners who are able to co-construct their learning intentions, learning strategies and learning outcomes in culturally meaningful ways with peers and adults (p.113).

Similarly, Corsaro (2011) argues that children engaged in peer culture play are able to enact control, autonomy and agency as they negotiate and protect their interactive play spaces within their early childhood settings (p. 161). From a sociology of childhood perspective, educators are likely to view children as competent actors capable of influencing their own learning with ideas and theories of pedagogical worth (Dahlberg et al. 1999, p. 48). With similar beliefs to those expressed by Dewey in the early twentieth century, Dahlberg et al. (1999) defined the 'new' sociology of childhood and the social construction of childhood:

> In this construction of the 'rich' child, learning is not an individual cognitive act undertaken almost in isolation within the head of the child. Learning is a cooperative and communicative activity, in which children construct knowledge, make meaning of the world, together with adults and, equally important, other children: that is why we emphasize that the young child as learner is an active co-constructor. Learning is not the transmission of knowledge taking the child to preordained outcomes, nor is the child a passive receiver and reproducer… he or she is born equipped to learn and does not ask or need adult permission to start learning (p. 50).

Postdevelopmental perspectives on play, whilst emphasising children's co-construction of knowledge in social contexts, also highlight the extent to which play is seen as open to interpretation. This includes seeing play in terms of the impact of gender, peer relationships, cultural experience and socioeconomic opportunities (Grieshaber and McArdle 2010). In early childhood education, this expanded understanding of play has resulted in the suggestion, that rather than seeing pedagogical play only as related to developmental or educational outcomes that educators think about how and why play is being used in early childhood education settings. In this way, play is thought about in terms of the 'context of application' in which it occurs and is used (Brooker and Edwards 2010). This can include developmental and educational outcomes, but also consideration of the impact of peer relationships on children's learning through play or the role of their cultural experiences on learning in early childhood settings. Importantly for early childhood environmental education, the context can and should consider the nature of children's play-based interactions of the world so that these may be orientated towards learning 'something' about the environment.

2.5 Conclusion

Early childhood education has been informed by a rich variety of beliefs and values over many generations of theorists and educators. Many of these ideas are still present in some form in multifaceted combinations of theories, images of the child and pedagogy. Long held views and traditions can be traced from the eighteenth Century through to contemporary thinking about pedagogical play. These include Rousseau's ideas about childhood innocence and protection; Froebel's notion of children being at work when playing in the children's garden; Dewey's focus of the active learner working on real life problems; Boyce's embedding of content knowledge in play; through to Piaget's exposition on the construction of knowledge through active exploration during play. More recently, ideas derived from Vygotsky's understanding about the social mediation of knowledge and learning, and play as a context for adult interaction are increasingly evident in approaches to early childhood education that now also value the role of the educator during play to support learning. The sociology of childhood highlights childhood agency, whilst notions of power relations between children and adults continue to shape discussion regarding the use of play-based learning in early childhood education. While play is gradually reconceptualised, the historical informants are still recognisable, and the Australian kindergarten described in the introduction of this chapter "for the small wee ones", may not be very different from the kindergartens now provided for young children in Singapore, New Zealand, the United States of America, the United Kingdom or Finland. This is not to say that pedagogical practices remain unchanged, rather to reflect on the extent to which early childhood education as a field evolves in relation to highly valued historical ideas about play, and the role of pedagogical play in the education and care of the very young. How these ideas manifest with the provision of early childhood environmental education forms the focus of the Chap. 3.

References

Ailwood, J. (2007). Motherhood, maternalism and early childhood education: Some historical connections. In J. Ailwood (Ed.), *Early childhood in Australia: Historical and comparative contexts*. Frenchs Forest: Pearson Education Australia.

Aries, P. (1962). *Centuries of childhood: A social history of family life*. New York: Knopf.

Bass, L. E. (2010). Childhood in sociology and society: The US perspective. *Current Sociology, 58*(2), 335–350. doi:10.1177/0011392109354248.

Blaise, M. (2009). "What a girl wants, what a girl needs": Responding to sex, gender, and sexuality in the early childhood classroom. *Journal of Research in Childhood Education, 23*(4), 450–460.

Bodrova, E. (2008). Make-believe play versus academic skills: A Vygotskian approach to today's dilemma of early childhood education. *European Early Childhood Education Research Journal, 16*(3), 357–369. doi:10.1080/13502930802291777.

Bredekamp, S. (1987). *Developmentally appropriate practice in early childhood programs serving children from birth through age 8* (Expanded ed.). Washington, D.C.: National Association for the Education of Young Children.

Bredekamp, S., & Copple, C. (1997). *Developmentally appropriate practice in early childhood programs* (Rev ed.). Washington, D.C.: National Association for the Education of Young Children.

Brooker, L., & Edwards, S. (2010). Introduction: From challenging to engaging play. In L. Brooker & S. Edwards (Eds.), *Engaging play* (pp. 1–10). London: Open University Press.

Corsaro, W. A. (2011). *The sociology of childhood* (3rd ed.). Thousand Oaks: Pine Forge Press.

Dahlberg, G. (2009). Policies in early childhood education and care: Potentialities for agency, play and learning. In W. A. Corsaro, M.-S. Honig & J. Qvortrup (Eds.), *The Palgrave handbook of childhood studies*. Basingstoke: Palgrave Macmillan.

Dahlberg, G. & Moss, P. (2005). The ethics and politics in early childhood education. Oxfordshire: Routledge Falmer.

Dahlberg, G., Moss, P., & Pence, A. R. (1999). *Beyond quality in early childhood education and care: Languages of evaluation*. New York: Routledge.

Department of Education. (2012). *Statutory framework for the early years foundation stage: Setting the standards for learning, development and care for children from birth to five*. London: Crown.

Department of Education, Employment and Workplace Relations (DEEWR). (2009). *Belonging, being and becoming: The early years learning framework for Australia*. Canberra: Commonwealth of Australia.

Dewey, J. (1956). *The child and the curriculum, and the school and society*. Chicago: Chicago University Press.

Dodd-Nufrio, A.T. (2011). Reggio Emilia, Maria Montessori, and John Dewey: Dispelling teachers' misconceptions and understanding theoretical foundations. *Early Childhood Education Journal, 39*(4).

Duhn, I. (2012). Making 'place' for ecological sustainability in early childhood education. *Environmental Education Research, 18*(1), 19–29. doi:10.1080/13504622.2011.572162.

Duncan, J. (2009). *Intentional teaching*. Retrieved from http://www.educate.ece.govt.nz/learning/exploringPractice/InfantsandToddlers/EffectivePractices/IntentionalTeaching.aspx

Edwards, S. (2003). New directions: Charting the paths for the role of sociocultural theory in early childhood education and curriculum. *Contemporary Issues in Early Childhood, 4*(3), 251–266.

Edwards, S., & Hammer, M. (2006). The foundations of early childhood education: Historically situated practice. In M. Fleer (Ed.), *Early childhood learning communities: Sociocultural research in practice* (Vol. 8, p. 237). Frenchs Forest: Pearson Education Australia.

Epstein, A. S. (2007). *The intentional teacher: Choosing the best strategies for young children's learning*. Washington, D.C.: National Association for the Education of Young Children.

Eun, B. (2010). From learning to development: A sociocultural approach to instruction. *Cambridge Journal of Education, 40*(4), 401–418. doi:10.1080/0305764X.2010.526593.

Fisher, J. (2008). *Starting from the child: Teaching and learning in the foundation stage* (3rd ed.). Maidenhead: McGraw Hill.

Fleer, M. (2010). *Early learning and development: Cultural-historical concepts in play*. Melbourne: Cambridge University Press.

Fleer, M. (2011). Conceptual Play: foregrounding imagination and cognition during concept formation in early years education, *Contemporary Issues in Early Childhood, 12*(3), 224–240.

Frijhoff, W. (2012). Historian's discovery of childhood. *Paedagogica Historica, 48*(1), 11–29. doi:10.1080/00309230.2011.644568.

Gibbons, A. (2007). The politics of processes and products in education: An early childhood metanarrative crisis? *Educational Philosophy and Theory, 39*(3), 300–311. doi:10.1111/j.1469-5812.2007.00323.x.

Goncu, A., & Gaskins, S. (2011). Comparing and extending Piaget and Vygotksy's understandings of play: Symbolic play as individual, sociocultural, and educational interpretation. In A. Pellegrini (Ed.), *Oxford handbook of the development of play*. New York: Oxford University Press.

Graue, E. (2008). Teaching and learning in a post-DAP world. *Early Education and Development, 19*(3), 441–447. doi:10.1080/10409280802065411.

Grieshaber, S. & McArdle, F. (2010). *The trouble with play*. Maidenhead: Open University Press.
Hatch, J. A. (2010). Rethinking the relationship between learning and development: Teaching for learning in early childhood classrooms. *Educational Forum, 74*(3), 258–268. doi:10.1080/00131725.2010.483911.
Hedges, H. (2010). Whose goals and interest? The interface of children's play and teachers' pedagogical practices. In L. Brooker & S. Edwards (Eds.), *Engaging play* (pp. 25–39). London: Open University Press.
Hedges, H., & Cullen, J. (2005). Subject knowledge in early childhood curriculum and pedagogy: Beliefs and practices. *Contemporary Issues in Early Childhood, 6*(1), 66–79.
Hedges, H., Cullen, J., & Jordan, B. (2011). Early years curriculum: Funds of knowledge as a conceptual framework for children's interests. *Journal of Curriculum Studies, 43*(2), 185–205. doi:10.1080/00220272.2010.511275.
James, A., Jenks, C., & Prout, A. (1998). *Theorizing childhood.* Cambridge: Polity Press in association with Blackwell Publishers Ltd.
Kessler, S. A. (1991). Early childhood education as development: Critique of the metaphor. *Early Education and Development, 2*(2), 137–152.
Kozulin, A. (2001). *Psychological tools: A sociocultural approach to education.* Cambridge: Harvard University Press.
Kozulin, A., Gindis, B., Ageyev, V. S., & Miller, S. (2003). *Vygotsky's educational theory in cultural context.* London: Cambridge University Press.
Krieg, S. (2010). The professional knowledge that counts in Australian contemporary early childhood teacher education. *Contemporary Issues in Early Childhood, 11*(2), 144–155.
Krogh, S., & Slentz, K. (2010). *Early childhood education: Yesterday, today, and tomorrow* (2nd ed.). New York: Routledge.
Lee, N. (2001). *Childhood and society: Growing up in an age of uncertainty*. Philadelphia: Open University Press.
Liebschner, J. (1993). Aims of a good school: The curriculum of Friedrich Froebel: Edited highlights from Froebel's writings. *Early Years: An International Journal of Research and Development, 14*(1), 54–57.
Lillemyr, O. F. (2009). *Taking play seriously: Children and play in early childhood education—an exciting challenge*. Charlotte: IAP, Information Age Pub.
Lim, S., & Genishi, C. (2010). Early childhood curriculum and developmental theory. In P. L. Peterson, E. L. Baker, & B. McGaw (Eds.), *International encyclopedia of education* (3rd ed., pp. 514–519). Oxford: Elsevier.
Malaguzzi, L. (1994). Your image of the child: Where teaching begins. *Early Childhood Educational Exchange, 96*, 52.
May, H. (2006). 'Being Froebelian': An Antipodean analysis of the history of advocacy and early childhood. *Journal of the History of Education Society, 35*(2), 245–262.
Ministry of Education. (1996). New Zealand curriculum document Te Whariki.
Ministry of Social Affairs and Health. (2004). *National curriculum guidelines on ealy childhood education and care in Finland.* Retrieved from http://www.thl.fi/thl-client/pdfs/267671cb-0ec0-4039-b97b-7ac6ce6b9c10
Moran-Ellis, J. (2010). Reflections on the Sociology of Childhood in the UK. *Current Sociology, 58*(2), 186–205. doi:10.1177/0011392109354241.
National Association for the Education of Young Children (NAEYC). (2009). *Developmentally appropriate practice guidelines: Position statement.* Washginton, D.C.: NAEYC.
Nolan, A., & Kilderry, A. (2010). Postdevelopmentalism and professional learning: Implications for understanding the relationship between play and pedagogy. In L. Brooker & S. Edwards (Eds.), *Engaging play* (pp. 108–122). London: Open University Press.
O'Brien, L. (2010). Let the wild rumpus begin! The radical possibilities of play for young children with disabilities. In L. Brooker & S. Edwards (Eds.), *Engaging play* (pp. 182–195). London: Open University Press.
Oelkers, J. (2002). Rousseau and the image of 'modern education'. *Journal of Curriculum Studies, 34*(6), 679–698. doi:10.1080/00220270210141936.

Platz, D., & Arellano, J. (2011). Time tested early childhood theories and practices. *Education, 132*(1), 54–63.

Pramling Samuelsson, I., & Asplund Carlsson, M. (2008). The playing learning child: Towards a pedagogy of early childhood. *Scandinavian Journal of Educational Research, 52*(6), 623–641.

Rogers, S. (Ed.). (2011). *Rethinking play and pedagogy in early childhood education: concepts, contexts and cultures*. Albingdon, England; New York: Routledge.

Shanahan, S. (2007). Lost and found: The sociological ambivalence toward childhood. *Annual Review of Sociology, 33*(1), 407–428.

Sherwood, S. A. S., & Reifel, S. (2010). The multiple meanings of play: Exploring preservice teachers' beliefs about a central element of early childhood education. *Journal of Early Childhood Teacher Education, 31*(4), 322–343. doi:10.1080/10901027.2010.524065.

Silin, J. (1987). The early childhood educator's knowledge base: A reconsideration. In L. G. Katz (Ed.), *Current topics in early childhood education* (Vol. 7, pp. 17–31). Norwood: Ablex Publishing Corp.

Siraj-Blatchford, I. (2009). Conceptualising progression in the pedagogy of play and sustained shared thinking in early childhood education: A Vygotskian perspective. *Educational and Child Psychology, 26*(2), 77–89.

Stephen, C. (2010). Pedagogy: The silent partner in early years learning. *Early Years: Journal of International Research and Development, 30*(1), 15–28. doi:10.1080/09575140903402881.

Thomas, L., Warren, E., & de Vries, E. (2011). Play-based learning and intentional teaching in early childhood contexts. *Australasian Journal of Early Childhood, 36*(4), 69–75.

Vygotsky, L. S. (1997). *Educational psychology*. Boca Raton: St Lucie Press.

Winsler, A., & Carlton, M. P. (2003). Observations of children's task activities and social interactions in relation to teacher perceptions in a child-centered preschool: Are we leaving too much to chance? *Early Education and Development, 14*(2), 155.

Wood, E. (2007). Reconceptualising child-centred education: Contemporary directions in policy, theory and practice in early childhood. *FORUM, 49*(1/2), 119–134.

Wood, E. (2010). Developing integrated pedagogical approaches to play and learning. In P. Broadhead., J, Howard., & E, Wood (Eds.), *Play and learning in the early years*. London: Sage Publications.

Wood, E. (2013). *Play, learning and the early childhood curriculum* (3rd ed.). London: Sage Publications.

Wood, E., & Attfield, J. (2005). *Play, learning and the early childhood curriculum* (2nd ed.). London: Paul Chapman.

Yelland, N. (2011). Reconceptualising play and learning in the lives of young children. *Australasian Journal of Early Childhood, 36*(2), 4–12.

Chapter 3
Environmental Education and Pedagogical Play in Early Childhood Education

Abstract This chapter turns the reader to critical debates and typologies in the environmental education research and literature. Such debates are contextualised within early childhood education and play pedagogies in particular. The authors initially discuss the concepts of sustainable development and sustainability, leading to further critical discussion around the apparent tensions between environmental education and Education for Sustainable Development (ESD)/Education for Sustainability (EFS). The authors challenge the dominant aligning of Education for Sustainability (EFS) and early childhood education, arguing that such alignment is grounded within traditional ideas about children's play. Rather the authors focus upon situating environmental education within contemporary play-based pedagogies. The chapter explores how understanding play-based pedagogy in terms of the role of the teacher is helpful because it widens understandings of 'play' so that content and educator interactions are valued alongside children's activities and interests. Such understandings are essential with respect to supporting children indeveloping ecocentric or biophilic dispositions.

3.1 Introduction

Environmental education is acknowledged as representing a core educational concern in the twenty-first century. This is because environmental education is understood as being an important response to the ways in which human interactions with the world can damage natural and finite resources and put at risk the habitats and ecosystems of different species. In 1972 at the Stockholm *United Nations Conference on the Human Environment*, environmental education was described as "one of the most critical elements of an all-out attack on the world's environmental crisis" (UNESCO-UNEP 1976, p. 2). In the intervening decades, environmental education developed a series of philosophical and research orientated perspectives, in which the purpose of environmental education was variously debated in terms of a range of ideological perspectives (Huckle 1991; Fien 2000;

A. Cutter-Mackenzie et al., *Young Children's Play and Environmental Education in Early Childhood Education*, SpringerBriefs in Education,
DOI: 10.1007/978-3-319-03740-0_3,

Jickling 1992; Jickling and Wals 2007; Sauve 2005). At the international policy level (UNESCO) there has been a notable shift in terminology from Environmental Education to Education for Sustainable Development (ESD) and Education for Sustainability (EFS). Such changes are part of a wider typology of different theoretical and pedagogical positionings or propositions. Sauvé (2005) argues that there are "15 currents" in environmental education whereby sustainable development (including the approaches ESD and EFS) is albeit one current. That argument aside though, the concept of sustainable development (and indeed ESD, EFS among other sustainability education iterations) has unquestionably infiltrated the field of environmental education.

Traditionally 'sustainable development' was defined as "development which meets the needs of the present without compromising the ability of future generations to meet their needs" (World Commission on the Environment and Development 1987, p. 8). However, as with any theory seeking political legitimacy, there are scholars and activists who oppose the ideas underpinning sustainable development (e.g. Jickling and Spork 1998; Selby 2009). One criticism of EDS/EfS is that these approaches derive from an anthropocentric perspective on the environment. An anthropocentric perspective emphasises the use of the environment for human gain, and so sustainability is associated for some scholars with responding to this use so that children become 'agents of change', working to protect the earth's resources from being depleted. Whilst this approach undoubtedly has value (in that children should be supported to understand the importance of not over-using the environment), critics argue that an ecocentric perspective is more appropriate. This is because ecocentrism seeks to value the environment for its own intrinsic value rather than what it offers humans as a resource (Dobson 2007; Eckersley 1992; O'Riordan 1981; Pepper 1984, 1986). Opponents of EfS therefore argue that EfS does not necessarily promote learning to value the environment for its own sake, nor allow children the option of developing their own worldviews about their relationship with the environment (see for example, Kopnina 2012). Hovardas (2013) argues:

> Belief in the intrinsic value of nature, namely, the value nature possesses independently of human valuers, is a strong indication of departing from anthropocentrism (i.e., justification of human conduct only in relation human motives and desires (Curry 2006, cited in text). Granting intrinsic value to nature is related to an ecocentric conceptualisation, according to which natural systems should be considered as bearers of intrinsic value (Gruen 2002, cited in text). Intrinsic valuation of nature and the adoption of ecocentrism might have a substantial effect on images of nature and sense of play (Korfiatis et al. 2009, cited in text). In this regard, environmental education might influence students' worldview to a substantial extent, rather than simply fostering environmental values. Overall, these reservations refer to the formulation of objectives in environmental education and to a potential controversy between endorsing the call for sustainable solutions and, at the same time, respecting learners' autonomy and self-determination (Wals 2010, cited in text) (pp. 1467–1483).

Thus, whilst ESD and EfS are increasingly evident approaches employed in school-based and public education campaigns, it is important for educators and scholars associated with early childhood education to be aware these approaches represent contested arguments in the broader environmental education literature

(Jickling and Wals 2007). This is not to discredit the role of EfS in helping build awareness about the critical importance of sustainability in educational circles, as clearly this been an important platform for getting environmental issues into the curriculum. Rather, the aim here is to alert those involved in early childhood education about how EfS and environmental education are positioned according to the ideological positions they hold about the environment and human relationships with the environment.

Environmental education has had a presence in primary and secondary education for a number of years, and recently emerged in the field of early childhood education in the form of EfS as an official concern (Littledyke and McCrae 2009). The first UNESCO international workshop on environmental education in early childhood was held in 2007, whilst the 2009 Bonn Declaration was amongst the earliest of international documents to recognise the role of early childhood education in environmental education. The 2007 UNESCO workshop resulted in a significant publication titled '*The contribution of early childhood to a sustainable society*' (Pramling Samuelsson and Kaga 2008), aimed at describing how EfS could be understood, used, taught and learned in early childhood settings. Whilst educators and researchers had been working in the area of early childhood environmental education prior to the release of the Pramling and Kaga (2008) document (see for example the significant works of Elliott and Davis 2009), the document served as a touchstone for increased public discussion and awareness regarding the relationship between the education of very young children and the role of sustainability as a core concern of the twenty-first century (Siraj-Blatchford 2009).

3.2 Environmental Education in Early Childhood

Since the publication of '*The contribution of early childhood to a sustainable society*' (Pramling Samuelsson and Kaga 2008) the notion of EfS in early childhood education has gained traction as the most frequently used term associated with environmental education in the early years. However, given debates in the broader environmental education literature about the ideological positions of different approaches to environmental education there is some concern that early childhood education should also be more open to these discussions (Cutter-Mackenzie and Edwards 2013), and so broaden awareness in the field beyond the concept of EfS into consideration of the educational function of environmental education in the first instance. Interestingly, in the history of early childhood sustainability education, it is the ecocentric, rather than anthropocentric perspective that has been most strongly emphasised. This is because the ecocentric perspective seeks to value the earth for its own sake in a way that aligns with historical beliefs in early childhood education about the significance of outdoor and nature-based play as a vehicle for learning about the environment. Pramling Samuelsson and Kaga (2008) argue this very point:

> There is a great deal in the history of early childhood education that aligns with education for sustainability e. g. *integrated curriculum approaches* (interdisciplinary), holism, outdoor play and learning, creating a sense of community, social justice etc. We do not have to create entirely 'new' pedagogies in order to 'do' education for sustainability. There is a tradition that could be built upon at the same time as it has to be renewed in terms of thinking about the content and [the need] to work [in] goal directed [ways] in the early years. It is important to raise the question of what the content in Early Childhood Education should be and also what the objectives have to be for fostering children for a life in Sustainability Development. We were also all convinced (from research) that it is not the traditional school subjects and ways of teaching knowledge that has the best effect on children's learning (p. 8).

This has resulted in the situation in which EfS has become somewhat of a default position for environmental education in early childhood education (even though EfS is more likely to orientate towards anthropocentric environmental position whilst early childhood education tends to express ecocentric tendencies towards outdoor play). Consequently, there has been more focus on educating young children about the importance of sustainability in early childhood education (see for example Duhn 2012; Prince 2010), then there has been on understanding how play-based learning connects with environmental education more broadly. Once again, this problem can be seen in the opening vignette for this book in which Seth's play episode largely echoed traditional beliefs about play-based learning in the outdoors, but lacked opportunities for children to engage with environmental learning that would further help them to understand biodiversity, develop biophilic dispositions towards nature and understand the natural habitat of the sea creatures they were incorporating into their play. Environmental education research suggesting that outdoor play *alone* is insufficient for helping children develop later pro-environmental dispositions as adults underscores the significance of this point (Blanchard and Buchanan 2011).

The need for more focused learning about the environment than that enabled by children's exploratory and outdoor based play is illustrated by the Vadala et al. (2007) study regarding the role of children's outdoor play experiences on their later adult-orientated environmental interests. They conducted extensive interviews with 61 participants aged 18–35 years, some who were involved in professional conservation related employment or volunteer activities. Participants were asked to recall and describe their childhood experiences in the outdoors. Interestingly, Vadala et al. (2007) identified two types of outdoor play, including 'child-nature play' and 'child–child play in nature'. Their findings suggested that children who participated in 'child–child play in nature' were more likely to use things found in nature (such as stones, sticks or walnuts) to play war games or build forts than were children who participated in 'child-nature play'. 'Child-nature play' was characterised by children's interests in collecting frogs, searching under logs for bugs and beetles or capturing fireflies. These adults also reported having their interest in nature actively supported by parents who provided access to books, field guides and magazines on natural history. One participant reported "you would just sit back and read them [field guides] like novels" (Vadala et al. 2007, p. 7). 'Child-nature play' adults were more likely to be involved in professional or volunteer conservation roles than those adults who participated predominately in 'child–child play in nature'. This meant that simply being outdoors was not necessarily enough to foster environmental knowledge or understanding in ways that contributed to meaningful environmental interests and behaviors in later adulthood. What mattered was the child's orientation to nature and the fostering of their interest via content supplied by parents. Being outside was not necessarily equated with understanding nature as for some adults the environment simply provided the resources for their childhood imaginative games and activities.

3.3 Biophilia and Biophobia

The Vadala et al. (2007) findings can be understood in relation to two important concepts in environmental education known as biophilia and biophobia. Biophilia is considered to be children's love of and affinity with nature (Wilson 1992). According to Hyun (2005) "biophilia is a theoretical notion that there is a fundamental, genetically based human need and propensity to affiliate with nature and life" (p. 200). Orr (1992) argues if biophilia is not encouraged and nurtured in the early years of life, the opposite occurs and children can develop a fear of nature which is described as biophobia. In the Vadala et al. (2007) study, opportunities for developing a biophilic disposition may be have been most likely to emerge from the experiences of those children participating in 'child-nature play' because this play was orientated towards meaningful engagement with and learning about nature, rather than simply using what nature offered as a resource for play. Research by Hyun (2005) regarding the ways in which children and adults perceive nature would concur with this suggestion. He found that children tend to engage more directly with nature "by doing more touching, smelling, drawing and pretending in a direct and descriptive manner than adults, who did not actively participate" (p. 205). Thus, a disposition towards biophilia is likely to require active opportunities to engage with nature, supported by later opportunities to engage with information about the experience. Seth's wading pool optimistically filled with sponges, sea weed and plastic sea creatures may in fact work to promote biophobia amongst the children—unless some means for later engagement with content knowledge about these creatures is provided.

An important point about biophilia and biophobia in early childhood education is the extent to which educators themselves are likely to express each disposition, and the consequent impact these dispositions have on educator capacities for engaging children in environmental educational experiences. Figure 3.1 presents two contrasting discussions between a child and educator exhibiting either a biophilic or biophobic attitude. Here, it can be seen that the educator leaning towards biophilia is able to support the child's learning needs with respect to understanding the importance of biodiversity and associated concepts such as habitat.

In these examples, the first educator exhibits a biophilic disposition. Her inclination towards respecting the 'snake' extends to helping the child learn the

<u>Biophilia</u>

Child: I saw a snake in my backyard yesterday

Educator: Aren't they so beautiful how they move?

Child: My Dad said I was very lucky to see a large python. So we took a photo. I asked Dad if I could keep him. I said he could sleep in my room. Dad said I couldn't because his home is in the bush

Educator: I know a book called 'The salamander room' (Mazer, 1991) that is about a little boy who tries to keep a salamander but found he couldn't unless he turned his house into a forest

Child: Can we read that now?

Educator: Sure. Let's tell all the other children about the snake you saw yesterday. I am sure we could find out lots more information on pythons too. About what they eat, where they sleep and so on

<u>Biophobia</u>

Child: I saw a snake in my backyard yesterday

Educator: Did your parents kill it?

Child: No, we took a photo of it

Educator: Did you tell your neighbors? You know snakes are very dangerous. They are poisonous and they bite. They could kill you.

Child: Dad said they are beautiful

Educator: Yeah, beautiful when they are dead

Fig. 3.1 Educator dispositions towards biophilia and biophobia

correct terminology (python) and to offering access to more information about the likely habitat and life needs of the python. In this way, the adult's biophilic disposition increases the likelihood of the child accessing the range of content material that the children in the Valdala et al. (2007) study were provided with by their parents—leading to an experience of nature that built and supported a respect for the environment that carried into adulthood. In contrast, the second educator promotes a view of nature that sees the snake as frightening and dangerous. The opportunity to learn more about the reptile is shut down by the suggestion that such a creature could only be beautiful when it was 'dead'. These examples show how environmental education in early childhood education requires more than providing children with outdoor play experiences in nature. Rather, opportunities for play that involve conversations with adults holding biophilic dispositions can be a necessary precursor to accessing content knowledge. In Chaps. 4, 5 and 6 of this book the biophilic dispositions held by Jeanette, Josh and Robyn were a significant influence on their decision making regarding the provision of content knowledge to the children during modelled and purposefully-framed play.

3.4 Pedagogical Play in Early Childhood Education

In Chap. 2 we outlined how theoretical and philosophical ideas about play have influenced understandings about pedagogy in early childhood education. An important idea in Western-European pedagogy has been that children's learning and development is most effectively supported through participation in open-ended and freely chosen play. This idea connects very strongly with ideas proposed by Piaget regarding children's active construction of knowledge and Froebel's and Dewey's arguments regarding the role of play in the child's life as a vehicle for purposeful learning (Wood and Attfield 2005). These ideas about play are strongly entrenched in understandings about early childhood education that are still typically expressed in curriculum documentation or different 'approaches' to early childhood education. For example, the Developmentally Appropriate Practice guidelines (Copple and Bredekamp 2009) suggest:

> Children of all ages love to play, and it gives them opportunities to develop physical competence and enjoyment of the outdoors, understand and make sense of their world, interact with others, express and control emotions, develop their symbolic and problem-solving abilities, and practice emerging skills (p. 14).

This orientation towards play in early childhood pedagogy continues to resonate with the field, and whilst the presence of play itself in early childhood education has not necessarily been critiqued, how play is used and understood in relation to young children's learning has attracted significant research attention. A particularly important body of play-based literature is focused on what young children are likely to learn whilst playing in early childhood settings. An initial concern in this literature was the extent to which young children were likely to learn content knowledge by participating in open-ended and interest-driven play.

Wood (2007) went to the heart of this concern by questioning the extent to which play could be argued to have an educational function if it relied predominately on children's interests in a way that did not deliberately connect with conceptual knowledge and the content associated with a particular learning area:

> It is not clear whether children's interests are themselves goals, whether children create their own goals through their interests and, if so, what those goals are. A further question focuses on whether educators recognise and act on those interests as personal and/or social goals. For example, whilst playing with materials in a water tray may enable children to observe that objects behave in different ways, they will not spontaneously learn the concept of floating and sinking, volume and mass without educative encounters with more knowledgeable others. In other words, play activities may stimulate learning-relevant processes, but may be content free which juxtaposes the developmental against the educational rationale for play (p. 125).

The line of argument expressed by Wood (2007) was largely initiated against a background of theoretical and philosophical change in early childhood education. Other researchers were raising similar questions and concerns regarding the assumed relationship between children's participation in interest-driven and open-ended play and the learning of content knowledge (Hedges and Cullen 2005;

Kallery and Psillos 2001). These investigations were characterized by interest in ideas derived from the sociology of childhood and sociocultural theory. Now broadly encapsulated in the idea of being 'post-developmental' these ideas were focused on addressing perceived limitations associated with traditional ideas about play-based learning such as those emerging from the works of Piaget, Froebel and Dewey amongst others (see Chap. 2). A core concern was focused on understanding the child in 'context', rather than focusing on the individual child and the construction of knowledge through play. Context included consideration of the role of relationships in children's learning and increasingly referenced the ways in which social and cultural experiences mediated what and how young children learned. Research investigating children's content learning during play drew on sociocultural ideas about learning and development derived from the work of Vygotsky (2004) and Rogoff (2003). These ideas included an emphasis on the role of the adult during play as a support to children's learning and the importance of children's intent participation during social and cultural activities in learning.

A stream of research emerged focussing on understanding the relationship between children's play and their learning of content during such play in early childhood settings (i.e. Pramling Samuelsson and Asplund Carlsson 2008; Robbins 2003). This research increasingly emphasised the importance of adult interactions during play as a means of supporting children's developing conceptual understandings as basis for building content knowledge (Jordan 2009). This included the concept of Sustained Shared Thinking (Siraj-Blatchford 2009) which emerged from the Effective Provision of Pre-School Education research conducted in the United Kingdom (Siraj-Blatchford et al. 2008). Sustained Shared Thinking was linked to the provision of high quality early learning experiences for young children and arguably characterised by interactions between children and adults that were focused on building knowledge and ideas in the context of play-based experiences. In Australia, Fleer (2010) proposed the idea of contextual inter-subjectivity during children's play. She suggested that interest-driven and open-ended play was an important and appropriate aspect of early childhood education. However, she argued that educators needed to ensure that they understood the context of children's play so that they were able to engage and interact with children in ways that supported learning rather than assuming that children were learning particular concepts through the provision of play experiences alone. In the United States the concept of intentional teaching was used to describe the importance of achieving a balance between child and teacher initiated activity and interactions:

> An effective early childhood program combines *both* child-guided and adult-guided educational experiences. The terms 'child-guided experience' and 'adult-guided experience' do not refer to extremes (that is, they are not highly child-controlled or adult-controlled). Rather, adults play intentional roles in child-guided experience; and children have significant, active roles in adult-guided experience. Each takes advantage of planned or spontaneous, unexpected learning opportunities (Epstein 2007, p. 3).

An important aspect of intentional teaching was the inclusion of content knowledge in the interactions children and teachers would have together. In Sweden,

Pramling Samuelsson and Carlsson (2008) noted that children should learn 'something' from their interactions during play. Like Bodrova and Leong (2011), they highlighted how learning 'something' was important for extending children's play so that children would have more knowledge to draw on to inform their play-scripts. Understandings about the relationship between adults, children and content during play-based learning have grown through the use of concepts such as intentional teaching, inter-subjectivity and sustained shared thinking. These concepts have supported the emergence of pedagogical ideas about play-based learning that focus on understanding play across a continuum of activity. In these arguments play is not focused on so much as an interest-driven and freely chosen activity in early childhood education as it is understood pedagogically as an experience encompassing a range of activities, including those that might be solely child-initiated and open-ended to those that are more adult directed and/or initiated. This also includes activities in between either end of the continuum that are likely to include a balance of child to child and adult to child interactions and engagements around both play and content learning.

The continuum idea is expressed in descriptions such as integrated pedagogies (Wood 2013) and pedagogical activity (Dockett 2011) that emphasise the importance of play for children's learning but also acknowledge the extent to which educators are able to support this learning when engaging in meaningful interactions with young children. This orientation towards play is evident in contemporary early childhood curriculum frameworks that refer to the role of the educator in engaging young children's learning. For example, the United Kingdom's Early Years Foundation Stage (Department for Education 2012) suggests:

> Each area of learning and development must be implemented through planned, purposeful play and through a mix of adult-led and child-initiated activity. Play is essential for children's development, building their confidence as they learn to explore, to think about problems, and relate to others. Children learn by leading their own play, and by taking part in play which is guided by adults. There is an ongoing judgement to be made by practitioners about the balance between activities led by children, and activities led or guided by adults. Practitioners must respond to each child's emerging needs and interests, guiding their development through warm, positive interaction (p. 5).

In the Australian Early Years Learning Framework (Department of Education and Employment and Workforce Relations 2009), the balance between adult and child-initiated play as a basis for learning is described as such:

> Early childhood educators take on many roles in play with children and use a range of strategies to support learning. They engage in sustained shared conversations with children to extend their thinking (Siraj-Blatchford and Sylva 2004, cited in text). They provide a balance between child led, child initiated and educator supported learning. They create learning environments that encourage children to explore, solve problems, create and construct (p. 5).

Interest-driven and open-ended play in early childhood education is still highly valued for the social, emotional, cognitive and language benefits it arguably provides for young children. However, as recent research suggests, and curriculum frameworks such as the Early Years Foundation Stage and Early Years Learning

Framework increasingly describe, interest-driven and open-ended play is also complemented by educator initiated experiences and interactions aimed at building the content knowledge associated with children's interests and activities. Trawick-Smith (2012) describes the movement towards intentional teaching in terms of three main approaches to pedagogical play, including the "trust in play approach", the "facilitate play approach" and the "enhance learning outcomes through play approach" (pp. 260–262). The "trust in play approach" involves educators providing children with opportunities to engage in open-ended activity in which content is associated with the nature of the materials provided. The "facilitate play approach" involves educators interacting with children during play to add complexity to play scenarios and to help children identify play content. The "enhance learning outcomes through play approach" involves teachers purposefully identifying content they intend for children to interact with during play in order to meet pre-determined learning outcomes. Trawick-Smith (2012) argues that play is used most effectively when teachers combine the approaches in various ways according to what they learn about children's learning through observation and assessment.

Earlier in this chapter we noted that early childhood environmental education needed to be based on more than children's experiences of outdoor play in nature. This was because research shows that play alone does not help children to develop pro-environmental dispositions and understandings (Davis 2010), and further, that adults disposed toward biophilic attitudes towards the environment help children access the content knowledge that extends nature play into understanding about the environment. The recent emergence in the field of early childhood education of the complementary use of different types of play, including both child and adult initiated play, provides a strong basis for beginning to understand how children's outdoor play may be connected with learning opportunities via educators who are interested in promoting environmental education with young children. This is because contemporary orientations towards play-based learning focus on the inclusion of content during play and the ways in which this play can be engaged by children and adults to support conceptual and content based learning. This means there is potential for considering how different forms of pedagogical play can be used by teachers in early childhood environmental education. As we noted in Chap. 1, the pedagogical play-types we have drawn on to inform our research with teachers include open-ended play, modelled play and purposefully-framed play.

3.5 Conclusion

Environmental education is recognised as a core educational concern for the twenty-first century. In recent years, this recognition has been extended to the field of early childhood education. Environmental education and early childhood education can involve more than aligning the values of EfS with the traditional ideas about children's play. It can also be focused on determining how environmental education can be located in early childhood education in a way that addresses needing to learn 'something' (Pramling Samuelsson and Carlsson 2008) about the environment using play-based learning. Recent advances in understanding play-based pedagogy in terms of intentional teaching are helpful because they widen understandings of 'play' so that both content and educator interactions are valued alongside children's activities and interests. This means there is space for considering environmental education in terms of content, but also in terms of the educator interactions that are necessary for realising this content so that children are supported in the development of pro-environmental dispositions and understandings. In the next three chapters we now consider how Jeanette, Josh and Robyn approached the use of play-based learning in early childhood environmental education.

References

Blanchard, P. B., & Buchanan, T. K. (2011). Environmental stewardship in early childhood. *Childhood Education, 87*(4), 232–238.

Bodrova, E., & Leong, D. (2011). Revisiting Vygotskian perspectives on play and pedagogy. In S. Rogers (Ed.), *Rethinking play and pedagogy in early childhood education: Concepts, contexts and cultures* (pp. 60–73). London: Routledge.

Copple, C., Bredekamp, S., & National Association for the Education of Young Children. (2009). *Developmentally appropriate practice in early childhood programs serving children from birth through age 8* (3rd ed.). Washington, DC: National Association for the Education of Young Children.

Cutter-Mackenzie, A., & Edwards, S. (2013). The next 20 years: Imagining and re-imagining sustainability, environment and education in early childhood education. In S. Elliott, Davis, J., Edwards, S., & Cutter-Mackenzie, A. (Eds.), *Best of Sustainability: Research, Practice and Theory* (pp. 61–67). Deakin West: Early Childhood Australia.

Cutter-Mackenzie, A., Edwards, S., & Widdop Quinton, H. (2013). Child-framed video research methodologies: Issues, possibilities and challenges for researching with children. *Children's Geographies.*

Davis, J. (2010). What is early childhood education for sustainability? In J. Davis (Ed.), *Young children and the environment: Early education for sustainability* (pp. 21–43). Cambridge: Cambridge University Press.

Department of Education, Employment and Workplace Relations, (DEEWR). (2009). *Belonging, being and becoming: The early years learning framework for Australia.* Canberra: Commonwealth of Australia.

Department of Education. (2012). *Statutory framework for the early years foundation stage. Setting the standards for learning, development and care for children from birth to five.* London: Crown.

Dobson, A. (2007). *Green Political thought* (4th ed.). London: Routledge.

Dockett, S. (2011). The challenge of play for early childhood education. In S. Rogers (Ed.), *Rethinking play and pedagogy in early childhood education: Concepts, contexts and cultures* (pp. 32–48). London: Routledge.

Duhn, I. (2012). Making 'place' for ecological sustainability in early childhood education. *Environmental Education Research, 18*(1), 19–29. doi:10.1080/13504622.2011.572162.

Eckersley, R. (1992). *Environmentalism and Political Theory: Toward an Ecocentric Approach.* London: UCL Press.

Elliott, S., & Davis, J. (2009). Exploring the resistance: An Australian perspective on educating for sustainability in early childhood. *International Journal of Early Childhood, 41*(2), 65–77.

Epstein, A. S. (2007). *The intentional teacher: Choosing the best strategies for young children's learning*. Washington, D.C.: National Association for the Education of Young Children.

Fien, J. (2000). Education for the environment: A critique- an analysis. *Environmental Education Research, 6*(2), 179.

Fleer, M. (2010). *Early learning and development: Cultural-historical concepts in play*. Melbourne: Cambridge University Press.

Hedges, H., & Cullen, J. (2005). Subject knowledge in early childhood curriculum and pedagogy: beliefs and practices. *Contemporary Issues in Early Childhood, 6*(1), 66–79.

Hovardas, T. (2013). A critical reading of ecocentrism and Its meta-scientific use of ecology: Instrumental versus emancipatory approaches in environmental education and ecology education. *Science & Education, 22*(6),1467–1483.

Huckle, J. (1991). Education for sustainability: Assessing pathways to the future. *Australian Journal of Environmental Education, 7*, 43–62.

Hyun, E. (2005). How is young children's intellectual culture of perceiving nature different from adults'? *Environmental Education Research, 11*(2), 199–214.

Jickling, B. (1992). Why I don't want my children to be educated for sustainable development. *Journal of Environmental Education, 23*(4), 5–8.

Jickling, B., & Spork, H. (1998). Education for the Environment: A Critique. *Environmental Education Research, 4*(3), 309–327.

Jickling, B., & Wals, A. (2007). Globalization and environmental education: looking beyond sustainable development. *Journal of Curriculum Studies, 40*(1), 1–21.

Jordan, B. (2009). Scaffolding learning and co-constructing understandings. In A. Anning, J. Cullen & M. Fleer (Eds.), *Early childhood education. Society and culture* (2nd ed., pp. 39–53). Los Angeles, CA: SAGE Publications.

Kallery, M., & Psillos, D. (2001). Pre-school teachers' content knowledge in science: Their understanding of elementary science concepts and of issues raised by children's questions. *International Journal of Early Years Education, 9*(3), 165–179. doi:10.1080/09669760120086929.

Kopnina, H. (2012). Education for sustainable development (ESD): the turnaway from 'environment' in environmental education? *Environmental Education Research, 18*(5), 699–717.

Littledyke, M., & McCrea, N. (2009). Starting sustainability early: Young children exploring people and places. In N. Taylor & C. Eames (Eds.), *Education for sustainability in the primary curriculum: a guide for teachers* (pp. 39–57). South Yarra, Vic.: Palgrave Macmillan.

O'Riordan, T. (1981). *Environmentalism*. London: Pion Limited.

Orr, D. W. (1992). *Ecological Literacy: Education and the Transition to a Postmodern World*. Albany: State University of New York.

Pepper, D. (1984). *The roots of modern environmentalism*. London: Groom Helm.

Pepper, D. (1986). *The roots of modern Environmentalism*. London: Routledge.

Pramling Samuelsson, I., & Asplund Carlsson, M. (2008). The playing learning child: Towards a pedagogy of early childhood. *Scandinavian Journal of Educational Research, 52*(6), 623–641.

Pramling Samuelsson, I., & Kaga, Y. (2008). *The contribution of early childhood education to a sustainable society*. Paris: UNESCO.

Prince, C. (2010). Sowing the seeds: Education for sustainability within the early years curriculum. *European Early Childhood Education Research Journal, 18*(3), 273–284. doi:10.1080/1350293X.2010.500082.

Robbins, J. (2003). The more he looked inside the more Piglet wasn't there: What adopting a sociocultural perspective can help us see. *Australian Journal of Early Childhood, 28*(2), 1–7.

Rogoff, B. (2003). *The cultural nature of human development*. Oxford: Oxford University Press.

Sauve, L. (2005). Currents in environmental education: Mapping a complex and evolving pedagogical field. Canadian Journal of Environmental Education, *10*, Spring, 11–37.

Selby, D. (2009). The Firm and Shaky Ground of Education for Sustainable Development. In B. Chalkley, M. Haigh, & D. Higgitt (Eds.), *Education for sustainable development: Paper in honour of the United Nations decade of education for sustainable development (2005–2014)* (pp. 199–213). New York: Routledge.

Siraj-Blatchford, I., Taggart, B., Sylva, K., Sammons, P., & Melhuish, E. (2008). Towards the transformation of practice in early childhood education: the effective provision of pre-school education (EPPE) project. *Cambridge Journal of Education, 38*(1), 23–36. doi:10.1080/03057640801889956.

Siraj-Blatchford, I. (2009a). Conceptualising progression in the pedagogy of play and sustained shared thinking in early childhood education: A Vygotskian perspective. *Educational and Child Psychology, 26*(2), 77–89.

Siraj-Blatchford, J. (2009b). Editorial: Education for sustainable development in early childhood. *International Journal of Early Childhood, 41*(2), 9–22.

Trawick-Smith, J. (2012). Teacher-child play interactions to achieve learning outcomes – Risks and opportunities. In R. C. Pianta, W. S. Barnett, L. M. Justice, & S. M. Sheridan (Eds.), *Handbook of early childhood education*. USA: Giuldford Publications.

UNESCO-UNEP. (1976). The Belgrade Charter: A global framework for environmental education. *Connect: UNESCO-UNEP Environmental Education Newsletter, 1*, 1–2.

Vadala, C. E., Bixler, R. D., & James, J. J. (2007). Childhood play and environmental interests: Panacea or snake oil? *Journal of Environmental Education, 39*(1), 3–18.

Vygotsky, L. S. (2004). Imagination and creativity in childhood. *Journal of Russian and East European Psychology, 42*(1), 7–97.

Wilson, E. O. (1992). *The diversity of life*. Cambridge, MA: Harvard University Press.

Wood, E. (2007). Reconceptualising child-centred education: Contemporary directions in policy, theory and practice in early childhood. *Forum, 49*(1/2), 119–134.

Wood, E., & Attfield, J. (2005). *Play, learning and the early childhood curriculum* (2nd ed.). London: Paul Chapman.

Wood, E. (2013). *Play, learning & the early childhood Curriculum* (3rd ed.). London: Sage Publications.

World Commission on Environment and Development. (1987). *Our common future*. Oxford: Oxford University Press.

Chapter 4
Jeanette: Pond Life

Abstract This chapter presents Jeanette's (an early childhood teacher) and the children's experiences in implementing the three different play types at Cornish College Early Learning Centre, Melbourne, Australia. Using Jeanette's knowledge of the children's past interests she planned an adventure to the pond (also referred to as the lake) in the grounds of the College as a learning opportunity to teach environmental education. Jeanette chose to focus on investigating concepts of sustainability, biodiversity and animal habitats. She used the play-types in the order of open-ended play, modelled-play to raise questions with the children to stimulate their learning, and purposefully framed play to engage the children with content to build their understanding about biodiversity. The order of play-types suited Jeanette as it was consistent with her typical approach to teaching. Whilst the open-ended play experiences helped Jeanette ascertain the children's existing knowledge base, for her it seemed to misconstrue what the children believed they would find in the pond (for example sharks and crocodiles). The later engagement of collecting the water and finding the creatures in the water in modelled-play and purposefully-framed play led the children to an understanding of the range of creatures that actually lived in the habitat. As such, purposefully framed play created a context for supporting children's understanding of life and supported the development of their own biophilia dispositions alongside Jeanette's disposition.

4.1 Jeanette and the Cornish College Early Learning Centre

Jeanette is an early childhood educator working at Cornish College Early Learning Centre. Cornish College Early Learning Centre is an early childhood education centre attached to a private Uniting Church school for children in kindergarten (aged 3–5 year) up to year ten (16 years) in the outer suburbs of Melbourne, Australia. The School opened in 1984 and from its onset had a strong environmental education and sustainability ethos to which Jeanette was strongly committed:

A. Cutter-Mackenzie et al., *Young Children's Play and Environmental Education in Early Childhood Education*, SpringerBriefs in Education,
DOI: 10.1007/978-3-319-03740-0_4, © The Author(s) 2014

> The vision of the Cornish campus founder, Richard B. Cornish, was to create a place of education where young people would be given the opportunity to understand and value the wisdom of living and working more sustainably (Cornish College 2012a).

Commencing in kindergarten, the College's educational philosophy is based on the following principles:

- A vision for the whole community of sustainable living based around sustainable thinking dispositions, including personal, socio-cultural, urban/technological and natural dimensions.
- Emphasis on creativity and the development of thinking skills.
- Differentiated curriculum to cater for different learning styles.
- Strong emphasis on building foundation skills for learning through structured inquiry.
- Children and staff work together collaboratively in a team structure (Cornish College 2012a).

In the Early Learning Centre, the College draws explicitly upon the educational principles associated with Reggio Emilia (Edwards et al. 1998) as informants to pedagogy, including:

1. *The child as a protagonist.* Children are rich, strong, and capable. All children have preparedness, potential, curiosity and interest in constructing their learning, negotiating with everything their environment brings to them. Children, teachers and parents are considered the three central protagonists in the educational process.
2. *The child as a collaborator.* Education has to focus on each child in relation to other children, the family, the teachers and the community, rather than on each child in isolation. There is an emphasis on work in small groups.
3. *The child as a communicator.* This approach fosters children's intellectual development through a systematic focus on symbolic representation, including words, movement, drawing, painting, building, sculpture, shadow play, collage, dramatic play and music which leads children to surprising levels of communication, symbolic skills and creativity. Children have the right to use many materials in order to discover and communicate what they know, understand, wonder about, question, feel and imagine. In this way, they make their thinking visible through their many natural languages.
4. *The environment as a third teacher.* The use of space encourages encounters, communication and relationships. Every corner of every space has an identity and a purpose, is rich in potential to engage and communicate and is valued and cared for by the children and the adults.
5. *The teacher as a partner, nurturer and guide.* Teachers facilitate children's exploration of themes, work on short and long term projects and guide experiences of joint, open ended discovery and problem solving. To know how to plan and proceed with their work, teachers listen and observe children closely.

Fig. 4.1 Cornish College grounds

Teachers ask questions; discover children's ideas, hypotheses and theories, and provide occasions for discovery and learning.

6. *The teacher as a researcher.* The teachers see themselves as researchers preparing the documentation of their work with children who they also see as researchers.
7. *The documentation as communication.* Careful consideration and attention are given to the presentation of the thinking of the children and the adults who work with them.
8. *The parent as partner.* The ideas and exchange of ideas between parents and teachers favour the development of a new way of educating, which helps teachers to view the participation of families not as a threat, but as an intrinsic element of collegiality and as the integration of different wisdom (Cornish College 2012b, p. 5; see also Cadwell 1997, pp. 5–6 from which the Cornish College principles were adapted).

The Early Learning Centre and School is situated on 42 hectares of marshland and has a farm, lake, orchard, an island and significant bush land (Fig. 4.1). This outdoor environment is important to learning at the centre and is not dissimilar to a Scandinavian nature kindergarten where Froebel's ideas about play are expressed in values that promote extensive nature and outdoor experiences, and few commercial toys (Waller et al. 2010).

At Cornish College Early Learning Centre information provided for parents includes a description of the outdoor experiences in which children attending the centre will participate:

> To increase their connection to nature, as well as many other educational benefits, the children will be spending extended periods of time outside. This will give them tangible ways of working with nature in a variety of settings (Cornish College 2012b, p. 17).

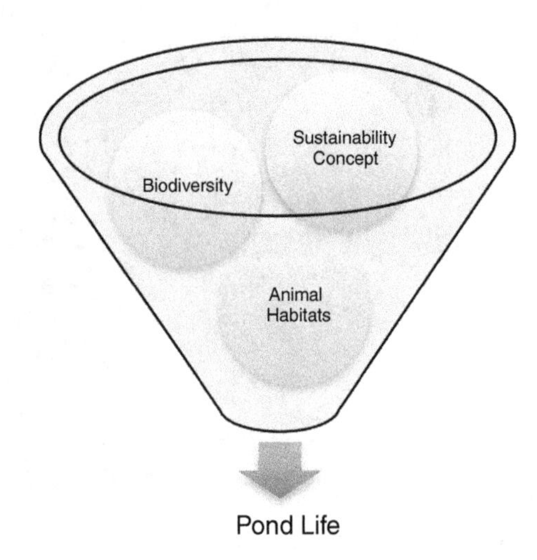

Fig. 4.2 A copy of Jeanette's teaching concept map

4.2 Focusing on Pond Life

During term two Jeanette noticed that the children were interested in mini-beasts (macro-invertebrates) whilst having spent some time planting seeds in the vegetable garden. Jeanette wrote in her teacher journal:

> Interest arose and a group of 5 children formed a project group called 'The Creatures House' to explore where some of these creatures live and what they need to stay alive. I decided to extend and further the interest in creature and their habitats (Fig. 4.2).

For her participation in the project Jeanette decided to capitalize on the Centre's strong commitment to children's outdoor experiences which meant she had access to a lake located on campus within walking distance of her classroom. This lake was quite a large body of water, and so considered larger than a pond. The term 'pond life' however is used to describe all aquatic creatures living in the lake. Jeanette believed that the lake would provide an appropriate opportunity for the children to engage in learning more about macro-invertebrates in way that would build logically on the existing interest in 'The Creatures House'. Her planning was developed around the order of play-types she had selected to examine as part of her participation in the project. This included an early focus on open-ended play, followed by modelled-play, and concluding with purposefully-framed play. Jeanette invited the five children who had established and maintained the 'The Creatures House' project to participate in the three consecutively implemented play-types. These children were Makayla, Lily, Isabelle, Ella and Mason.

4.3 Open-Ended Play

Jeanette gathered the children on the mat whilst they finished their morning tea. They began by discussing creatures. Jeanette asked the children, "Do you think any creatures live in the lake around the island?" One child very excitedly said "a crocodile lives in the lake". Another said "a shark". The children focused on identifying larger creatures rather than smaller bugs and fish in the initial discussion. Jeanette carried on with her questioning and asked, "What will we need to go down to the lake?" The children were well accustomed to going to the lake and knew exactly what was needed. The children put their wet-weather overalls on followed by their gumboots (wellingtons). They also had a red cart with equipment to search for pond life as well as a picnic blanket and other essentials such as a first-aid kit. Once the children were ready to go they made their way down to the lake which was a 10 min walk through a dense 'fairy' garden and farm area. Tracy, one of the researchers attending the walk with Jeanette and the children, described it in her journal as "no ordinary walk. They jumped, ran, skipped, splashed. They took risks—jumping 1 metre off the pier. Their experience was not so much a walk but an adventure".

When they got to the lake Jeanette stopped at a safety sign that said "Danger. Deep Water. Keep Clear". She asked the children what the sign meant. Makayla explained "clear means you can see through it". Meanwhile, Mason thought, "there might be crocodiles". Jeanette agreed with Makayla, saying "clear does mean that, but what this sign also reminds us to do is to be careful and safe around the water." Jeanette and the children moved down to the lake. Jeanette asked the children "How deep is it?" She encouraged the children to walk slowly into the water as it was only a few centimeters deep at the edge. Jeanette provided each child with a magnifying glass and asked them "What can you see?" The children looked around, explored and gradually came together to look more closely together. Jeanette provided the children with some prompts, such as "What can you see when you put your hand in?" "What can you hear?" Lily replied, "I can hear froggies." Jeanette asked "Where might they be?" Lily pointed to a deeper area and they made their way over and looked for a short time. Makayla and Isabelle wanted to go back to the shallow area. The children focused their observations on the plants they could see rather than on finding or identifying any macroinvertebrates as they had discussed at the Centre prior to leaving for their walk. Jeanette observed, "We can see lots of things growing out of the water" and asked, "What might be in the water?" She used further prompts, asking the children "Is there anything swimming in there?" "What's at the bottom?" Ella said "crocodiles" again, but Mason quickly replied, "Crocodiles are not insects" (Fig. 4.3).

As a group the children and Jeanette decided to move to a different location at the lake to try and find more pond life. They were going to walk along the water's edge but Makayla was uncomfortable because she had a hole in her gumboot and her foot was getting wet. Makayla described feeling "scared" several times whilst the children and Jeanette were gathered at the edge of the water. The group then walked a long way around to the pier and the children spent some time leaping

Fig. 4.3 'Crocodiles are not insects' What lives in the lake?

from the pier. The researcher noted in her journal that Makayla's fears seemed to have waned at this point "perhaps because this is what she expects when doing this experience?" Once the children had jumped several times, Jeanette asked "The water is deeper here. Shall we see what we can see in the water?" Makayla, Ella and Jeanette went to the water's edge near the pier to look for more creatures.

Jeanette then gathered the children onto the picnic blanket. She asked them, "Who remembers why we came to the lake? What were we looking for?" Mason replied, "We were looking for bugs". Jeanette then said, "Did we find any?" The children offered a collective "no". So Jeanette asked them another question—"Is there anything else we could use to make it easier to find creatures?"

Makayla: We need to go out into the deep water, but we might sink.
Jeanette: What could we do instead to get to the water?
Lily: We need a boat. Lots of boats.
Ella: Or ride on something.
Mason: I went on holidays once and went on a motorboat.
Jeanette: What could we use to get some of the deep water?
Ella: We could float on the water to collect some? We could use the tree.
Jeanette: These are special trees so we couldn't use those as the birds need them. I think we need to think about how we could get the water for next time so we can see some of the creatures.
Ella: We could get a bowl and scoop it up.
Jeanette: That's a great idea. Ok, we're going to go back now and get warm.

4.4 Modelled-Play

Jeanette's modelled-play experience was implemented 5 days after the open-ended experience. She gathered the children on the mat and asked, "Remember when we went down to the lake to look for creatures?" Was it hard to find them?" Ella

Fig. 4.4 Look and see if you can see anything

replied "They were hiding" and Mason suggested "They were hiding because they were deep in the water". Jeanette had a fish tank on table located near the mat, and so she asked the children "Would it be easier to see the bugs in the tank?" She also pointed out that she had collected some glass jars, nets, trays and magnifying glasses for the children. She said that last time that they had gone to the lake Ella had the idea of collecting some water. Jeanette said "I have got a bucket so we can collect some water as it will be too difficult to take the glass fish tank down to the lake." Jeanette and the children then talked about the different equipment and how it could be used. They discussed how they might use the trays and magnifying glasses to look closely at the bugs. Makayla observed "Some of the bugs might be dead or squished". Jeanette asked her, "How can we tell if they are dead or alive?" Makayla replied, "They won't be moving if they are dead." Jeanette then said that they needed to put on their wet-weather overalls so that they could go to the lake and suggested Makayla wear different gumboots so she didn't get cold feet again.

Like the first time Jeanette and the children made their way down to the lake exploring and discovering along the way. When they got to the edge of the water Jeanette gave each child a net and jar. Together they talked about the holes in the net and how they might catch bugs. Jeanette encouraged the children to go a little deeper into the water and to fill up their jars and then place the water from their jars in the larger bucket. Jeanette observed:

> See how soily this water is? Let's walk really slowly so we can get some cleaner water. We need to go very slowly. When we take it back to the fish tank it needs to be clear so we can see the pond creatures.

Mason and Lily quickly understood what needed to be done. Jeanette encouraged the other children as they were collecting clearer water. Once the children filled the bucket Jeanette asked the children to tip some of the water from the bucket into their trays which were laid out on the picnic blanket. She asked them to "look and see if they could see anything?" They all gathered and began looking at

Fig. 4.5 Ella observing and drawing using the magnifying glass

what they had found in the water (Fig. 4.4). They tended to differentiate between a bug and a plant by whether or not it was moving. When the children found a moving bug they placed it in a jar and watched it swimming and said "let's take the bugs back to the Centre".

4.5 Purposefully-Framed Play

Six days after the modelled-play experience Jeanette gathered the children around a table where she had a fish tank centered in the middle. The fish tank was filled with the water the children had collected from the pond and carried back to the centre in the bucket. Placed around the table was a seat for each child, and at each seat was a tray, a laminated identifying chart, a marker pen, paper and a magnifying glass. Jeanette talked to the children about putting some water from the fish tank into the tray. She initially asked the children "What can you see?" The children were very excited and quickly ascertained that there were many bugs. Jeanette emphasized "We need to remember to 'to look, look and look again'". She asked the children "How is the bug moving?" "How is he swimming?" She said to them "Look at that shape" And asked—"What sort of shape is that?" Ella responded "It's like a spoon because it has a round bit on the bottom." Jeanette prompted Ella and the other children to look at their charts and draw what they saw under the magnifying glass (Fig. 4.5). Ella said "I think it is a beetle". Jeanette then worked with the children attempting to identify the creatures. She continued to use the phrase "look, look and look again" to encourage the children to carefully observe the creatures.

Mason found a snail during his examination of the creatures. Mason and Jeanette then discussed the snail's hard shell. Jeanette also encouraged Mason and

Lily to look at the pond book she had set up on the table to find out more about snails. They found the section on snails and Jeanette asked them "Would you like me to read it to you?"

Jeanette: It says that at first all pond snails look alike as they are very small. When you look carefully you see the shells are very delicate and often like a spiral. Can you see that? Does your snail have a spiral shell?
Mason: No
Jeanette: Have a look, does it have a pointy end?
Lily: It has a sharp bit.
Ella: Look I found a tadpole [consulting the same book as Lily and Mason].
Jeanette: Did you see that in the book that Ella is looking at? There is another pond snail so there are lots of different types of pond snails.

Jeanette continued to engage with the children, exploring other macro-invertebrates and identifying their unique characteristics. To look even more closely at the macro-invertebrates they got the digital microscope and discussed the characteristics of each creature—trying to identify them according to the information in the book. They photographed each creature with the digital microscope and compared them to what they could see in the book.

4.6 Pedagogical Play and Environmental Education

Pedagogical play is understood to encompass a range of play-based activities, including open-ended through to more purposefully-framed play (see Chap. 3). Drawing on a combination of pedagogical play-types forms a more 'intentional' approach to teaching (Epstein 2007) that is arguably of value in environmental education because children require access to content knowledge to engage effectively with environmental concepts, such as biodiversity and animal habitats (Palmer 1993). Jeanette wrote in her journal that she was concerned about the open-ended play experience and the extent to which she would be able to leave this as largely exploratory. Her preference was to engage the children during such play to prompt their thinking and raise possible areas of investigation. She wrote:

> My main concern is the open-ended play as I tend to observe children in these experiences and then ask questions to provoke thinking and hopefully extend knowledge and the experience but I know for this research project I must just watch during this session. I do wonder how I will go.

During her interview Jeanette talked about her role in the children's open-ended play in more detail:

> I probably talked more than what was recommended for just that play experience because of being at the lake and trying to get them to see. In hindsight I probably would go to another spot next time. I saw frogs there last year so I was hoping to find them again but really I think that there was another place that would have been better to go to that had clearer water to begin with and so perhaps if I had looked at that myself before I went out that is probably one thing I would have done differently. The second time in just providing

> those materials for them and then taking them out is something that we would do and then the third time pretty much the same thing. Probably what I would do more so is only have two or three children in that final experience when we had five because normally we would only have two or three and then take them.

Whilst Jeanette did talk during the open-ended play, much of her dialogue was in the form of questions which is a feature of the pedagogical approach used in her Centre. Jeanette went on to say that commencing with open-ended play "was a great way to see any prior knowledge the children have". She also said that this is normally where she commences an experience, with open-ended play. She explained:

> [Open-ended play] provides an experience where you can see where they are going with it and then being there to see. So sometimes with the experience we may not necessarily do that three times. It may have been brought down to two or sometimes a similar experience we may have taken that moment when they discovered something—found some creatures and then brought them back to class that day, so it would really be how they are going. But asking the questions and trying to get them to respond and look. One of the things when we were on the second walk was what I learned from Tracy [the research assistant]. She was talking about the 'look, look and look again' approach and I have been using that a lot lately because I would say to them 'look and look' but that real 'look, look and look again' to see what they can see I think that is a good one.

Jeanette indicated that the order of play-types she implemented was consistent with her normal approach to supporting children's learning. She suggested that implementing a different order of play-types would have been particularly challenging for her as she used the open-ended as a basis for establishing the children's existing knowledge base and the modelled and purposefully-framed play for building knowledge by connecting more strongly into the biodiversity content she associated with the children's learning. Whilst research suggests intentional teaching is characterised by the use of a range of child-centred to more teacher orientated activities, the exact order or 'blend' of these experiences as a basis for supporting learning tends to remain at the level of teacher discretion (Trawick-Smith 2012, p. 265). In the context of early childhood environmental education, this raises interesting questions because it is not known whether or not children benefit most from the exploratory play first, or would benefit from exposure to the more purposefully-framed play prior to opportunities to engage in the open-ended experiences.

Jeanette's implementation of the play experiences also highlights the need for early childhood environmental education to draw on identified principles for using play-based learning, rather than relying on a conception of play as 'freely chosen' and associated with valuing outdoor activity. Jeanette was asked during her interview what she was hoping the children would learn by the end of the third play-type. Here Jeanette's own disposition towards biophilia was evident, and highlights the important relationship between educator dispositions and the use of play-based learning in early childhood environmental education:

> That there are creatures in the water and that they are really tiny and that the creatures they [the children] all thought about were going to be big, they thought that they would see fish, crocodiles and really big things but that there are tiny things that live there and that we

need to be careful with them. One died when we tried to get it out last time and since then when we have used it, it is hard to get them out even with a teaspoon and that we do have to be careful with small creatures.

Whilst the open-ended play helped Jeanette ascertain the children's existing knowledge base, it seemed to misconstrue what they believed they would find in the lake (i.e. sharks and crocodiles). It was the later engagement collecting the water and finding the creatures in the water that led the children to an understanding of the range of creatures that actually lived in the habitat. As such, purposefully-framed play created a context for supporting children's understanding of life and therein also supported the development of their own biophilia dispositions alongside Jeanette's. Working towards biophilic dispositions therefore requires using principles of play-based learning that allow biophobic ideas to be explored via the provision of content knowledge with an engaged and supporting educator.

Later in her interview Jeanette was asked why the chart she used with the children during the purposefully-framed play included the heading 'macro-invertebrate' even though she did not explicitly use this term with the children. She went on to say "I didn't use that term but I will do so as we continue on". When asked how far she would go with engaging the content knowledge via the play purposefully-framed play type, she said:

Probably as a class not so far but individually it will go further depending on the child's interest…I think that we are part of the learning experience so along with the Reggio philosophy we have got the teacher, the environment as well as the experiences, so all of those are important, so if you look at the environment being the teacher, the teacher being the teacher and so on. I think other children they learn so much from each other and you saw that with Lily and Mason and it becomes that scaffold of learning.

An important part of Jeanette's planning in using the three play-types was accessing the outdoors and using the lake as a learning opportunity. During the interview Jeanette was asked to comment on her understanding of the relationship between pedagogical play and the outdoors. This included parental perceptions of the children's experiences on the walks to the lake and activity around the pier:

Jeanette: They are quite mixed. It is interesting we had two of the new parents come yesterday. It was the second time the parents came to the centre and this is week four so they have only been involved in the centre for four weeks and they have been on one other walk and the father is a doctor so I don't know if that has any bearing on it but he was really out of his comfort zone watching Makayla climbing the tree. He stood there and he said how high should we let her climb?
Amy: He said that?
Jeanette: Yes and he said I don't want to step into the boundary of education and I know that you must have a reason for it but he said I find it really uncomfortable and I said to him well safety is a concern and our first concern is always safety and we know that she has climbed a lot of trees before now and that we talk about those safe branches and things like that but having you there in case she falls is a great thing. But it was interesting and on the way down he wanted to lift her down and I said I know but if we can teach her how to get down if we can just guide her, and I said we might need to lift her in parts, but if we can guide her then that is a better thing because then she knows what to do the next time

and he did and at the very end because it was hard to get her leg to the next point he did lift her a bit and that was fine. And he even said afterwards that he found that hard because of that safety thing.
Amy: It was confronting for him?
Jeanette: Yes it was confronting for him and another dad came on a walk and he spent less time involved and it was the first walk that he had been on and he just watched and watched a lot and at the end he said to me "you always said to come on a walk and I thought that we would just walk and I didn't realize how much the children did".

To Jeanette, going on the walk was an important part of the children's learning as it provided access to opportunities for children to be in the environment and to experience nature. Sobel (2008) says that such walks are not 'just a walk':

> If I suggested to my children that we were going on a walk, they complained. However, if I opened with, "Let's go on an adventure," they were much more recruitable. Walks are for adults. You staidly put one foot in front of the other, you chat about boring things with your friends, you wind up at outlooks and say, "Oh what a beautiful view." Snoresville. Adventures mean you don't know what's going to happen when you start out (p. 21).

Jeanette's walks with the children could be understood from an 'adventurous' perspective. However, they also were underpinned by a deliberate consideration of pedagogy because they were not only about the children's outdoor play, but provided a vehicle for engaging Jeanette's own disposition towards biophilia in a way that worked to build the children's knowledge about the environment. Jeanette viewed this as an important aspect of her work:

> Children don't have the same experiences of playing outside as much. Their lives are more controlled I think. We give them those experiences just to play in the environment because they discover as they go. But it is being there to support that discovery so if they find something outside, like we found a dead frog yesterday on the walk, so it is looking at that and talking about that and where could have the frog lived and what might have happened to it.

4.7 Conclusion

The combination of play types implemented by Jeanette was consistent with her normal approach to planning for children's learning. In Jeanette's work there is evidence of the two principles of play-based learning informing her approach to early childhood environmental education. These are:

Principle One:

Valuing different play-types according to their pedagogical potential for engaging with aspects of environmental education

This is seen in Jeanette's use of open-ended exploratory activity to promote initial interest in learning about the macro-invertebrates, and then more adult orientated activity via modelled and purposefully-framed play to further engage children with the content knowledge associated with the initial interest.

Table 4.1 Jeanette's combination of play-types and planned experiences according to the pedagogical value she attributed to the play-types and her associated environmental learning goals

Principle one Pedagogical value Jeanette attributed to play-type	Principle two Combination of play-types Jeanette decided to implement	Planned experience according to play-type	Environmental learning goal associated with play-type
Opportunity to observe children and ask questions to provide insight into existing levels of understanding	Open-ended	Initial discussion: what might we find at the lake? Walk to the lake Search for pond life Concluding discussion: what did we find at the lake?	Exposure to the outdoors, opportunities for risky play and interactions with nature
Raising questions with children that build on existing levels of understanding	Modelled	Initial discussion: remember when we went to the lake? Walk to the lake Collect pond water Examine pond water: what can we see? Take some pond water back to the classroom	Biodiversity: characteristics of macro-invertebrates
Engaging content knowledge to build levels of understanding that contribute to an appreciation of the life needs of other creatures	Purposefully-framed	Fish tank filled with pond water Tray, laminated identification chart, marker pen, paper and magnifying glass Place drops of water into trays Use magnifying glasses: what can you see? Draw what you see Digital microscope and digital photographs Compare digital images to non-fiction text	Biophilic dispositions towards nature

Principle Two:

Creating combinations of play-types that support engagement with different aspects of environmental education

This is evident in Jeanette's combination of open-ended, modelled and purposefully-framed play orientated towards the active building of biophilic dispositions and the acquisition of content knowledge about the macro-invertebrates found living in the lake.

Table 4.1 provides a summary overview of the articulation of the principles to Jeanette's planned play experiences and her environmental learning goals for the children.

References

Cadwell, L. (1997). *Bringing Reggio Emilia home*. New York: Teacher's College Press.

Cornish College (2012a). *Information handbook: Early learning centre*. Retrieved from http://www.cornishcollege.vic.edu.au.

Cornish College (2012b). *Cornish College Educational Philosophy*. Retrieved from http://www.cornishcollege.vic.edu.au/content/educational.

Edwards, C., Gandini, L., & Forman, G. (1998). *The hundred languages of children* (2nd ed.). Greenwich, CT: Ablex.

Epstein, A. S. (2007). *The intentional teacher: Choosing the best strategies for young children's learning*. Washington, D.C.: National Association for the Education of Young Children.

Palmer, J. (1993). Development of concern for the environment and formative experiences of educators. *Journal of Environmental Education, 24*(3), 26–30.

Sobel, D. (2008). *Childhood and nature: Design principles for educators*. Portland, Maine: Stenhouse Publishers.

Trawick-Smith, J. (2012). Teacher-child play interactions to achieve learning outcomes—risks and opportunities. In R. C. Pianta, W. S. Barnett, L. M. Justice, & S. M. Sheridan (Eds.), *Handbook of early childhood education*. USA: Giuldford Publications.

Waller, T., Sandseter, E., Wyver, S., Arlemalm-Hagser, E., & Maynard, T. (2010). The dynamics of early childhood spaces: Opportunities for outdoor play? *European Early Childhood Education Research Journal, 18*(4), 437–445.

Chapter 5
Josh: Small Is Beautiful

Abstract This chapter presents Josh's (an early childhood teacher) and the children's experiences at St Kilda and Balaclava Kindergarten, Melbourne, Australia. The outdoor environment at the kindergarten provided opportunities for children to find and observe living things and explore their habitat. Josh orientated the implementation of his three play-types on an investigation of macro-invertebrate habitats. Josh implemented the play-types in the following order: open-ended play, modelled-play, and then purposefully-framed play. In the open-ended play experience the children explored various habitats with Josh observing the children. During the modelled play Josh modelled finding macro-invertebrates in their habitats, citing their names and characteristics. Josh's purposefully-framed play session began with exploratory learning of the environment, and then matching photographs of the macro-invertebrates with pictures, name, characteristics and habitat. As the children participated in the play-types the level of their biophobic expressions declined and they began to show more biophilic orientated dispositions. Josh was challenged by implementing an open-ended play approach only. He explained he would not normally teach in this manner, instead choosing to follow up the children's emerging interests immediately. However he reflected that he found value in listening to the children's ideas initially without questioning and interacting with the children.

5.1 Josh and the St Kilda and Balaclava Kindergarten

Josh and the children attending his centre are from St Kilda and Balaclava Kindergarten, an inner city childcare centre in Melbourne, Australia. The centre has a strong philosophical approach to teaching environmental education, and has been actively doing so for 10 years. The centre's philosophy states:

A. Cutter-Mackenzie et al., *Young Children's Play and Environmental Education in Early Childhood Education*, SpringerBriefs in Education,
DOI: 10.1007/978-3-319-03740-0_5,

In providing open-ended experiences, children are able to explore, experiment, create, invent and extend upon their innate curiosity using the natural wonders of the world. This helps children in the process of developing knowledge, skills and attitudes necessary to take environmentally responsible action.

The outdoor environment at St Kilda and Balaclava Kindergarten provides opportunities for children to find and observe living things and explore their habitat. Josh orientated the implementation of his three play-types on an investigation of macro-invertebrates habitats for insects, spiders, millipedes and centipedes. The outdoor environment at the centre contained a compost bin, logs, rocks, shrubs and trees, and water tanks. Prior to participating in the project Josh had been focussing on environmental education in his programming with the children for at least 6 months. This included learning about aspects of sustainability, such as recycling, growing food and establishing a composting system.

Josh implemented the play-type combination as open-ended play, followed by modelled-play, and finally purposefully-framed play. Josh began his open-ended play session with five children from the 3-year-old room, including Mitchell, Charlie, Jackson, Netra, Kayne and Anne (Fig. 5.1). One girl, Anne chose not participate in the open-ended play however she participated in the modelled and purposefully-framed play experience.

5.2 Open-Ended Play

Josh asked the children to see what living things they could find in the outdoor area. His goal was to extend and broaden the children's understanding of living things. Throughout the three play sessions he took photographs of the children's findings. The children quickly dispersed throughout the playground as they excitedly suggested where the mini-beasts could be. For example, several children went to the compost bin to see what that could find (Figs. 5.1 and 5.2).

Josh accompanied the children around the yard, and initially the children explored one of the compost bins. One child said he could see spiders, although none were actually evident on this day. This child then asked "Where have all the spiders gone?" demonstrating the child's previous experience with looking in the compost bin. When the compost bin door was first opened another child asked if he could sit on Josh's lap, and Josh reassured the child by saying "it's OK". The first compost bin yielded no living things so the second compost bin was opened. Josh questioned the children about whether there was anything in this bin, while refraining from taking the lead in the exploration. A millipede was found in this bin and Josh asked the children what it was. Netra said "it is a caterpillar", and while the other children knew it was not a caterpillar they did not know its name. At this point Netra began saying in a loud voice "kill it, kill it", while pointing at the millipede. Josh responded by asking Charlie what he thought about killing things. Charlie responded by saying "it is not good". Charlie wanted to touch the

Fig. 5.1 Looking for living things in the outdoor area

Fig. 5.2 Josh and the children looking for living things in the compost bin

millipede and Josh advised just to look at it. Two children picked up leaves and tried to make the millipede move. There was no definitive answer on what it was from the children, and Josh did not tell the children what it was called.

Josh then encouraged the children to look elsewhere prompting "Where else do you think we might find some living things?" Mitchell suggested looking under logs. Stones were turned over first, with children advising their peers to watch their feet. The first stone uncovered some living things, and Netra proceeded to try to kill whatever it was on the ground. Josh advised him to keep his feet back, and a child said it would "snap him". Jackson expressed a desire to hit a snapper bug with a spade, however Josh reminded him of the ethics of caring—"that we look after these bugs". Josh helped the children turn the rocks back over and followed them to the next suggested habitat—some logs under trees. The children assisted each other in turning over the logs, and Josh asked the children if there was anything present. Netra was delighted to find a feather, and asked if he could take it home to which Josh replied "yes". Josh proceeded to accompany the children and helped them to move the logs.

5.3 Modelled-Play

Three weeks after the open-ended play session Josh planned and implemented the modelled-play session. Josh's goals for the session were for the children to think about macro-invertebrates' habitats, their names and characteristics. He also wanted the children to develop a growing appreciation for caring for the mini-beasts by returning them to their habitats after examining them. He led five children—Mitchell, Charlie, Jackson, Kayne and Netra—on a modelled-play experience to achieve these goals. Three of the five children had been involved in the previous open-ended play experience. Mitchell and Netra led the way with enthusiasm to find the living things in the yard. Mitchell declared "Don't kill the bugs, don't kill the bugs". Josh responded to this declaration by gathering the group together and asking Mitchell "how should we treat the bugs?" Mitchell repeated "No killing the bugs, and don't touch them" leading Josh to ask the children "So what could we do? Is it OK if we look at them?" There was general agreement all round regarding this suggestion. Throughout this modelled-play experience Netra, who had expressed interest in killing the bugs in the open-ended play experience, was heard to state on at least six occasions "I'm not killing them".

Josh began this modelled-play session by first going to the compost bins followed by three children holding magnifying glasses. They found a spider's web, no spiders, and some slaters. One child confidently picked up a slater to examine it more closely. There was no response by Josh to this action. With prompting from Josh, the group moved on from the compost bins to look underneath some logs, and whilst making their way to the logs Charlie used his magnifying glass to closely examine the bark of a tree (Fig. 5.3). Upon regrouping the children found a worm and an earwig under the bamboo matting. Netra declared that he wouldn't kill the earwig and Josh thanked him. When the earwig kept crawling into dark areas Josh talked about how it was seeking the dark to be safe. Netra again repeated his declaration that he would not kill it.

Josh's language supported the children's understanding of the habitat associated with the macroinvertebrates. He asked the children questions about the bugs they had found—such as what is its name, characteristics, food and preferred habitat? The children's understanding of the type of habitat the macroinvertebrates preferred was reinforced when the group found plastic under the bamboo matting and Josh asked the children whether the bugs were likely to live in plastic. The children all said "no". Each time Josh uncovered a macroinvertebrate habitat he talked

Fig. 5.3 Charlie using a magnifying glass to examine habitat

about how he was "carefully" returning the cover for the bug, whether it was a log, a rock or the bamboo matting, thus modelling an ethic of care for the living things in the environment, a biophilic disposition.

The discovery of faeces in the yard led the children to speculate that it may have come from a squirrel or even from an elephant. This discussion took a new turn when Netra asked if he could kill the faeces. Josh responded by asking him "is it alive?" Netra said "no" and proceeded to stomp on the faeces. Another sample of faeces was found in the lower branches of a nearby wattle tree, and owing to its size was identified by the children as most likely to be possum faeces. The children agreed that elephant "poo" was probably going to be too large to be found in their yard.

5.4 Purposefully-Framed Play

One week after the modelled-play session Josh began the purposefully-framed experience at the first compost bin with Anne, Netra, Jackson and Jake. Josh began the session by reminding the children of the macroinvertebrates they had found the previous week. He prompted them to remember their search and discoveries. Together Josh and the children examined the layers of rotting matter in the compost bin, found various bugs and discussed the names of the creatures they could see and the food they ate. They found spider's eggs but no spider. Netra asked "where is the spider?" Josh replied that he was unsure. Netra knew that spiders came out of spider eggs, and when he asked if the eggs were edible, Josh replied "we do eat some eggs, but not spider eggs".

The exploration for bugs continued in the yard and each time Josh and the children found a living macroinvertebrate they would discuss its characteristics and try to remember its name. When Anne said she was unable to remember the name of an earwig she said "It was one that Mitchell told us about".

Fig. 5.4 Josh and the children matching found mini-beasts with images placed on a photograph board

In the second compost bin were some tools that did not belong there, including a spade, a ribbon, a piece of plastic and a bucket. The children had established a sense of where things belong in the environment and insisted that these objects be removed. No further bugs were visible so Josh encouraged the children to come and look at photos he had printed of the bugs they had found last week. However the children were still keen to find living things, and proceeded to turn over rocks, and look around the yard. The children were engaged in exploring and discovering more living things in the yard.

Josh began the purposefully-framed play session by stimulating exploratory learning of the environment to find living things. He intended to teach content associated with macro-invertebrates during this session as a follow on from modelled and open-ended play. He planned for the children to match photographs of the macroinvertebrates with pictures (Fig. 5.4), name the macroinvertebrate, and identify its characteristics and habitat. He intended for this knowledge to contribute to the children's appreciation for natural environments, and most importantly to him the development of an ethics of care for living things.

The pictures of spider's eggs that Josh downloaded off the internet were compared with the photograph of spider eggs found in the compost bin the week before during the modelled-play session. The key difference identified by the children was that the spider eggs they had found were "soily" compared to the picture from the internet. However, despite this difference the children did agree that they were the same type of egg. The group agreed to pin the photo of spider eggs next to a photo of two spiders—one male and one female of the brown house spider. The children were interested that the smaller of the spiders was the male, and one child said "girls are small, boys are big". Josh explained how female spiders are bigger than male spiders, and some girls are bigger than boys at kindergarten. Josh then led the children to review what they had seen, and a discussion followed about the differences between millipedes and centipedes, confusion over the names (including calling the centipede a caterpillar) with one child suddenly arriving with a live millipede in his hand. Josh used this opportunity to explain the differences between these macroinvertebrates. At times during this purposefully-framed play experience Anne struggled to find the words to express her understanding, however she was delighted to identify the picture of the worm and she said she knew it was a worm "because it was lumpy". Josh focused the children's attention on the characteristics of each creature—for example the number of legs.

There was some discussion about whether the centipede was dangerous. Netra asserted that all the macroinvertebrates were dangerous, including the centipede, millipede, brown house spider, slug, earwigs, slaters, worms and snail. There was general disagreement about the danger of the macroinvertebrates, although there was agreement that the brown house spider could bite and make one feel unwell.

5.5 Pedagogical Play and Environmental Education

The children responded keenly to investigating what living things were to be found in their yard, and as a result exhibited some knowledge about biodiversity. This included learning the names of the macroinvertebrates, their habitats, and characteristics, and how to care for them in their environment. One week after the purposefully-framed play the children were shown a video of themselves participating in the three play experiences, and asked what they remembered about these experiences. They recalled their knowledge about the body characteristics of spiders, the behaviour of mini-beasts seeking the dark for safety, the names of slaters, spiders, worms, and snappers—however, they still disagreed on the name of the millipede/centipede.

Josh employed several pedagogical strategies during the implementation of the three play-types, including open questioning and speculating during open-ended play, demonstrating in modelled-play, and explaining and engaging in shared thinking and problem solving during purposefully-framed play. Josh's engagement with the children during the implementation of the play-types was a significant support to the children's interactions during each experience. For example, he supported the children to access places in the yard where the macro-invertebrates were to be found, and was available to comfort children when they were uncertain about their findings. This was evident when children expressed fear and some biophobic dispositions towards certain macro-invertebrates. However, given Josh himself held a biophilic disposition he was able to deploy the different play-types to engage the children in rich discussions about the macroinvertebrates. As the children participated in these discussions the level of their biophobic expressions declined and they began to show more biophilic orientated dispositions. This was illustrated by Netra at first wanting to kill and squash the macro-invertebrates and then later being able to say that he would not hurt them.

Josh's teaching style was challenged by implementing an open-ended play approach in one session. He explained that normally he would not teach in this manner, choosing instead to follow up the children's emerging interests within the same day by beginning with open-ended play, then modelled-play and finally purposefully-framed play. This implementation was staggered across a number of weeks, which was not his preferred approach. When Josh reflected upon the open-ended play he said he had found it difficult to refrain from telling the children about the creatures, and as a consequence he realised the value of listening to the children. When asked whether there were any surprises for him by teaching open-ended, modelled and purposefully-framed play Josh replied:

> I was surprised that it was quite hard to stick to them (open-ended questions) because I feel like I use open-ended questioning all the time and a lot of things we do are open-ended but that once I tried to limit what I was saying and the input that you have over the play experience, and I found that really difficult because I always thought I was generally quite quiet and didn't talk a lot but then I thought I do talk all the time when I am working with the children.

Josh realised that his teaching style was interactive and he found it difficult not to influence the children's activity during the open-ended play experience. However each of the three play-types influenced the way he engaged with the children. When using open-ended play Josh restrained himself from giving the children direct content knowledge. As a result, Josh believed he learnt more about the children's thinking and what they were curious about. This included deeper insight into their working knowledge and theories about the macro-invertebrates. During an interview conducted with Josh following the implementation of the three play-types, he was asked whether or not this level of insight was beneficial for supporting the children's learning. He replied:

> Yes trying to not have too much influence over what they were doing... it was an eye opener for me.... it's beneficial for me to recognise that and also it's beneficial just to find out what the children are thinking and what they want to find out and what their knowledge is to stand back a bit.

Josh's insight into the role of open-ended play in learning suggests that such play is a useful starting point for both children and teachers. In Josh's case, the open-ended play was pedagogically valuable when he refrained from too much interaction because it helped him to find out more about what the children were thinking. Trawick-Smith (2012) notes this as a key advantage of the 'trust in play' approach. Interestingly for Josh, this approach was also paired with consideration of the significance of using purposefully-framed play with the children. During his interview Josh was asked to comment on the children's responses to watching the video footage of themselves engaged in the different play-types. Here the children indicated that they preferred the purposefully-framed play when Josh was more fully engaged with them. Josh believed the children preferred this play-type because "they have a real thirst for knowledge, and interest in the subject". Purposefully-framed play enabled him to engage this thirst for knowledge with the children, however, having first implemented open-ended play he was also able to build on what he understood to be the children's current thinking about the macroinvertebrates. In this way interest driven and open-ended play were complemented by Josh's planned experiences and interactions with the intention of building the content knowledge associated with learning about biodiversity.

For Josh, this meant that there was pedagogical value in the combination of the play-types he implemented, commencing with open-ended play, followed by modelled-play and finishing with purposefully-framed play. Josh was aware of raising the children's interest in the topic and hence valued the role of open-ended and modelled-play as a vehicle for establishing this initial interest. Josh felt that if he had begun immediately with purposefully-framed play then only those children with a prior interest in the topic would have continued with the experiences. He believed that beginning with open-ended and modelled-play provided time and opportunity for the children to talk about the concepts and to formulate ideas and questions that were later realised when he explicitly engaged the content knowledge via the purposefully-framed play.

5.6 Chapter Conclusion

Josh believed the combination of all three play-types supported the children's engagement with biodiversity. This was because each play type enabled a range of exploration, reflection and opportunity to participate in discussions that allowed the children to grow their awareness about biodiversity. For Josh, learning and teaching about biodiversity was not so much a matter of choosing to engage with only one type of pedagogical play, rather it meant understanding the benefits of each approach and how they could be combined to realise his goals for the children's learning and their engagement with the natural world. In Josh's work there is evidence of the two principles of play-based learning informing his approach to early childhood environmental education:

Principle One:

Valuing different play-types according to their pedagogical potential for engaging with aspects of environmental education

This is evident in Josh's understanding of the three play-types providing different opportunities for learning that are considered equally valuable. He learned that open-ended play would provide him with insight into the children's thinking, whereas he could use modelled-play to explicitly build children's ethical awareness of how to care for the macro-invertebrates. Purposefully-framed play he viewed as an avenue for addressing the children's 'thirst for knowledge'.

Principle Two:
Creating combinations of play-types that support engagement with different aspects of environmental education

This is seen in Josh's suggestion that modelled and purposefully-framed play extended children's initial open-ended exploratory interests and provided a platform for engaging children in the development of biophilia dispositions.

Table 5.1 Josh's combination of play-types and planned experiences according to the pedagogical value he attributed to the play-types and his associated environmental learning goals

Principle one Pedagogical value Josh attributed to play-type	Principle two Combination of play-types Josh decided to implement	Planned experience according to play-type	Environmental learning goal associated with play-type
Opportunity to observe children and ask questions to provide insight into existing levels of understanding	Open-ended	Explore the outdoor area: where can we find living things? Where else could you look?	Broaden awareness of living things located in the outdoor area Ethics of care for living things
Discussing content to support knowledge building Discussing content to provide a rationale for ethics of care	Modelled	Take the children to the compost bins/logs/ matting: what can we see using the magnifying glass? Let's put things back where we find them	Biodiversity content knowledge about macroinvertebrates habitat, names and characteristics Ethics of care for living things
Engaging content knowledge to build levels of understanding that contribute to an appreciation of the life needs of other creatures	Purposefully-framed	Explore the outdoor area: where can find living things	Biodiversity content knowledge about macroinvertebrates' habitat, names and characteristics
		Photograph matching board: what did we find?	Ethics of care for living things Biophilic dispositions towards nature

The use of these principles by Josh in his provision of early childhood environmental education are summarised in Table 5.1.

Reference

Trawick-Smith, J. (2012). Teacher-child play interactions to achieve learning outcomes—risks and opportunities. In R. C. Pianta, W. S. Barnett, L. M. Justice, & S. M. Sheridan (Eds.), *Handbook of early childhood education*. USA: Giuldford Publications.

Chapter 6
Robyn: Worms Underground

Abstract This chapter presents Robyn's (an early childhood teacher) and the childre's experiences. Robyn's kindergarten was located in an outer suburban part of Melbourne, Australia. Robyn focused on worms and making a wormery (a worm farm) owing to the children's interest in worms, and her goals were to provide children with greater understanding of worms and their habitats. Robyn's play order was purposefully framed play, modelled play and open-ended play. Robyn brought in a large clod of soil rich in worms for the children to explore. She initiated purposefully framed play asking children in-depth questions about worms, used correct terminology and built a worm farm with the children. She used nonfiction books and scientific tools to enhance the children's learning. During the modelled play children made their own worm farms under guidance from Robyn, and in the open-ended play they were given free rein to make their worm farm. This led to some of worms being drowned by the children using too much water, leading Robyn to step in to save the worms. Robyn identified that normally she would use all three strategies in the same play session rather than in isolation or separately. This articulation of the combined play types to environmental education is important for early childhood education as educators move in and out of teaching strategies depending on the children's cues, their interests and the intent of teaching.

6.1 Introducing Robyn and Hallam Kindergarten

Robyn's kindergarten was located in an outer suburban part of Victoria, Australia. There were many children from diverse cultural backgrounds and from lower to mid socioeconomic circumstances in Robyn's kindergarten. Robyn valued outdoor play for young children because of the opportunities she perceived it provided for children's learning about the environment. She was particularly interested in supporting children to be respectful of other living creatures and viewed outdoor play as an avenue for achieving this goal. Robyn believed in the importance of

A. Cutter-Mackenzie et al., *Young Children's Play and Environmental Education in Early Childhood Education*, SpringerBriefs in Education,
DOI: 10.1007/978-3-319-03740-0_6, © The Author(s) 2014

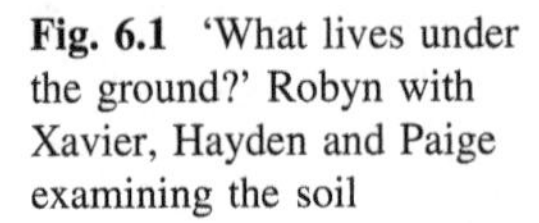

Fig. 6.1 'What lives under the ground?' Robyn with Xavier, Hayden and Paige examining the soil

what she called 'direct' teaching as well as open-ended play because she felt the cultural experiences of the children she worked with warranted strong interactions and engagements to foster learning.

During her participation in the project Robyn decided to focus on worms and making a wormery (a worm farm). Robyn mentioned that the children were already interested in worms, and said that "every time they found one they were extremely excited and then they just waned off". Taking this reflection into consideration, Robyn felt that the children's interest needed to be extended to provide "greater understanding about worms" not just encouraging basic "observation skills". Consequently, Robyn decided to commence with purposefully-framed play, then implemented a modelled-play experience and ended with open-ended play. Robyn intended for the children to learn how the worms moved, what they needed to survive and the nature of their habitat.

Three boys (Hayden, Xavier and Sam) and two girls (Paige and Tahima) participated in the three play experiences. While many children had parental permission to participate (and also provided self-consent), these five children were chosen by Robyn either because they were particularly interested in worms, or because they were "always playing in the soil". Robyn's approach to making a wormery was resourceful and constructive. Robyn particularly wanted the children to appreciate that worms live in the natural world "under the ground" not just in an artificial, plastic worm farm. This meant the basis of the physical setup for her experiences was a large grassy topped clump of soil freshly dug up from her paddock at home because she considered the soil at the centre to be "not good for digging" and not "bug rich" (Fig. 6.1).

6.2 Purposefully-Framed Play

While the rest of the children in the centre continued to play inside with other educators, Robyn gathered the five children to work outside on "something special", walking past the native grasses to sit at a small table with bench seats under

Fig. 6.2 Xavier showing Robyn a worm in the book similar to those in the wormery

the eucalyptus trees. A large plod of grass covered soil nearly covered the whole table top and the children were invited to sit and discuss "what lives under the ground?" The first question the children wanted to know was "where did you get this ground from?" showing an immediate awareness that this piece of earth was different to the soil at their centre. Robyn explained that the soil came from her paddock at home and the children helped to lift the heavy piece of rich earth upside down, so the soil was exposed under the grass to aid their investigation. The children were instantly engaged, excited and interested in finding "what was under the ground", whilst Robyn asked several questions—"What do you think might live under the ground?" and "How will you know if it's a worm you've found under the ground?" Correct scientific terminology was used by Robyn and the concept of habitats was explained. There was a focus on asking biophilia orientated questions such as, "Are worms safe for us to touch?" and "What do you think worms do under the ground?" Robyn's questions punctuated the children's activity, with the children responding, and saying "I found a big giant worm" and "I found a baby worm because he is little", as they carefully sorted through the soil, finding and picking up worms.

The children were then invited to build a worm house together. Robyn asked the children what they would need to make the worm house similar to the soil they had just examined. Next to the table where they were playing with the soil Robyn had placed a number of containers with sand, additional soil, compost/food and newspaper, along with small shovels for the children to collect materials to make the wormery. The children were again invited to collect small amounts of these materials to pour into the large glass fronted wormery in layers, before covering it in black paper to simulate the darkness of under the ground (see Fig. 6.2). This session was 45 min long, requiring sustained periods of concentration on the children's part. Perhaps because of this, Tahima started to wander away to the swings and tended to come back and forth, while Xavier was more involved in the 'Earth Worm' picture story books nearby than the actual worms in the soil, exclaiming to Robyn, "Look, a worm" pointing to the pictures.

For the other children water was added to the mix of materials to make the habitat for the worms more life-like. Robyn continued to pose questions, such as, "Do worms like it wet or dry?" Hayden speculated, "Wet… so worms can live underground at the beach too!" Sam suggested the wormery should stay outside "because it's much cooler outside, and worms like it cold!!" These comments seemed to demonstrate the children's developing understanding about the nature of the habitat needed by the worms.

6.3 Modelled-Play

The following week, the same five children—Hayden, Paige, Sam, Xavier and Tahima -were invited to look at worms again, but this time the session was held inside. At the beginning of this experience, the children gathered around Robyn for a discussion about "what do we need to do to make this wormery like under the ground for the worms?" This time the children were invited to make their own individual wormeries using a plastic bottle inside another half bottle, with soil and other materials inserted in the space between, then eventually covered in black paper to make it dark "like under the ground". They talked about what the worms needed to live happily, and how the wormery would need drainage holes. The children appeared engaged and interested in the experience and were eager to start.

Back at the table was another huge plod of grassy earth waiting for the children to discover "what lay under the ground". On the floor, surrounding the table were the same materials the children had used to make the large wormery during their purposefully-planned experience including, containers of sand, soil, newspaper with spoons and small cups. Additional resources including non-fiction books about worms and magnifying glasses were also provided. This time, the children knew immediately what to do, and collectively started to lift the heavy patch upside down with exclamations of "I found a wriggling worm" and shortly afterwards, "Look everyone, I found a worm… He's with his family." This statement led Robyn to state that "He belongs under the ground!" which triggered the children to start making their own individual wormeries to remedy the situation of homeless worms.

This session lasted for 65 min and was characterised by the children's sense of innovation as they made their own wormeries. The children readily drew on the resources available, selecting what they believed was necessary to create their worm farms. All of the children took care and time to compact soil, sand and compost (for food) into their bottles, with added "decorations" on top to make their wormeries look like the "grassy patch". The children had understood the concept that worms live "under the ground", and that they needed to replicate that habitat. Occasionally there were issues of worm ownership, with Xavier saying, "That's my worm" while Hayden asked, "Please can I have one of your worms?" Overall, the worms were carefully collected, examined, shared and located in each child's own wormery (See Fig. 6.3). During this experience some children chose to use the spoons provided for their investigation and collection of worms while others used only their bare, muddy hands.

During this experience, Robyn sat at the table with the children asking questions such as, "Are you trying to find out what the worms like in their house?"

Fig. 6.3 Robyn modelling the making of a womery with Hayden and Xavier

The children continued to experiment and investigate, answering Robyn's questions whilst they engaged in the experience. While Robyn was clearly involved and interested in their activity, she was not directing the children, instead adding comments and questions that deepened the children's inquiry into worm life. For example, at one stage, Robyn asked, "Do worms have babies?" to which Sam answered quickly, "Yes, because they have families!" Another question posed by Robyn about how worms eat, was answered by Hayden who said, "Worms are small, so they eat small stuff like compost." Robyn's questions and comments appeared to provoke the children's scientific thinking. This notion was especially evident when Robyn commented about one worm's travels, saying "Look, he went all the way down to the bottom. I wonder how he did that. How does a worm get all the way through the soil?" The children's answers show the collective peer thinking and learning occurring throughout this play with Hayden answering:

> A worm is very small, and doesn't have any hands, so he pushes his way through with his head.

Sam listening close by added, "He has very strong brains." It was at this stage that Robyn mentioned to the children, "If the worms are going to live in there, they'll need it to be a little bit wet!" This comment had unforeseen ramifications for what was to occur during the children's participation in the open-ended play experience a week later.

6.4 Open-Ended Play

Another week passed before the open-ended play type session was planned for the children. Once again, the play was set up inside the preschool, with Robyn inviting the children to make their own wormeries centred on the tray of soil, materials and

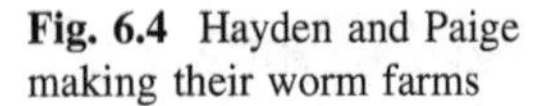

Fig. 6.4 Hayden and Paige making their worm farms

resources they had used before, and then she stepped away from the group. This time, spray bottles of water, plus torches were added to the experience in an attempt to provide an additional mode of investigation of worms in the earth (Fig. 6.4) Another addition was a raised, clear tray of soil for children to be able to see worm action from underneath.

Raised children's voices were heard back and forth across the table with comments ranging from "There's no worms here!" to "Found one" and then, "Wow, look at this worm!" The children flicked the torches on and off and experimented with the magnifying glasses. The spray bottles of water were constantly in use, but it was not the occasional squirt of water to dampen the soil that was happening—instead large muddy puddles of water were appearing over the table top and on the floor. At one stage, worms were being flicked into children's faces. Some of the children tried to rectify the issues saying to each other, "Don't take another worm!" Eventually it was the appearance of the drowning worms that drove Robyn to return to the table, where she quickly reverted to commenting and questioning the children in her effort to save the worms. Robyn asked the children with a horrified look on her face, "Do they look like they are moving in there? Can worms swim?" and then she said, "Do you think the worms would like the water or the soil to live in?" In Robyn's presence the investigation once again became richer, with children commenting "I found something too small to be a worm, and too small to be a caterpillar." Their behaviour also became more respectful towards the worms who were less flooded and more gently treated. After an extended period of sorting and collecting worms, the children started to make wormeries again as suggested at the beginning of the session. Robyn reminded the children that "he's got soft skin, if you touch him too hard he'll be hurt." Conversations about other minibeasts added another dimension, with Tahima suggesting that she had "just touched a little green worm, but I dropped it and it runned away." Robyn enquired, "Oh, could you see its legs?" which in turn developed into further discussion about the attributes of worms.

Eventually, Paige, Tahima and Xavier decided they had had enough play with the worms, and wandered away from the table. The final two boys, Hayden and Sam, who were left at the table, appeared to be totally immersed in the sensory elements of the wormery-making play, including making up musical rhymes in the mud. Robyn wondered aloud after an hour, "How will you know when it's finished?" which was answered by one of the boys saying, "I'll tell you, because I love building it." Robyn replied, "I'm sure the worms appreciate you being gentle!" Finally Robyn suggested to Hayden and Sam they had been working there for such a long time, that perhaps they could come back later and check how the worms were in their wormeries? The boys thought this was a great idea, and decided, "We'll come back later!"

6.5 Pedagogical Play and Environmental Education

Robyn reflected on the relationship between the three play-types, her planning for the children's learning, and the learning she believed had occurred during the children's experiences. Although Robyn initially planned to have all the play experiences outside, she felt it was difficult to "contain the children" and that being outside was more of a distraction for the children who at times wandered away from the purposefully-framed play experience. For the subsequent play types, Robyn arranged these to be set up inside while the other children were playing outside:

> I thought that being outside would make it more natural, more getting into the experience more readily, but to me it was more of a distraction than an enhancement.

Robyn was asked if she thought her teaching style influenced the way she interacted with the children differently in each play type. She commented that as a teacher she considers herself to be "quite directive", she was surprised how difficult it was "to separate the mix of all three different play-types", and to manipulate the teaching in the way she had intended:

> You can see I was trying to pull it back to a more purposefully-framed experience. And it was interesting because I find that quite often as a teacher I am quite directive and frame some of the experiences quite firmly, and yet when I tried to make it definitely a purposefully framed thing and when it went into a slightly different direction I found it really hard to bring it back to that.

On reflection, Robyn concluded that as a teacher "you just automatically jump in and out of the different play-types based on what you need." This was supported in an entry recorded in her journal where she wrote "teachers blend teaching strategies to help children work constructively towards goals." Robyn's claim of "blending" play-types acknowledges existing ideas regarding intentional teaching in early childhood education, including the argument that children benefit in terms of knowledge construction from experiences that contain a balance of adult-initiated and child-centred activity (Epstein 2007; Wood 2013). The articulation of the combined play-types to environmental education is important for early childhood education as it suggests using a range of pedagogical play for supporting children's engagement with environmental knowledge, rather than relying solely on one play-type to enable learning.

One of the most significant concerns to emerge during Robyn's implementation of the three play-types was that environmental education for young children needs engaged educator support and not just self-discovery through open-ended play experiences. It seemed from Robyn's reflections and journal writing that this engagement included using a combination of the play-types to support children's learning. For example, it was during the implementation of the open-ended play where the children began to over-water the worms that Robyn said, "I couldn't help myself" and felt she had to intervene during the play when "creatures were being hurt". It was clear in this situation that open-ended play suggested opportunities for the children to mistreat the worms in a way not consistent with the messages of nurturing and caring for living things. Robyn was asked if she thought the children's learning about the worms would have been as engaged if only open-ended play had been used:

> No…when we had open-ended play here I was trying to stay out of it, but when the worms were getting stretched and hammered and drowned, I just couldn't do that.

Pearson and Degotardi (2009) suggest that children's learning about sustainability in early childhood is important because research shows that biophilic attitudes towards the environment are formed during the early years. These attitudes may not develop in a meaningful way in situations where open-ended play lessens the access children have to adults for supporting their interactions with other living things. For example, the children in this study tended to default to harmful behaviour towards the worms when there was less adult support available to them during the open-ended play experience than they had exhibited during the purposefully-framed and modelled play activities. This finding is interesting because Robyn felt she and the children had already done a "fair bit of work" about respecting all living things prior to their engagement in the final open-ended experience. However, Robyn concluded that a biophilic attitude takes time to establish:

> Just that the bugs we don't have to harm them that they are living things and they breed like us. 'They don't like to be hurt, do you like to be hurt?' 'They've got soft bodies, do you like your body to be hurt?' 'They don't have big bones like we do'. I just try to create an understanding and empathy I suppose about creatures, and I guess that comes from my belief that we are all entitled to live. Even with spiders we will put them in a container so we can watch them. We have a lot of Red Backs [small highly poisonous spiders] around here so even when we remove them from the environment, we do it so the children don't see how they are removed, so we often catch them in a container and then they are removed later. But other spiders we will put out into the garden because they've got a job to do. So I think all of those attitudes build up over time it's not just something that you teach in one hit.

Robyn also suggested that it can be difficult to support biophilia when there is minimal support for this type of environmental learning from the children's home, and said, "I don't think they spend a lot of time outside in the outdoor environment as a family." Robyn was particularly clear about her attitude and believed that "a bit of soil doesn't hurt us" in relation to encouraging the children to experience the reality of worms and the soil without the use of "latex gloves". At times throughout the worm sessions, there were comments from some of the children demonstrating their anxiety about "the mess" being created in the play, with one child warning others "don't touch, it's dirty". Such comments are somewhat typical signs of the formation of early biophobic attitudes towards nature.

The conversation about the range of play-behaviours exhibited by the children during their participation in the the open-ended and purposefully-framed play triggered some interesting comments from Robyn regarding the rhetoric associated with open-ended play and its role in young children's learning. Robyn was asked if she thought it was still the dominant pedagogy used in early childhood settings:

> I think there are some places where perhaps it is, but I am not fully sure that everyone knows what open-ended means. It is not my predominant thing. I would probably say I use more supported and modelled and guided play and I probably use guided more than purposeful…
>
> I think that if you don't have a purpose for what you put in the room, my belief is that everything you model and say and do from the minute you walk in the door sets the scene and influences what happens in the day.

The role of the adult in children's learning is a significant aspect of contemporary perspectives on intentional teaching (Fleer 2010; I. Siraj-Blatchford 2009). This appeared to be the case for Robyn, whose implementation of the purposefully-framed and modelled-play, included using in-depth questioning, the use of correct terminology and extensive visual cues such as the clump of earth, non-fiction books and scientific tools. These pedagogical strategies supported the children's engaged and extended play with complex biodiversity concepts, such that children participated in the experiences for up to sixty minutes. For example, during the purposefully-framed play experience the children talked about what the worms looked like, what they ate and what constituted a worm family. In the modelled-play experience, they discussed what worms need for their habitat and how such a habitat could be re-created in a wormery. The combination of these strategies possibly contributed to the type of "deep learning" Littledyke and McCrea (2009) claim is necessary for young children to engage with scientific content (p.43). Robyn reflected on the nature of this "deep learning", indicating that she "would never have anticipated the length of engaged time that evolved" during the purposefully-framed play, and that she was surprised that even more information emerged during the modelled-play type in the subsequent session. It was noted that Robyn's provision of multiple "visual cues" together with asking in-depth questions were highly successful pedagogical aids that assisted the children's extensive engagement in the experiences:

> That's probably my style that I try to include some of the information into the question, provocations for them but try to only give it in small amounts until it seems that they are ready for the next bit, so I think with the saddle someone noticed that he had a 'band-aid' [sticking plaster] so it was giving him the actual name [by mentioning the saddle].

Table 6.1 Robyn's combination of play-types and planned experiences according to the pedagogical value she attributed to the play-types and her associated environmental learning goals

Principle one Pedagogical value Robyn attributed to play-type	Principle two Combination of play-types Robyn decided to implement	Planned experience according to play-type	Environmental learning goal associated with play-type
Supports strong interactions and engagements for fostering learning	Purposefully-framed	Large clump of soil: what lives under the ground? How do you know? Why do you think worms live under ground? Are they safe for us to touch?	Move children beyond 'just looking' at worms towards acquiring content knowledge about worms: habitat, characteristics
		Use correct terminology: worm, soil, saddle, castings	
		Build a large worm together	
		Cross reference worm farm with non-fiction books	
Allows teacher to 'set the scene' influencing the type of learning that occurs	Modelled	Materials for making individual worm farms	Content knowledge about habitat: moisture, drainage
		How can we make these farms look like under the ground?	Respect for living things
		Look at the clump of soil	
		Show how to use magnifying glass to examine worms	
		Provide non-fiction books about worms	
Exploration and access to nature (opportunity to get dirty)	Open-ended	Provide materials for making individual worm farms	Biophilic dispositions
		Spray bottles of water for moistening soil	

6.6 Conclusion

Robyn's implementation of the three play-types illustrated the importance of adult interactions during play to support the children's engagement with the biodiversity content forming the basis of the experiences. In Robyn's situation adult interaction involved questioning, providing information and prompting the children's understanding about the worms and their habitats. During the open-ended play experience, the absence of these interactions meant that the children began to engage in what was undoubtedly satisfying exploratory play for them—but considerably less so for the worms. This led Robyn to reflect on the extent to which open-ended play alone would be a satisfactory pedagogical approach in relation to early childhood environmental education. This reflection is consistent with contemporary research regarding the role of open-ended play in early childhood education in relation to children's engagement with content knowledge—particularly where this has shown that children are more likely to build conceptual knowledge via interactions with adults. Importantly for environmental education, such child–adult interactions seem to be important for addressing early signs of biophobia amongst children and supporting the development of biophilic dispositions.

Principle One:

Valuing different play-types according to their pedagogical potential for engaging with aspects of environmental education.

This is evidenced in Robyn's understanding that whilst open-ended play supports children to become comfortable with aspects of nature (such as playing with soil), that modelled and purposefully-framed play provides a basis for learning why it is important to be respectful towards other living creatures.

Principle Two:

Creating combinations of play-types that support engagement with different aspects of environmental education.

This is reflected in Robyn's ideas about "just jumping in and out of the different play-types based on what you need" to support learning. Sometimes Robyn blended play-types within one type (for example stepping in with modelled play when she saw the worms being harmed by the children during the open-ended experience).

The use of these principles by Robyn in her provision of early childhood environmental education are summarised in Table 6.1.

References

Epstein, A. S. (2007). *The intentional teacher: Choosing the best strategies for young children's learning*. Washington, D.C.: National Association for the Education of Young Children.
Fleer, M. (2010). *Early learning and development: Cultural-historical concepts in play*. Melbourne: Cambridge University Press.
Littledyke, M., & McCrea, N. (2009). Starting sustainability early: Young children exploring people and places. In N. Taylor & C. Eames (Eds.), *Education for sustainability in the primary curriculum: A guide for teachers* (pp. 39–57). South Yarra, Vic.: Palgrave Macmillan.
Pearson, E., & Degotardi, S. (2009). Education for sustainable development in early childhood education: A global solution to local concerns? *International Journal of Early Childhood, 41*(2), 97–111.
Siraj-Blatchford, I. (2009). Conceptualising progression in the pedagogy of play and sustained shared thinking in early childhood education: A vygotskian perspective. *Educational and Child Psychology, 26*(2), 77–89.
Wood, E. (2013). *Play, learning and the early childhood curriculum*, (3rd ed.). London: Sage Publications.

Chapter 7
A Challenge Reconsidered: Play-Based Learning in Early Childhood Environmental Education

Abstract In this chapter, the authors discuss the two principles that emerged from this research project, and that can be applied for play-based learning in early childhood environmental education. These principles are (1) Valuing different play-types according to their pedagogical potential for engaging with aspects of environmental education; and (2) Creating combinations of play-types that support engagement with different aspects of environmental education. These two principles go beyond the traditional thinking of learning 'naturally' through play. This is because the principles allow educators to identify pedagogical value associated with a play type and to combine this with other play types to achieve environmental learning goals with children. Simply providing children with access to open-ended play in an outdoor setting is insufficient to support environmental learning. Environmental learning in the early years needs to provide children with opportunities for acquiring content knowledge that allow them to build understandings about their world and develop biophilic dispositions toward nature. This is a necessary basis for engaging children in discussion about the need for sustainability and sustainable actions in their own lives and communities.

7.1 Introduction

The opening vignette for this book described four children happily playing with some materials placed in a wading pool at their kindergarten. It was noted that the materials had been selected to help the children learn about the biodiversity associated with their local beach. Whilst the children initiated a play-script drawing on their knowledge of SpongeBob Squarepants, their teacher (Seth) approvingly noted the positive nature of their social interactions. Such play-experiences are not uncommon in early childhood education, and are believed to help children learn to respect other living things and to develop an ecocentric appreciation for the environment. Our argument, in the context of emerging research into the use of pedagogical play in early childhood (see Chaps. 2 and 3),

A. Cutter-Mackenzie et al., *Young Children's Play and Environmental Education in Early Childhood Education*, SpringerBriefs in Education,
DOI: 10.1007/978-3-319-03740-0_7,

and the debates associated with environmental education (see Chap. 3), is that such activity is not enough to support children's environmental learning.

In this book we have considered the history of play-based learning and seen that critiques of the historically valued use of open-ended play have resulted in new conceptions of pedagogical play that value the role of adults in children's activity. Variously conceptualised as intentional teaching (Epstein 2007), sustained shared thinking (Siraj-Blatchford 2009), integrated pedagogies (Wood 2013), pedagogical activity (Dockett 2011) and inter-contextuality (Fleer 2011), these positions suggest that adult-child interactions during play support conceptual learning. In this book we have drawn on three different play-types to show how such interactions can be realised by teachers engaging children in environmental education. Broadly, the play-types used in this book mirror those established by Trawick-Smith (2012) as the 'trust in play', 'facilitate play' and 'learn and teach play' approaches, and include open-ended play, modelled play and purposefully-framed play.

In Chap. 4 we saw how Jeanette used open-ended, modelled and purposefully-framed play to foster children's learning about pond life. Jeanette suggested that the combination of play-types she used was a significant aspect of how she understood the relationship between play-based learning and environmental education. This was because Jeanette believed that it was important to provide children with opportunities to explore and examine the environment via open-ended play prior to participating in more adult-initiated experiences such as modelled and purposefully-framed play. However, Jeanette, like Robyn, noted that open-ended play alone was insufficient for dispelling misconceptions the children held about the likely creatures to live in the lake and the promotion of biophilic dispositions towards nature. Here, both Jeanette and Robyn valued purposefully-framed and modelled play as play-types that enabled them to create direct relationships between the children's open-ended experiences and the range of content knowledge that both dispelled misconceptions and helped to reduce biophobic dispositions. This was clearly the case when Robyn intervened in the children's open-ended play to protect the worms from being "overwatered, stretched and hammered" by the children.

Chapter 5 highlighted Josh's understanding of the play-types as providing the children with different but equally valuable opportunities for engaging and supporting learning. Josh suggested that open-ended play was useful because it allowed him to observe and listen to the children in ways that alerted him to what they already knew and understood about macroinvertebrates. Modelled-play was perceived as providing a prime opportunity for demonstrating ethical ways of engaging with macroinvertebrates and for challenging biophobic tendencies. Meanwhile, purposefully-framed play was viewed as significant because it allowed Josh to support the children's interests and gave them access to information that further supported their developing ethical perspectives. For example, learning that insects prefer dark spaces helped the children decide to return them to their habitat after they had finished looking at them. This stance on purposefully-framed play was echoed by Jeanette and Robyn, each of whom reflected on the extent to which actively engaging the children in content knowledge about biodiversity later prompted more ethical and respectful interactions with the environment on the children's behalf.

Chapter 6 focussed on Robyn's implementation of the three play-types commencing with purposefully-framed play, then modelled play and ending with open-ended play. Here, Robyn argued that a fundamental environmental concern of hers was that the children would learn to respect the life needs and rights of all creatures—including worms. Robyn was also keen for the children to understand worm habitats, and created an ingenious series of experiences where children were able to see, touch and explore a large clump of soil from above, the side and from underneath prior to constructing their own worm farms. Purposefully-framed play mattered because being able to talk to the children about worm habitats provided a basis for engaging in conversation about the 'rights' of the worms during open-ended play. Thus, like Josh, ethical and biophilic dispositions towards nature were enabled by Robyn when she used content knowledge as a basis for talking with the children about the characteristics of the worms and their preferred habitats.

7.2 Two Principles for Using Play-Based Learning in Early Childhood Environmental Education

The perspectives held by Jeanette, Josh and Robyn suggest two principles for using play-based learning in early childhood environmental education. As noted in Chap. 1 the first principle is concerned with the pedagogical *value* associated with each play type, whilst the second principle is concerned with the *combination* of play-types educators use to achieve different environmental learning goals. These principles were represented in Tables 4.1, 5.1 and 6.1 at the end of Jeanette, Josh and Robyn's chapters in relation to the experiences they planned and implemented for the children according to the goals they held for the children's environmental learning outcomes. In summary, the principles may be understood as:

Principle One

Valuing different play-types according to their pedagogical potential for engaging with aspects of environmental education.

This principle is based on the idea that no one play type is more valuable than another. Each play-type offers particular experiences and opportunities that help teachers to think about children's learning, and therefore their approach to teaching environmental education. Open-ended play can support the exploration that exposes children to nature and biodiversity. As Jeanette and Josh noted, open-ended play can also provide teachers insight into children's current modes of thinking. Modelled-play can promote opportunities for teachers to illustrate respectful relationships with the environment. Purposefully-framed play can enable access to content knowledge that further promotes biophilic dispositions. Valuing play-types for the different pedagogical potential they provide teachers means open-ended play does not have to be promoted over and above the other play types. This is consistent with contemporary research regarding the use of 'integrated' play-based pedagogies (Wood 2013) because it highlights the unique pedagogical value of each play-type.

Principle Two

Creating combinations of play-types that support engagement with different aspects of environmental education.

The play-types do not need to be fixed in a given sequence to usefully support teachers and children engaged in environmental education. Instead, the play-types can be used in flexible combinations to meet teacher goals for children's learning according to the value they attribute to a play-type. For example, Josh valued open-ended play because it provided him with insight into the children's current levels of thinking and understanding. In turn he appreciated purposefully-framed play because it helped him to support children's ethical encounters with the macroinvertebrates. Modelled play was valued because it allowed Josh to share his own biophilic dispositions. If Josh's goal was to promote biophilic dispositions with the children he might deliberately begin with modelled play, prior to moving to purposefully-framed play and then open-ended play. Conversely, if Josh was more focused on engaging the children in learning about the habitats of the macroinvertebrates he might commence with open-ended play so that he could gain insight into their current thinking and then use this as a basis for planning some purposefully-framed activity. Here there is no need to use all three play-types in a particular order. Rather iterations of play-types can be selected and sequenced by teachers to achieve their environmental learning goals for children, whether these are orientated towards supporting biophilic dispositions, the acquisition of content knowledge associated with biodiversity, developing eco-centric perspectives on the environment or engaging with sustainability.

7.3 Re-considering Play-Based Learning in Early Childhood Environmental Education?

In the introduction to the book we suggested the two principles for using play-based learning in early childhood environmental education could be used to re-consider the provision of Seth's initial experience for the children gathered around the wading pool. The activity as first described could be taken as an open-ended play experience. If like Josh, Seth valued open-ended play for the potential insight it was likely to give him into the children's thinking he may have noticed that the children related the sea creatures to SpongeBob Squarepants and his sea star sidekick Patrick. This could have alerted Seth to the fact that the children had some pre-existing knowledge of sponges and sea stars. Seth's next step could be to consider what he valued as the pedagogical potential for both modelled and purposefully-framed

Table 7.1 Seth's re-considered approach to early childhood environmental education using the two principles of play based learning

Principle one	Principle two		
Pedagogical value Seth attributes to play-type	Combination of play-types Seth decides to implement	Planned experience according to play-type	Environmental learning goal associated with play-type
Provides insight into children's existing knowledge base as informed by their media viewing	Open-ended	Place seaweed, sea stars and plastic sea animals in wading pool	Identifying sea creatures
Engaging children in content knowledge to expand existing media-informed knowledge	Purposefully-framed	Place seaweed, sea stars and plastic sea animals in wading pool Locate books and/or iPad with information/ video about characteristics of seaweed and sea stars near wading pool/ Watch Sponge Bob Squarepants Read, watch, share and discuss video and information	Content knowledge about biodiversity: characteristics of seaweed, sea stars, octopus, fish
Opportunity for modelling biophilic dispositions	Modelled	Visit the beach Search for sea creatures Return creature to habitats Photograph habitats Create photographic habitats for plastic creatures and/or characters from Sponge Bob Squarepants	Respecting living things Content knowledge about the relationship between creatures and habitat

play. If purposefully-framed play was perceived by Seth as providing opportunities for engaging children in content knowledge about sea creatures he may plan to build on what they already recognised as the difference between the sponge and the sea star. Several possibilities are evident here—perhaps Seth would choose a website or some video footage to show the children using an iPad; perhaps he would source some books and engage the children in discussion about the different features on each creature. Maybe they would watch an episode of Sponge Bob Squarepants and discuss the various creatures represented as characters in the program. Having done this, Seth might be interested in expanding the children's awareness of the habitats associated with each creature. Using modelled play he may plan to re-visit the beach showing the children how to search for the creatures and being careful to return what he found to the correct habitat. Photographs could be taken of the different habitats and on return to the centre the children could use these images to create 'homes' for the plastic sea animals used in the initial play-experience. Alternatively, the children may be invited to create or paint appropriate habitats for the different characters from the Sponge Bob Squarepants program.

Re-thinking Seth's provision of early childhood environmental education using the two principles of play-based learning highlights how considering the *value* (Principle One) associated with a play-type informs why a teacher might decide to use that type, and consequently the *combination* (Principle Two) of types a teacher might decide to implement to achieve particular environmental learning goals. This is because we can see that Seth's decision to use modelled play and then purposefully framed after the open-ended play is based on providing the children with access to the some content information (modelled) and the building on this information to extend their understandings of habitat (purposefully-framed). The two principles of play-based learning articulate with each other to provide Seth with a framework for approaching early childhood environmental education that allows him to move beyond simply providing experiences to engaging in learning about biodiversity with the children.

Like the examples provided for Jeanette, Josh and Robyn (Tables 4.1, 5.1 and 6.1) it is possible to illustrate Seth's re-considered approach to early childhood environmental education using the two principles of play based learning (Table 7.1).

7.4 Conclusion

In the opening chapter of this book we suggested that traditional play-based practices posed a challenge for early childhood environmental education. This is because simply providing children with access to open-ended play, the outdoors and nature is not enough to support environmental learning. Environmental learning in the early years needs to provide children with opportunities for acquiring content knowledge that allow them to build understandings about their world and develop biophilic dispositions toward nature. This is a necessary basis for engaging children in discussion about the need for sustainability and sustainable actions in their own lives and communities. Furthermore, research in play-based learning over the last decade has suggested multiple ways of thinking about how adults can most effectively engage with children during play-based activities to promote learning. Our work with educators and children suggests that the two principles of play-based learning we have identified in this book can be readily articulated to the provision of early childhood environmental education. This is because the principles allow educators to identify the pedagogical *value* they associate with a play-type and to *combine* this with other play-types in order to achieve environmental learning goals with children. Whilst there will always be challenges associated with how best to engage young children in environmental education, these two principles go some way to providing educators such as Seth with a starting point for more readily integrating such education into the early years. In this way, children are able to transcend traditional notions of environmental learning (such as swirling seaweed or stretching worms) to participating instead in deeply rich play-based early childhood environmental education.

References

Dockett, S. (2011). The challenge of play for early childhood education. In S. Rogers (Ed.), *Rethinking play and pedagogy in early childhood education: Concepts, contexts and cultures* (pp. 32–48). London: Routledge.

Epstein, A. S. (2007). *The intentional teacher: Choosing the best strategies for young children's learning*. Washington, D.C.: National Association for the Education of Young Children.

Fleer, M. (2011). 'Conceptual Play' foregrounding imagination and cognition during concept formation in early years education. *Contemporary Issues in Early Childhood, 12*(3), 224–240.

Siraj-Blatchford, J. (2009). Editorial: Education for sustainable development in early childhood. *International Journal of Early Childhood, 41*(2), 9–22.

Trawick-Smith, J. (2012). Teacher-child play interactions to achieve learning outcomes—Risks and opportunities. In R. C. Pianta, W. S. Barnett, L. M. Justice, & S. M. Sheridan (Eds.), *Handbook of early childhood education*. USA: Giuldford Publications.

Wood, E. (2013). *Play, learning and the early childhood curriculum*, (3rd ed.). London: Sage Publications.

About the Authors

Amy Cutter-Mackenzie is Associate Professor in the School of Education in the area of Sustainability, Environment and Education. She is the Director of Research for the School of Education, and the Research Leader of the Sustainability, Environment and Education (SEE) Research Cluster. Amy commenced her career as a primary school teacher in Queensland Australia and later moved into academia after completing her Ph.D. Amy's research is clearly situated in the area of children's and teachers' thinking and experiences in environmental education and sustainability in a range of contexts and spaces (including early childhood education, schools, teacher education, higher education, research and communities). Amy is the Editor of the Australian Journal of Environmental Education (Cambridge University Press) and Consulting Editor for the Journal of Environmental Education, the International Journal of Early Childhood Environmental Education (NAAEE) and International Journal of Environmental and Science Education. She has been recognised nationally for teaching excellence in "leading school-community teaching and learning practices and partnerships to influence, motivate and inspire pre-service education students and schools to engage in environmental education and sustainability" (OLT 2008, 2010).

Susan Edwards is the Deputy Director of the Centre for Early Childhood Futures at Australian Catholic University. She works in the area of early childhood education and specialises in researching aspects of the early childhood curriculum, including play-based learning, teacher thinking, digital technologies and environmental education. Susan has achieved national recognition for teaching excellence in the tertiary sector and has published a number of key texts associated with early childhood education. She is the co-author of Early Childhood Curriculum: *Planning, Assessment and Implementation* published by Cambridge University Press and a co-editor of *Engaging Play* published by Open University Press. Associate Professor Edwards is currently one of two editors for the Asia Pacific Journal of Teacher Education.

Deborah Moore is a Ph.D. candidate in the Centre for Early Childhood Futures at Australian Catholic University. With a background of over 25 years as a Preschool teacher and Preschool Field Officer, Deb was also the inaugural Early Years Sustainability Officer for a local government in Victoria. Deb has worked for many years for Play Australia as one of their Early Childhood Outdoor Play

A. Cutter-Mackenzie et al., *Young Children's Play and Environmental Education in Early Childhood Education*, SpringerBriefs in Education,
DOI: 10.1007/978-3-319-03740-0, © The Author(s) 2014

seminar presenters. Deb's Ph.D. research is based around young children's imaginative play places, and her research interests include environmental education for young children and their outdoor play places.

Wendy Boyd is a Lecturer in Early Childhood Education at Southern Cross University (SCU). She was an early childhood educator for 25 years before moving into academic life. Having completed her Ph.D. in 2011, Wendy has collaborated to research and publish in the areas of pre-service teachers' attitudes to child care, early childhood education for sustainability, pre-service teachers' attitudes to mathematics, and teaching in higher education. Her approach to teaching pre-service early childhood teachers has been recognised through the 2011 SCU's Vice Chancellor's Citation Award for Excellence in Teaching. Wendy is an editor for the New Zealand Research in Early Childhood Education Journal.

Author Index

A. Cutter-Mackenzie et al., *Young Children's Play and Environmental Education in Early Childhood Education*, SpringerBriefs in Education,
DOI: 10.1007/978-3-319-03740-0, © The Author(s) 2014

Subject Index

A. Cutter-Mackenzie et al., *Young Children's Play and Environmental Education in Early Childhood Education*, SpringerBriefs in Education,
DOI: 10.1007/978-3-319-03740-0,

CPSIA information can be obtained
at www.ICGtesting.com
Printed in the USA
LVHW020803270523
748233LV00029B/441

9 783319 037394

Emblème de l'Alliance

ALLIANCE FRANÇAISE

ASSOCIATION NATIONALE

POUR LA

PROPAGATION DE LA LANGUE FRANÇAISE

DANS LES COLONIES ET A L'ÉTRANGER

SIÈGE SOCIAL

27, rue Saint-Guillaume, 27

PARIS

ALLIANCE FRANÇAISE

ASSOCIATION NATIONALE

POUR LA

PROPAGATION DE LA LANGUE FRANÇAISE

DANS LES COLONIES ET A L'ÉTRANGER

SIÈGE SOCIAL

27, rue Saint-Guillaume, 27

PARIS

SOMMAIRE

ALLIANCE FRANÇAISE

ASSOCIATION NATIONALE POUR LA PROPAGATION DE LA LANGUE FRANÇAISE

DANS LES COLONIES ET A L'ÉTRANGER

CE QUE C'EST QUE L'ALLIANCE FRANÇAISE

L'Alliance française[1] a été fondée en juillet 1883; elle a commencé à fonctionner en janvier 1884; elle existe depuis *cinq ans* et quelques mois. Le premier jour, nous étions neuf, réunis dans une petite salle du cercle Saint-Simon[2], nous sommes aujourd'hui plus de **quinze mille**, en France, dans les colonies et à l'étranger, sur tous les points du globe.

Notre association a été reconnue comme *établissement d'utilité publique* par décret du Président de la République en date du 23 octobre 1886.

Nous avons amassé un fonds de réserve de *cinquante mille francs;* notre budget annuel, d'abord très modeste, est aujourd'hui d'environ *quatre-vingt mille francs;* nous avons déjà dépensé plus de cent mille francs de subvention en argent, en médailles, en livres d'enseignement, fournitures classiques et livres de prix distribués aux écoles françaises situées hors de France. Grâce à la générosité des éditeurs parisiens, cette somme de cent mille francs représente une valeur effective bien plus considérable.

---

1. **L'emblème de l'Alliance française.** — L'*Alliance française* a pris pour blason les **couleurs nationales** sur champ d'azur. L'azur, c'est à la fois le bleu de la mer et le bleu du ciel, l'espace immense et l'idéal. Puisse notre chère langue française, symbolisée par le drapeau tricolore, franchir les mers azurées, résonner sur les plus lointains rivages! Puisse-t-elle en même temps donner chaque jour une forme à la fois plus précise, plus énergique et plus universelle à ces hautes vérités, à peine entrevues et encore mal vérifiées qui, pareilles aux astres, se cachent dans le ciel profond de la pensée humaine.

2. MM. Ant. Bernard, Paul Bert, Paul Cambon, l'abbé Charmetant, Pierre Foncin, Jusserand, Lœb, Machuel, Alfred Mayrargues.

L'**Alliance française** a pour but de **propager la langue française dans les colonies et à l'étranger.**

Son œuvre est double. Elle recueille en France des ressources qu'elle dépense au dehors. Ces ressources, elle les obtient par une propagande incessante que dirige

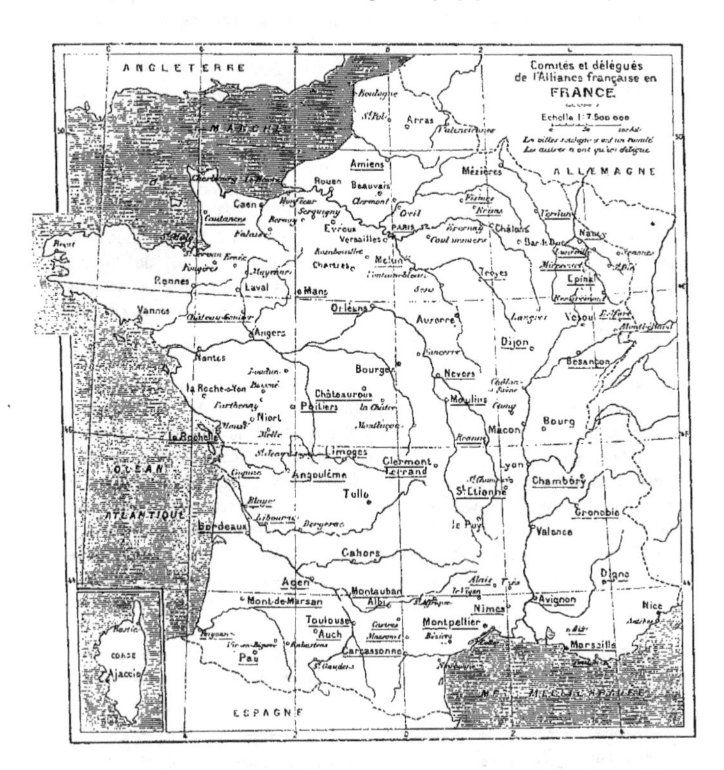

le Secrétariat général assisté d'une **Commission générale de propagande**. Elles sont distribuées par le **Conseil d'administration**, composé de cinquante membres élus en Assemblée générale, organe souverain de l'Association. Le travail d'information préalable sur les demandes de subventions est confié au Secrétariat général et les votes du Conseil sont rendus sur les propositions de commissions d'étude ou sections dont la plus importante est la *section du Levant*. — La trésorerie centralise les fonds et veille à l'expédition des envois votés.

Le *siège de l'Association* est à Paris, **27, rue Saint-Guillaume**, où l'École des sciences politiques nous a accordé, moyennant une modeste location, une précieuse hospitalité [1].

Propagande à Paris. — L'Alliance a créé à **Paris** des *comités de propagande* dans chacun des vingt arrondissements : ceux de la Bourse, du Panthéon, de Passy, de la place Voltaire sont les plus florissants. Elle a organisé des conférences et donné des fêtes destinées à faire connaître l'œuvre. C'est ainsi qu'en 1887 M. Ernest Renan, en 1888 M. Jules Simon, ont parlé de la langue française, au Vaudeville, dans des matinées dramatiques et musicales auxquelles les artistes les plus distingués de l'Opéra et de la Comédie-Française ont prêté leur gracieux concours. Plus récemment à la Sorbonne, sous la présidence de M. Gréard, assisté de M. de Brazza, M. Deschamps et M. le général Tcheng-Ki-Tong ont fait connaître la situation de la langue française dans le Levant et en Chine. Il serait trop long de citer les autres conférences faites à Paris sous notre patronage.

Propagande en province. — Dans les *départements*, nous avons 62 *délégués* et 40 *comités de propagande régionaux* ou *locaux*. Les Comités de Nancy, Reims, Moulins, Limoges, Saint-Étienne, Bordeaux, Cognac, Mont-de-Marsan, Alger, Oran, Constantine, etc., se sont particulièrement distingués par leur activité. Aux efforts de leurs conférenciers tels que MM. Gavet, Leroy, Ed. Petit, Trolliet, Gide, Imbart de La Tour, Rinn, de Cardaillac, Radet, Agoulon, a répondu le zèle de nos conférenciers envoyés de Paris, MM. Puaux, Wahl, Hément, Brau de Saint-Pol-Lias, Guillot, Normand, de Mahy, de Lanessan. A l'Université, à ses professeurs des Facultés, des lycées, des collèges, revient l'honneur principal de ces campagnes entreprises en faveur de l'œuvre.

Congrès de 1889. — A l'occasion de l'Exposition universelle, nous publions un *Annuaire*, nous organisons un **banquet** et un **congrès**. Nous prenons une part brillante à **l'Exposition** elle-même.

---

1. **Commission générale de propagande** : M. Armand Colin, *président*. MM. le vicomte de Begouën, Brau de Saint-Pol-Lias, Bougier, Biétrix, Bernard, Bonnaire, Bureau fils, Chamerot, Cranney, Cosnard, docteur Charvot, Callet, Chênebenoit, Couderc, Collombier, Clunet, Delalain, E. Duruy, David-Mennet, Deligny, Failliot, Faroy, Fernoux, Fontin, de Frézals, docteur Frère, Franck, Gaudefroy-Demombynes, Gomel, Guillot, Guérie, docteur Gaube, Godard, Garnier, Hément, Huguet, Jandet, Jost, Junot, Kœchlin (Raymond), Lecène, Lourdelet, Lebon, Leroy, Lesoudier, Mathorel, Mayrargues, Mamy, Mesnard, Mouttet, Moullé, Muzet, Née, Nathan, Normand, Ollendorff, Petit, docteur de Pradel, Rochard, de Royou, Salle, Saint-Denis, Viénot, Vaquez, Wahl.

Comités des colonies et de l'étranger. — Nous avons fondé *hors de France* des **comités d'action** en grande partie *autonomes*, qui ont leurs ressources propres dont ils disposent, en se conformant à nos statuts et sauf approbation de leurs actes par le Conseil d'administration.

École Arabe française en Tunisie.

En **Algérie**, nos comités de propagande sont en même temps comités d'action. Tous trois ont créé des cours d'adultes et contribué à rendre l'opinion publique favorable à l'instruction des indigènes. Le comité d'Oran est le plus important. Celui de Constantine a donné des fêtes brillantes au profit de l'Association.

Colonies et pays de protectorat. — **L'Alliance** a des comités à Tunis, à Saint-Louis du Sénégal, aux Antilles, à la Guyane, dans l'Inde à Pondichéry, dans l'Indo-Chine à Hanoï et à Saigon. Le comité de Tunis, dirigé par M. Machuel, a réuni l'adhésion d'un grand nombre d'indigènes. Celui du Sénégal subventionne les écoles militaires fondées par le colonel Gallieni au Soudan français et celles des PP. du Saint-Esprit. Celui de Pondichéry fondé récemment par M. Martinet a créé des comités locaux à Mahé et Karikal et obtenu le gracieux concours de plusieurs dames qui ont résolu d'enseigner elles-mêmes le français à de jeunes Indoues.

A l'**étranger**, notre association a des comités au Caire et à Alexandrie (Égypte), à Constantinople, à Smyrne, à Syra, à Mételin, à Salonique ; à Madrid, à Valence et à Barcelone (Espagne), à Zurich, à Copenhague, à Londres, à Port-Louis (Ile Maurice ou de France), à Rio-Janeiro, à Montevideo, etc. ; elle entretient des relations ami-

École française du Levant.

cales avec les Français de Bâle, avec l'Alliance française de Prague, le Cercle français de Budapest, le Cercle littéraire de Bombay, l'union des Sociétés françaises de New-York, l'Union française de la Nouvelle-Orléans, la Société de langue française de Tokio (Japon). Le comité du Caire a fondé une école importante à Syout; ceux de Madrid et de Valence ont chacun leur école franco-espagnole. Celui de Maurice donne des fêtes annuelles ; il a créé des concours de français et institué des bourses.

Nos *délégués* sont disséminés de tous côtés. Il faut signaler surtout : **MM.** Knapp à Neuchâtel, Bresson à Rotterdam, Baale à Amsterdam, Van Hamel à Groningue, Gullberg à Kalmar, Muller et Schulhtess à Stockolm, Berstène à Saint-Pétersbourg, Lyautey à Odessa, d'Aubigny à Port-au-Prince (Haïti), Fréchette au Canada, etc.

Subventions aux écoles. — La majeure partie de nos **subventions** a été accordée, après avis de la **section du Levant**[1], aux écoles françaises du Levant, *catholiques pour la plupart*, ou grecques, arméniennes, syriennes, israélites, laïques. Nous avons secondé les efforts de Mgr Azarian, patriarche des Arméniens catholiques, de Mgr Altmayer, archevêque de Bagdad, des ordres religieux et des missionnaires : Lazaristes, Frères des Écoles chrétiennes, Dominicains, Franciscains, Assomptionnistes, Filles de la Charité, Sœurs de Saint-Joseph, Dames de Sion, Oblates de l'Assomption, etc. Nous avons servi ainsi la cause de l'*influence française*.

Nous avons encouragé la propagation du français en Algérie, en Tunisie, à Madagascar, en Indo-Chine, dans les colonies et travaillé ainsi à la **conquête morale** des indigènes placés sous la protection de la France. Le **seul rôle** digne d'une grande nation est de **conquérir jusqu'à l'âme des peuples** qui s'abritent sous les plis de son drapeau.

Nous avons noué des relations avec les États de l'Europe amis de la France, avec les républiques de l'Amérique espagnole, avec le Brésil, avec le Canada, avec les Français établis aux États-Unis. Nous avons réveillé les sympathies littéraires que la France a conservées dans la plupart des pays civilisés. Nous avons travaillé ainsi, dans la mesure de nos forces, à l'extension de l'influence nationale, au développement du commerce national. Car tout *lecteur d'un livre français* devient un **ami de la France**, et tout ami de la France est un **client naturel des produits français.**

Tout cela a été fait, qu'on ne l'oublie pas, en cinq années. Que ne ferons-nous pas avec le temps ?

Caractère de l'Association. — L'Alliance française agit au grand jour ; il est aisé d'en connaître l'*esprit* et le caractère. Son *Bulletin* tient ses adhérents exactement au courant de ses moindres actes.

---

1. **Section du Levant** : MM. **Amiable**, maire du IVe arrondissement ; **Avril** (baron d'), ministre plénipotentiaire ; **Colonna Ceccaldi** (comte), ministre plénipotentiaire, conseiller d'État, vice-président du Conseil d'administration ; **Dunoyer**, conseiller d'État ; **Guérin** (V.), docteur ès lettres ; **Kahn** (Z.), grand rabbin de Paris ; **Laporte**, magistrat ; **Leroy-Beaulieu** (A.) ; **Marmier** (commandant) ; **Mayrargues**, trésorier de l'Alliance française ; **Mas Latrie** (comte de), de l'Académie des inscriptions et belles-lettres ; **Maspero**, membre de l'Institut, professeur au Collège de France **Melon** (P.) ; **Parmentier** (général) ; **Reinach** (J.), publiciste ; **Rey**, ancien chargé de missions scientifiques en Syrie ; **Royou** (de).

C'est une *association indépendante* et libre de toute attache officielle. Respectueuse du gouvernement de son pays, elle s'efforce de le seconder partout où il est chez lui et le maître ; elle peut agir à sa place, là où il risquerait de se compromettre.

Elle n'a qu'une cocarde, celle de **la France**[1] ; elle a adopté pour *emblème* les **couleurs nationales** sur champ d'azur, image du rayonnement de la France par delà les mers les plus lointaines ; elle reste étrangère à toute querelle entre les personnes, et même à tout débat entre les idées ; elle appelle, elle groupe dans une communauté d'efforts patriotiques *les hommes de bonne volonté de tous les partis*. Des catholiques, membres du comité de l'Œuvre des Écoles d'Orient ; de israélites, membres de l'Alliance israélite universelle ; des protestants ; un prêtre, un rabbin, un pasteur ; des penseurs libres ; en un mot des hommes de toute nuance politique ou religieuse font partie de son Conseil d'administration.

École militaire dans le Soudan français.

Elle s'adresse en particulier aux **femmes françaises**, aux mères qui sont les premières institutrices de leurs enfants, qui leur apprennent les premières à balbutier la langue française et qui ont reçu en dépôt dans leur berceau l'*âme de la patrie*. « Ce qui est gravé dans le cœur de la femme est assuré de l'immortalité. Heureux le peuple chez qui la femme s'associe aux aspirations nationales ! La victoire et l'avenir sont à lui[2] ».

Elle a été fondée par des hommes d'étude, elle a été surtout propagée jusqu'ici par des *professeurs* ; c'est dire assez combien sa **propagande est désintéressée.** Mais elle s'adresse en même temps au *commerce français* dont elle est l'alliée naturelle ; car la propagation de la langue française est *la clé des marchés extérieurs*.

Si elle sert les intérêts de la France hors de ses limites continentales, elle

1. M. le ministre de la guerre et M. le ministre de la marine ont spécialement autorisé MM. les officiers des armées de terre et de mer à faire partie de l'*Alliance française*.
2. Paroles prononcées par Mgr Strossmayer, archevêque des Croates.

contribue par surcroît à affermir dans la mère patrie, **l'union de tous les bons citoyens.** Il faut avoir séjourné à l'étranger pour comprendre avec quelle poignante humiliation on y entend nos ennemis rire de nos discordes. L'Alliance fran-

École française Annamite.

çaise ne fait pas de politique, mais *elle a une politique :* **la concorde au dedans, le rayonnement pacifique au dehors.**

Loin de haïr l'étranger, elle lui tend la main. Un nombre important d'**étrangers,** Grecs, Roumains, Russes, Danois, Suédois, Norvégiens, Hongrois, Suisses, Espagnols, Arabes, Levantins, Indous, Annamites, sont ses délégués ou font partie de ses comités. *Créer des écoles est de toutes les concurrences la plus loyale et en même temps la plus profitable à l'humanité.*

S'il est vrai que tout homme ait deux patries : la sienne et la France, il est possible d'espérer qu'un jour la *langue française*, sans abolir les langues nationales, devienne la **langue universelle.**

P. Foncin,
Secrétaire général de l'Alliance française.

COMITÉS ET DÉLÉGUÉS

DE L'ALLIANCE FRANÇAISE A L'ÉTRANGER

A l'étranger, l'Alliance française s'efforce principalement de ranimer ou d'éveiller les *sympathies littéraires* qui unissent depuis des siècles la nation française aux autres peuples, tout en s'abstenant avec le plus grand soin de s'immiscer dans leurs affaires intérieures. Elle ne saurait oublier d'autre part que la langue française est la langue nationale du Canada, de la Louisiane, de l'île Maurice (ancienne île de France), que la Belgique wallone, la Suisse romande parlent français et qu'un grand nombre de Français dispersés par petits groupes sur divers points du globe ont toujours les yeux fixés sur la mère patrie, l'aimant d'autant plus qu'ils en sont plus éloignés et moins connus.

EUROPE

ILES BRITANNIQUES. **Londres.** — COMITÉ : Société nationale des professeurs de français : *Président*, M. Ragon ; *Secrétaire*, M. Huguenot.

BELGIQUE. **Bruxelles.** — DÉLÉGUÉ : M. Chassaing, publiciste.

PAYS-BAS. **La Haye.** — DÉLÉGUÉ : M. C. H. Hofman, directeur d'école primaire supérieure. — **Amsterdam.** — DÉLÉGUÉ : M. Baale, professeur de français. — **Rotterdam.** — DÉLÉGUÉ : M. Brosson, pasteur de l'Église wallonne. — **Groningue.** — DÉLÉGUÉ : M. Van Hamel, professeur à l'Université.

DANEMARK. **Copenhague.** — COMITÉ : *Président*, M. le général Tvernoos, inspecteur de l'infanterie ; *Vice-président*, M. Kragenbühl, pasteur de l'Église réformée ; *Secrétaires*, MM. Nyholm, docteur en droit ; A. Abraham, professeur de langues ; *Trésorier*, M. Monrad Bay, négociant.

SUÈDE et NORVÈGE. **Stockholm.** — DÉLÉGUÉS : MM. le Dr Joseph Müller et Schulthess. — **Kalmar.** — DÉLÉGUÉ : M. Gulberg, professeur de français au gymnase royal.

RUSSIE. **Saint-Pétersbourg.** — DÉLÉGUÉ : M. Borstène, attaché à la Banque d'escompte. — **Odessa.** — DÉLÉGUÉ : M. Lyautey, professeur au deuxième gymnase. — **Kiev.** — DÉLÉGUÉ : M. Louis Pécus, lecteur en langue française. — **Vasa** (Finlande). — Mademoiselle Augusta Krook, professeur.

BOHÊME. **Alliance française de Prague.** — COMITÉ : *Président*, M. Sobeslav Pinkas ; *Vice-président*, M. le général de division baron Friedberg-Mirohorsky ; *Secrétaire*, M. L. Pinkas ; *Trésorier*, M. Charles Voiti, commerçant ; *Comptable*, M. E. Fourneaux, chimiste.

ROUMANIE. **Jassy.** — COMITÉ : *Président*, M. Weitzsecker, professeur au Lycée national ; *Vice-président*, M. Cazabon, président de la Société française d'assistance ; *Secrétaire*, M. Forgues, professeur ; *Trésorier*, M. G. Doucet, professeur.

SUISSE. **Bâle.** — COMITÉ : Société de l'École française : *Président*, M. Huguenin. — **Zurich.** — COMITÉ : *Président*, M. A. Petit, professeur à l'École polytechnique. — **Genève.** — DÉLÉGUÉS : MM. Rod et Scheler, professeurs à l'Université. — **Neuchâtel.** — DÉLÉGUÉ : M. Knapp, professeur, archiviste bibliothécaire de la Société neuchâteloise de géographie.

ESPAGNE. **Madrid.** — COMITÉ. Société française de bienfaisance : *Président*, M. J. Barat. — **Barcelone.** — COMITÉ : *Président*, N. — **Valence.** — COMITÉ : *Président d'honneur* : M. Joseph Pellio, consul de France ; *Président*, M. d'Yechet ; *Secrétaire*, M. Santi ; *Trésorier*, M. Lacombe ; *Conseillers*, MM. Fontès, Lauriol, Mourgues et Gondard. — **Alicante.** — DÉLÉGUÉ : M. le baron Rousseau, consul, chargé du vice-consulat de France.

ASIE

SIBÉRIE. **Irkoutsk.** — DÉLÉGUÉ : M. Deloscaut, professeur au Gymnase.
SIAM. **Louong-Prabang.** — DÉLÉGUÉ : M. Pavie, vice-consul de France.
JAPON. **Tokio.** — DÉLÉGUÉ : M. Camille Giraud, professeur de langue française.

AFRIQUE

ILE MAURICE (ancienne Ile de France). **Port-Louis.** — COMITÉ : *Président*, M. le docteur Clarenc ; *Vice-présidents*, MM. Honorable, H. Leclésio, Ch. Baissac, J. Coutanceau ; *Secrétaire*, M. Martial Noël ; *Secrétaire-archiviste*, M. A. Daruty de Grandpré ; *Trésorier*, M. G. Bouic.

AMÉRIQUE

CANADA. **Montréal.** — DÉLÉGUÉ : M. Louis Fréchette.

ÉTATS-UNIS. **New-York.** — COMITÉ. Union des sociétés françaises : *Président*, M. A.F. Blank. — **Nouvelle-Orléans.** — COMITÉ. Union française : *Président*, M. Tujague. — **San-Francisco.** — DÉLÉGUÉ : M. Édouard

Larcher, professeur. — **Philadelphie.** — DÉLÉGUÉ : M. A. de Villeroy, chef d'institution. — **Chicago.** — DÉLÉGUÉ : M. P. M. Loubrie.

MEXIQUE. **Mexico.** — DÉLÉGUÉ : M. Pierre Martin, négociant.

HAITI. **Port-au-Prince.** — DÉLÉGUÉ : M. Ch. d'Aubigny, président de la Société française de secours mutuels.

BRÉSIL. **Rio-de-Janeiro.** — COMITÉ : *Président :* M. Tisserandot, professeur à l'École polytechnique ; *Vice-présidents,* MM. Gambaro, directeur du Collège international, Hellot, pharmacien ; *Secrétaire,* M. Madée ; *Trésorier,* M. Robillard de Marigny, négociant ; *Archiviste,* M. Gabalda, professeur.

GUATEMALA. — DÉLÉGUÉ : M. Vié, agent général de la Compagnie transatlantique.

PÉROU. **Lima.** — DÉLÉGUÉ : M. Dupeyrat, directeur du Collège français.

CHILI. **Santiago.** — DÉLÉGUÉ : M. Lambert, représentant du Creuzot. — **Valparaiso.** — COMITÉ. Chambre de commerce française : *Président,* M. Raymond Devès.

VÉNÉZUELA. **Caracas.** — DÉLÉGUÉ : M. Waltz, secrétaire de la Chambre de commerce française.

COMITÉS DE L'ALLIANCE FRANÇAISE DANS LE LEVANT

La France, jadis, a entraîné l'Europe occidentale dans le grand mouvement des croisades qui ont mis en contact le monde chrétien et le monde musulman. Elle a été la première alliée de l'empire ottoman. Elle a conservé le protectorat des catholiques de l'Orient. Elle a fait l'expédition d'Égypte, la guerre de Crimée, l'expédition de Syrie. Elle s'est passionnée, elle a versé son sang pour l'indépendance des Hellènes. Elle a percé l'isthme de Suez. Les noms de saint Louis, de Bonaparte et de Ferdinand de Lesseps résument son influence en Orient. Marseille, son premier port de commerce, a noué, depuis le moyen âge, d'étroites *relations commerciales* avec tout le bassin oriental de la Méditerranée que sillonnent ses paquebots. Aussi la langue française, bien que menacée par des langues rivales, est-elle toujours prépondérante sur le Nil, à Smyrne, à Athènes, dans les Échelles du Levant. L'Alliance française a entrepris de l'y défendre et de l'y propager, elle y est en même temps, d'une manière indirecte, mais efficace et certaine,

la tutrice de notre *influence* plusieurs fois séculaire et de nos intérêts commerciaux. Elle sait qu'elle peut compter dans le Levant comme ailleurs sur le concours bienveillant de nos représentants consulaires. Elle a, d'autre part, formé plusieurs comités importants et actifs en Égypte et dans la mer Égée (voir la carte ci-contre).

LEVANT

CYCLADES. **Syra**. — COMITÉ : *Président*, M. Eyssartier, ingénieur; *Vice-présidents*, MM. Calloudis, agent de la compagnie des Messageries maritimes; Toman, avocat, ancien député au Parlement grec; *Secrétaire*, M. Stoychich, chancelier du Consulat de France; *Trésorier*, M. Bambacarry, employé à l'agence des Messageries maritimes.

TURQUIE D'EUROPE. **Constantinople**.— COMITÉ: *Président*, M. Lacoine, conseiller technique des postes et télégraphes ottomans; *Vice-président*, M. le baron de Vandeuvre; *Secrétaire*, M. Sarret, professeur au lycée impérial ottoman; *Trésorier*, M. Baudouy, banquier.

TURQUIE D'ASIE. **Smyrne**. — COMITÉ : *Président*, M. Élie Guiffray; *Vice-président*, M. Ch. Darvant; *Secrétaire général*, M. Alf. Arlaud; *Secrétaire-adjoint*, M. Lascaris; *Comptable*, M. E. Pagy: *Archiviste*, M. A. de Courson. — **Mételin**. — COMITÉ : *Président d'honneur*, M. D. Bernardaki, président de l'Éphorie; *Président*, M. G. Bernardaki, directeur du Gymnase; *Vice-président*, M. Lucas, membre du conseil municipal; *Secrétaire*, M. J. Luciani, professeur de français au Gymnase; *Trésorier*, M. J. Emmanuel, propriétaire; *Conseillers*, MM. A. Baudouy, inspecteur des contributions indirectes, et M. Spadaro, agent de la régie.

ÉGYPTE. **Le Caire**. — COMITÉ : *Président*, M. Le Chevalier, commissaire directeur de la caisse de la Dette publique; *Vice-président*, M. Barrois, secrétaire général du ministère des travaux publics; *Secrétaire*, M. Peltier Bey, directeur de l'école normale Towfik; *Secrétaire-adjoint*, M. Lesieur; *Trésorier*, M. Guiguen-Bey, directeur de l'école khédiviale d'arts et métiers: *Trésorier-adjoint*, M. Baccus, professeur à l'école normale de Towfik.— **Alexandrie**.— COMITÉ : *Président*, M. Gilly, avocat; *Vice-présidents*, MM. Dervieux, banquier, et Jaquin; *Secrétaire*, M. Suzzarini; *Trésorier*, M. Escoffier, directeur de l'agence du Crédit lyonnais.

COMITÉS ET DÉLÉGUÉS DE L'ALLIANCE FRANÇAISE

DANS LES PAYS COLONIAUX

Dans la première moitié du dix-huitième siècle, la puissance coloniale de la France, égalait, si elle ne la surpassait pas, celle de l'Angleterre. Nous étions, grâce à Dupleix, les maîtres de l'Inde, et nous possédions encore le Canada. De nos jours, nous avons conquis l'Algérie, acquis la prépondérance en Indo-Chine, assis notre protectorat en Tunisie et notre influence à Madagascar, occupé le haut Sénégal et une partie du Soudan occidental. Les ouvriers de cette grande œuvre sont presque tous des dignitaires de l'Alliance française. Pour ne citer que les vivants et les plus illustres, ils se nomment Paul Cambon, Le Myre de Vilers, Savorgnan de Brazza, Faidherbe. Mais la conquête matérielle n'est rien sans la *conquête morale* et les indigènes placés sous notre protectorat ne pourront devenir Français de cœur que s'ils ont appris à parler notre langue. Encourager l'enseignement du français aux indigènes des pays coloniaux est une des tâches essentielles de l'Alliance française. Elle y favorise les efforts de l'armée, de l'administration et des missionnaires. Elle y est secondée elle-même par des comités et des délégués qui ont déjà fourni la preuve de leur zèle patriotique.

SÉNÉGAL. **Saint-Louis**. — COMITÉ : *Président*, M. Hubler, chef du service des Postes et des Télégraphes; *Secrétaire*, M. Carpot, négociant; *Trésorier*, M. Pécarrère, percepteur.

TUNISIE. **Tunis**.— COMITÉ : *Président*, M. Machuel, directeur de l'Enseignement public en Tunisie; *Secrétaire*, M. Dolmas, professeur au collège Sadiki.

GOLFE DE BÉNIN. **Grand Popo**. — COMITÉ : *Président*, M. Victor Ballot, administrateur commandant les établissements français du golfe de Bénin; *Secré-*

taire, M. A. d'Albéca, administrateur colonial à Grand Popo.

OBOCK. **Obock**. — DÉLÉGUÉ : M. Émile Proche, attaché au cabinet du Gouverneur.

INDE FRANÇAISE. **Pondichéry**. — COMITÉ : *Président d'honneur*, M. Piquet, gouverneur ; *Vice présidents d'honneur*, Mgr Laouennan, archevêque de Pondichéry ; M. Mathivet, directeur de l'Intérieur ; *Président*, M. Montbrun, maire de Pondichéry ; *Vice-présidents*, MM. Pordijon, Paul Pernon et Chanemougom, conseiller général ; *Secrétaire général*, M. Lippmann, chef de bureau ; *Trésorier*, M. Filatriau, chef de bureau ; *Secrétaire archiviste*, M. Coulandu, professeur ; *Rédacteurs de séance*, MM. Gnanadicam, Rajagobalou et Sirop (Alfred).

COCHINCHINE. **Saigon**. — COMITÉ : *Président*, M. Navelle, secrétaire général de la Cochinchine ; *Secrétaire*, M. Ulysse Mercier ; *Trésorier*, M. Marc, publiciste.

TONKIN. **Hanoï**. — COMITÉ : *Président*, M. Dumoutier, inspecteur de l'Enseignement. DÉLÉGUÉ, M. Duchemin.

ANNAM. **Hué**. — DÉLÉGUÉ : M. André Petit, officier d'administration du service de l'Intendance militaire. — **Vinh**. — DÉLÉGUÉ : M. Lemire, résident de France.

GUADELOUPE. **Pointe-à-Pitre**. — DÉLÉGUÉ : M. Arnaud, professeur au lycée de la Pointe-à-Pitre. — **Basse-Terre**. — DÉLÉGUÉ : M. Lasocki, conseiller à la Cour d'appel à la Basse-Terre.

MARTINIQUE. **Port de France**. — COMITÉ : *Président d'honneur*, M. le Gouverneur ; *Membre d'honneur*, Mgr Carméné, évêque de la Martinique ; *Président*, M. Garaud, vice-recteur ; *Vice-président*, M. Dupont, conseiller à la Cour ; *Secrétaire*, M. Revel, secrétaire du vice-rectorat.

ÉCOLES FRANÇAISES DU SÉNÉGAL

A peine l'Alliance française venait-elle de se fonder à Paris, qu'à la prière du général Faidherbe, qui est un de ses présidents d'honneur, M. Seignac, gouverneur du Sénégal, instituait à Saint-Louis, par décret du 3 juin 1884, un comité régional de l'œuvre. Il lui allouait en même temps un modeste crédit, auquel s'ajoutèrent divers dons, ainsi que le produit des cotisations.

Bientôt, le Conseil général, entraîné par une généreuse émulation, votait une subvention annuelle de 10 000 francs en faveur du Comité de Saint-Louis. Depuis lors, sous la présidence de M. Delort, conseiller général, puis de M. Hübler, chef du service des postes et des télégraphes, ce Comité a consacré des sommes relativement importantes à la fondation et à l'entretien d'écoles indigènes.

Les PP. du Saint-Esprit surtout ont bénéficié de sa libéralité ; ils ont étendu leur action dans les rivières du Sud et y ont fondé plusieurs écoles de missions, notamment à Boffa (Rio-Pongo). Leurs établissements de Sedhiou et Zighinchor (Casamance), de Palmérin, Fadiout, Poponguine (pays des Serrères), etc., sont également subventionnés par notre Association.

Notre Comité de Saint-Louis a créé directement plusieurs écoles dont le succès est désormais assuré, à Boké (Rio-Nunez) et à Dagana (sur le bas fleuve).

De son côté, l'autorité militaire a pu, grâce aux encouragements de l'Alliance, organiser des écoles dans les vastes régions du Soudan français récemment soumises à notre influence. C'est à M. le lieutenant-colonel Gallieni que revient le principal honneur de ces fondations. A Bakel, Kayes et Bafoulabé sur le haut Sénégal, à Bammako, sur le Niger, à Kita, dans la région qui s'étend entre les deux fleuves, sur plusieurs points occupés par nos troupes, les petits noirs qui jadis couraient à demi-nus dans la brousse, apprennent aujourd'hui à parler notre langue et sont initiés à notre civilisation.

Des sous-officiers, des militaires européens et indigènes, dirigés par leurs chefs dans cette tâche nouvelle, se sont improvisés instituteurs. Ils instruisent les fils de ceux qu'ils combattaient la veille et se hâtent de réparer de leur mieux les maux que la guerre toujours traîne après elle.

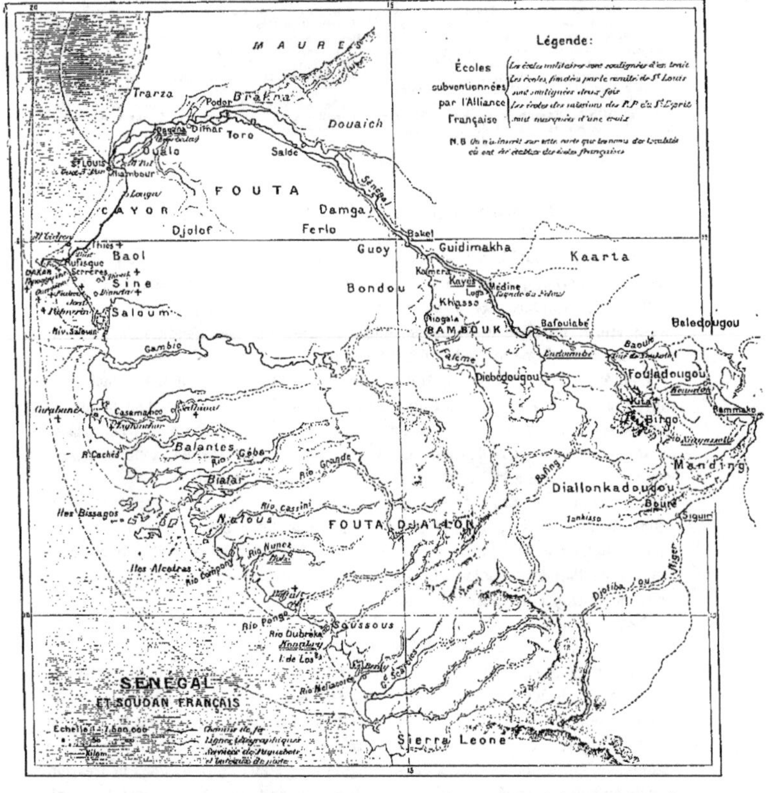

C'est ainsi que, pour la première fois peut-être, chaque étape de la conquête a été marquée par un progrès moral et que partout où notre drapeau a été planté sur le faîte d'un fort, il a en même temps abrité de ses plis une école. Grand exemple, digne d'être suivi dans toutes nos possessions extérieures. P. F.

ÉCOLES DU LEVANT

QUI ONT REÇU DES SUBVENTIONS DE L'ALLIANCE FRANÇAISE

GRÈCE	**Athènes et le Pirée**	Sœurs de Saint-Joseph.
	Cyclades	Ursulines de Naxos; Sœurs de Saint-Joseph à Syra; Ursulines de Tinos.
TURQUIE D'EUROPE	**Constantinople**	École grecque du Phanar; — École grecque commerciale de Halki; — Écoles de Mgr Azarian; — Oblates de l'Assomption; — Augustins de l'Assomption; — École des sœurs de l'hôpital français de Péra; — P. P. Géorgiens; — Frères des écoles chrétiennes; — Collège de M. Faure; — Institution de MM. Deveaux et Schaffner; — Institution de Mme Becognano; — Institution de MM. Charrol et Astier.
	Salonique	École des sœurs à Kou-Kousch; — Écoles diverses de Salonique; — École de M. Hypert.
	Philippopolis	Augustins de l'Assomption.
	Andrinople	Écoles grecques; — Augustins de l'Assomption; — Oblates de l'Assomption — P. P. Mineurs conventuels; — Résurrectionnistes; — École des religieuses françaises à Karagatch.
ASIE MINEURE ou ANATOLIE	**Brousse**	Sœurs de la Charité; — Augustins de l'Assomption.
	Smyrne	Frères des écoles chrétiennes.
	Chypre	École des sœurs à Larnaca.
	Trébizonde	Écoles arméno-grégoriennes; Gymnase grec; — Frères des écoles chrétiennes.
ARMÉNIE	**Erzeroum**	Écoles de Mgr Melchisédech: — Frères des écoles chrétiennes; — Sœurs de Saint-Joseph.
	Samsoun	Écoles arméniennes.
	Erzinguian	École arménienne populaire privée.
MÉSOPOTAMIE	**Mossoul**	Dominicains; — Séminaire syro-chaldéen; — Écoles de Monseigneur Benni.
	Bagdad	Écoles de garçons et de filles de Mgr Altmayer.
SYRIE	**Beyrouth**	Écoles diverses.
	Aïn-Tab et Marache	Écoles arméno-grégoriennes; — P. P. de Terre Sainte; — Franciscains.
	Adana et Tarse	Écoles de Mgr Alsanian.
	Alep	Sœurs de Saint-Joseph; — Écoles de Mgr Balitian; — Écoles grecques catholiques.
	Alexandrette	P. P. Carmes.
	Antioche et Salima	P. P. Capucins.
	Abey	P. P. Capucins.
	Akbès	Orphelinat des P. P. de la Trappe.
	Batroun et Becherré	P. P. Carmes; — Écoles maronites.
	Balbeck	Écoles grecques catholiques.
	Byblos (Mont Liban)	Collège de M. Chéhadé (maronite).
	Caïffa	Dames de Nazareth. — Frères des écoles chrétiennes.
	Dahr Safra	École maronite.
	Damas	École patriarcale; — Écoles des Lazaristes.
	Diarbékir	École catholique.
	Deir Makhaldèc	Séminaire maronite.
	Hasbeya	P. P. Capucins.
	Jérusalem	Frères des écoles chrétiennes; — Dames de Sion; — Sœurs de Saint-Joseph; — Sœurs du Rosaire; — École de M. Rochais.
	Kornet-Chaouan	Collège de Mgr Zoghi.
	Latakieh	École grecque orthodoxe; — École maronite.
	Markab	École maronite.
	Nazareth	École des religieuses françaises.
	Ramleh	Sœurs de Saint-Joseph.
	Saïda et El Kancor	École de Mgr Aggiar.
	Sgorta	École des P. P. Carmes; — École maronite.
	Tripoli	Sœurs de la Charité; — Frères des écoles chrétiennes.
ÉGYPTE	**Alexandrie**	École gratuite de la marine; — Écoles diverses.
	Le Caire	Écoles diverses.
	Port-Saïd	Sœurs du Bon Pasteur; École maronite; École laïque internationale de garçons.
	Ismaïlia	École des religieuses françaises; — École de la Mission franciscaine.
	Zagazig et Tantah	École de la Mission catholique.
	Syout ou Assiout	École copte; — École catholique; — École de l'Alliance française.
	Haute-Égypte	Écoles de Louxor, de Neggadeh, de Kench, Ermont et Girgeh.
TRIPOLITAINE	**Tripoli et Benghazi**	Écoles françaises congréganistes.

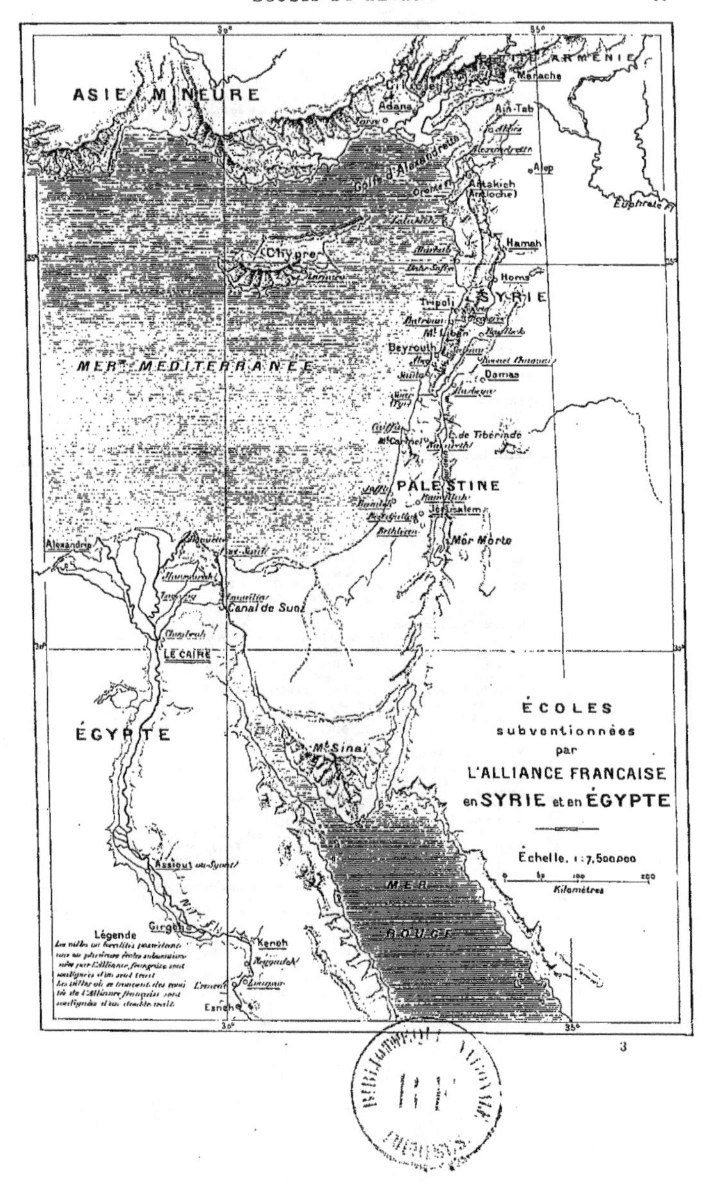
ASIE MINEURE
ARMÉNIE
Marache
Adana
Aïn-Tab
Alep
Golfe d'Alexandrette
Antakieh (Antioche)
Euphrate Fl.
Hamah
Chypre
Homs
SYRIE
Tripoli
Mt. Liban
Beyrouth
Damas
MER MÉDITERRANÉE
Mt. Carmel
Lac de Tibériade
PALESTINE
Jérusalem
Mer Morte
Alexandrie
Canal de Suez
LE CAIRE
ÉGYPTE
Mt. Sinaï
Assiout
Girgeh
Kenéh
Esneh
MER ROUGE
ÉCOLES
subventionnées
par
L'ALLIANCE FRANCAISE
en SYRIE et en ÉGYPTE
Échelle. 1 : 7,500,000
0 50 100 200
Kilomètres
Légende

LA LANGUE FRANÇAISE DANS L'AMÉRIQUE DU NORD

La France n'a conservé de ses anciennes possessions de l'Amérique du Nord que les ilots minuscules de Saint-Pierre et Miquelon.

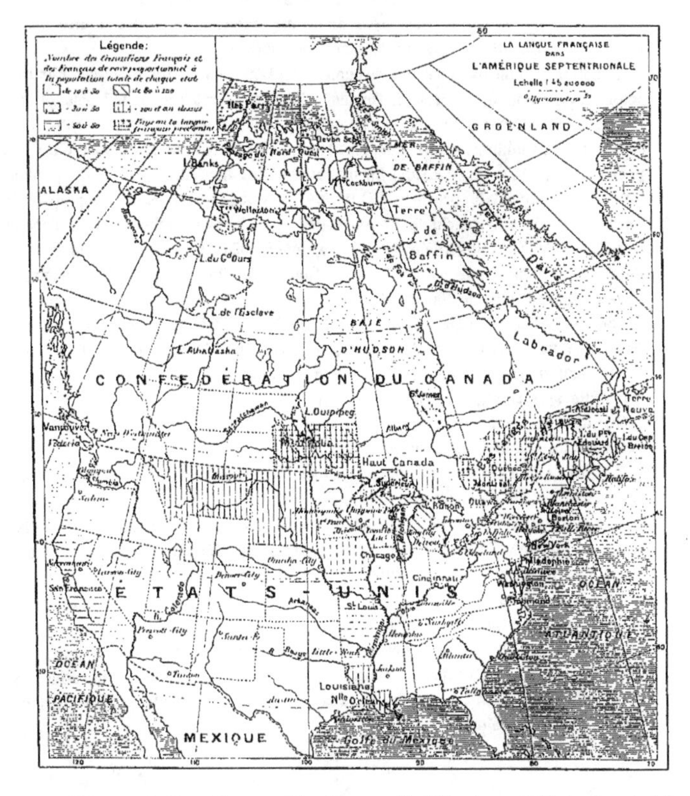

Elle a perdu Terre-Neuve et l'Acadie au traité d'Utrecht en 1713. Le Canada lui a été enlevé par le traité de Paris en 1763. La Louisiane a été vendue aux Etats-Unis par Bonaparte en 1803.

Cependant, la langue française subsiste et se développe au delà de l'Atlantique dans ce Nouveau-Monde où l'avaient apportée nos pères au temps de Jacques Cartier, de Champlain et de Cavelier de la Salle. En dépit de désastres tels que la dispersion et la déportation des Acadiens, la mort de Montcalm sous les murs de Québec, la ruine des États du Sud après la guerre de Sécession, cette langue vigoureuse a poussé si avant ses racines dans le sol américain que rien ne peut l'en arracher et qu'elle y étend de divers côtés de puissants rameaux.

Les 60 000 Français que le gouvernement de Louis XV abandonna à la domination anglaise ont multiplié prodigieusement ; ils ont conservé, avec leur langue et leur foi, un pieux attachement à la patrie perdue ; ils sont un peuple aujourd'hui, un peuple de deux millions d'âmes ; ils seront demain peut-être une grande nation. De la province de Québec (Bas-Canada) où ils forment les neuf dixièmes de la population, ils ont envahi la province d'Ontario (Haut-Canada) et les vastes prairies du Nord-ouest. Ils ont franchi la frontière des États-Unis et débordé dans l'ancien domaine de la Nouvelle-Angleterre. On estime à 500 000 au moins le nombre des Canadiens français fixés aujourd'hui aux États-Unis. Dans le seul État de Massachusets, ils sont plus de 100 000. Ils sont près de 30 000 dans le New-Hampshire, de 40 000 dans l'État de New-York, de 20 000 dans le Rhode-Island. Ils ont leurs églises, leurs curés, leurs écoles, leurs journaux. Sur plusieurs points toutefois et notamment dans les grands centres tels que Chicago et Détroit, ils ont abandonné en partie leur langue maternelle. Mais ils sont soutenus et encouragés par leurs frères du *vieux pays* qui les surveillent avec un soin filial et s'efforcent de maintenir chez eux les traditions nationales.

L'Acadie, dont le clergé est en grande partie étranger, a plus de peine à conserver et à accroître le domaine de sa langue.

La Louisiane, isolée, lutte courageusement. L'*Athénée louisianais*, l'*Union française* de la Nouvelle-Orléans, plusieurs écoles libres défendent avec persévérance, sur les bords du Missisipi, le culte de la langue et de la littérature françaises.

La Californie est le siège de plusieurs groupes importants de Français qui ont donné maintes preuves de leur patriotisme.

Nos émigrants en quête de colonies de peuplement ne sauraient en trouver beaucoup de meilleures que ces quatre centres français de la Californie, de la Louisiane, de l'Acadie et surtout du Canada, principal berceau de la Nouvelle-France dans le Nouveau-Monde.

P. F.

LES PRÉSIDENTS DE L'ALLIANCE FRANÇAISE

Les présidents d'honneur de l'Alliance française sont : M. le vicomte Ferdinand de Lesseps, le général Faidherbe et le vice-amiral Jurien de la Gravière.

Le Président du Conseil d'Administration de l'Œuvre est M. Victor Duruy.

Le vicomte FERDINAND DE LESSEPS, né à Versailles en 1805, suivit d'abord la

M. de Lesseps.

carrière diplomatique ; en 1833, il géra le consulat général d'Alexandrie, puis se distingua en Espagne et à Rome. A partir de 1854, date de son second séjour en

Égypte, il n'eut plus qu'une pensée, l'exécution du grand projet qu'il avait conçu, le percement de l'isthme de Suez. Malgré des difficultés inouïes, à force d'énergie et on peut le dire d'héroïsme, il réussit enfin, et le canal de Suez fut solennellement inauguré en 1869. Il a entrepris depuis, avec non moins de ténacité enthousiaste et

M. le général Faidherbe, grand chancelier de la Légion d'honneur.

jusqu'ici moins de bonheur, le percement de l'isthme de Panama. Une seule de ses œuvres grandioses suffirait à immortaliser sa mémoire. Conférencier charmant, écrivain et savant distingué, il est membre de l'Académie des sciences et président de la Société de géographie.

Le général **Faidherbe** est né à Lille, le 3 juin 1818. Il est ancien élève de l'École polytechnique et de l'École d'application de Metz. Après avoir servi en Algérie, il passa au Sénégal et en fut nommé gouverneur peu de temps après. On peut dire qu'il est le véritable fondateur de la colonie du Sénégal, vieille pourtant de plu-

M. le vice-amiral Jurien de la Gravière.

sieurs siècles. Les Sénégalais reconnaissants lui ont élevé une statue à Saint-Louis. mais son plus beau titre de gloire est d'avoir commandé l'armée du Nord pendant la guerre néfaste de 1870, et d'avoir tenu les Allemands en échec à Pont-Noyelles.

Le froid, la fatigue, les privations pendant cette cruelle campagne ont ruiné sa santé déjà altérée par un long séjour aux colonies.

M. Victor Duruy, ancien ministre de l'instruction publique, 1863-1869.

Le général Faidherbe est aujourd'hui sénateur du Nord et grand chancelier de la Légion d'honneur. Il a publié de nombreux travaux de linguistique et il est membre de l'Académie des sciences.

Le vice-amiral Jurien de la Gravière, né en 1812, est le fils d'un brave marin qui fut lui-même vice-amiral et pair de France. Chargé en 1861 du commandement de la division navale du golfe du Mexique, il signa, de concert avec nos alliées, l'Espagne et l'Angleterre, la convention de Soledad qui, si elle eût été ratifiée par le gouvernement, eût coupé court à cette guerre désastreuse. En 1870, il réorganisa la flotte de la Méditerranée. En 1871, il fut nommé directeur du dépôt des cartes de la Marine. Il est aussi brillant écrivain qu'habile marin et loyal patriote. Il a publié de nombreux travaux sur les guerres maritimes contemporaines et sur l'histoire de la marine. Il est Président d'honneur de l'Œuvre des Écoles d'Orient. Il fait partie de l'Académie des sciences.

M. Victor Duruy est né à Paris en 1811, d'une famille d'artistes employés aux Gobelins. Mais sa vocation était l'histoire qu'il professa dès 1833 au lycée Henri IV, presque au sortir de l'École normale. On lui doit nombre de volumes classiques qui ont servi à l'instruction de plusieurs générations d'écoliers et deux œuvres magistrales, l'*Histoire des Romains* et l'*Histoire de la Grèce ancienne*. Ministre de l'instruction publique de 1863 à 1869, il entreprit la réorganisation de l'Université, il prépara la plupart des réformes qui ont été accomplies depuis, il en indiqua plusieurs qui n'ont point été réalisées encore. Il est à la fois membre de l'Académie française, de l'Académie des sciences morales et politiques et de l'Académie des inscriptions et belles-lettres. Par son libéralisme éclairé, son labeur incessant, son ardent patriotisme, l'intégrité de sa vie, il a su imposer le respect à tous les partis.

En écrivant au frontispice de son œuvre les noms de Faidherbe, Jurien de la Gravière, de Lesseps et Duruy, l'Alliance française a voulu surtout honorer en eux la qualité maîtresse de tous les grands caractères, le patriotisme.

P. F.

OEUVRES FRANÇAISES

POURSUIVANT UN BUT ANALOGUE A CELUI DE L'ALLIANCE

L'œuvre des Écoles d'Orient. — Il y a maintenant près de 35 ans que l'œuvre des Écoles d'Orient est née en France. C'était à la fin de la guerre de Crimée, et les perspectives nouvelles qu'ouvrait le Hatti-Humayoun proclamant la liberté religieuse dans l'Empire ottoman furent l'occasion de la fondation de cette œuvre dont le but, sous un nom modeste, était de travailler au retour à l'unité des Églises orientales.

Les premières réunions eurent lieu, en 1855, dans le salon d'un membre éminent de l'Académie des sciences, le baron Cauchy. Un autre membre de l'Académie des inscriptions et belles-lettres était l'âme de cette Société naissante. Je veux parler de M. Charles Lenormant, qu'une mort prématurée a ravi à la science et à la France.

A cette époque, quelques écoles dirigées par les congrégations françaises des Frères de la Doctrine chrétienne et des Sœurs de la Charité existaient déjà dans le Levant. Les Lazaristes étaient en Egypte, en Syrie, à Constantinople et à Smyrne. Les Jésuites venaient d'ouvrir à Ghazir, dans le Liban, le premier séminaire du clergé Oriental. Enfin, les Sœurs de Saint-Vincent de Paul avaient commencé à Alexandrie, à Beyrouth, à Smyrne et à Constantinople leur apostolat de charité.

Les choses en étaient donc là quand l'œuvre fut entreprise.

L'année suivante, M. Wallon, acclamé secrétaire général de l'Association naissante, rendait compte de ce premier essai. En une année, et avec beaucoup d'efforts, on n'avait recueilli que 16 000 francs.

C'est alors que fut mis à la tête de l'œuvre un jeune professeur de la Sorbonne, sous l'impulsion duquel elle prit un grand développement. Ce jeune professeur était l'abbé Lavigerie, aujourd'hui cardinal et primat de l'Église d'Afrique.

Les événements dont la Syrie fut le théâtre durant l'année 1860 grandirent rapidement le rôle de l'œuvre des Écoles d'Orient, qui maintenant aide et subventionne dans l'Empire ottoman, tant en Asie Mineure qu'en Syrie, en Égypte et en Mésopotamie près de 200 écoles fréquentées par plus de 40 000 élèves dont 27 000 environ apprennent le français. En Perse les écoles, au nombre de onze, comptent environ 1 600 élèves dont 190 étudient notre langue.

Les allocations des dernières années s'élèvent environ à 890 000 francs.

E.-G. Rey.

Écoles protestantes de langue française. — Les persécutions dirigées contre les protestants, avant la Révolution, provoquèrent une émigration considérable qui amena la formation d'églises protestantes de langue française à l'étranger, mais surtout dans les pays du Nord. Quelques-unes subsistent encore et par ce fait même servent la cause de l'Alliance, car la prédication et le culte se font toujours dans notre langue. Nous citerons simplement les noms de ces diverses églises : **Suède**, Stockholm; **Danemark**, Copenhague; **Russie**, Saint-Pétersbourg, Odessa, Moscou; **Allemagne**, Berlin, Hambourg, Dresde, Stuttgart, Hanau, Francfort-sur-le-Mein, Friedricksdorf, Kœnigsberg; **Hollande**, Amsterdam, Arnheim, Bois-le-Duc, Breda, Delft, Dordrecht, Groningue, Harlem, La Haye, Leyde, Maestricht, Middelbourg, Nimègue, Rotterdam, Utrecht, Zwolle; **Angleterre**, Londres, Cantorbery, Brighton, Southampton, Edimbourg. On trouve aussi de très nombreuses églises protestantes de langue française en Amérique, au Canada, dans les vallées vaudoises du Piémont, dans les îles de la Manche. Nous ne saurions oublier les grandes églises qui, en Alsace-Lorraine, maintiennent dans le culte l'emploi de la langue française.

Mentionnons encore l'œuvre importante d'instruction due à l'activité de la Société des Missions évangéliques qui a créé des écoles où l'enseignement du français est obligatoire à Tahiti, au Sénégal et au Gabon.

F. Puaux.

L'alliance israélite universelle. — L'Alliance israélite universelle apporte un utile concours à l'œuvre entreprise par l'Alliance française. Elle entretient en Orient et dans l'Afrique du Nord 53 écoles réparties entre la Turquie d'Europe, à Constantinople, Andrinople, Salonique, aux Dardanelles; la Turquie d'Asie, à Smyrne, Brousse, Alep, Beyrouth, Caïffa, Jérusalem, Damas, Bagdad; la Bulgarie, à Sofia, Philippopolis, Choumla, Varna etc; la Tunisie, à Tunis et à Sousse; le Maroc, à Fez, Mogador, Tanger, Tétuan. Plusieurs de ces écoles ont une importance considérable, celles de Constantinople groupent 2 098 élèves, celles de Tunis 1 652, celles de Salonique 517. Toutes ensemble comptaient dans la dernière année scolaire 10 331 élèves: 7 153 garçons et 3 178 filles. A part l'école de Botochani en Roumanie, où l'enseignement est donné en roumain, l'école de filles de Salonique où il est donné en italien, l'école allemande mixte de Galata à Constantinople où il est donné en allemand, le français est partout employé comme la langue principale et devient aussi familier que la langue maternelle aux nombreux enfants qui fréquentent ces écoles[1].

Une *École normale orientale* établie à Paris forme des maîtres pour les écoles de l'Alliance israélite.

M. Wahl.

1. Deux autres associations françaises poursuivent un but voisin du nôtre, mais très différent. La *Ligue de l'Enseignement* encourage l'instruction privée en France et à l'étranger, sans se préoccuper de la question des langues. L'*Académie des palmiers* distribue des récompenses aux meilleurs ouvrages publiés à l'étranger.

LA PROPAGATION DE LA LANGUE TCHÈQUE

ET L'ENSEIGNEMENT DU FRANÇAIS EN BOHÊME

Associations tchèques. — La plus ancienne est l'*Union scolaire tchèque* (*ústredni matice skolska*), fondée en décembre 1880, quelques mois après le Schulverein allemand de Vienne. Cette association, dont le président est M. Ladislas Rieger, compte actuellement 247 sous-comités ou succursales dont 205 en Bohême et 42 en Moravie et Silésie. Elle s'occupe surtout des contrées voisines de la limite ethnographique entre les populations allemande et slave et des localités à population mixte. Elle fonde, entretient ou soutient des écoles tchèques, organise des conférences, publie un bulletin, des brochures, etc. Outre les cotisations régulières de ses trente-cinq mille membres, dont la moitié environ paye 1 florin, l'autre moitié 5 ou 10, elle trouve des ressources dans les collectes faites à son profit dans les réunions et cérémonies, mariages, baptêmes, etc., dans la vente de cartes de visite nationales, de formulaires imprimés pour dépêches télégraphiques, etc. Dans les cafés et restaurants de la Bohême et de la Moravie, on fait circuler des jouets représentant soit un petit tireur, soit une petite boulangère, qui lance dans une tirelire en forme de cible ou de four la pièce de monnaie qu'on lui confie pour l'Union scolaire. Souvent un procès commencé se termine par une transaction en forme d'arbitrage : la partie perdante verse alors dans la caisse de l'Union une somme égale à l'amende ou à l'indemnité qu'elle aurait dû payer si l'affaire avait suivi son cours. Grâce au concours de ces moyens ingénieux, l'Union scolaire tchèque a pu recueillir, depuis sa fondation jusqu'au mois d'août 1883, 1 242 725 florins (environ 3 millions de francs). Elle entretient entièrement dans 41 localités : 2 lycées, 28 écoles primaires, 31 écoles maternelles ; elle accorde en outre des subventions aux écoles publiques de 30 communes et elle a organisé 45 bibliothèques scolaires. 12 écoles fondées et à l'origine entièrement entretenues par elle ont été, en raison de leur importance, transformées en écoles de l'État. Aucune des écoles fondées par l'Association scolaire allemande n'a pu réunir le nombre d'élèves exigé par la loi pour obtenir cet avantage. Il existe d'autres associations tchèques, comme la *Narodni jednota severoieská* (Union nationale du nord de la Bohême) qui groupe dans cette région plus de 10 000 adhérents, crée des écoles, des bibliothèques, organise des conférences, des expositions locales ; comme la *Narodni jednota Posumavská* (Union nationale de la Sumava ou Boehmerwald) qui compte 25 000 membres dans le sud-ouest de la Bohême ; comme l'Union nationale du sud-ouest et du nord-est de la Moravie. Toutes ces associations doivent d'ailleurs se fondre en une grande *Union nationale centrale des pays de la couronne de Bohême.*

Université tchèque. — La loi qui a établi à la place de l'ancienne Université de Prague (désignée comme utraquiste à cause d'un nombre insignifiant de cours faits en langue Bohême) deux Universités distinctes, l'Université « Carlo Ferdinandea » tchèque et l'Université « Carlo Ferdinandea » allemande, reconnaît à chacune d'elles la même continuité historique des droits et privilèges de l'ancienne. Il y a donc eu un partage, une scission si l'on veut dans l'ancienne Université, plutôt que la création d'une Université nouvelle et plus jeune que l'autre. Toutes deux ont la même origine et partant le même âge. C'est ainsi que les deux recteurs ont siège l'un et l'autre à la diète du royaume.

Au dernier semestre d'été 1888, il y avait à l'*Université tchèque*, 2 291 étudiants; à la Faculté de droit, 1 070 dont 69 extraordinaires; à la Faculté de médecine, y compris 21 pharmaciens, 1 029 dont 29 extraordinaires; à la Faculté de philosophie, lettres (et sciences), 192 dont 13 extraordinaires. A la même époque, il n'y avait à l'Université allemande que 1 470 étudiants y compris 229 théologues dont la grande majorité est de nationalité tchèque. Ceux-ci sont obligés en effet de suivre les cours de l'Université allemande parce que la Faculté de théologie fait encore défaut à l'Université tchèque malgré l'insistance que l'on met à la réclamer.

Enseignement du français. — La langue française est très répandue en Bohême et enseignée dans un grand nombre d'écoles (voir la carte ci-jointe). L'Alliance française de Prague, dont le président est M. S. Pinkas et le secrétaire M. L. Pinkas, docteur en droit, compte près de trois cents adhérents. Il y a des cercles français à Chrudim, Jindrichuv, Hradec, Rychnov, etc. Dans la seule ville de Prague, on compte plus de 300 professeurs de français.

Dernièrement, s'est constitué un nouveau « cercle français » à Slané, ce qui porte à douze le nombre des sociétés françaises de Bohême, en y comptant la Société de secours française, belge et suisse de Prague.

S. Pinkas.

LA LANGUE FRANÇAISE ET L'ESPRIT FRANÇAIS

C'est la logique qui gouverne notre parole jusque dans la forme de nos périodes. Je ne trouve cela dans aucune autre langue du monde ; cela nous coûte peut-être quelque chose pour la facilité et quelquefois pour la grâce, mais cela nous donne une solidité, une fermeté et une clarté incomparables.

Je crois qu'on peut dire que la langue française est celle dans laquelle il est le plus difficile de déraisonner. Jamais on ne déraisonne et jamais on n'équivoque quand on parle français, sans être forcé de convenir immédiatement que ce n'est plus le français qu'on parle.

J'aime à insister sur cette qualité de notre chère langue, parce que, en le faisant, il me semble que j'insiste aussi sur la qualité de notre cher pays. Nous ne manquons pas d'extravagances, mais ne pensez-vous pas que toutes ces extravagances sont comme cette écume qui vient à la surface d'un beau lac? Le vent la chasse; les eaux demeurent pures et profondes. On a beau me harceler des bruits de la tribune et de la rue... Où est notre âme? Où est notre volonté? Où est notre avenir? C'est dans le bon sens, dans la fermeté de nos esprits et de nos pensées. J'avoue qu'il faut que nous ayons un grand fonds de bon sens pour qu'il nous en reste encore après ce que nous voyons.

Les autres peuples ont comme nous des accès de fièvre, et, après chaque accès, le malade est un peu plus affaibli qu'il ne l'était auparavant. Mais nous, messieurs, nous nous retrouvons entiers après la crise. On nous croyait affolés; nous retrouvons tout à coup la robuste solidité de l'esprit français. Telle est la langue, tel est le peuple.

JULES SIMON.

(Extrait d'un discours prononcé à la matinée-conférence du Vaudeville le 20 décembre 1888).

LA LANGUE FRANÇAISE APPRÉCIÉE PAR UN ÉTRANGER

.....Tout en faisant de l'étude du français une science sérieuse, je ne saurais oublier qu'elle est en même temps un art, et un des plus exquis, puisque son objet est une des langues les plus artistiques qui aient jamais été parlées. Il y a des savants qui font du français comme ils feraient du chinois et du cafre. J'avoue franchement que cela m'est impossible. Je sais qu'au point de vue de la science pure, le plus petit patois alpestre vaut la langue littéraire la plus brillante. Mais je ne saurais oublier que toute langue est une musique en même temps qu'une pensée et que si rien n'est clair comme la pensée française, il est peu de musiques aussi douces à l'oreille que le parler de la France. Ah ! messieurs, nous pourrons étudier et analyser cette langue, en faire l'anatomie et l'histoire naturelle, nous ne serons que des Français de formation savante ; pareils au botaniste qui classe dans son herbier les fleurs dont la jeune fille rieuse se fait une parure vivante, nous regarderons souvent d'un œil d'admiration et d'envie cette foule heureuse qui fait tomber de ses lèvres les mots les plus justes, les sons les plus harmonieux sans y penser, qui ne sait pas analyser sa langue comme un professeur étranger, mais qui la comprendra toujours mieux que nous. J'aime donc à me dire que l'étude artistique du français mérite sa place à côté de l'étude philologique, qu'on ne connaît pas la langue française à moins d'être devenu sensible à son admirable clarté, à son élégance exquise, à cette diction simple et naturelle qui n'exclut pas l'élévation, mais qui est surtout inséparable de l'esprit, qui appelle l'éloquence, mais qui repousse la déclamation pompeuse, — à toutes ces qualités de pensée, de forme, de timbre, d'accentuation rapide qui font du français la langue de la diplomatie et celle des confidences, la musique bruyante des foules et le chant discret des cœurs tendres, un murmure dans l'intimité, un éclat de rire dans les salons et un tonnerre à la tribune.....

A.-G. Van Hamel.

(Extrait d'un discours prononcé à l'occasion de son installation comme professeur ordinaire à la Faculté des lettres de l'université de Groningue (Pays-Bas).

LA LANGUE FRANÇAISE

Elle naquit un jour, en pleine barbarie,
Dans un berceau gaulois et d'un germe latin,
Naïvement aimable en sa sauvagerie,
Et jetant vers les cieux sa chanson du matin.

Car dès sa jeune aurore elle se sent poète.
Même avant de parler, elle chante; et sa voix
Redit, tantôt cigale et tantôt alouette,
Ton soleil, ô Provence, ô Bretagne, tes bois.

Elle chante, et la note attendrie ou sévère,
Au Nord écho de guerre, au Sud écho d'amour,
Retentit, âpre et rude, aux lèvres du trouvère,
Ou mollement soupire au luth du troubadour.

Elle chante, et l'Europe à sa voix rajeunie,
Pour la première fois regarde, en tressaillant,
Se lever sur le monde, au souffle du génie,
Un Achille chrétien qu'on appelait Roland.

Car c'est le doux parler de la vieille patrie,
Qui fit partout éclore au seuil du temps nouveau,
Ces deux fleurs de lumière et de chevalerie,
Le culte de la femme et le culte du beau.

Tout mot venu de France emportait dans sa course
Un sourire; et dès lors, notre langue a jeté,
Sur le jeune Occident, comme une jeune source,
Sa fraîcheur printanière et sa limpidité.

. . . .

Ah ! ne fais pas rougir le front des jeunes hommes,
Mais tourne leur regard du côté des hauteurs ;
Ils ont besoin, surtout à l'époque où nous sommes,
De mâles conseillers et non de corrupteurs.

Car elle peut sonner bientôt l'heure suprême
Où nous devrons, nous tous, aux frontières courir,
Et pour sauver la France et peut-être toi-même,
Choisir tout simplement entre vaincre... ou mourir.

Parle-nous donc d'honneur, de vertu, de courage,
Mûris-nous pour l'épreuve et l'intrépide effort,
Pour qu'au jour où viendront la bataille et l'orage,
Notre esprit reste calme et notre bras soit fort.

Porte avec toi la flamme et porte la lumière ;
Sois l'hymne du devoir et l'hymne de beauté ;
Et du juste amoureuse et du grand coutumière,
Chante pour la patrie et pour l'humanité.

Illumine la route, ô langue maternelle,
La route où sous les cieux s'avance l'univers,
Du préjugé nocturne ennemie éternelle,
Élargis tous les cœurs et brise tous les fers.

Va consoler tous ceux qui se tournent encore
Vers l'étoile de France en dépit des revers ;
Oui, dépassant du bout de ton aile sonore
La coupole des monts et la coupe des mers,

Va dire à ces amis obstinés et fidèles,
Qui, n'oubliant jamais quel pays mit au jour
Les saintes libertés aux lueurs immortelles,
De la France vaincue ont l'invincible amour ;

Va leur dire qu'elle est, même après ses défaites,
La terre de bravoure et d'affranchissement,
Et qu'ils en ont menti ces déloyaux prophètes,
Qui vont criant partout à son abaissement.

. . . .

Pour les déshérités sois la bonne nouvelle,
Et pour les égarés le flambeau du chemin ;
Chercheuse de lumière et d'équité, révèle
Aux semeurs d'aujourd'hui la moisson de demain.

ÉMILE TROLLIET.

LES AUTEURS ÉTRANGERS QUI ONT ÉCRIT EN FRANÇAIS

Le besoin d'une langue universelle s'est toujours fait sentir. Le nombre des idiomes parlés sur la surface du globe est infini, et l'on ne peut raisonnablement demander aux savants, aux diplomates ou aux commerçants de les connaître tous : leur vie s'y consumerait sans fruit pour l'objet particulier de leurs travaux. Dans l'antiquité, ce fut le grec qui fut la langue universelle ; le latin lui succéda au moyen âge, et le français, après la Renaissance, prit la place du latin. Tout à cette époque concourut à donner la prépondérance à notre langue : d'abord ses qualités propres, sa netteté, sa clarté, sa précision qui la rendaient plus précieuse encore aux sciences qu'aux lettres ; ensuite notre situation politique, l'éclat de nos victoires ; pourquoi n'ajouterais-je pas nos fautes elles-mêmes et en particulier la Révocation de l'Édit de Nantes qui se trouva servir, à l'étranger, par un contre-coup inattendu, la cause de la civilisation française.

Le français fut partout en Europe au dix-septième siècle la langue des honnêtes gens, comme on disait alors ; mais il fut aussi autre chose qu'un moyen pour la société polie de se distinguer du vulgaire. On ne parla pas seulement, on écrivit en français ; il y eut une littérature française hors de France, phénomène unique dans les temps modernes.

Sans parler de la Savoie qui nous a donné l'œuvre aimable et pieuse de saint François de Sales, il y eut alors en Europe trois grands foyers de culture française, la Hollande, l'Angleterre, l'Allemagne. La Hollande, pays d'élection des esprits libres, fut une sorte de seconde France. C'est à Leyde que Descartes publia son Discours de la méthode en 1637 ; c'est à Leyde que professa Saumaise ; à Rotterdam, P. Bayle et Jurieu, arrivés en 1681, ne s'y trouvèrent pas dépaysés et c'est en français que Jurieu y fit ses leçons, pour être compris, dit Bayle, de ceux qui ne connaissaient pas le latin. Jacques Basnage fut, dans la même ville et plus tard à La Haye, pasteur de l'église wallonne. Les journaux rédigés en français étaient alors très nombreux en Hollande ; tels étaient : *Les nouvelles de la république des lettres*, la *Bibliothèque universelle*, les *lettres historiques*, le *Mercure historique*, l'*esprit des cours de l'Europe*, etc. Ces gazettes venues de Hollande étaient lues à Versailles et firent plus d'une fois froncer le sourcil olympien de Louis XIV.

En Angleterre, le goût et l'usage du français étaient aussi répandus. La cour des Stuarts était entièrement française ; Saint-Evremond et le chevalier de Grammont y furent tout de suite à leur aise, et ils y retrouvèrent cette chose subtile, insaisissable et qui s'évapore si facilement au dehors, qu'on appelle l'esprit français. C'est précisément le beau-frère du chevalier de Grammont, un Écossais, Antoine Hamilton (1646-1720), qui nous a laissé « *les Mémoires du chevalier de Grammont* », cette merveille de laisser-aller, de bonne humeur et de finesse.

Dans le nord de l'Europe et surtout en Allemagne, la langue française dut beaucoup aux femmes qui y trouvaient les qualités qui leur sont chères et qui, encore aujourd'hui, ont gardé pour elle une véritable affection. Christine de Suède, la princesse Élisabeth de Bohême, la duchesse de Hanovre, la margrave de Brandebourg, toutes femmes d'un esprit sérieux et solide, avaient fait du français leur langue de prédilection. Le grand électeur encourageait ces tendances ; le grand philosophe et mathématicien Leibnitz (1646-1716) était l'âme des cours de Hanovre et de Brandebourg ; avec lui le français devint la langue scientifique et philosophique de l'Europe ; c'est en français que cet homme illustre écrivit la *Théodicée* et ses *Nouveaux essais sur l'entendement humain*.

Loin de perdre son empire au dix-huitième siècle, la langue française l'accrut encore en y annexant la Russie. Paris et l'étranger purent alors échanger leurs savants, leurs philosophes, leurs hommes d'esprit, sans qu'aucun d'eux, de chaque côté, parût souffrir du déplacement. Voltaire allait à Berlin, Diderot à Saint-Pétersbourg ; mais l'Allemand Grimm (1723-1807) et l'Italien Galiani (1720-1787) faisaient les délices des salons parisiens ; le premier rédigeait sa célèbre *Correspondance littéraire* ; le second ses *Dialogues sur les Blés* et c'était lui qui, une fois revenu à Naples, disait en soupirant : « J'étais une plante parisienne. » Un autre Italien, Goldoni (1707-1793), écrivait en français une comédie : *le Bourru bienfaisant*, qui eut le plus grand succès à Paris. Un Anglais, Horace Walpole, correspondait en français avec madame du Deffand ; un autre, un des plus grands historiens de l'Angleterre, Gibbon (1737-1794), écrivit ses premiers ouvrages en français. Et je ne parle pas à dessein des écrivains nés à l'étranger dans un pays de langue française, tels que Necker et Jean-Jacques Rousseau (1712-1778) dont l'influence, si grande et si décisive, balança celle de Voltaire.

Au dehors, la littérature française était aussi active et aussi florissante ; nous ne pouvons citer tous les noms, mais nous prendrons pour type la cour de Berlin, où le maître, Frédéric II, entouré de Français, fut lui-même un remarquable écrivain français. Ses écrits : l'*Anti-Machiavel*, les *Mémoires de la maison de Brandebourg*, l'*Histoire de mon temps*, sont tous rédigés en français. Autour de lui les membres de l'Académie royale de Prusse, fondée en 1701, Maupertuis et tant d'autres contribuaient par leurs écrits à développer l'influence française en Allemagne. Ce que nous disons de Berlin peut s'appliquer à Saint-Pétersbourg, où régnait Catherine II, et à la Russie tout entière dont l'aristocratie a gardé jusqu'à nos jours le culte de la langue française. Enfin, nous ne pouvons terminer cette trop rapide revue des écrivains étrangers de langue française au dix-huitième siècle, sans citer au moins le nom du prince de Ligne (1735-1814) dont le seul défaut, si c'en est un, dans ses *Mélanges militaires*, fut d'avoir trop d'esprit.

Le français, langue universelle au dix-huitième siècle, perdit ce rôle après la Révolution et on ne saurait trop le déplorer. Il était sans doute légitime que chaque peuple eût une littérature nationale ; mais la philosophie et les sciences ne sont-elles pas comme la diplomatie un terrain neutre où l'avantage serait grand d'employer partout la même langue? Ne nous exagérons pas pourtant le recul du français au dix-neuvième siècle ; sans doute les écrivains étrangers qui écrivirent en français devinrent très rares, pourtant on pourrait encore en citer quelques-uns et non des moins grands : Malte-Brun, le célèbre géographe, né en Danemark en 1775 et qui, après s'être compromis dans son pays par son zèle pour la Révolution française, vint chercher un asile à Paris où il devint rédacteur du *Journal des Débats* et où il publia en français sa Géographie mathématique, physique et politique de toutes les parties du monde (1807) et son précis de Géographie universelle (1810) ; le grand voyageur et naturaliste allemand de Humboldt (1769-1859) qui vécut vingt ans à Paris, de 1807 à 1829, et qui pendant cette période y publia ses principaux ouvrages ; Henri Heine (1799-1856), le poète railleur et plaintif de l'*Intermezzo*, le conteur charmant des *Tableaux de voyage* (Reisebilder), qui quitta son pays pour venir vivre à Paris et qui s'appelait lui-même « un Prussien libéré ». Enfin, même de nos jours, quelques étrangers distingués pour qui la France est une seconde patrie, celle de l'esprit et de l'intelligence, écrivent encore en français : c'est ainsi qu'un homme d'État viennois, le baron de Hübner, a publié aussi dans notre langue ses charmantes Promenades autour du monde.

Dans l'histoire de la langue française, au dix-neuvième siècle, en dehors de la France proprement dite, comment oublier la Belgique et la Suisse? La première a eu des historiens, des hommes d'État, des journalistes : elle a aujourd'hui une école littéraire qui soutient le bon combat contre les Flamands et dont les productions donnent quelquefois raison à ceux qui pensent que Bruxelles est un second Paris ; la Suisse, peut-être plus originale et moins portée à imiter Paris, a mis son cachet d'esprit sérieux et ferme sur les œuvres de ses principaux écrivains. Je ne puis en parler longuement ici ; mais leur valeur est assez grande pour qu'il suffise de rappeler leurs noms : Benjamin Constant de Rebecque (1766-1830), qui trouva dans la politique française un vaste champ d'activité que la scène un peu restreinte de sa patrie n'aurait pu lui offrir ; le littérateur Bonstetten (1745-1832); le célèbre physicien et naturaliste H.-B. de Saussure (1740-1799) ; l'historien Sismonde de Sismondi (1773-1842) qui vécut, lui aussi, à Paris ; R. Toppfer (1799-1846), l'auteur aimable et doucement spirituel des *Nouvelles Genevoises* et des *Voyages en Zigzag ;* le pasteur Vinet, né à Ouchy, près de Lausanne, en 1797 et mort en 1847 après une vie d'études incessantes et de méditation ; le poète Juste Olivier ; Amiel et tant d'autres que le défaut d'espace m'empêche de citer, mais qui tous ont contribué à faire de Genève et de Lausanne une seconde France littéraire, avec des qualités et des défauts qui lui sont propres et qui lui constituent une individualité particulière.

Enfin, comment ne pas dire un mot de nos colonies qui, si éloignées qu'elles soient de la mère patrie, ne laissent pas d'en ressentir la bienfaisante influence? Chose curieuse, elles ont produit beaucoup de poètes. La Guadeloupe a donné naissance à Léonard (1744-1793) et à Campenon (1772-1843), auteurs de poésies fugitives. Plus féconde et plus heureuse, l'île de la Réunion (ancienne île Bourbon) nous a donné le chevalier de Parny (1753-1814), Lacaussade, né en 1820, et surtout Leconte de l'Isle, né à Saint-Paul en 1818.

Toute cette énumération est bien rapide et bien défectueuse. Elle sert pourtant à montrer que trois siècles de production incessante où les chefs-d'œuvre ne se comptent pas, n'ont épuisé ni la sève ni l'action de la langue française. Loin d'être un organe en décadence, elle se transforme de génération en génération en acquérant une vitalité nouvelle, et son empire, en dépit des révolutions qui se sont accomplies à notre époque, ne se borne pas entièrement à ses frontières naturelles. Le français est resté jusqu'à nos jours la langue des relations internationales et aussi un peu partout la langue favorite de la bonne compagnie ; notre littérature trouve encore un écho dans tous les pays du monde où l'on aime les belles choses, dites simplement et avec goût ; beaucoup de savants étrangers écrivent encore leurs mémoires en français, afin qu'ils se répandent plus facilement, en particulier en Suède, en Russie. La Société de géographie de Budapest publie un compte rendu abrégé en français ; les annales de l'Observatoire impérial de Rio-de-Janeiro sont publiées simultanément en portugais et en français ; il y a des journaux français en Portugal, en Russie, en Turquie, en Égypte, dans tout l'Orient. Le français, Dieu merci, est encore la langue de la littérature et de l'art et son domaine, qui est resté si considérable, peut encore s'agrandir dans l'avenir : c'est notre confiance, c'est notre espoir ; c'est le but pour lequel nous travaillons et nous luttons.

Ch. Normand.

DIALECTES FRANÇAIS COLONIAUX

LA FABLE DU *Loup et de l'Agneau* (patois nègre de la Martinique).

Yon ti mouton, les ault fois,
Té ka boué dans larivié.
Yon gros loup sôti dans bois,
Li vini tou pou li boué.
Loup là, dent li té rouillé,
Li pas té trouvé mangé;
On a dit li te fé carême;
Guiole li té longue, li té blême
Comme yon patate six simaine,
Maig comme yon nèg qui dans chaine.
Quand li voué ti mouton là,
Tout suite khé li té content.
Li dit mouton : « Pourquo fé
To, rhadi, ka vini boué
Dans larivié, pou troublé
Dleau là? To fè ça exprès
Pour chaché train ékec moin.
To pas té tini bousoin
Fé ça, moin te save déjà
Dans l'année qui passé là
Lassous moin to mal palé. »
Ti mouton là dit : « Mouché,
Pitètt c'était yon laut moune,
Piss moin p'enco té dans moune
Dans temps on ka palé la. »
Gros loup lui réponne comça :
« Si c'est pas to, c'est papa
Yche maman to. » — « Mais moin pas
Ni papa, moins c'est bata. »
— « C'est foué to pouloss, mon fi. »
— « Foué, mais moin com Titiri
Moin pas tini piess parent.
Dépi moin lassous lаté
Moin pas jamais ni bonhé
Connaître yonne; anni maman... »
— « To ka raissonneis, joucrué
Qui monne ça to ka palé?
Comment, to p'enco ni dent
Et to déjà insolent.
M'a fé to voué to ni to
Vini ici fé guiole fò. »
— « Mais moin pas dit ou enguien,
Mouché, ché maîte. » — « Pas bousoin
To mandé grâce, à présent. »
Quand li dit ça, li fé : houan!
Ça fé, li ba li yon coup
D'dents pas coté dérié cou.
Pauve ti mouton la fé : béh!
Li tombé mô raide à té.
Loup là prend tout, viano come yo
Valé : floupé com yon Gombo.

Un petit mouton autrefois
Buvait dans la rivière.
Un gros loup sortit dedans le bois,
Qui venait aussi pour lui boire.
Ce loup là, ses dents de lui étaient rouillées,
Il n'avait pas trouvé à manger;
Vous auriez dit qu'il avait fait carême;
La gueule de lui était longue, il était blême,
Comme une patate de six semaines,
Maigre comme un nègre sous la chaîne.
Quand il vit le petit mouton là,
Tout de suite le cœur de lui fut content.
Il dit au mouton : « Comment
Toi hardi (tu as la hardiesse) de venir boire
Dans la rivière pour troubler
Cette eau là? Tu fais ça exprès
Pour chercher dispute avec moi.
Tu n'avais pas besoin
De faire ça, je savais déjà
Que dans l'année passée
Sur moi tu as mal parlé. »
Ce petit mouton là lui dit : « Monsieur,
Peut-être c'était une autre personne,
Puisque moi pas encore dans ce monde
Dans le temps dont vous parlez là. »
Le gros loup répond comme ça :
« Si ce n'est pas toi, c'est le père
De l'enfant de ta mère. » — Mais je n'ai pas
De papa, moi c'est un bâtard. »
— « C'est ton frère pour lors, mon fils. »
— « Frère, mais je suis comme les Titiri [1]
Je n'ai aucun parent.
Depuis que je suis sur la terre,
Je n'ai jamais eu le bonheur
D'en connaître un, excepté maman... »
— « Tu raisonnes, je crois.
A quel individu parles-tu ainsi?
Comment, tu n'as pas encore de dents
Et toi déjà insolent.
Je vais te faire voir que tu as tort
De venir ici faire forte gueule. »
— « Mais je ne vous ai dit rien
Monsieur, cher maître. » — « Pas besoin
De demander grâce, à présent. »
Quand il dit ça, il fait : houan!
Ça fait qu'il lui donne un coup
De dents du côté de derrière le cou.
Ce pauvre petit mouton là fait : béh!
Il tombe raide mort à terre.
Ce loup là prend tout, viande comme os
Et les avale : floupe, comme un Gombo [2].

D'après le général FAIDHERBE.

1. Frai d'une petite espèce de poissons des Antilles; les nègres croient que ces poissons naissent spontanément.
2. Gombo. Petit fruit à enveloppe grasse, glissante, de sorte qu'on peut l'avaler d'un coup sans mâcher.

LES OEUVRES ÉTRANGÈRES

TENDANT A PROPAGER LES LANGUES ALLEMANDE, ITALIENNE, ANGLAISE

Allemagne. — *Deutsch schulverein. Association scolaire allemande.* Cette association a son siège à Berlin; elle a été fondée en 1881 sous le patronage de la Société de géographie commerciale de cette ville. Deux ans après sa fondation, au mois de décembre 1883, elle comprenait 77 comités locaux et près de 10000 membres; plusieurs comités sont composés de dames et de jeunes filles. Elle reçoit les adhésions collectives des corps ou sociétés et surtout celles des sociétés académiques d'étudiants. Elle a pour but de conserver au germanisme les Allemands établis à l'étranger et de les aider à rester Allemands ou à le redevenir. Pour atteindre ce but, elle soutient ou fonde des écoles, place et secourt des instituteurs, crée des bibliothèques, subventionne des journaux, publie des livres. Son attention se porte surtout sur l'Autriche-Hongrie, où l'antagonisme des nationalités se traduit par le conflit des langues. Mais elle s'occupe aussi des autres pays d'Europe, des États américains, des contrées de l'Extrême-Orient. Partout aux progrès qu'a faits depuis 1870 l'influence politique et commerciale de l'Allemagne correspond une diffusion plus grande de la langue allemande.

Autriche-Hongrie. — *Deutsch schulverein* d'Autriche-Hongrie. Cette association a son siège à Vienne. Elle a pour but de défendre ou de propager la langue allemande dans tous les pays de la monarchie austro-hongroise, en luttant surtout sur le terrain de l'école contre les langues et les nationalités rivales. Lors de sa première assemblée générale constitutive, le 2 juillet 1880, elle comptait déjà plus de 3000 membres. Elle compte actuellement 120000 membres dont près de *trente mille femmes*. Les recettes qu'elle a réalisées depuis sa fondation jusqu'en mai 1888 au moyen de cotisations de 1 florin (2 fr. 50), se montent à 1760000 florins. En 1887 elle a dépensé 300000 florins pour ses écoles. Elle entretient 40 écoles primaires et 59 écoles maternelles et accorde des subventions à 56 écoles primaires et à 29 écoles maternelles. Indépendamment de ses ressources propres, elle est soutenue par l'Association de Berlin, Son action s'exerce surtout en Bohême, mais elle y rencontre l'énergique opposition des sociétés tchèques dont la propagande s'exerce en sens inverse (voir plus haut pp. 28 et 29).

Italie. — Le gouvernement italien a réorganisé en novembre 1888, d'après un plan d'ensemble, les écoles italiennes à l'étranger. Toutes ces écoles sont laïques et rattachées au ministère de l'Instruction publique. Elles sont administrées par quatre directeurs résidant à Constantinople, Smyrne, Alexandrie et Tunis et visitées par des inspecteurs. Soixante-dix instituteurs et institutrices ont été expédiés tant dans le Levant que sur la côte septentrionale d'Afrique, et ce premier envoi sera suivi de plusieurs autres.

Les écoles italiennes sont destinées d'une part à faire concurrence aux écoles religieuses tenues par les missionnaires dont la société de protection est à Florence et qui relèvent directement du Saint-Siège, d'autre part à propager la langue italienne et à combattre l'influence française.

Voici les noms des quatre directeurs :

Le professeur Girolamo del Luca Aprile, directeur du bureau de l'imprimerie, au ministère de l'Intérieur, a été envoyé en mission à Constantinople, chargé de la direction centrale des écoles italiennes de la Turquie d'Europe, de la Bulgarie, de la Roumanie et de la Grèce.

Le professeur Giuseppe Ayra, directeur des Écoles techniques élémentaires de Tunis, a été nommé directeur central, à Smyrne, des écoles italiennes de la Turquie d'Asie.

Le professeur Carlo-Felice Restagno, secrétaire du ministère de l'Instruction publique, a été envoyé en mission à Alexandrie, chargé de la direction centrale des écoles de la Haute et Basse Égypte.

Ces deux derniers fonctionnaires, les professeurs del Luca Aprile et Restagno, avaient été chargés, précédemment, de l'élaboration de l'ordonnance sur les écoles italiennes à l'étranger.

M. Mario Mandalari, professeur au lycée et à l'école normale de Caserta, a été envoyé à Tunis comme directeur central des écoles italiennes en Tunisie et en Tripolitaine.

Sociétés anglaises. — Il n'existe pas en Angleterre d'association pour la propagation de la langue anglaise, mais les diverses sociétés religieuses qui agissent au dehors en tiennent largement lieu. « Les missionnaires débarquent sur les côtes, ils s'établissent sur les ilots les moins habités, en même temps qu'ils se frayent un chemin jusqu'au cœur des grands continents..... ils y fondent des missions qui deviendront peut-être un jour des colonies, car en même temps qu'ils prêchent l'évangile, ils répandent les idées et propagent l'influence de la mère patrie. Puissamment aidés par les missions médicales, ils attirent à eux des populations qu'ils soulagent dans leurs misères et qu'ils secourent dans leurs maladies ; les écoles s'ouvrent, elles sont de deux sortes, écoles quotidiennes et écoles du dimanche ; dans les premières ils enseignent les connaissances les plus élémentaires et en arrivent progressivement à enseigner leur langue ; dans les secondes l'enseignement est purement religieux ».

En dehors des sociétés qui s'occupent exclusivement de la publication des Bibles et des livres religieux (l'une d'elles la *British and foreing bible society* a imprimé, distribué ou vendu, en 1887-88, 186 229 bibles, 612 427 nouveaux testaments, plus de 1 100 000 autres livres religieux); les sociétés actives sont au nombre de 40. Trois d'entre elles, qui sont dites *missions médicales*, ont pour objet de mettre à la disposition des diverses sociétés, des missionnaires ayant fait des études médicales complètes, et susceptibles par là d'exercer une influence toute particulière sur les populations indigènes. Presque toutes ces sociétés sont protestantes; il existe cependant aussi des missions catholiques anglaises. Quelques-unes sont très anciennes, la création de la « Compagnie de la Nouvelle-Angleterre » remonte à 1649.

Quelques chiffres donneront une idée de leur puissance et de l'action qu'elles exercent pour le plus grand profit de l'influence anglaise. La société des *Missionnaires de l'Église*, fondée en 1799, dispose d'un revenu annuel de 221 000 livres sterling, soit plus de 5 millions de francs, elle compte 182 000 adhérents, entretient 280 stations et 1 859 écoles, fréquentées par 71 814 écoliers. La société des *Missionnaires méthodistes wesleyens* a 88 000 adhérents, 130 000 livres de revenu, 236 stations, 752 écoles avec 53 000 écoliers. La société *pour la propagation de l'Évangile à l'étranger* a 281 000 adhérents, 110 000 livres de revenu, 464 stations, 802 écoles et 32 000 écoliers. La société des *missionnaires de Londres* a 339 000 adhérents, 105 000 livres de revenu, 1 787 stations, 2 719 écoles et 142 000 écoliers. Les missions catholiques anglaises entretiennent 4 500 écoles fréquentées par 110 000 élèves.

M. WAHL.

RÉCOMPENSES ACCORDÉES PAR LE CONSEIL D'ADMINISTRATION

DANS SA SÉANCE DU 9 JUIN 1889

COMITÉS DE PARIS

2e et 11e arrondissements	Médaille d'argent grand module.
5e et 6e id.	Médaille d'argent petit module.

COMITÉS DES DÉPARTEMENTS

Alger, Bordeaux, Cognac, Constantine, Limoges, Moulins, Nancy, Oran, Reims, Saint-Étienne	Médaille d'argent grand module.
Bayonne, Belfort, Castres, Mazamet, Mont-de-Marsan, Montpellier, Nimes	Médaille d'argent petit module.
Besançon, Coutances, Dijon, Libourne, Melun, Roanne, Toulon, Troyes, Verdun	Mention honorable.

COMITÉS DE L'ÉTRANGER ET DES COLONIES

Port-Louis (Ile Maurice)	Médaille de vermeil grand module.
Le Caire, Madrid, Valence	Médaille d'argent grand module.
Prague, Saint-Louis, Syra, Tunis	Médaille de vermeil petit module.
Pondichéry, Saïgon	Médaille d'argent petit module.
M. Mazoyer, directeur de l'école de l'Alliance française à Assiout (Egypte)	Livres.

ENVOIS FAITS A L'EXPOSITION UNIVERSELLE DE 1889

PAR LES ÉCOLES, COMITÉS ET DÉLÉGUÉS DE L'ALLIANCE FRANÇAISE

Lieu	Expéditeur	Envois
Constantinople	Mesdames Devaux et Schaffner	Cahiers. — Cartes. — Broderie. — Lingerie.
Id.	Madame Bocognano	Devoirs. — Cartes. — Vue de l'école.
Id.	Communauté arménienne catholique (Mgr Azarian).	
Id.	Collège Faure	Devoirs.
Salima	Capucins	Cèdres.
Papaz-Keupru	P. P. Géorgiens	Devoirs. — Photographies. — Plan de l'école.
Lattaquié	École grecque	Cahiers.
Andrinople	École hellénique de jeunes filles	Lingerie. — Broderie.
Smyrne	Pensionnat héllénique de jeunes filles (Homéreïon).	Photographies. — Cahiers. — Broderie.
Id.	Consul de France	Journaux.
Trébizonde	École des Frères	Cahiers.
Akbès	Trappistes	Cartes. — Reproduction d'inscriptions sur pierres.
Larnaca (Chypre)	Sœurs de Saint-Joseph de l'Apparition	Lingerie. — Broderie. — Cahiers de devoirs.
Athènes	Sœurs de Saint-Joseph de l'Apparition	Cahiers. — Lingerie. — Broderie. — Photographies.
Tinos	Ursulines	Devoirs. — Lingerie — Broderie.
Naxos	Id.	Devoirs. — Dessins. — Cartes.
Philippopoli	Augustins de l'Assomption	Photographies. — Devoirs. — Notice.
Assiout	École de l'Alliance française	Devoirs. — Insectes.
Port-Saïd	Sœurs du Bon Pasteur	Lingerie. — Broderie. — Cahiers.
Assinie	École française d'Elima	Cahiers.
Porto-Novo	École des Missions africaines de Lyon	Devoirs.
Sénégal	Colonel Galliéni (Écoles du Haut-Fleuve)	Cahiers.
Port-Louis	Comité de l'Alliance française	Journaux et livres.
Constantine	M. Emile Jean, directeur d'école communale	Carte. — Tableaux de lecture.
Bâle	École française	Devoirs. — Livres. — Documents relatifs à la Société française.
Bruxelles	M. Chassaing	Journaux et livres.
Amsterdam	M. Baale	Livres.
Rotterdam	Écoles wallonnes (M. le pasteur Bresson)	Tableau des écoles wallonnes. — Livres.
Groningue	M. Van Hamel	Livres. — Journaux. — Photographies.
Copenhague	Sprogselskabet (Comité de l'Alliance française).	Livres.
Kalmar	M. Gotthard Gullberg	Livres.
Prague	Alliance française (M. Pinkas)	Carte de Bohême — Diagramme de la progression de l'enseign. du français.
New-York	École française d'Hudson County	Cahiers d'élèves.
Tokio	Sœurs de Saint-Paul de Chartres	Devoirs (4 ou 5 dictées).
Ouargla	École française (Envoi de M. le lieutenant Estève).	Devoirs. — Plan. — Renseignements historiques sur l'école.

Paris. — Imp. E. Capiomont et Cie, rue des Poitevins, 6.

MEMBRES D'HONNEUR DE L'ALLIANCE FRANÇAISE

PRÉSIDENTS D'HONNEUR

MM. **Lesseps** (FERDINAND de), Membre de l'Académie française et de l'Académie des Sciences.

Faidherbe (le Général), Sénateur, Grand Chancelier de la Légion d'honneur, membre de l'Académie des Inscriptions et Belles-Lettres.

Jurien de la Gravière (le Vice-Amiral), Membre de l'Académie française et de l'Académie des Sciences.

MEMBRES D'HONNEUR

MM. **Billot**, Ministre de France à Lisbonne.

Brazza (SAVORGNAN de), Commissaire général de la République française au Congo et au Gabon.

Cambon (PAUL), Ambassadeur de France à Madrid.

Charton, Sénateur, Membre de l'Académie des Sciences Morales et Politiques.

Dietz-Monnin, Sénateur.

Freycinet (de), Sénateur, Ministre de la Guerre.

Galliéni (le Lieutenant-Colonel).

Gréard, Membre de l'Académie française et de l'Académie des Sciences Morales et Politiques, Vice-Recteur de l'Académie de Paris.

Hébrard (ADRIEN), Sénateur.

Jourde, Directeur du journal *Le Siècle*. Président du Syndicat de la Presse.

Leboucher, Gouverneur de la Guadeloupe.

Le Myre de Vilers, Résident général à Madagascar.

Levasseur, Membre de l'Académie des Sciences Morales et Politiques, Professeur au Collège de France.

Lockroy, Député, Ancien Ministre.

Massicault, Résident général en Tunisie.

Paris (GASTON), Membre de l'Académie des Inscriptions et Belles-Lettres, Professeur au Collège de France.

Pasteur, Membre de l'Académie française et de l'Académie des Sciences.

Piquet, Gouverneur général de l'Indo-Chine.

Pressensé (de), Sénateur.

Renan, Membre de l'Académie Française et de l'Académie des Inscriptions et Belles-Lettres, Administrateur du Collège de France.

Ribot, Député.

Rothan, Ancien Ministre Plénipotentiaire.

Rousse, Avocat, Membre de l'Académie française.

Say (LÉON), Sénateur, Membre de l'Académie française et de l'Académie des Sciences Morales et Politiques.

Simon (JULES), Sénateur, Membre de l'Académie française et de l'Académie des Sciences Morales et Politiques.

Spuller, Député, Ministre des Affaires Étrangères.

Taine, Membre de l'Académie française.

Thomson, Député de l'Algérie.

Vogüé (Marquis de), Membre de l'Académie des Inscriptions et Belles-Lettres, Ancien Ambassadeur

CONSEIL D'ADMINISTRATION DE L'ALLIANCE FRANÇAISE

MM. **Président :**

Duruy (Victor), membre de l'Académie française, de l'Académie des sciences morales et politiques, de l'Académie des inscriptions et belles-lettres.

Vice-Présidents :

Colonna Ceccaldi (comte), ministre plénipotentiaire, conseiller d'État.
Maspéro, membre de l'Institut, professeur au Collège de France.
Maunoir, secrétaire général de la Société de géographie.
Parmentier (Th.), général de division.

Secrétaire général :

Foncin (Pierre), inspecteur général de l'Instruction publique.

Secrétaire général adjoint :

Kœchlin (Raymond), publiciste.

MM. **Trésorier :**

Mayrargues (Alfred), ancien professeur.

Trésorier-Adjoint :

Puaux, secrétaire de la Société historique.

Contrôleur :

M. **de Royou.**

Secrétaires :

Bernard (Antoine), inspecteur des chemins de fer.
Izoulet, professeur de philosophie au lycée Condorcet.
Reinach (Joseph), publiciste.
Rey (E.-G.), ancien chargé de missions scientifiques en Syrie.

Archiviste :

Duchesne (l'abbé), maître de conférences à l'École des hautes études.

MM.

Avril (baron d'), ministre plénipotentiaire.
Bardoux, sénateur, ancien ministre de l'Instruction publique.
Bigot (Charles), publiciste.
Cambourg (baron de), de la Société des études coloniales et maritimes.
Colin (Armand), éditeur.
Granney, juge de paix.
David-Mennet, manufacturier.
Drapeyron, directeur de la Revue de Géographie.
Dreyfus (Ferdinand), avocat à la Cour d'appel, ancien député.
Dubard, chef du service de l'inspection au ministère de la Marine.
Grandidier, membre de l'Institut.
Guérin (Victor), docteur ès lettres.
Hébert (de la maison Didot).
Jacquemart, directeur au ministère du commerce.
Jost, inspecteur général de l'Instruction publique.
Kahn (Zadoc), grand rabbin de Paris.
Laporte, magistrat.
Leger (Louis), professeur au Collège de France.
Maës, membre de la Chambre de commerce de Paris.

MM.

Marcilhacy, secrétaire de la Chambre de commerce de Paris.
Masson (Georges), éditeur.
Mas-Latrie (comte de), membre de l'Académie des inscriptions et belles-lettres.
Melon (Paul).
Meurand, directeur honoraire au ministère des affaires étrangères, président de la Société de géographie commerciale.
Meyer (Paul), directeur de l'École des Chartes.
Morel (Georges), inspecteur général de l'Enseignement secondaire.
Niox (colonel).
Reinach (Salomon), conservateur adjoint au Musée de Saint-Germain.
Tranchant, ancien conseiller d'État.
Vandal, professeur à l'École des sciences politiques.
Vaquez, avocat, adjoint au maire du XVIe arrondissement de Paris.
Vignes (contre-amiral).
Villard, ingénieur civil.
Wahl, professeur d'histoire au lycée Lakanal.
Zeller (Jules), membre de l'Académie des sciences morales et politiques, inspecteur général de l'Instruction publique.

MEMBRES HONORAIRES DU CONSEIL D'ADMINISTRATION

MM.

Charmes (Francis), directeur des Affaires politiques au ministère des Affaires étrangères.
Geffroy, directeur de l'École française de Rome.
Jusserand, conseiller de l'ambassade de France à Londres.
Lamothe (de), gouverneur de Saint-Pierre et Miquelon.
Lavisse, professeur à la Faculté des lettres de Paris.

MM.

Liard, directeur de l'enseignement supérieur au ministère de l'Instruction publique.
Machuel, directeur de l'enseignement public en Tunisie.
Mouttet, secrétaire général des directions de l'intérieur, de l'Indo-Chine.
Parieu (de), membre de l'Institut.
Richet (le docteur), professeur à la Faculté de médecine, directeur de la *Revue scientifique*.
Zévort (Edgar), recteur de l'Académie de Caen.

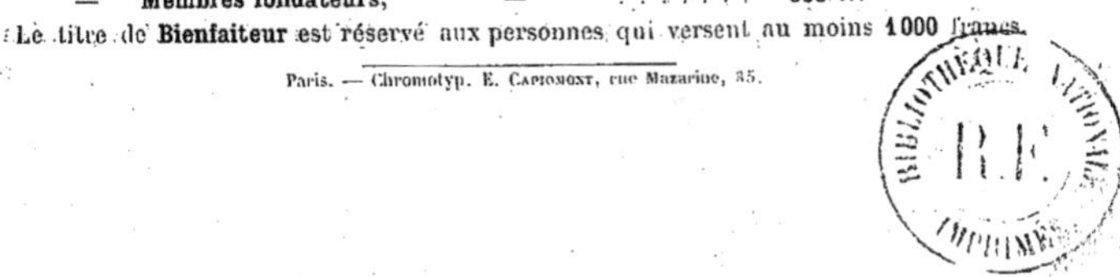

Conditions d'adhésion à l'Alliance française :

Pour les **Sociétaires annuels**, le versement est de.	6 fr.	(*minimum*)
— **Sociétaires perpétuels**, —	120 fr.	(*une fois versés*)
— **Membres fondateurs**, —	500 fr.	—

Le titre de **Bienfaiteur** est réservé aux personnes qui versent au moins **1000** francs.

Paris. — Chromotyp. E. Capiomont, rue Mazarine, 35.

CPSIA information can be obtained
at www.ICGtesting.com
Printed in the USA
LVHW020803270523
748233LV00029B/442

9 782012 786004